The Muses of Resistance

A cottage girl shelling pease.
W. R. Bigg Pinxit/P. W. Tomkin Sculpt./30 May 1787

The Muses of Resistance

Laboring-Class Women's Poetry in Britain, 1739–1796

Donna Landry
Department of English, Wayne State University

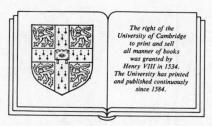

The right of the
University of Cambridge
to print and sell
all manner of books
was granted by
Henry VIII in 1534.
The University has printed
and published continuously
since 1584.

Cambridge University Press
Cambridge
New York   *Port Chester*
Melbourne   *Sydney*

Published by the Press Syndicate of the University of Cambridge
The Pitt Building, Trumpington Street, Cambridge CB2 1RP
40 West 20th Street, New York, NY 10011, USA
10 Stamford Road, Oakleigh, Melbourne 3166, Australia

Cambridge University Press 1990

First published 1990

Printed in Great Britain at the University Press, Cambridge

British Library cataloguing in publication data

Landry, Donna
    The muses of resistance: laboring-class women's poetry in Britain, 1739–1796.
    1. Poetry in English, 1702–1800 – Critical studies
    1. Title
    821'.5'09

Library of Congress cataloguing in publication data applied for

ISBN 0 521 37412 X

CE

Contents

Illustrations

Acknowledgments

The research for this study was undertaken in the British Library, London; the Bodleian Library, Oxford; the Cambridge University Library; the Wren Library, Trinity College, Cambridge; the William Andrews Clark Memorial Library of UCLA; the Huntington Library, San Marino; the National Library of Scotland, Edinburgh; the Glasgow University Library; and the John Rylands Library, Manchester. I should like to thank the American Council of Learned Societies and the National Endowment for the Humanities for financial assistance in traveling to these institutions, and I am grateful to Marshall Cohen, Dean of Humanities at the University of Southern California, for allowing me to take a semester's and later a year's, leave. Final revisions were produced at the Society for the Humanities at Cornell; many thanks to the fellows and to the members of my seminar for stimulation, especially Sheila Lloyd, Laura Mandell, Lisa Moore, Charlotte Sussman, and Martin Wechselblatt, and to Jonathan Culler and Dominick LaCapra for making the opportunity possible. I wish to thank the librarians and staffs of these institutions as well as the staffs of the British Library, the Folger Library, the Central Library, Bristol, and the Bristol Records Office for providing me with copies of documents in their collections.

Special thanks to Betty Rizzo for sharing her extensive knowledge of Mary Leapor, to Richard Greene for sharing his of Leapor and Elizabeth Hands, and to Morag Shiach and Mary Waldron for letting me read their forthcoming work. If I had been able to read Bridget Hill's invaluable *Women, Work, and Sexual Politics in Eighteenth-Century England* (Basil Blackwell, 1989) when I was first beginning this project, it might well have turned out differently; hers is the book with which future studies of eighteenth-century women and work ought to begin. I am very grateful to her for sending me page-proofs so expeditiously.

I owe my readers for the press, Laura Brown, Isobel Grundy, and John Richetti, many thanks for meticulous commentary. Andrew Brown, Kevin Taylor, Josie Dixon, and Christine Lyall Grant made the business of

viii

publishing as painless as possible. A version of chapter two appeared in *The New Eighteenth Century*, edited by Felicity Nussbaum and Laura Brown (New York and London: Methuen, 1987), and I wish to thank them both for their helpful suggestions. Material from that essay is reprinted here by permission of Routledge, Chapman and Hall, Inc.

Many friends and colleagues have contributed to making this a better book than could have been written in isolation, providing suggestions or encouragement and provoking disagreements and rethinking, especially Paul Alkon, Carol Barash, Leo Braudy, Carol Briggs, Marie-Florine Bruneau, Margaret Doody, Moira Ferguson, Heather Findlay, Brean Hammond, Elaine Hobby, Mary Jacobus, Linda Kauffman, Katie King, Martha Malamud, Peter Manning, Don McGuire, Tita Rosenthal, Hilary Schor, Gayatri Spivak, Susan Staves, Rajani Sudan, James Turner, Martha Vicinus, Rachel Weil, James Winn, and Winnie Woodhull. The late Irvin Ehrenpreis, who directed my dissertation on another topic, would have been, I think, both surprised and pleased by this book. Gerald MacLean, with whom collaboration is not only pleasurable but possible, helped most to bring it into being, with varied assistance from Angela and the girls, David, Carol and the cats, Elaine, Chris, Tim, Mollie, Jo, Charlotte, Christopher, *les ménages* at Skaigh and Creaber, Christine, Ian, Jude, and Sid, to all of whom it is dedicated.

'I certainly esteem myself a steady, reasonable kind of body,' she said;
'not exactly from living among the hills and seeing one set of faces, and
one series of actions, from year's end to year's end; but I have
undergone sharp discipline, which has taught me wisdom: and then, I
have read more than you would fancy, Mr. Lockwood. You could not
open a book in this library that I have not looked into, and got
something out of also: unless it be that range of Greek and Latin, and
that of French; and those I know one from another: it is as much as you
can expect of a poor man's daughter.'

(Emily Brontë, *Wuthering Heights*)

She would notice her; she would improve her; she would detach her
from her bad acquaintance, and introduce her into good society; she
would form her opinions and her manners. It would be an interesting,
and certainly a very kind undertaking; highly becoming her own
situation in life, her leisure, and powers. . . . [Harriet's] early attachment
to herself was very amiable; and her inclination for good company, and
power of appreciating what was elegant and clever, shewed that there
was no want of taste, though strength of understanding must not be
expected.

(Jane Austen, *Emma*)

Introduction

HOBNELIA seated in a dreary Vale,
In pensive Mood rehears'd her piteous Tale,
Her piteous Tale the Winds in Sighs bemoan,
And pining Eccho answers Groan for Groan.

. . .

But hold – our *Light-Foot* barks, and cocks his Ears,
O'er yonder Stile see *Lubberkin* appears.
He comes, he comes, *Hobnelia*'s not bewray'd,
Nor shall she crown'd with Willow die a Maid.
He vows, he swears, he'll give me a green Gown,
Oh dear! I fall *adown, adown, adown!*[1]   (John Gay, *The Shepherd's Week*)

She, wretched matron, forced, in age, for bread,
To strip the brook with mantling cresses spread,
To pick her wintry faggot from the thorn,
To seek her nightly shed and weep till morn;
She only left of all the harmless train,
The sad historian of the pensive plain.[2]

(Oliver. Goldsmith, *The Deserted Village*)

On those occasions when the laboring woman has appeared in canonical eighteenth-century verse, she has been represented as an object of satire or pathos. Yet between the publication of Gay's pastorals and Goldsmith's elegy to the English georgic a poetic discourse was developed both by and about women of the laboring classes, a discourse coextensive with, yet in some ways discontinuous from, the eighteenth-century verse of traditional literary history. Satire and pathos may be found there, but, once read, these women's texts forever complicate our notions of plebeian female consciousness and the culture of an emergent "working class" to which high literary representation alludes but which it also effaces. If the project of a feminist literary history necessitates a thorough questioning and overhaul of existing literary-historical canons, a materialist feminist literary history attends to issues of class, race, and sexuality as well as gender in the encounter with traditional valuations. No feminist literary history that seeks to trace a "female" tradition while

I

remaining blind to the operations of class difference, conflict, and deliberate or unconscious repression will come close to giving a sufficiently nuanced account of women's literary production in previous centuries.

Gay's Hobnelia represents the resituation of neoclassical pastoral in a vernacular English context, a move which allows the satire to extend two ways. A slavish neoclassicism is rendered ludicrous as a means of representing rural life in Britain, but that very "rural life" is itself subjected to satire, to a privileged fixing of forms and imaginative possibilities from which both the significance of labor and the subjectivity of the laborer are excluded. This exclusion is particularly noticeable where women are concerned. When women's work does surface in *The Shepherd's Week* – as when we read of what Marian the milkmaid is *not* doing because she is lovelorn:

> *Marian* that soft could stroak the udder'd Cow,
> Or with her Winnow ease the Barly Mow;
> Marbled with Sage the hard'ning Cheese she press'd,
> And yellow Butter *Marian*'s Skill confess'd;
> But *Marian* now devoid of Country Cares,
> Nor yellow Butter nor Sage Cheese prepares – [3]

we are reminded that Gay's poem began with a literary quarrel between Pope and Ambrose Phillips and Thomas Tickell over "realism" in English pastoral, and that Gay took Pope's side. The interest of labor represented thus is intended to lie with its impropriety, its ludicrousness and potential bawdiness as a feature of the eclogue. We are supposed, not to delight in the skill signified by Marian's milking, her sage cheese, and her use of a sieve to reduce a heap of barley, but to find in her actions a comically lascivious potential, a low joke for men only. Thus it should come as no surprise that the repetitions of Hobnelia's sorrow are easily cut short by the belated reappearance of Lubberkin, and that Hobnelia's mock resistance to sexual urgency seals her fate with a slapstick swoon. Even the reading that finds a delightful "realism" in Gay's satire bespeaks a certain repressive recuperativeness in relation to the jolly quaint labors and sorrows of poor country-dwellers, a certain neutralizing of class differences – a function of the text that leaves the polite reader unthreatened by the possible otherness of working-class subjectivity. When the history of rural life is written from above, and from London, the possibility of complex subjectivities, let alone political consciousness, among "the folk" is cancelled in advance.

When Goldsmith gives us his "sad historian of the pensive plain," of the vanishing village communities whose fate is sealed by the last phase of eighteenth-century enclosure, he makes her poor, old, and female, the most marginal of the already marginalized rural poor. But her history is never delivered, her narrative of Auburn never written; Goldsmith's narrator writes it for us, forever rendering her silent and pathetic, downtrodden and weeping, most powerless of the powerless. The sad historian of "the harmless train," seen as inarticulate, comes to stand for the laboring poor as objects of pathos, incapable of self-representation, incapable of political consciousness, incapable of protest. A whole tradition of oral political culture is banished from the scene, the figure of the laboring woman as "historian" at once cancelled and preserved.

Gay's and Goldsmith's figures of the laboring poor are class- and gender-specific productions; they represent two forms of an important tradition in English literary history, but not "the" tradition. Ironically, against the silencing and objectification of female labor to be found in high literary discourse, we can place a countertradition of poetic production by working-class women. It is a discourse marked by many constraints, a far from unfettered radical discourse, but its historical and subjective complexity, political consciousness, and strategies of protest work against any simple critical acquiescence in either Hobnelia's comedy or the wretched silence of Goldsmith's "sad historian." These muses of resistance demand that a new, and feminist, literary history be written from below.

Each of the terms of this book's title requires some qualification. The subjects of this study, who are women poets from the laboring classes publishing in eighteenth-century Britain, attend to the "muses of resistance," but it is never entirely clear where the resistance is coming from. The political desires, both theirs and mine, out of which such an investigation and reconstruction emerge can never be fully articulated. The project of a materialist feminist literary history would, however, be unthinkable without the grounding provided by the discontinuous theories and practices of marxist historical writing, feminism, what is called in Britain "cultural materialism," and its Foucauldian counterpart in the United States, "New Historicism." And so such a project announces its awareness of the inevitability of political engagement in advance.

This is a study of the social–textual articulation of class and gender in a largely forgotten literary discourse. But neither class nor gender can be addressed unproblematically. Social historians, following suggestions made by E. P. Thompson, Gareth Stedman Jones, and others, have advised us to treat class "with some skepticism, as at most an ideal type, reworked and developed to take account of a much wider and more subtle range of social formation," while we learn to pay attention to "significant social phenomena which too rigid a class interpretation can overlook or underestimate, such as gender and religion or nationalism and regionalism."[4] In this respect the work of Stedman Jones and much of what is published in *History Workshop Journal* seems to me exemplary. As Stedman Jones comments, "in England more than in any other country, the word 'class' has acted as a congested point of intersection between competing, overlapping or simply differing forms of discourse – political, economic, religious and cultural – right across the

political spectrum." Rather than beginning with an essentialist definition of
"class" or "the social" as something existing outside and logically prior to its
articulation through language, he argues, "we should start out from the other
end of the chain":

Language disrupts any simple notion of the determination of consciousness by social
being because it is itself part of social being. We cannot therefore decode political
language to reach a primal and material expression of interest since it is the discursive
structure of political language which conceives and defines interest in the first place.
What we must therefore do is to study the production of interest, identification,
grievance and aspiration within political languages themselves.[5]

As Joan Scott has remarked, Stedman Jones himself fails to pay sufficient
attention to signification (the ways in which meanings and texts are constructed) and the symbolic operations of gender within such meaning-
construction:

We cannot understand how concepts of class acquired legitimacy and established
political movements without examining concepts of gender. We cannot understand
working-class sexual divisions of labor without interrogating concepts of class. There
is no choice between a focus on class or on gender; each is necessarily incomplete
without the other . . . To study [the history of the material link between gender and
class] requires attention to "language" and a willingness to subject the very idea of the
working class to historical scrutiny.[6]

I would like to refocus the concept of "political languages" to include such
arguably gender- and class-specific texts of interest, identification, grievance,
and aspiration as the printed collections of poems and other forms of writing
produced in Britain between 1739 and 1796 by women characterized therein
as members of the laboring classes.

   It is not, however, a simple matter of adding the categories of gender and
sexuality to a pre-existing class analysis, even if that analysis were linguistically
based and informed by the textual subtlety of post-Althusserian and post-
structuralist criticism. A feminist critique and a marxist or materialist one will
always be discontinuous, at crucial moments threatening mutual subversion
rather than lending themselves easily to analyses of their mutual construction.
For the social historian, as Sally Alexander notes, the problem of this
discontinuous articulation poses itself as follows:

How can women speak and think creatively within marxism when they can neither
enter the narrative flow as fully as they wish, nor imagine that there might be other
subjectivities present in history than those of class (for to imagine that is to transgress
the laws of historical materialism)? . . .

Feminist history has to emancipate itself from class as the organizing principle of history, the privileged signifier of social relations and their political representations.[7]

This does not mean the abandoning of class, as both Alexander and Scott make clear, but rather the interrogation of those historical and textual moments when what Pierre Macherey has called "the unconscious which is history"[8] emerges around these categories, erupts in contradictions, fissures, gaps. Within the discipline of social history, Alexander suggests, "The questions for the historian of feminism are why at some moments does sexual difference and division take on a political significance – which elements in the organization are politicized, what are the terms of negotiation, and between whom?" (Alexander, p. 135).

Within the discipline of literary history, one is more immediately concerned with textual readings. Here the work of Gayatri Spivak, dedicated to the mutually interruptive discourses of literary criticism and history, and alert to the textual pressures and effects of gender, class, and race, has been most helpful.[9] Such a model requires a sophisticated notion of ideology, and Louis Althusser's sense of it as a "representation" of the imaginary, lived relation between individuals and their real conditions of existence is indispensable.[10] At the same time, an historical understanding of the concept of ideology in its various usages, such as Raymond Williams provides, is illuminating for a study of eighteenth-century writing.[11] Particularly in the interrogation of the textual politics of literary productions of the past, with their half-suppressed, often inchoate or incompletely articulated traces of resistance or desire which may be both uncannily familiar and historically alien to us, a model of ideology as a field of contestation and change is essential. I have found Macherey's discussion of ideology and the literary text as typically possessed of contradictory projects, tendencies, and desires especially useful.[12] At the level of the sentence and even the individual word, Mikhail Bakhtin's notion of heteroglossia, of historical and ideological struggle enacted within language, makes legible the dialogic potential of much eighteenth-century English verse, though Bakhtin himself gives pride of place to the novel as the genre of linguistic conflict and dialogism.[13]

It would not be misleading to read the scene of writing for these laboring women, these upstarts, these cookmaids, milkmaids, laundresses, field hands, and women of obscure parentage, as a site of resistance. Although the desire to imitate the upper classes, sometimes aroused in servants by their "having been introduced to new tastes, new forms of beauty in the furnishing, decorations, flowers and gardens of the houses where they worked," may be one possible source of working-class conservatism,[14] the experience of domestic service among these women produces a social critique. For the laboring population maintained many forms of elaborately coded class opposition, and, as social historians have shown, "Resistance could take other forms than flight or the escape into fantasy of servants' romantic literature" (Davidoff, p. 136). Writing verse that ventriloquizes and thus challenges the verse forms and values of mainstream culture is a way of speaking out, and of altering social discourse. This is ventriloquism in the sense employed by Margaret Doody and others,[15] that is, ventriloquism with a subversive twist. It is as if the dummy did not merely serve to demonstrate the master's skill at speaking through another's body, but took on a life of its own, began to challenge the master by altering the master's texts.

Theirs is a discourse that comes to reflect satirically on its own mode of production, reception, and poetic conventionality, as exemplified by the servant Elizabeth Hands's "A Poem, On the Supposition of an Advertisement appearing in a Morning Paper, of the Publication of a Volume of Poems, by a Servant Maid" (1789):

> A servant write verses! says Madam Du Bloom;
> Pray what is the subject? – a Mop, or a Broom?
> He, he, he, – says Miss Flounce; I suppose we shall see
> An Ode on a Dishclout – what else can it be?
>
> . . .
>
> For my part I think, says old lady Marr-joy,
> A servant might find herself other employ:
> Was she mine I'd employ her as long as 'twas light,
> And send her to bed without candle at night.
> Why so? says Miss Rhymer, displeas'd; I protest
> 'Tis pity a genius should be so deprest!
> What ideas can such low-bred creatures conceive,
> Says Mrs. Noworthy, and laught in her sleeve.
> Says old miss Prudella, if servants can tell
> How to write to their mothers, to say they are well,
> And read of a Sunday the Duty of Man;
> Which is more I believe than one half of them can;
> I think 'tis much *properer* they should rest there,
> Than be reaching at things so much out of their sphere.[16]

(11–14, 21–34)

Here we have the use of tetrameter, a popular meter for lightly handled satire, in the service of a class-conscious and protofeminist critique of working-class women's subordination, the simultaneous suffocation and exploitation of their talents and desires. If Swift or Butler has served as inspiration, Hands manages not to sound exactly like either of them. This is far from a slavish form of imitation, if imitation it can be called. As Luce Irigaray has hypothesized, feminine imitation of masculine forms also serves to subvert mimesis because women are simultaneously outside and inside the discourse that they imitate:

If she can play the role so well, if it does not kill her, quite, it is because she keeps something in reserve with respect to this function. Because she still subsists, otherwise and elsewhere than where she mimes so well what is asked of her.[17]

The existence of this form of literary production signifies that working-class consciousness and working-class feminism have histories that predate their usual association with the nineteenth century. The achievement of this marginal writing, from the perspective of our disciplinary practice as literary historians, ought to be the vindication of modes of literary production hitherto denigrated or ignored: writing that has been dismissed as derivative, conventional, or imitative needs now to be reread for its dialogic, innovative, and critical possibilities, for its muted protests and attempts at subversion, its curtailed yet incorrigible desires.

There are a number of historical and aesthetico-critical grounds upon which this study has been built. I have defined a poetic discourse by delineating its shifting margins in terms of both chronology and critical reading. This is a comparative study in the sense that Ann Messenger means when she suggests that, whatever one's commitment to feminist politics, women historically have not written in strict homosocial segregation and so, "Men's writing cannot be ignored . . . I look at these writers in their various relations to other writers," including "the better known ones of the opposite sex."[18] Any such study thus implicitly engages questions of the canon and of valuation. As Morag Shiach comments in her study of popular culture, the female "peasant poets" she examines were doubly marginalized by virtue of their gender and class positions, and any attempt to redress the balance must confront the obstacle of "hundreds of years of cultural neglect" that cannot simply be wished away: "The challenge of producing interesting and powerful accounts of poetic writing which has never before been part of critical discussions is daunting, particularly when set beside the proliferation of critical responses to the work of James Thomson, Stephen Duck or John Clare."[19]

Between 1739 and 1796 an identifiable discourse of working-class women's poetry emerges in Britain, only to fold back on itself after the turn of the century with the increasing popularity of working-class prose autobiography, a gradual defusing of working-class combativeness, and increasing class defensiveness. Thus Mary Collier's *The Woman's Labour* (1739) and Ann Yearsley's *The Rural Lyre* (1796) mark important moments in the history of this discourse. They are also texts that yield a great deal, critically speaking, when read with feminist and marxist questions in mind, texts whose textuality enacts struggle, contradiction, and ideological and subjective contestation. After 1796, I shall argue, there is a waning of engagement and affect within this discourse, which rapidly becomes "residual" in Ann Candler and Elizabeth Bentley.[20]

But what of earlier women writers of less than genteel origins, and how is one to determine what constitutes for the period the "working classes?" Mary Barber (1690?–1757), for instance, was the wife of a wool clothier, and in 1837 we find her coupled with Mary Leapor by a writer in *Blackwood's Magazine* because of their lower-class situations, and the consequent expectation that they will write enthusiastic religious verse:

Mary Barber was the wife of a shopkeeper in Dublin, and Mary Leapor a cook, but neither of them had so much of the *mens divinior* as might have been expected from their occupation.[21]

Similarly, Mary Masters (1706?–1759?) is introduced in Colman and Thornton's *Poems by Eminent Ladies* as having been "shut out from all commerce with the polite world," with her desire to write poetry "always brow-beat and discountenanced by her parents."[22] But if we read Barber and Masters carefully, their social circumstances appear incomparably more genteel than Collier's or Yearsley's, and there is no question of their ever having been "in service." Mary Barber is not only a friend of Swift, but of Mary Caesar, the wife of a Tory M.P. Her poems address such topics as dining with Lord Carteret and the Speaker of the House of Commons, the marriage of Lady Margaret Harley, daughter of the former Tory Lord Treasurer Robert Harley, and the education of her son Constantine, who would become President of the College of Physicians in Dublin. Her verses were approved by Swift, and both Pope and his mother subscribed to them, along with the Lords Bathurst and Cobham, the Duke and Duchess of Buckingham, the Duchess of Ormonde, Sir Robert Walpole, and Sir William Windham.[23] Of Mary Masters we know rather less, but her verses were perhaps revised by Samuel Johnson, she may have lived with the publisher Edward Cave, and the *D.N.B.* claims that she "seems to have been known to most of the *literati* of the day."[24] She was certainly patronized by the Earl of Burlington. Here, too, signs of genteel social connection work against equating "laboring class" with what it might mean to be of "humble" or "obscure" birth. And so, while I have discussed Masters's poem "To the Right Honourable the Earl of Burlington" as a representative response to Pope, I have not analyzed Masters's entire corpus, because to do so would be to militate against the claims of those poets of the laboring classes whose literary production was even more exceptional.

A marginal case in the determination of social class, Elizabeth Bentley (1767–1839) represents a later instance of a lower-class poet whose *œuvre* I have not treated fully because of the relative "respectability" of her circumstances. The only daughter of a journeyman cordwainer or shoemaker who suffered a stroke which reduced him to hawking garden produce until he was appointed bookkeeper for a coaching company, Bentley was poor, but there is no evidence of her ever having gone into service. She eventually became proprietor of a small school.[25] Her situation and literary identification with her social superiors suggest the importance of education and the possession of both mental and manual skills among the artisanal class. In her case, this distancing of herself from the laboring poor through a resolute clinging to relatively genteel work like writing and teaching is linked with anti-Jacobinism and other forms of political conservatism.[26] Although I discuss several of her poems, I have limited the scope of my analysis of her work in recognition of her borderline status as a "working-class" woman poet.

This question of the specificity of a woman writer's "class" is of paramount importance because the class position of the women whose writing this study investigates was, in every case, explicitly identified during their brief moments of literary recognition as "low," "menial," or "obscure," but, as we have seen, such labels did not necessarily designate members of the laboring population. Even such apparently common strategies among women writers as the appropriation of poetic languages and styles from master texts by men may manifest themselves differently when the social and economic circumstances of literary production and reception differ as widely as they do for a penurious middle-class woman and a female agricultural laborer or domestic servant.

The writers I have chosen to examine at length were all "working class" in that they were employed in laboring occupations, and all were the daughters of laboring families. I am thus interested in addressing certain historical, political, and discursive continuities between the experience of the laboring classes in a still predominantly agrarian economy, in which capitalism was already emergent, and the experience of their descendants during industrialization – a usage of "working class" sanctioned by the documentary work of Ivy Pinchbeck, E. P. Thompson, Stedman Jones, and other social historians. Across this economic history of developing capitalism, relations of patronage and clientage function in a backward-looking way, reminiscent as they are of "traditional," that is, feudal, social relations and exchanges of service. The supplementary use of such terms as "laboring class" and "poor" or "plebeian" writers emphasizes, in each case, a slightly different valence: for "laboring class," read workers in an agrarian economy; for "the poor," a need on the part of contemporaries to signify a certain pathos within socio-economic hierarchies; for "plebeian," the mainly cultural opposition to "patrician" or "polite."

The aesthetico-critical grounds for selection of writers to explore at length are more problematical than the historical delimiting outlined above. It is arguable that Susannah Harrison's (1752–84) *Songs In The Night: By a Young Woman under deep Afflictions* (1780), which by the 1820s had gone through fifteen British and six American editions,[27] was in terms of reception and impact on possible readerships the most important publication by a plebeian female poet. It may be that in another historical moment, such highly conventional devotional verse, so popular in its day, but now nearly unreadable according to our post-Romantic critical codes, will seem more interesting and important than Leapor's or Yearsley's, or that another of the poets mentioned here will prove a more crucial discovery for another critical agenda. But in our moment the literary innovations, and protofeminist and potentially radical social criticism offered by the writing of Collier, Leapor, Yearsley, Hands, Little, and Wheatley cannot fail, I think, to engage us most fully.

This is not a book about the literary representation of female agrarian workers, domestic servants, or plebeian prodigies. Nevertheless, readers will doubtless encounter the relatively unfamiliar texts of Elizabeth Hands and others in this book with certain representations of working-class women already in mind. I hope that the testimonies of these laboring women of letters will help resituate and reinflect our readings of such figures as Emily Brontë's Nelly Dean and the unholy couple formed by Emma Woodhouse and Harriet Smith in Jane Austen's *Emma*.

Nelly, whose self-discipline, devoted service to masters, vicarious familialism, and intense narration mark the socially repressive, politically containing functions of literacy and middle-class acculturation among the working classes: Nelly works behind the scenes, between the lines and in the margins of her own narration, to bring about traditional propertied and wedded closure. Apparently working against her own interests because she has identified them so totally with the family she serves, she is the chief agent of patriarchy, of the rule of the father, within Emily Brontë's novel, the chief prop of traditional hierarchies and exclusions.[28]

But we cannot now "rescue" Nelly, nor can we protest the repressive function of those scars, those marks of the "sharp discipline" she has undergone, without risking entrance as well into the role of the do-gooding, ultimately self-serving middle-class patron: Jane Austen's Emma, who appoints herself sponsor of Harriet Smith. Emma patronizes Harriet without understanding her, interprets Harriet's needs and desires to suit her own. Neither Emma nor Austen credits the socially inferior Harriet with much intelligence. And where "strength of understanding must not be expected," it may also be found suspect, if not distinctly objectionable, as we shall see. Clever complicity with one's own subjection, or insufficient intellect to challenge it: between these two possible relations to subjection, this simple dichotomy, lie many others, many actual practices of reading, writing, and self-representation by laboring-class women.

Chapter 1

Sensibility and slavery: the discourse of working-women's verse

Textuality and subjectivity: the politics of unlettered female genius

For a materialist feminism, engaged in historicizing the categories of class, race, and sexuality as well as gender with an eye towards intervening in their historical effects, working-class women's histories constitute an important site of investigation. A materialist feminist literary history might well ask how, at a given historical moment, both women and men of the laboring classes are engaged in cultural production, in social criticism, in a signifying practice we might identify as in some sense political as well as "literary." Between the eruption of printed texts by lower-class sectarian women during the English Civil Wars and the contributions of working-class women to autobiographical and radical utopian discourse in the nineteenth century, what might plebeian women have been writing?[1] In eighteenth-century Britain a specific form of literary production emerges, the publication by subscription of volumes of verse by laboring-class women. From 1739, and the appearance of *The Woman's Labour: An Epistle To Mr. Stephen Duck* written by Mary Collier, the "washerwoman of Petersfield," until 1796, when Ann Yearsley, the "Bristol milkwoman" published her last volume, *The Rural Lyre*, a discourse composed of plebeian poetry by women flourished alongside a better-known discourse of plebeian poetry by men.

Both occupy a marginal terrain with respect to laboring-class cultural production in the period. Between the oral culture of story and ballad and high-literary modes there lies a vast range of publications, but few are by or precisely directed to the laboring majority of the population. By far the largest category among those publications with something of a working-class fix is the anonymous flood of broadsides. Eighteenth-century laborers of both sexes, like middle- and upper-class women, doubtless enter literary history before the nineteenth century most often as Anon. But the fact is that female agricultural workers, domestic servants, laundresses, cookmaids, and dairy-women began to publish poetry under their own names in this period, concurrently with the male farm-workers, bricklayers, and shoemakers with whom readers of eighteenth-century literary history will be familiar. Stephen Duck, Robert Tatersal, James Woodhouse, Robert Bloomfield, John Bryant, Robert Burns, and John Clare have at least entered the literary-historical record, though they may not have received the scholarly attention they deserve. But the names of Mary Collier and Ann Yearsley, Elizabeth Hands and Elizabeth Bentley, Mary Leapor, Mary Masters, Janet Little, Phillis Wheatley, Susannah Harrison, and Ann Candler are far from familiar even to eighteenth-century specialists, though Wheatley is beginning to be known in the context of African American writing.[2]

The work of these writers lies between the anonymous balladry of popular culture and the most celebrated poetry of the period, neither radically plebeian in aesthetic nor entirely derivative of mainstream aristocratic and middle-class verse. The phenomenon of the laboring writer was identifiable by her entrance into a discourse that could be understood as unproblematically literary, and, in this period, in obvious if insubstantial contradiction with the popularity of the novel, that discourse was poetry. A largely neoclassical aesthetic that shifts throughout the century to accommodate the styles of Milton, Dryden, Pope, Swift, Thomson, Young, Johnson, and Gray, finally giving way to the modifications in aesthetic represented by Burns, Blake, Wordsworth, the dominance of the novel, and the new genre of working-class prose autobiography, constitutes the grounds of and conditions this textual movement.

Paradoxically, in order to engage in public self-representation, cultural intervention, social criticism, or the "literary," women of the lower classes in this period had to learn to write like the privileged masters of high-literary discourse. Although Mary Collier, Elizabeth Bentley, and Ann Candler, at least, wrote short prose autobiographical texts in response to enquiries about their authenticity as laboring-class poets, such prose productions were unusual. Not until the nineteenth century would lower-class women be able to publish their own narratives, their own self-representations as individual and class subjects explicitly as such, and even then, as Julia Swindells has argued, we had best beware of reading their autobiographies as unsubjugated self-expression.[3] A number of these eighteenth-century working-class women poets model themselves on Pope, while looking back to Dryden, and, via translation, Virgil, Ovid, and Homer; others pay homage to Milton, Swift, Thomson, Young, and Johnson. There is comparatively little explicit engagement with either vernacular plebeian poetry or women's writing, though Mary Collier replies to Stephen Duck, Janet Little to Robert Burns, and several of the poets implicitly to a sapphic epistolary tradition we might associate most clearly with Katherine Philips as an "English Sappho." Philips, as one of the most accomplished female poets of the seventeenth century, may well have influenced subsequent generations of women readers sufficiently to have been accessible to plebeian poets, and her work brings the celebration of erotic female friendships to a fine pitch.

This is a discourse elaborately coded and formalized: the same genres, modes, tropes, and preoccupations occur again and again, apparently without mutual recognition. If Collier turns the georgic to plebeian feminist protest against male workers' scorn and refusal even to "see" women's labor as productive, Leapor turns the pastoral dialogue, the neoclassical epistle and the country-house poem to surprisingly unconventional ends. Yearsley's uses of landscape poetry, philosophical meditation, classical imitation, and topical political verse are often innovative if not textually radical in their parodic and polemical effects. Hands reappropriates the pastoral as a mode appropriate for the representation of laboring-class experience. The texts of Little and Wheatley pose particularly difficult and timely questions regarding relations between gender and class marginality and the further marginalizing functions of linguistic, national, and racial difference. We can characterize this verse by the predominance of class-conscious georgic and pastoral poems, verse epistles to women, poems critical of marriage and of women's condition in general, poems in response to much-admired (usually male) poets, and versified narratives from the Scriptures. Like every other occasional poet of the period, these women wrote many elegies, but their elegiac poems remain among their most purely conventional, least critically interesting experiments, and do not help us to distinguish this discourse as such. There is also relatively little acknowledged engagement with a female literary tradition, and, where there is, considerable ignorance of literary history is shown.[4] But these women poets respond to the question of a male literary establishment in ways remarkably similar to those of their middle- and upper-class counterparts, except where the issue of class itself presses.

This is, then, a far from servile discourse, though it can teach us much about emergent class-consciousness in this period before industrialization. The clever, skillful, sometimes brilliant appropriation of mainstream literary culture by these women, these examples of *les voleuses de langue*, the thieves of language who steal and fly, produces a discourse potentially more culturally critical in its implications than many later, more "authentic," working-class self-representations.[5] With Spivak and the Subaltern Studies group, we should remember that it may be that "only the texts of counter-insurgency or élite documentation . . . give us the news of the consciousness of the subaltern."[6] Even where a woman of the laboring class attempts her own self-representation, the textual traces of élite literary culture overdetermine the site of "her own" textual production. But that is no reason not to read against the grain of those overdetermining traces, alert to the possibility of some "news of the consciousness of the subaltern."

Ironically, laboring-women's verse as a print phenomenon largely disappears with the waning of revolutionary fervor in the wake of the turmoil of the 1780s and 1790s. There seems to be an inverse relation between the socially critical, textually innovative edge of this discourse and the apparently open and "freeing" possibility of autobiographical expression. Stephen Duck was presented to the world with a long covering narrative by the Rev. Joseph Spence, making much of his class privations and his thus nearly incredible poetic genius. This is only the first stage in Duck's assimilation by the political and literary establishments, the containment of his poetry of social protest through public evocations of his misery and the need for his consequently radical deracination. Duck's female counterparts cannot be so easily deracinated, so easily accommodated in the higher social ranks; they tend to remain poor and laboring until their deaths, though some improvement in their circumstances may result from publication. But they also come down to us less covered by biographical preface and autobiographical statement than their male counterparts. Beyond a statement of their authenticity as plebeian writers, and sometimes a few facts about their families and employment, their works are made to stand by themselves – the curious productions of a "natural genius," a working-class prodigy, but not the self-examinations of an autobiographical subject whose "lived experience" in itself can be considered worthy of public textualization. As Morag Shiach has observed, polite interest in this poetry in the eighteenth century lay in the extent to which it could "support particular theories about the relations between nature and poetic writing, rather than in any desire to re-evaluate the cultural and social role of the peasantry."[7] The poetry itself may suggest other aims, but only if read against the grain of its presentation by polite patrons.

Eighteenth-century laboring male writers may be remembered for their lives rather than their literary works,[8] and they are worthy of a good revisionist study, but laboring-class women of the period are hardly remembered at all. That is why their historical recovery seems to me at the moment to be more urgent than the recovery of their male counterparts. Dwight L. Durling, for example, briefly discusses Duck, Woodhouse, Bloomfield, Burns, and Clare but not a single laboring woman poet. The women writers mentioned in his study are upper- or middle-class, the incomparably more familiar names of Margaret Cavendish, Duchess of Newcastle, Anne Finch, Countess of Winchilsea, Aphra Behn, and Anna Laetitia Barbauld.[9] Plebeian male poets constitute a discourse, one that intersects in many places with the texts examined in this study, but that differs with regard to the politics of gender. When James Woodhouse, "Journeyman Shoemaker," as the title page to his poems proclaims him, complains about his hard lot, his wife "Daphne" is offered as both comfort and burden to his manly sensibility:[10]

> Not that my Daphne's charms are flown,
>   These still new pleasures bring;

'Tis these inspire content alone,
  'Tis all I've left of Spring.

The dew-drop sparkling in her eye,
  The lily on her breast,
The rose-buds on her lips supply
  My rich, my sweet repast.

Her hair outshines the saffron morn;
  To her harmonious note
The thrush sits list'ning on the thorn,
  And checks his swelling throat.

Nor wish I, dear connubial state,
  To break thy silken bands;
I only blame relentless fate,
  That ev'ry hour demands.

Nor mourn I much my task austere,
  Which endless wants impose;
But – oh! it wounds my soul to hear
  My Daphne's melting woes!

Ixion like, her fate she moans,
  Whose wheel rolls ceaseless round;
While hollow sighs, and doleful groans,
  Fill all the dark profound.

For oft she sighs, and oft she weeps,
  And hangs her pensive head;
While blood her furrow'd fingers steeps,
  And stains the passing thread.

When orient hills the sun behold,
  Our labours are begun;
And when he streaks the west with gold,
  The task is still undone.   (77–108)

As we shall see repeatedly in texts by laboring-class women, texts frequently critical of gender ideology in protofeminist ways, Woodhouse's objectification of "his" Daphne as a source of sensual pleasure and a source of psychic suffering is traditional, and objectionable.

Feminism is a political, social, and intellectual movement grounded in Enlightenment discourses critical of customary prejudices and inequities of power based upon sexual difference.[11] As early modern archival evidence amply demonstrates, well before the advent of the organized women's movements of the nineteenth century, "feminist," or more accurately, protofeminist arguments were in circulation. To generalize about a diverse global movement like feminism is necessarily to distort its history and reduce its specificities, but under the sign of feminism here, I wish to invoke particularly a tradition of critiques of the cultural construction of gender as a rationale for the deployment of hierarchical differences, and of the socio-political relations, in all their intimate affectivity, that this gendered symbolic order subtends. Such a system of relations is often loosely referred to as "patriarchy." Strictly speaking, patriarchy designates the rule of the father, but much feminist theory has expanded its implications to cover various forms of male domination generally.[12] I shall use the term sparingly, to signify the rule of the father, and the adjective "patriarchal" to describe social relations that combine "a public dimension of power, exploitation or status with a dimension of personal servility."[13] The interweaving of sexualized and gendered affectivity with power in social relationships, families, households, workplaces, and political and legal institutions distinguishes the operations of patriarchal power from other kinds of power and makes resistance to it peculiarly difficult.

In Woodhouse's poem, Daphne is at once an object of desire, a pleasurable plaything, an irritant to the poet's sensitive nature, an economic liability, and a vehicle for the expression of his own pathos – one that does not threaten his manhood, externalizing his pain and locating it in an industriously spinning yet apparently financially dependent wife. As the muses of resistance, laboring women poets publishing in Britain in the course of the eighteenth century can be seen to question cultural assumptions such as the gender ideology that constructs Woodhouse and "his" Daphne in mutually exploitative ways.

The unhappy alliance of Ann Yearsley and Hannah More: a parable for feminism

In the case of Hannah More and Ann Yearsley lies a parable for feminists of our own times, a cautionary tale for those within the discipline of English studies engaged in writing a "properly historical" or materialist feminist literary history. Hannah More (1745–1833) was a writer whose Sunday Schools and essays, especially her enormously successful Cheap Repository tracts, penny-pamphlets aimed at promoting laboring-class morality and economy, were attempts to reform popular culture and defuse radical social protest in England in the wake of the American and French revolutions; Ann Cromarty (or Cromartie) Yearsley (1753–1806)[14] was a milkwoman who claimed that poetry helped her survive hard work, poverty, and near-starvation. Winters were especially hard on the laboring poor, with male agricultural workers usually jobless. Early in 1784 the pregnant Yearsley, her husband, five children, and her aged mother "all got together into a stable," expecting to die of hunger. They were saved when a Mr. Vaughan "acciden-tally look[ed] into the stable," though relief came too late to preserve old Mrs.

Cromartie.[15] In the summer of 1784, Yearsley became the object of More's philanthropy. In 1785 their alliance ended, acrimoniously.

There they are, the middle-class reformist and the working-class poet.[16] The abolitionist with a cottage salubriously named Cowslip Green, and the milkwoman whose chief delight lay in composing verses and offering them to an audience like that of More's cook, from whom Yearsley obtained the "hogwash" with which to feed her pig. They first cross paths in More's kitchen in Bristol, brought together by this nameless cook, who shows her mistress Yearsley's poems.

The relation between the cook and Yearsley is curiously both feudal and capitalist, one of those social relations in which a shift in the general mode of production can be distinctly marked. In some sense, Yearsley gives service to the cook by taking away the slops. The kitchen is the province of the cook, her fiefdom; over its rights and privileges she has control. The relation is feudal, a relation of personal service between members of two estates. But a super-imposed capitalist model can be seen in these features of the relation: Yearsley pays the cook for the "privilege" of taking away the slops; there is an annual contract, paid for in advance.

This mixed mode of socio-economic relation becomes a nexus of bad feeling between Yearsley and More after their quarrel; we know nothing of the cook's opinion.[17] More resents the "vulgarity" of Yearsley making public such demeaning economic details; she also feels that her own charity has been impugned. Yearsley, more accustomed to a public discourse of money and such arrangements as are necessary to material survival on the margins, tries to make a virtue of social and economic necessity by speaking openly of her contract with More's cook. More can neither publicly acknowledge the cook's feudal prerogative, which gives her servant a certain relative independence, nor, as a good traditionalist, can she endorse the trace of commercial practice that has entered her household: hence More's wounded pride, for which Yearsley's "obnoxious" – that is, class-specific – behavior is responsible.

How is the privileged middle-class reformist to avoid "patronizing," wounding, and exploiting her protégée? How is the laboring poet to make use of the offer of sisterly alliance without sacrificing her dignity and independence, confronted by middle-class propertied confidence, self-righteousness, fear of insurrection, and the authority of "educated" speech? A materialist feminist project must remain vigilant against replicating both the exploitative and the sentimental tendencies of eighteenth-century "discovery" and patronage. To fail do so so would be to court what Dominick LaCapra describes as "the vicious paradox by which a certain class of scholars establish their own disciplinary hegemony through a vicarious appeal to the oppressed of the past."[18] And while we may wish to position strategically the writing of those most exploited by the dominant culture at a given historical moment, we must recognize that "the mere pluralization of voices and traditions (a currently fashionable and sentimental gesture) is inadequate to the ultimate problem of linking repressed and master voices as the agon of history, their abiding relation of class conflict."[19] There is a danger, too, in reading as texts of liberation texts that encode merely more subtle forms of subjection, fantasies of servitude that please the master (or mistress), as Julia Swindells has argued.[20] These are questions which any study of eighteenth-century social relations ought to take into account, and to which a feminist literary history ought particularly to attend.

Reading in Yearsley's poems the high-literary skill or sense that the century called "genius," so sought after and here so mysteriously acquired, More recognizes a prodigious talent in these "unlettered verses."[21] As she writes to her friend and fellow patron, Elizabeth Robinson Montagu, "All I see of her, raises my opinion of her genius . . . Confess, dear Madam, that you and I know many a head competently stored with Greek and Latin which cou'd not have produced better verses. I never met with an Ear more nicely tuned."[22] Yearsley herself will be favorably judged more sober and industrious than More might have expected. She also elicits upper-class sympathy as the victim of an arranged marriage, against which the English bluestockings protested. More writes to Montagu, "and what will excite your compassion for a Woman of *Sentiment*, [she] was sacrificed for *money* at 17 to a silly Man whom she did not like; the Husband had an Estate of near *Six pounds* a year, and the marriage was thought too advantageous to be refused."[23] According to the parish records, Ann Cromarty married John Yearsley at twenty-one, but whether she or More was responsible for this inaccuracy cannot now be determined, as Mary Waldron points out:

this departure from the exact truth, whoever was responsible for it, throws some of the rest into doubt. The whole thing has a somewhat sensational air which does not accord well with what we know of Ann's mother, who seems unlikely to have forced a beloved daughter into an uncongenial marriage.

Waldron adds in a footnote: "It is possible that she was encouraged to marry against her real inclinations, but hardly 'sacrificed'."[24] For More, writing to Montagu and hoping to make the best case for Yearsley as a deserving client, laboring-class marriage without romance or recognizable property must be seen as a form of martyrdom. Comparable rhetorical and ideological slippage marks encounters between More and Yearsley throughout the documentary evidence.

As time passes and money does and doesn't change hands in their partnership, More appears to Yearsley increasingly condescending, and the servility of clientage becomes unbearable. And once Yearsley comes close to attaining an independent, private income – the basis of More's own class privilege – More will have nothing more to do with her. The mutual ideological tensions of class expectation and antagonism, always present, finally make continued alliance impossible. Yearsley uses her capital to establish a circulating library. According to Southey, she dies in straitened circumstances, though the evidence for this conclusion is obscure. She seems to have spent the last years of her life at Melksham in Wiltshire with her one surviving son, John, who had established himself in the Trowbridge clothing trade and who buried her at Clifton; Tompkins comments, "and as a stone was raised over the grave it is unlikely that the family was destitute."[25] It is more likely that Yearsley's failure to publish anything after 1796 has contributed to the frequent construction of a melancholy ending to her story.

For More, Yearsley represents that attempt to resolve contradictions in eighteenth-century literary theory, the "natural genius," "one who writes under every complicated disadvantage," not the least of which is being a woman. Poverty exacerbates the ordinary female exclusions from learning and literature.[26] Hence More's dwelling on Yearsley's combining of "the genuine spirit of Poetry" with what renders it "still more interesting," "a certain natural and strong expression of misery."[27] But More cannot countenance the move towards fracturing the "natural" connection between literature and middle-class privilege that Yearsley's independent pursuit of a literary career might bring about.

We are up against the limits of class ideology in this period, the limits of what social subjects like More and Yearsley would have been likely to expect from one another, and not some villainous failure of understanding for which More can be held accountable. Indeed, it would be a mistake to underestimate the progressive agenda with which More identified her projects, from the Cheap Repository to her patronage of the milkwoman. As recent essays by Mitzi Myers and Susan Pedersen demonstrate, arguments about the Cheap Repository tracts as instruments of social control tend to reproduce an orthodoxy that is more than a little gender-biased and certainly reductive. As Pedersen claims, "The anti-Jacobinism of the tracts has blinded us to the fact that More's aims extended far beyond fostering political loyalty"; her essay contends that the Cheap Repository should be read in the context of popular literature, for it represents "a broad evangelical assault on late eighteenth-century popular culture."[28] According to Myers, we should situate More within "that bourgeois renovation of manners and morals which marks the transition from the eighteenth to the nineteenth century," and within which female reformers were notably instrumental: "More's tracts present not so much a brief for Tory political stasis as for a woman's brand of bourgeois progressivism – pedagogy, philanthropy, and purification her cures for the old order's social ills."[29] Though More came eventually to reject her own earlier interest in promoting literacy among the laboring classes, for years she devoted herself to the cause of popular education and the encouragement of self-sufficiency and prudent domestic management among the poor.

More's own benevolent intentions and their humanitarian effects notwith-standing, there remains a conservative connection between literature as social propaganda, exemplified in More's depoliticizing if also sometimes practically useful tracts for the poor,[30] and the deradicalizing function of literary patron-age if it succeeds in providing a member of the laboring class with certain ameliorations and amenities while reconciling her to her "rightful place." This is the shifting limit of More's reformism, the counter-revolutionary tendency of her interest in Yearsley, and the liberal feminist dilemma writ large: "a good heart and an inadequate methodology."[31]

From the perspective of a feminist analysis, it is not sufficient merely to mark, as H. Gustav Klaus does in an otherwise sound study, "only a superficial contradiction" in More's attempts on one hand to procure subscribers for Yearsley's poems while on the other restraining Yearsley from writing for a living. These may indeed be "two complementary sides of a paternalism" as Klaus argues, but the fact that these interventions are conducted by women, both in the case of More and in that of her friend Elizabeth Montagu, deserves further scrutiny. It is not clear from the evidence that the marked class antagonisms which make More's patronage of Yearsley increasingly untenable necessarily denote a simple relation in which the bourgeois patron "can toler-ate no opposition, no independence and no subjectivity" in her protégée.[32] Rather, what unfolds is a gradual recognition on both sides of the limits of each woman's class-produced ideological field, which renders any further cross-class alliances too great a strain. More runs up against her propertied attitude towards the dangerous unsuitability of "letters" as a means of live-lihood for Yearsley. Yearsley resents and resists More's paternalist circum-scription of what looks like an emerging literary career. More's intervention is in fact dependent upon her early recognition of Yearsley's imaginative oppo-sition to and relative freedom from her material circumstances as they produce, without completely determining, her class-specific subjectivity.

So long as Yearsley remains a member of the working class, supplying milk to her customers around Clifton Hill, and merely using the limited income paid out to her by More and Montagu (the trustees of her subscription earn-ings, now invested in the "funds") for furniture and clothing, More is grati-fied. More even supplies her with "a *little* Maid, to help feed her pigs, and nurse the little ones, while she herself sells her Milk."[33] But once the basis of More's own class privilege, that discretionary management of the private income, becomes Yearsley's chief desire, More retreats into indignation and class hostility. Promoting the working-class prodigy does not mean pro-moting working-class deracination, as had happened with Queen Caroline's patronage of Stephen Duck, the "Thresher Poet," in the 1730s; that is one thing that More is very clear about. To Montagu, she writes: "I am *utterly* against taking her out of her Station. *Stephen* was an excellent Bard as a *Thrasher*, but as the Court Poet, and Rival of Pope, detestable."[34]

This would seem to suggest that Yearsley's excellence as a poet rests with her remaining a "Poetical Milkwoman," and not with anything ineluctably literary about her verses at all. The appeal of the plebeian poet would then lie in a surplus of production, poetic production in addition to productive labor. The value of her poetry would be clearly determined by her cultural deprivation, so that a further surplus of industry and talent was necessary to supplement a lack of education. Yet More herself claims that Yearsley's poetry already surpasses mere middle-class competence; preventing her rise in the social scale may preserve her from imitating conventional high-literary verse as Duck had done, but we have no reason to think that Yearsley would choose such hackneyed imitation – and so, for purely aesthetic purposes, no such constraint ought to be necessary. So it is not so much a matter of Yearsley's verse losing its value if she ceases to belong to the laboring classes; the complaint has more to do with a middle-class fear of social mobility generally, especially if it can be obtained through a literary livelihood. There is something too near idleness about the life of writing for More to countenance Yearsley's taking it up; better that the leisured classes occupy themselves in such a way than that a useful member of the laboring force be encouraged in relative inactivity: "You judge with your usual wisdom in saying that she shou'd not be corrupted by being made *idle* or *useless*."[35]

For Yearsley to work seriously at her writing would be for her not to "work" at all, and More seems to fear that a social rise like Duck's might prove dangerous. More does not mention Duck's suicide, but she might well have thought that his tragic end was a likely consequence of such radical deracination. Regardless of her talents, the plebeian poet is not to think of achieving reputation, fame, or immortality through verse. A little pocket-money and some assurance that starvation will be kept at bay are all that Yearsley is entitled to seek, according to More. For the laboring-class poet, writing is material, instrumental – transparently a means to an end. As readers we are not to forget the hardships, poverty, and inadequate education that lie "behind" the verse, but to keep them before us imaginatively at all times, as the true measure of the laboring poet's achievement.

For More, there was, on the one hand, the "natural" writer with the "nicely tuned," genteel-sounding ear, and, on the other, the plebeian subject, doomed to perpetual subordination. Yearsley's texts, and the texts of Collier, Leapor, Wheatley, and others tell a different story, of the politicization of the laboring-class writer encountering bourgeois subjectivity and making a contradictory, sometimes radical accommodation to it.

Feminist scholars and literary critics, beware! We will not succeed in liberating the Yearsleys of history by casting them as historically liberated already, nor by tokenizing them through selective canonization of their "exceptional" plebeian texts. Nor can we allow ourselves to feel paralyzed into silence, or into silencing the discourse that is always exceptional because it has been made public, entered the public sphere at considerable risk, for fear of working a canonization.[36] It would not be banal or misleading to see in Yearsley's contradictory situation a warning to feminist scholars who seek to create a new literary canon of women's works. To incorporate a few of Yearsley's poems, or Mary Collier's *The Woman's Labour* or Mary Leapor's *Crumble-Hall* into any canon without simultaneously questioning and historicizing the hierarchical and exclusionary practices of canon formation would be to replicate these poets' experience of patronage as tokenization. To praise exceptional merit in such individualist terms, while leaving the complex politics of class relatively untouched, is to help perpetuate the very conditions of More and Yearsley's *mésalliance* and Collier's resignation to continued exploitation. The limits of liberal inclusionism lie in the making of exceptions only to prove the rule of unchanging class hierarchies and inequities of power: these are class-bound, depoliticizing tactics that a radical and emancipatory feminist criticism cannot afford to endorse. Surely we should be at least as bold, in the context of our own historical moment, as many of these poets were in theirs.

Pastoral and georgic transformations

> . . . all in bright array
> The Cherubim descended; on the ground
> Gliding meteorous, as Ev'ning Mist
> Ris'n from a River o'er the marish glides,
> And gathers ground fast at the Laborer's heel
> Homeward returning.   (*Paradise Lost* XII, 627–32)

Thus the cherubim descend on Eden, arriving like the evening mist that pursues the country worker home. What we have here, concordant as well as concurrent with Eve and Adam's departure from paradise, is the transformation of the landscape from a pastoral prospect to a scene of labor, and the return of the georgic mode. If medieval and Renaissance pastoral had expanded to encompass both romance and the georgic, eighteenth-century pastoral verse becomes increasingly preoccupied with and finally crowded out by a georgic discourse of labor and industry.[37] With this georgic emphasis on the representation of the toil of labor becoming increasingly dominant in English poetry, especially after 1744 and the death of Pope, that purveyor of "pure" neoclassical pastoral, it is hardly surprising that there should have arisen at least a marginal movement of writers who were themselves agrarian workers: a movement towards a georgic mode written from inside the experience of rural labor instead of from without, in the Virgilian manner. What the poetry of Stephen Duck, Robert Bloomfield, John Clare, Mary Collier, Ann Yearsley, and others establishes is a new point of view, a new discursive stance, both within the tradition of the English georgic and counterposed to it: it is the perspective of the laborer previously "represented' from outside and at a distance but not (re)produced as such and thus effectively silenced as a discursive possibility. Within the domain of plebeian georgic, it is the male laborer whose point of view emerges first and remains dominant, but the few laboring-class women poets who achieved publication constitute a counter-discourse to this class-conscious, largely masculine tradition.

Undoubtedly the popularity of Virgil's *Georgics* in eighteenth-century Britain helped prepare the way for working-women's verse. Once the preference for "realistic" representations of rural life was firmly established,[38] a certain polite curiosity about what the laborers might have to say for themselves became possible. Dryden's translation of "the best Poem by the best Poet"[39] penetrated even the remoter parts of Britain. When asked in Bristol in 1784 who her favorite authors were, Ann Yearsley replied that "Among the Heathens" she had "met with no such Composition as Virgil's Georgics."[40] But certain changes in the countryside itself also helped prepare the way for such writing, if not always in the most salutory sense. Although the tradition of English "country" verse had tended to obscure the functions of labor, to naturalize the productivity of the soil as magical plenitude,[41] plebeian georgic emerges as a discourse of protest – against class oppression and against the silencing and effacement of labor wrought by the leisured pastoral tradition. Thus we may speak of working-women's verse in relation to "georgic transformations" of at least two kinds: this discourse simultaneously testifies to the important transformations within British agriculture of the eighteenth century that are still the subject of debate among historians, and it helps produce transformations within the georgic mode, and hence within English literary history.

Recent historical scholarship has established that a certain capitalization of British agriculture occurred in the eighteenth century. Beyond this assessment, however, historical interpretations of the evidence vary, and vary in usefulness with regard to understanding laboring-class women's poetry in the period. For R. S. Neale, following Maurice Dobb, what is most important about this development of agrarian capitalism is that the "revolutionary class," the class that contributed most towards the establishment of a modern bourgeois state and prepared the ground for industrialization, was in Britain not to be found among the urban bourgeoisie but among the rural land-owners. The rationalization of agricultural technologies, the formation of a laboring class supporting itself entirely by means of wage labor, and the ideology of intensive estate improvement and industry at home that Britain might rule an empire abroad all preceded the industrialization of manufacturing *per se*: "What Dobb argues, and what a good deal of recent research shows, is that because of various peculiarities in English agriculture and society *capitalism and capitalists developed within the rural sector*."[42] Working from demographic evidence, David Levine argues for the "proletarianization" of eighteenth-century agricultural and artisanal labor. According to Levine, the factory system of the nineteenth century did not so much implant a new work regimen and new "industrial" social relations on a previously antithetical agrarian model as "superimpose" the demands of the factory as a workplace upon an already deracinated and struggling rural proletariat. The capitalization of agriculture and cottage industries helped to bring about demographic upheaval, a certain independence of individuals from traditional village communities, a lowered marriage age, and a consequent rise in the laboring population at the same time that wage labor ceased to represent only a phase in a worker's life cycle and became the norm. As a result: "Not only were the workers replacing themselves at a very rapid rate, but any sustained period of prosperity occasioned the influx of new recruits into the industry . . . Because labor was both cheap and plentiful there was little incentive to undertake capital investments in order to raise productivity." Following Clifford Geertz, Levine describes this "vicious circle" as "industrial involution."[43] Both Neale and Levine provide historical models for understanding the emergent class consciousness evident in much working-women's verse and seemingly "in advance" of what previous historiography would have harnessed firmly to the industrial revolution of the nineteenth century. If the emergence of this literary and sometimes socially critical discourse in rural and provincial communities rather than in London, where female literacy rates were higher,[44] might once have seemed odd, Neale and Levine usefully illumine a possible link between early capitalization and the potential need for, if not the inevitability of, forms of agrarian protest and social criticism in Britain, including poetry.

K. D. M. Snell's study of changing patterns of agricultural labor amply demonstrates that previous discussions of a possible rise in the standard of living of the rural poor in the later eighteenth century, based on wage levels, have been too narrow, and that the grounds of protest were many. One of the major considerations from a contemporary laborer's perspective would have been the prospects of women's employment and thus women's contributions to the family income. Here we find the capitalization of agriculture creating an increasingly gender-specific division of labor and a consequent undermining of women's earning capacities, at the very moment when the last wave of enclosures made it most difficult to supplement the family income by keeping livestock, planting, and growing vegetables.[45] Summarizing detailed statistical evidence, Snell describes an important shift in women's agricultural labor that transpires during the latter half of the eighteenth century, the period of the working-class women's poetic production:

So from an environment with a relatively high degree of sexually shared labour, in which gender differences appear to have been almost a matter of indifference to employers, we have moved to a situation indicating an unprecedentedly marked sexual specialisation of work. Women had come to be most secure from unemployment during a period of the year characterised in the east by relatively slight labour costs and by a low demand for labour [the spring, as opposed to harvest time]. The change was long-term, and its origin can certainly be dated from a period before 1793 – almost certainly between 1750 and 1790. This description of change affecting female work and the sexual division of labour, with its implications of a decline in annual female participation rates and potential earning capacity, can be well supported by long-term trends in male and female money wages, and by early nineteenth-century literary evidence for the region.[46]

Snell's thesis is well supported by such reformist proposals as David Davies's *The Case of Labourers In Husbandry Stated And Considered* (1795), which argues for a rise in wages, the rationalization of the distribution of poor-rates, and encouragement of employment among the poor, especially the gender-specific work of "knitting, spinning, sewing, and the like" for women and girls, which would make them more desirable as prospective wives:

And as such women would be then more courted than the ignorant and unskilful, this might induce the women in general to learn these easy and useful arts: and having learnt them, they would know their value, and teach their children the same.[47]

Snell's study thus seeks to account for the growing split between "North and South" in Britain after 1770 in a variety of ways, combining economic history with a social focus on women and the family. In characterizing the difference between "the impoverished and stolidly comic figure of 'Hodge' in the agrarian south" and "his unionised and assertive northern counterparts," Snell helps to shed light on the shifting limits of laboring-class women's consciousness and the consciousness of the middle- and upper-class patrons who subscribed to their volumes of verse. From C. Holdenby's *The Folk of the Furrow* (1913), Snell offers the following painful misrecognition of laboring consciousness by yeoman or gentry observers:

"Wages and beer are the only things I've found a countryman keen on, and I've worked with 'em pretty often." This was as far as my friend had got after twelve years' farming on his own land. No wonder countrymen are reserved . . . they have also a reserve born of poverty, of being under-valued, of being alienated from the land, or being mere lodgers upon it.   (Quoted in Snell, p. 5)

To the deformations of subjectivity attributed to the laboring classes as a whole, we must add those specific to female laborers if we are to understand their discourse in historically nuanced ways.

In analyzing the representation of the rural poor in English painting of the period, John Barrell identifies a peculiar asymmetry between portrayals of laboring men and women. Particularly in the figure of the milkmaid, there seems to be a conflation of the rustic and the polite that effaces female labor as productive work and reestablishes the country woman solely as an object of the spectator's desire. Barrell discusses this phenomenon in terms of class and representation only and without reference to any feminist critique. Thus the milkmaid, like many other female figures in later eighteenth-century painting who are rustic or poor but attractive, finer-featured, and better-dressed than their male counterparts, hover:

between a courtly and a rustic identity, as the art of rural life hovers between idyll and actuality. The polite viewers of this landscape [Gainsborough's *Landscape with a Woodcutter Courting a Milkmaid*], then, had the possibility of identifying with the milkmaid, and so with the cleanly and delicate-featured woodcutter, who is, precisely, "courting" her, which they did not have, and certainly would not have wanted, with the ploughman.[48]

According to Barrell, this painting by Gainsborough offers us "the image of a society divided between those who must, and those who need not work, and secures the pastoral present for the consumer, while deferring the happiness of the laborious producer to the distant georgic future" (Barrell, *The Dark Side of the Landscape*, p. 41).

If even the extant representations of rural female laborers in the period are really those of courtly ladies in disguise or purely erotic objects to excite the polite consumer's pleasure, then laboring women have been doubly effaced. Reading the poems written by two milkwomen, Ann Yearsley and Janet Little, in the light of social and economic history reorganizes our sense of what representations of eighteenth-century milkmaids could possibly signify, beyond their relatively hygienic picturesqueness and the psychosexual dynamics of their skill in milking and their metonymic association with bountiful lactation. If we are to move on from Barrell and make the material conditions of rural women's labor "speak," we can begin by recognizing that dairying was the most economically valuable and the most arduous form of women's agricultural work.[49] A certain prestige attaches to it on both counts, which may have contributed to the preference for milkmaids in English landscape painting and poetry in important ways.

We should value the discourse of working-women's verse not least for its representations of the hard physical labor to which women of the lower classes in Britain were accustomed in the centuries before industrialization, and to which women in less developed countries remain accustomed today. Such representations from within this class position should forever give the lie to assumptions about the essential "backwardness" of those who labor, though the exceptional status of the few laboring women who not only wrote but published their works must also be acknowledged. The aesthetic polish of Mary Leapor's description of the fatigue produced by field work in *Complaining Daphne. A Pastoral* (1751) must have been achieved at great imaginative cost:

> Oft, I remember, in my Infant Pride,
> When *Daphne* wander'd by her Mother's Side;
> When, fledg'd with Joy, the dancing Minutes flew,
> Nor Grief nor Care this guiltless Bosom knew;
> As oft she led me at Meridian Day,
> To weed our Corn, or turn the fragrant Hay;
> If then I sunk beneath the parching Heat,
> And my quick Pulse with flutt'ring Motion beat,
> While fainting Sweats my weary Limbs invade;
> Her Care convey'd me to a Beechen Shade.
> There with her Hand she press'd my throbbing Head,
> And laid me panting on a flow'ry Bed;
> Then sat beside me in the friendly Bow'r;
> Long Tales she told, to kill the tedious Hour;[50]   (78–91)

here we are reminded that the women of cottager families in the period must painfully combine the necessities of a subsistence economy with minding children.[51] Pastoral convention, however, permits a temporary, idyllic retreat beneath the shade, in which stories can be told and the possibilities of women's poetic composition are established.

The most common forms of women's work in the century are not nearly so visible or so often represented as the forms of agricultural work, but they nevertheless make their way into laboring-class women's georgic poetry. Housekeeping, in cottages and in the houses of the middle class, gentry, and aristocracy, remains the primary form of women's work. Changes in the structure of "service" in the course of the century in fact mark a transition from the tradition of servants in husbandry – farm servants considered as part of the household and who were often the children of other farming families – to a sharper division between the landed and the landless, with a class of laborers both agrarian and domestic emerging, a ready supply of labor for the factory system of the nineteenth century.[52] By the end of the eighteenth century, women had become much more extensively employed in service than in earlier periods, while male servants were now being drawn from a distinctly lower social class than formerly. "Even the upper servants," writes Dorothy Marshall, "were in the majority of cases the sons of labourers, artisans or small farmers rather than recruits from the ranks of reduced gentlemen."[53] For women, especially, the shift in service from the category of servants in husbandry, who might serve only in youth before marrying and setting up their own households, to the category of lifelong domestic servants, was crucial. As late as 1851, domestic service remained the second largest occupational group after agriculture for both sexes and easily the most important for women, and the second half of the nineteenth century saw an increase in the number of domestic servants, primarily female servants, roughly twice as rapid as the growth of the population as a whole (Marshall, in Burnett, p. 137).

The georgic mode of course offers possibilities of representation beyond the description of husbandry and domestic economy, notably political possibilities. Virgil's poem simultaneously celebrates domestic cultivation and imperial might, industrious peace at home and militant expansionism abroad. Mainstream English georgic poetry, from Denham's *Coopers Hill* (1642, 1655) through Dryden's translation of Virgil (1697), John Philips's *Cyder* (1708), Pope's *Windsor-Forest* (1713, 1717), Gay's *Rural Sports* (1713, 1720), James Thomson's *The Seasons* (1726–30), William Somerville's *The Chace* (1735) and *Hobbinol* (1740), Christopher Smart's *The Hop-Garden* (1752), John Dyer's *The Fleece* (1757), James Grainger's *The Sugar-Cane* (1764), Richard Jago's *Edge-Hill* (1767), Goldsmith's *Deserted Village* (1770), George Crabbe's *The Village* (1783), and William Cowper's *The Task* (1785), to much of the work of Burns and Clare, works out in different ways the relations of power between domestic agriculture and empire, between a gradual agricultural revolution and the expansion of the scene of "British" industry to nearly global proportions.

The plebeian georgics of Duck, Woodhouse, Burns, Clare, Bloomfield, and the female poets to which this book is devoted add to this conception of power the specific dimension of laboring-class experience. What is distinctive about female plebeian georgic is its protofeminist insistence upon the injustice and absurdity of sexual relations as they cut across and adumbrate oppressive class relations. In *The Woman's Labour* (1739), Mary Collier explicitly sets out to supplement the lack of a feminine perspective in Duck's *The Thresher's Labour* (1730, 1736). Mary Leapor's *Crumble-Hall* (1751), which combines plebeian georgic, satirical country-house and pastoral modes, provides a critique of familial and sexual relations in addition to sardonic commentary on the experience of domestic service. Elizabeth Hands's superficially conventional and leisured pastorals are intercut with criticism of increasingly formal, contractual marriages among the poor, for which Hands would like to substitute indigenous moral integrity and love; her perspective is at once nostalgic and resistant to later eighteenth-century images of the poor as cheerful, humble, and without any trace of the boisterous wit which characterized representations of them earlier in the century. The criticism of contractual relations can also be read as a protest against the increasing legalization of, and intervention by the juridical system in, social and sexual relations, the control of much-feared protest and disturbance on the part of the laboring classes through the gradual incorporation into a system of power deployed within the most intimate relationships.[54]

Certain aspects of the English georgic tradition, and the imperial mode generally, operate symbolically in ways hostile both to eros and to the female gender, who must bear the sign of eros, must be "the sex," themselves the embodiment of "sexuality." None of our plebeian female poets comments on this aspect of the *Georgics* or the georgic, not even Yearsley who professed such interest in Virgil's poem. And yet the transformations in the georgic mode wrought by these poets very much concern a desire to rectify, and to equalize, relations between the sexes. In their verse, we hear less about British imperium and more about eros, though the war between the sexes often drives female characters off into the shady groves with one another. What they appear to be seeking there is left ambiguous; they seem to retreat to a pastoral green world as much in the interests of a certain defiance of male control as for the satisfaction of desire.

But we shall find that the critique of sexual relations, though it spills over into georgic representations of agrarian and domestic labor, is really concentrated elsewhere in their *œuvres*, in a poetic mode that ranges generically from philosophical satire to amorous epistle and biblical narrative. These are among the most explicitly feminist poems of the eighteenth century, exposés of male dominance and of patriarchal privilege, poems that strive to provide an alternative to the existing sexual order.

Disputing the rule of the fathers

The dangers we despise, doth this truth prove,
Though boldly we not fight, we boldly love.
   Ingage us unto Books, *Sappho* comes forth,
Though not of *Hesiod*'s age, of *Hesiod*'s worth.
If Souls no Sexes have, as 'tis confest,
'Tis not the he or she makes Poems best:
Nor can men call these Verses Feminine,
Be the sence vigorous and Masculine.[55]

(Philo-Philippa, *To the Excellent Orinda*, 87–94)

By the time Mary Collier publishes her plebeian female georgic that is also a protofeminist polemic in 1739, the grounds of debate over "the woman question" and the politics of gender have been well established in Britain for at least a century.[56] It is not so much a matter of these laboring-class poets initiating a feminist poetics, therefore, though their intervention in the debate marks a definite departure in class terms from much of what had gone before. With the exception of plebeian contributions to this storm over the gender question during the 1640s and 1650s, the debate had been mainly between middle- and upper-class women and men. Thus, although the plebeian Mary Cary published prophecy concerning the future of women as spiritual leaders in 1651,[57] a gesture fraught with political implications, there would seem to be little memory of her intervention in 1694 when Mary Astell published *A Serious Proposal To the Ladies, For the Advancement of their true and greatest Interest*,[58] advocating the development of women's spiritual and intellectual powers as if she were broaching a nearly new subject. Cary had claimed that the times were changing, that women of all ranks and unlettered men were beginning to speak publicly and prophetically as instruments of God's will; the revolution of the saints was underway:

Indeed, they have tasted the sweetness of the Spirit; and having tasted, are longing for more, and are ready to receive from those few that are in any measure furnished with the gifts of the Spirit for prophesying; . . . But the time is coming, when this promise shall be fulfilled, . . . and not onely men, but women shall prophesie; not onely aged men, but young men; not onely superious [*sic*], but inferiours; not onely those that have University-learning but those that have it not; even servants and handmaids.[59]

By contrast, Astell's pious but more secular discourse sets out to supply privileged women with something approaching a university education; the plebeian aspirations towards political participation that would have constituted a social revolution and that were thinkable in 1651 have no place in Astell's better known and more strictly, if class-specifically, feminist text.

The debates on gender, sexual relations, marriage, and the family that are carried through from the seventeenth into the eighteenth century in Britain find their way into women's, and thus working women's, poetry with some frequency. At times their theoretical position approaches what we would now call radical feminism: a thoroughgoing critique of patriarchy, male domination, heterosexism, the double standard of sexual morality, and men's exploitative control over the means of representation, production, and reproduction. This theoretical position tends to be coupled with a desire for strong female friendships, sometimes for female separatism and lesbian attachments. Radical feminists logically attempt to distance themselves critically from patriarchal relations in as many respects as possible.

Mary Astell, whose texts are persuasive rather than polemical, and whose feminism is not so radical as that of many women writing before and after her, nevertheless advocates the establishment of a female seminary, the forerunner of the women's college, so that women may develop their intellectual abilities and moral understanding apart from men:

You are therefore Ladies, invited into a place, where you shall suffer no other confinement, but to be kept out of the road of sin . . . You will only quit the Chat of insignificant people, for an ingenious Conversation; the froth of flashy wit for real wisdom; idle tales for instructive discourses. The deceitful Flatteries of those who under pretence of loving and admiring you, really served their *own* base ends, for the seasonable Reproofs and wholsom Counsels of your hearty well-wishers and affectionate Friends; which will procure you those perfections your feigned lovers pretended you had, and kept you from obtaining.[60]

As Bridget Hill has shown, the idea of a "Protestant nunnery" in England recurred persistently from the closing of Catholic convents in the sixteenth century to the founding of women's colleges in the nineteenth.[61] Phyllis Mack concludes, "As the feminist writer Mary Astell saw things in 1697, the best alternative to domesticity, for almost all women, was still the convent."[62] This separatist strain comes to be joined with a preference for female friendship and the adoption of a received notion of "Sappho" as a literary predecessor, as we shall see.

As a site of conflict over gender ideology, the institution of marriage remains unrivalled in the period. There is every reason to doubt that eighteenth-century marriages were significantly more equitable than marriages in previous centuries; the tradition of the feme covert continued, with women legally absorbed under their husbands' names and authority.[63] The marriage debate and the questioning of marital custom prove fertile subjects for women poets. Astell argued that a husband's domestic tyranny was structurally comparable with monarchical tyranny, and would be resisted, especially if – an ironical masterstroke – women were not educated sufficiently to understand the patriarchalist necessity of their subjection. Mocking from a Tory point of view the disparity in Willliamite Englishmen's thinking between a rejection of "Passive-Obedience" at the political level and an insistence on women's submission to patriarchal authority within marriage, Astell represents women's relative powerlessness within that institution as a form of slavery:

Patience and Submission are the only Comforts that are left to a poor People, who groan under Tyranny, unless they are Strong enough to break the Yoke, to Depose and Abdicate, which I doubt wou'd not be allow'd of here. For whatever may be said against Passive-Obedience in another case, I suppose there's no Man but likes it very well in this; how much soever Arbitrary Power may be dislik'd on a Throne, Not *Milton* himself wou'd cry up Liberty to poor *Female Slaves*, or plead for the Lawfulness of Resisting a Private Tyranny.[64]

Jocelyn Harris, who points correctly to connections between Locke's treatises and Astell's arguments in spite of partisan political differences between them, also astutely quotes Mary Leapor on the question of women's domestic slavery:

Locke's influence is obvious, too, upon (for instance) the gardener's daughter Mary
Leapor, whose work Richardson printed and published by subscription. Where
Locke had written derisively that under Filmer's patriarchal scheme "there will be as
many Kings as there are Fathers" (I. 70), she in her *Essay on WOMAN* wrote "Unhappy
Woman's but a Slave at large", because, as she explained in *Man the Monarch*, men
take to themselves the prerogatives of kings.

> Sires, Brothers, Husbands, and commanding Sons,
> The Sceptre claim; and ev'ry Cottage brings
> A long Succession of Domestic Kings.[65]

Thus, when Leapor employs the terms of an anti-absolutist political stance to
expose the injustice of female subjugation, she is not so much inventing new
arguments as transposing into poetry what had already been argued often in
prose, and transposing it with a polemical clarity unusual in women's poetry
of the period.

Particularly in the genre of epistles exchanged between women, we can
find a complex, if largely unacknowledged, intertextuality with female poetic
precursors. The poetry of Katherine Philips (1631–64), for instance, offers
both criticism of marriage and sexual relations and a sapphic alternative.
Although we cannot locate a tradition of explicit admiration for Philips's
poetry in these working-class women's *œuvres*, her influence as an "English
Sappho" may well have left its mark, traceable in the popularity of a sapphic
retreat, a pastoral green world of women's passionate friendships, within their
discourse. The questioning of women's subordination within marriage posed
by "An Answer to another perswading a Lady to Marriage":

> FObear bold Youth, all's Heaven here,
>   And what you do aver,
> To others Courtship may appear,
>   'Tis Sacriledge to her.
>
> She is a publick Deity,
>   And were't not very odd
> She should depose her self to be
>   A petty Household God?[66]   (1–8)

may be usefully articulated with such erotic tributes to other women as
Philips's "To Mrs. Mary Awbrey":

> SOul of my Soul, my Joy, my crown, my Friend,
>   A name which all the rest doth comprehend;
> How happy are we now, whose Souls are grown,
> By an incomparable mixture, one:[67]   (1–4)

especially when we consider what value Philips placed on female friendship:

> Nobler than Kindred or then Marriage-band,
>   Because more free; Wedlock-felicity
> It self doth only by this Union stand,
>   And turns to Friendship or to Misery.[68]   (13–16)

Both explicit admiration for Sappho and epistles traversed by women's complex and often contradictory desires regarding other women are characteristic of Leapor's *œuvre*. Elizabeth Hands would seem to have found this latter a fit subject for literary parody; Janet Little continues the tradition with a straight face.

Most mysteriously, Ann Yearsley's manuscript papers include a love poem to an unspecified other prefaced with the following epigraph:

> Sappho,   Justified,   either way.[69]

The two ways in which Sappho might be justified are not finally decidable, but the epigraph probably refers most literally to the concluding lines of Pope's *Sapho to Phaon*, an imitation of Ovid's *Heroides* and a poem with which all these poets seem familiar. Rejected by Phaon, her young male lover, Sappho contemplates leaping from the Leucadian cliffs in order to drown herself:

> If not from *Phaon* I must hope for Ease,
> Ah let me seek it from the raging Seas:
> To raging Seas unpity'd I'll remove,
> And either cease to live or cease to love![70]   (256–9)

Thus the question implicit in Yearsley's "either way" could be that Sappho was justified whether or not she committed suicide. Or if Yearsley were reading Pope's final line very closely, she might be claiming that Sappho's suicide was equally "justified" as a way of ending her life and her unrequited love, since they have become inextricable in Pope's text. Sappho insists on seeking ease for her burning desire, even at the risk of drowning. In Pope's version, not acting on desire implicitly already represents for Sappho a kind of death. We may think of Blake's "Sooner murder an infant in its cradle than nurse unacted desires."[71]

The poem to which the epigraph is attached is an epistle addressed to "✶✶✶✶✶✶," in which Yearsley discourses upon freewill and causality in relation to a forbidden love – literally, a love that "dare not speak its name,"[72] concluding:

> And Yet, – if pow'r of Acting is not mine!
> What Virtue's in Me, if I Joy resign?
> To choose, what we may deem, a *Virtuous* grief
> That mourns, yet never will accept Relief.

> There, am I at a pause! nor will my Song
> Remove, my doubt, but ev'ry doubt prolong
> Therefore I will not strain the studious lay
> To Reason ev'ry softer sense away!
> But own my Soul, moves in a pure degree
> And Boasts her Freedom, in pursuing *Thee*.   (25–34)

The text, like the writer's "Soul," boasts its own freedom by rejecting virtuous restraint and expressing a desire for the forbidden, the unnameable, but Yearsley dares not risk naming the object of her affections. Only this unspecified object of desire, the poem's "true" addressee, will be able to recognize the referent of that emphatic "*Thee*." If we consider what "Sappho" has come to represent as a cultural sign both within and outside the immediate context of Pope's imitation of Ovid, then Sappho's being justified "either way" acquires another significance. For Sappho's pursuit of Phaon has supplanted her more famous relations with women on the island of Lesbos:

> No more the *Lesbian* Dames my Passion move,
> Once the dear Objects of my guilty Love;
> All other Loves are lost in only thine,
> Ah Youth ungrateful to a Flame like mine!   (17–20)

The doubleness of Sappho's passions, fixed exclusively on neither male nor female lovers, gives her fragmentary texts and her eighteenth-century reputation a certain undecidability and a certain transgressive power, the power of the illicit. In Pope's version, Sappho's lesbian loves are clearly classified as "guilty" ones. In Yearsley's poem, pursuit of the loved one is somehow transgressive – simultaneously forbidden and liberating, a sign of freedom in its breach of virtue. For Yearsley, a married woman who most often writes as a married woman, any extramarital passion would constitute a breach of virtue. Sappho's erotic doubleness, as well as her threat of defiant suicide in Pope's poem, may well represent for Yearsley an imaginary resolution to her own dilemma of unspeakable desire. Because the love that dare not speak its name is so powerfully exacting, as Yearsley's poem testifies, Sappho's agency in its doubleness, from illicit passion for lovers of both sexes to the undecidability of whether or not she killed herself, is always already justified.

In the sapphic textuality of amorous epistolary discourse between women, a powerful alternative to oppressive heterosexual relations is made possible, if only discursively. Disputing the rule of the fathers can take many forms; working-class women poets appear to follow the tradition of more privileged female precursors most clearly when they situate their poetic protests regarding marriage and sexual relations within the context of a sapphic alternative to female "slavery."

To return to Mary Collier's questioning of working-class male authority, with which we began this section, we might see her contribution to a protofeminist discourse of protest, specifically addressed as it is to a former fellow worker, as a move belonging to the history of female interventions in a traditionally male working-class politics. Sheila Rowbotham characterizes this scene of intervention most memorably in a modern British context when she writes:

Women's liberation has mounted an attack on precisely those areas where socialists have been slow to resist capitalism: authoritarian social relationships, sexuality and the family . . . The predicament of working-class women is the most potentially subversive to capitalism because it spans production and reproduction, class exploitation and sex oppression . . . They are thus compelled to develop both sisterhood and solidarity or be crushed. They need each other, they need the support of male workers, and their fight at work connects immediately to their situation at home.[73]

Rowbotham could nearly be describing the content of Collier's protest to Duck, its focal points of interest, identification, grievance, and aspiration. Disputing the rule of the fathers preoccupied many early modern women writers, for whom publishing, if not writing itself, often represented a struggle against convention and the prejudices of a largely masculine literary establishment. Women poets of the laboring class contribute unequivocally to the debates about gender, but their style of disputation is marked by an emergent consciousness of class as well.

Versifying the Scriptures

Reading the Scriptures was crucially formative for working-class women poets. Elizabeth Montagu, while a patron of Ann Yearsley, went so far as to exclaim:

Avaunt! grammarians; stand away! logicians; far, far away, all heathen ethics and mythology, geometry, and algebra, and make room for the Bible and Milton when a poet is to be made. The proud philosopher ends far short of what has been revealed to the simple in our religion.[74]

Neither Yearsley nor any of the other writers treated at length in this study were so entirely bound to religion in their reading as Montagu would have them; neoclassical mythology in particular seems to have been indispensable for the eighteenth-century poet. In its minimalist form, however, laboring-class women poets' versifying of the Scriptures could consist mainly of elaboration on the Letter of the Law.

Susannah Harrison's devotional verses begin with quotations from the Scriptures and perform incantatory explications of and meditations on these lessons for the day. A domestic servant stricken with a lingering and

eventually fatal illness that rendered her unfit for service, Harrison taught
herself to write as an aid to prayer. According to the anonymous preface to
the first edition of *Songs In The Night* (1780), she never intended publication
during her lifetime, but thought the posthumous issuing of her verses might
bring some comfort to other sufferers. When she was unexpectedly spared,
she agreed to publication anyway.[75] The second and fourth editions include
additional poems, up to "Song XVIII. *I am as a wonder unto many: let my mouth
be filled with Thy praise and with Thy honour all the day.* – Psalm lxxi. 7,8,"[76]
which is described in a concluding note as her last composition: "★This piece
is dated October, 1783, in the MS. and appears to have been the last time of
Her using a pen." What began as prayer and therapy for Harrison would
seem to have found a ready audience who sought similar consolations in
reading.

Harrison positions herself discursively as an instrument of divine praise, a
handmaid to the Lord:

> LET Praise employ my Heart and Tongue:
>   Let Grace, free Grace, be all my Song,
>   While Life and Breath remains:
> In this sweet Work I love t'engage,
> And when I quit this earthly Stage,
>   I'll sing in nobler Strains.[77]   ("XVIII")

She sometimes speaks directly to an audience of servants and laborers with
uplifting or prudential advice for their continued forbearance in service:

> Ye that are Servants, seek for Grace,
> If to your Masters you'd be dear;
> And thus fill up your humble Place,
> Serve them in Faith, with holy Fear.
>
> Labour while Heav'n allows you Strength,
> Let all your Work to God be done;
> A sure Reward shall come at length,
> And everlasting Life be won.
>   ("XLIX. *A certain Centurion's Servant was dear unto him.*
>   – Luke vii. 2," 17–24)

Unlike her fellow laboring poets, however, she advises against seeking after
any knowledge other than knowledge of the Scriptures, the knowledge
necessary to faith. Harrison would seem to exemplify Montagu's divinely
instructed, and religiously preoccupied, poet. But that model proves too
narrow for Harrison's contemporaries, too intellectually constricting. It also
leads to precepts not unlike Hannah More's strictures on the spread of learning among the poor:

What is the Knowledge he requires?
What are the Things his Soul desires?

. . .

He seeks to know himself aright,

. . .

Earnest he seeks Jehovah's Face,

. . .

He seeks for Pardon thro' the Blood
Of Jesus, the incarnate God;

. . .

He seeks to prove his Faith sincere,

. . .

This is the Knowledge he requires;
And God will grant his pure Desires;
Jesus will bless him from the Skies,
And make him to Salvation wise.

("L. *The Heart of him that hath Understanding, seeketh Knowledge.*
Prov. xv. 14," 3–24)

Historically, we can say that this knowledge seems not to have proved sufficient for the majority of laboring women who put pen to paper in the
eighteenth century, though religion could also provide consolation. Powerful religious writing of Harrison's decade attests to the struggle with faith
and the constraints of religious community that an intelligent, literate
woman was likely to face, a struggle especially evident in the Quaker discourse of Dorothy Gott.[78] But Harrison's texts do not inscribe this struggle,
they represent faith as assuring the transcendence of it. And as poetic texts,
they are least aesthetically interesting where they adhere to Scripture most
closely.

In "CXIX. To Young Women. *Beauty is vain, but the Woman that feareth the
Lord she shall be praised.* – Prov. xxxi. 30," Harrison attempts a more secular
discourse within the tradition of poetic advice to young women on such
topics as vanity, dress, frivolity, and piety, of which Pope's *The Rape of the
Lock* (1717 version) and *Epistle to a Lady* (1735) and Young's *Satires V* and *VI*
"On Women" in *Love of Fame. The Universal Passion* (1725–8) were probably the most famous:

HOW oft doth Beauty lead to Sin.
    And tempt the Heart to stray;
It charms awhile, then hides again,
    And soon it fades away!

Not all the Art, and Pains, and Care
　　Of Man can make it sure;
Nor can the fairest of the Fair
　　The transient Bliss secure.

Sickness and Pain may soon disgrace
　　The most admired Charms;
Soon must they sleep in Death's Embrace,
　　And lose their lovely Forms.

How vain is Beauty, then, my Muse!
　　Unworthy of thy Lays;
Turn, and a nobler Subject chuse,
　　Let Virtue have thy Praise.   (1–16)

At this juncture, the poem returns to Harrison's usual liturgical style, after a brief effort at the secular advice poem, a momentary rapprochement with mainstream poetic culture in the period. Harrison's texts have more in common with hymnal verse than with what circulated as poetry *per se* in the latter part of the century. In their very assurance of the joys of divine salvation, Harrison's poems resist aesthetic response and critical scrutiny, as they prostrate themselves humbly before the anticipated heavenly future.

More typical of plebeian women's poetic appropriation of the Scriptures in the period is the long narrative poem that rewrites an episode from the Old Testament. Like the long poem on a classical or antique subject, Phillis Wheatley's *Niobe in Distress for her Children slain by Apollo, from Ovid's Metamorphoses, Book VI. and from a View of the Painting of Mr Richard Wilson* (1773) or Ann Yearsley's *Brutus. A Fragment* (1796), such poems on biblical events give these poets an ambitious range of possibilities for exploring ideas and aesthetic effects not otherwise readily accessible in the poetry of the day. With a biblical model in view, a poetic project was likely to pass ideological muster. And, like a classical subject, an Old Testament episode was bound to offer imaginative scope beyond the provincialism of much occasional, elegiac, pastoral, or georgic verse.

Thus we should not be surprised to find these writers attracted to biblical moments when the question of women's power, and their status as religious, discursive, and political subjects, comes to the fore. Again and again we find these women returning to the problem of gender and power, seeking some assurance from the insistence of the Letter, some consolation from the divine Word. Mary Collier's *The First and Second Chapters of the First Book of Samuel Versified* (1762) and Elizabeth Hands's *The Death of Amnon. A Poem* (1789) both rework biblical episodes in which women feature. Both, ironically, eventually turn from the most radical implications of the narratives they have chosen to versify in order to reassure themselves and their readers that the patriarchal order of God's law and eighteenth-century English social custom remain firmly in alignment. The burden of scriptural versification, then, would seem to lie in reworking texts that can be read radically, and often had been during the English Civil Wars and Interregnum, while staying within the pale of contemporary orthodoxy. In *On Jephthah's Vow, Taken In A Literal Sense* (1787), Yearsley challenges these conventions of scriptural versification most boldly, going so far as to question the patriarchalist prejudices of the Old Testament fathers themselves. But this is a maneuver of unusually radical political insight, to which we shall return. More representative of the discourse of laboring-class women's poetry in the period are Collier's and Hands's complex compromises.

It is hard not to imagine that Collier was drawn to 1 Samuel 1–2 because of Hannah's eloquence when her faith is rewarded, not only by her giving birth to Samuel, but by the gift of prophecy. Hannah, wife to Elkanah, has endured in silence the disgrace of barrenness and the insults of Peninnah, Elkanah's other wife who has born him sons, until the year when she prays for a son, promising God that she will make him a priest. Although the biblical narrative emphasizes Elkanah's as well as Peninnah's provocation – he asks her why she weeps and does not eat, adding "*am* not I better to thee than ten sons?" (1 Samuel 1: 8) – Collier's version stresses Hannah's silent martyrdom until she takes relief in prayer:

> While thus She did disclose her pain and Grief
> To him, who able was to grant relief,
> No Friend on Earth was privy to her moan,
> Unto pure Omniscience She pray'd alone.
> Her voice not heard, only her lips did move.   (72–6)

Here "Christian" forbearance and an appeal to divine authority explicitly replace social action – the possibility of Hannah confronting her husband and Peninnah with her faith and grief. Instead she prays for heavenly intervention and gets it. Samuel is born, and she successfully offers him to the Lord as a priest, as promised. Her joy unleashes a flow of eloquent predictions for a divinely sanctioned levelling social transformation. This eloquence, we must suppose, more than compensates for her former silent suffering, and may have attracted a laboring poet like Collier, struggling with plebeian female modes of critical articulation. In Collier's version, Hannah's thanks locates her explicitly as a poor "Handmaid" of the Lord, in the tradition of Mary Cary. Like Cary's, Hannah's social powerlessness is displaced by the divine strength (of speaking, at least) guaranteed by faith. Her predictions promise a generalized vindication of the faithful at the expense of the enemies of the Lord:

> Her grateful tongue those joyful words Exprest,
> My heart and soul doth in the Lord rejoice,

Who heard the sighing of his Hand-maids voice;
My glory, and my Strength he doth appear,
What cause have I the Race of man to fear?

. . .

He is the Lord Supream of life and Death,
When brought to Dust he can restore our breath,
From abject State can raise unto a Throne,
The Earth with all its Kingdoms are his own;
'Tis he protects his Saints and will display,
His Sov'reign Grace to keep them in the way;
But from his hands the Slaves of vice shall share
Woes, scenes of Death, horror, and despair,
Destruction Shall his Enemies attend,
Amazing Thunder he from Heav'n will send;
His Judgments shall upon the Earth appear
That Men may learn, Almighty Jove to fear;
The just shall live, uplifted by his Arm
Untouch'd by danger, and dreadless of harm.   (105–41)

What is most remarkable about this passage is the way it plays down the political suggestiveness of the King James version, which is far more radical in its social implications, especially its insinuation that the meek who shall inherit the earth are specifically the underclass, the socially downtrodden:

5 *They that were* full have hired out themselves for bread; and *they that were* hungry ceased: so that the barren hath born seven; and she that hath many children is waxed feeble.
6 The LORD killeth, and maketh alive: he bringeth down to the grave, and bringeth up.
7 The LORD maketh poor, and maketh rich: he bringeth low, and lifteth up.
8 He raiseth up the poor out of the dust, *and* lifteth up the beggar from the dunghill, to set *them* among princes, and to make them inherit the throne of glory: for the pillars of the earth *are* the LORD's, and he hath set the world upon them.

(1 Samuel 2: 5–7)

Collier's reworking may have drawn some of its initial excitement from these prophetic verses, but her version flattens out the social specificity of the biblical text. Unconsciously or deliberately, she steers away from writing the levelling polemic that her own text could so easily have become.

In *The Death of Amnon*, Elizabeth Hands employs a similar strategy of biblical recuperation: a potentially radical text featuring a woman in some sexual difficulty is rewritten so as to shift emphasis from the woman's victimization to the need for a structure of mastery and loyal servitude within the domestic sphere. Once again, self-effacement, the turning from the "woman question" to the seeking of some reassurance, no matter how meagre, in the texts of the Fathers, marks these poems as representing both the beginnings of a protofeminist discourse — a critique of patriarchal ideology — and the means of that discourse's recontainment within patriarchal ideology. The biblical narrative of the death of Amnon, 2 Samuel 13, stresses David's son Amnon's incestuous desire for his sister Tamar, his will to power over her, and their brother Absalom's cool and calculated plan to have his servants murder Amnon in retaliation. The biblical focus is on the brothers' rivalry, the father's mortification; Tamar is allowed to protest and display her shame publicly, but not to reflect on the social meaning of her situation: the biblical text is concerned above all with patriarchal succession and the necessary rivalries between men that accompany a patriarchal order. Hands's rewriting allows Tamar to reflect briefly on her victimization as a social phenomenon, but otherwise the rape itself is played down in favor of exploring the relation between Absalom, the admirable master, and his faithful servants who are prepared to commit murder for him. In this poem, Hands's desire to rationalize submission to mastery claims her so entirely that her entry into the biblical story is by way of the servants' entrance, not Tamar's silent suffering. Yet she seems to have expected her audience to think of *The Death of Amnon* as "about a rape"; at least her satirically projected gentry readers discuss the poem in these terms in *A Poem, On the Supposition of the Book having been published and read*, in which Hands anticipates the reception of her verse.[79] It would seem that class preoccupations overrode the further examination of Tamar's fate, once the sensationalism of her rape had been briefly captured. Indeed the disgrace of the rape itself is conceived of in class terms when Tamar wonders how she will bear the social consequences:

> . . . tho' by the dignity of birth
> Protected from low insult, can I 'scape
> The meaning leer, the vain contemptuous smile,
> Or the more humbling pity of the proud?   (Canto III, 230–3)

So much for the "woman question." The longest digression from the biblical original concerns how masters can best assure their servants' loyalty, a class-specific address from servant to master in the manner of literary advice to the king from a courtier-writer:

> Too oft do masters, void of judgment, check,
> By froward peevishness and discontent,
> The many little assiduities,
> Which otherwise a servant's zeal would mark,
> Nor make distinction between good and bad;
> But Absalom, with nicest judgment, scans

Their merits and defects; he in reproof
Is slowly cautious, and exactly just;
No clam'rous oaths re-eccho thro' his hall,
No mutt'ring servants whisper imprecations;
Tho' affable and courteous, yet he ne'er
To low familiarity descends;
But with great dignity is nobly kind,
Reigns in their hearts, and by enliv'ning smiles
Encourag'd, they spontaneously attend,
And love completes their servitude with joy.   (Canto III, 159–74)

We can see how reworking biblical narratives provides these poets at once with imaginative scope for addressing questions of some urgency to them in their subservient situations and with the means of exacting comfort from the spiritual promises of the Scriptures. Even the enormity of a conspiracy to murder one violent brother for another, it seems, can be accommodated within the discourse of the courtesy book, put to use simultaneously as retribution for a woman's violation and as proof of servants' unquestioning loyalty to deserving masters. *The Death of Amnon* reproduces a biblical episode in a poetically attractive but ultimately horrifying way. We are led to question, at the very least, the possible applicability of lessons from Old Testament stories to contemporary lives. As elsewhere in her *œuvre*, here Hands exposes but does not resolve some of the social contradictions that inhere in the forms of representation with which she was most culturally familiar and which were not easily subjected to such critical scrutiny.

Versifying scriptural narratives offered women poets of the laboring classes an occasion for tackling difficult philosophical questions that they were accustomed to framing as matters of biblical interpretation. Attempting to write within such a discourse enabled ambitiously long poems on important religious subjects – on matters of familial and social duty, the testing of faith, the consolations to be expected from piety. Empowered by the Word, these poets could write as handmaids of the Lord whether they were churchwomen or Dissenters, putting to use their knowledge of sermons, clerical precepts, and prayers. Rewriting the Scriptures yoked biblical exegesis with imaginative composition, the dramatization of psychic and philosophical conflicts, the meditative practices of prayer and hymn-singing. But if these poems functioned in some sense as acts of piety or songs of praise, they also represented figurations of Woman, femininity – probings and testings of the ideological construction of the proper duty of women within Judaeo–Christian discourse.

Thus the consolations to be derived from faith and from spiritual exercises, including the writing of religious verse, were inflected by discourses that questioned the ways in which the figure of Woman was to be read within biblical narratives and the applicability of such object lessons to real women's actions. As men's and women's spheres were increasingly defined as gender specific and separate, and the social meanings of sexual difference were elaborated in the course of the eighteenth century, such a focus on locating and sometimes querying women's spiritual position as represented within religious discourse is understandable. The distance from revolutionary out-pourings of religious inspiration in the mid-seventeenth century is conspicu-ous, not least because both class and gender divisions seem to have solidified in the interim. The discourses that bear hardest on women's representation within Judaeo–Christian tradition by the end of the eighteenth century are the Enlightenment querying of custom and prejudice as insufficiently accountable to reason, and more faintly discernible, the memory of a plebeian radical tradition of direct spiritual inspiration and empowerment which, combined with the Enlightenment discourse of liberty and natural rights, contributed to the popular unrest and occasional insurrections that marked the last decade of one century and the first several decades of the next.

In 1837, we may recall, it was assumed by a critic in *Blackwood's Magazine* that lower-class women poets of the previous century, like Mary Leapor and Mary Barber, were likely to be primarily writers of enthusiastic religious verse, and that such a breach of literary taste might prevent their recuperation by later audiences. As we have seen, though these poets' most ambitious works may sometimes be scriptural narratives versified, religious poetry by no means dominates their *œuvres*, with the exception of Susannah Harrison's, and her verse is exceptional for a number of reasons. In the years between 1739 and 1796, the poetic productions of the *mens divinior* and "poetry" as such were far from synonymous, and in this respect the range of verse genres produced by laboring women poets of the eighteenth century was little different from the preferences of their more genteel contemporaries.

That ravishing supplement

If a certain less than reverent imitation of celebrated male authors marks women's writing in the period generally, casting them as bricoleurs who steal where they can, recombining textual voices ironically and disputatiously, laboring-class women's poetic homage to the masters is representative of contemporary women's writing as a whole. Except, that is, where class itself enters the discourse and laboring women's specific situations assert them-selves. A poet like Lady Mary Wortley Montagu may steal Pope's and Swift's language and poetic form from text to text to produce such scathing satires on them both as "The Reasons that Induc'd Dr. S[wift] to write a Poem call'd the Lady's Dressing room" and "P[ope] to Bolingbroke," but she inscribes herself therein as both a bitter rival and their social superior.[80] What gender fails to provide, the reliance on class power supplies: magisterial scorn for the very poets from whom she derives such excitement, such irritation, and such literary vitality.

Like Montagu, Anne, Viscountess Irwin, takes Pope directly to task for his arguments in *Epistle to a Lady*, particularly his contempt for women's intellectual powers. These female contemporaries of Pope would seem to agree with the modern feminist critics who claim that, despite his obvious interest in writing about, and so in "representing," women, Pope's stance on the "woman question" is very much of his time and so complicit with antifeminist ideology, though it may seem initially less misogynist than Swift's preoccupation with the grotesque female body.[81] As Ellen Pollak and Felicity Nussbaum have argued, Pope is a master of condescension to his female readers, granting them a spurious sexual power at the same time as he casts doubt on their ability to reason and advises them to minimize their otherness, to become "softer men." In *Epistle to a Lady*, the idealized character of Pope's friend Martha Blount, whose spinsterhood is "normalized' by granting her a husband and children, represents a cluster of contradictions which Pope's forceful rhetoric insists that women accept and, however exhausting it may prove, attempt to live within. Martha Blount's submission to the will of an imaginary husband is offered magically as evidence of her power to influence a man without his ever recognizing it: "Charms by accepting, by submitting sways, / Yet has her humour most, when she obeys" (263–4).[82] We might think that Pope is agreeing with Astell, that within the institution of marriage as traditionally conceived, in accordance with the concept of the feme covert, women are legally subject to their husbands' will and so must find ways of influencing without contradicting them. But Pope represents women as justly subject: as "characterless," as blank spaces without intellectual or moral integrity upon whom men naturally inscribe their fantasies and desires. As if to add insult to injury, the key to this aspect of his argument is attributed to Martha Blount:

> NOTHING so true as what you once let fall,
>   "Most Women have no Characters at all."   (1–2)

Thus not even a woman will defend women as a sex; and even the best women (those who succeed in maintaining their good humor while pleasing men) represent a contradiction in terms, a cipher that is also simultaneously a lack of sexual difference:

> And yet believe me, good as well as ill,
> Woman's at best a Contradiction still.
> Heav'n, when it strives to polish all it can
> Its last best work, but forms a softer Man.   (269–72)

Within Pope's mapping of gender ideology here, women are doubly in/ different, doubly nothing at all.[83] They are also doubly barred by this logic from the profession of letters. Pope's relations with women writers seem to have been vexed at best; he may have praised Judith Cowper, but he quarrelled with Lady Mary Wortley Montagu, failed to acknowledge his poetic debts to Katherine Philips and Anne Finch, Countess of Winchilsea, and ruthlessly satirized Eliza Haywood, Susannah Centlivre, and the very notion of the aspiring woman of letters.

After challenging such assumptions about female characterlessness and subjection, Lady Irwin concludes *An Epistle to Mr. Pope* by appealing to Pope's poetic powers to encourage women's education rather than denounce their follies:

> Wou'd you, who know th' arcana of the soul,
> The secret springs which move and guide the whole;
> Wou'd you, who can instruct as well as please,
> Bestow some moments of your darling ease,
> To rescue woman from this *Gothic* state,
> New passions raise, their minds anew create:
> Then for the *Spartan* virtue we might hope;
> For who stands unconvinc'd by generous *Pope*?
> Then would the *British* fair perpetual bloom,
> And vie in fame with ancient *Greece* and *Rome*.[84]   (111–20)

Irwin simultaneously recognizes the persuasiveness of Pope's poetic rhetoric, its effectiveness at inculcating ideology at an unconscious level, the level of "secret springs," and attempts to enlist him on the side of protofeminist arguments for women's education. It is not enough to refute Pope and have done; somehow he must be persuaded to take up women's cause in spite of his complicity with certain antifeminist commonplaces.

After Pope's death, his persuasive, even seductive, style becomes the object of appropriation for many women poets, especially for women poets of the laboring class, who, unlike their upper-class contemporaries, do not take Pope to task explicitly for his antifeminism. Thus Leapor, in "An Essay on Woman" and "Man the Monarch," implicitly turns Pope's representation of women's characterlessness around as well as upside down, stealing from Pope his language and poetic form without naming him, using his style to undermine antifeminist prejudices, but without confronting him directly. Women's situation within a patriarchal social order, whether they be daughters, sisters, wives, or mothers, is not that of a pleasurable and happy compliance with a masculine will, but a form of slavery: "Unhappy Woman's but a Slave at large."

The fact that Pope himself, as a social victim of exclusion on religious, political, and physical grounds, seems to have identified with female powerlessness, complicates his texts and works against his complicity with the gender ideology of his time.[85] Indeed one might argue that women poets were particularly drawn to reading and responding discursively to Pope because of this very identification, which goes against the grain of many of his poems' explicit pronouncements. *Eloisa to Abelard* may serve as a key text in this respect, given its ventriloquism of a ravished and desiring female voice whose only remaining power is the power to yearn for what she can never possess; it is also, so far as we know, the only poem of Pope's specifically mentioned by a working-class woman poet as the occasion of her own writing.[86] Pope's muse may be female, but Pope's discursive positioning of himself within his texts may be read as remarkably "like a woman's."[87] One might say that a sapphic tendency is already present within Pope's texts in the form of an encounter between his feminized persona and his female muse. The grounds upon which female poets might pay homage to Pope through identification with this image of him or his muse are fruitful indeed.

For the female laboring poet, transference on to a poetic text often involves a class-conscious dynamic compounded of ambition and humility, eroticism and homage. Ravished by the beauty of a poetic discourse which is alien to her, and from which she is often specifically excluded, yet ironically aware of the space occupied within that discourse by subservient female figures in the form of muses, she raids and ravishes by both praising and appropriating what she admires. Sometimes the object of her ravishment would seem to be an image of the great male bard as himself erotically ravished in the act of writing. Sometimes she pursues a desire for union with the bard's female muse.

Particularly in these plebeian responses to Pope, questions of gender and sexuality enter in a disruptive way that no "anxiety of influence" can account for and that might be described as the "supplement" of writing. The supplement contains within itself a certain doubleness that aptly describes the double relations of homage and resistance manifested in these texts: "The supplement adds itself, it is a surplus, a plenitude enriching another plenitude, the *fullest measure* of presence . . . But the supplement supplements. It adds only to replace. It intervenes or insinuates itself *in-the-place-of* . . . Compensatory [*suppléant*] and vicarious, the supplement is an adjunct, a subaltern instance which *takes-(the)-place* [*tient-lieu*]."[88] Pope, the poet who writes women back into their place, who satirizes women writers and would deny them the pleasures of writing while writing "on their behalf," inspired by a female muse, is a recognizable Pope to these plebeian poets. But for them Pope is also a poet ravished by the poetic fit, whose lines exude incomparable sensuous beauty attributed to a rapturous overpowering of his being by the muse. Plebeian women's writing in particular thus "supplements" Pope's texts by demonstrating that educated men's literary authority, men's writing on behalf of and in the name of "Woman," is presumptuous, perhaps even a little preposterous. As a humbly "subaltern instance" of Popean literary production, these poems both pay homage to, enrich the plenitude of, Pope's texts, and show up their exclusions and lacks, effectively supplanting Pope and clearing space for laboring-class women's own production. Such writing turns the female muse and the woman writer into conspirators in the stealing of men's previously exclusive pleasure in inspiration, writing, and fame. Other poets may sometimes be approached in this fashion, but Pope's preeminence within working-class women's poetic discourse seems to cast him as the master of that ravishing textuality to which they would most often aspire, the master of masters.

Neither the Bloomian agon between fathers and sons, a contest of virility displaced on to a struggle for literary prowess, nor Gilbert and Gubar's female bogey, against the spectre of which women writers must struggle, adequately describes relations between eighteenth-century working-class women writers in Britain and their male contemporaries.[89] By understanding the ways in which these poets work to supplement and take pleasure in the style though not the gender ideology of Pope's texts, we shall begin to develop a paradigm of how they make use of poetic precursors without resorting to the Bloomian "family romance," from which both women and feminist concerns are categorically excluded, or to Gilbert and Gubar's own family romance through which a class-specific model comes to dominate a too-homogeneously gendered literary history.

There are, of course, exceptions to this focus on Pope, as we shall see: Mary Collier addresses herself most directly to her fellow plebeian poet, Stephen Duck. Janet Little must needs compare her hybrid Anglo-Scottish poetics with Robert Burns's, while making Samuel Johnson her antagonist. Elizabeth Hands owes a large debt to Butler and Swift, and, as Margaret Doody has argued, Swift dominates the scene of eighteenth-century women's comic verse generally.[90] Early in her career Ann Yearsley claims to be most inspired by a translation of the *Georgics*, and by Milton and Edward Young – "the latter she said had an ardour and boldness in his Imagination that was very delightful to her"[91] – but even she writes Pope a poetic tribute, pays homage to his monumental reputation by striving, briefly, to imitate him in his metonymic groves at Twickenham. In the poems of writers otherwise as various as Yearsley, Little, Hands, and Mary Leapor, Mary Masters, Phillis Wheatley, and Elizabeth Bentley, Pope emerges as the master poet and Pope's textuality as a master text, the quintessence of the high literary mode to which their writing must achieve some relation in order to be considered "literary" at all.

By contrast, contemporary male plebeian responses to Pope may employ a comparable desire for supplementation but they also tend to conform in some sense to the Bloomian oedipal and antagonistic paradigm. Stephen Duck, for instance, wishes for inspiring bodily "Warmth" from Pope's muse, but in order that his description of Richmond Park and the Thames might displace Milton's Eden as a paradise supreme:

> Wide, round her Domes, the spacious Forest shines,
> Tho' brighter much in POPE's harmonious Lines:
> O! would his tuneful Muse my Breast inspire,
> With equal Warmth, with her sublimer Fire;
> Then *Richmond* Hill renown'd in Verse should grow,
> And *Thames* reecho to the Song below;
> A second *Eden* in my Page should shine,
> And MILTON's *Paradise* submit to mine.[92]   (57–64)

Duck's wish to supersede both Pope and Milton here echoes Pope's parallel wish to supersede Milton, and is therefore in one sense a tribute to Pope. But that desire for Milton's text to submit to his suggests a rivalry between Duck and his poetic precursors represented explicitly as a contest for power in which hierarchical dominance is desirable. This male oedipal dynamic is conspicuously absent from the laboring women's poems.

It should also be said that praise for Pope's "ravishing" muse is by no means restricted to these poets, but is, in fact, traditional. Of the two anonymous commendatory poems on his *Works* of 1717, for example, the first contains these lines:

> Smit with thy lays, we join'd the *Sylvan* throng,
> And heard with rapture the enchanting song,
> The ravish'd fancy, thro' the painted meads,
> Travels well-pleas'd, where'er thy musick leads.
>
> ("To Mr. Pope," 5–8)

The second anonymous poem ends: "When all is just, and regular, and great, / We own the mighty master's skill, as boundless, as compleat" ("To Mr. Pope," 77–8). By contrast, Anne Finch, Countess of Winchilsea ("A. Winchelsea"), lectures to Pope on writing well and on not being too much moved by either "Censure or Praise" ("To Mr. Pope," 43).[93] And yet the laboring women poets' construction of their own acts of writing as acts of ravished and ravishing supplementation goes beyond such transparently conventional praise.

Of these various eighteenth-century working-class female responses to Pope, I shall focus here on four differently representative texts; others will be discussed in the chapters that follow. Ann Yearsley's "Written On A Visit" (1787) is perhaps the best example of poetic homage rapturously supplemented. But Mary Masters's "To The Right Honourable The Earl of Burlington" (1733), Mary Leapor's "On the Death of a justly admir'd Author" (1748), and Elizabeth Bentley's "On Reading Mr. Pope's Poems. 1786" (1791) provide a range of responses that nevertheless participate in a certain erotically charged supplementarity in their relation to the bard.

Mary Masters begins her first volume of verse with what looks like an obligatory poem of thanks to her chief patron, but "To Burlington" turns out to be more a self-dramatization of our heroine at the scene of writing than a poem to or about the noble lord who had also recently patronized Pope:[94]

> *My* LORD,
> WHILE you in gilded Palaces reside,
> The *Muses* Patron, and a Monarch's Pride;
>
> . . .
>
> Far far remote I live, a lowly Maid,
> In humble Solitude and rural Shade;
>
> . . .
>
> How shall I then, in so obscure a State,
> Ah! with what Confidence address the Great?
> Unskill'd in Converse, and in Schools untaught,
> Artless by Words, and unrefin'd my Thought:
> What Numbers shall I chuse, to form a Lay
> Th' incumbent Debt of Gratitude to pay?   (1–16)

Masters thus characterizes herself as lowly, rustic, uneducated, and obscure: the very type of the plebeian female poet, at least in relation to Richard Boyle, one of the greatest landowners in England and a noted patron of the arts.[95] In such a situation of inequity Masters wishes fervently that she could have even the briefest of trysts with Pope's "vast Genius," from whom "Floods of Harmony" are sure to flow – an image of textuality as erotic "spending" or dissemination:

> O happy POPE, blest with auspicious Fate!
> On whom the *Muses* and the *Graces* wait,
> Who never o'er the Silver Quill did bow,
> But Floods of Harmony were sure to flow.
> Would thy vast Genius lend me half its Fire,
> And one short Hour my panting Breast inspire;
> By just Degrees the stately Verse should grow,
> And with strong Sense the strong Expression glow;
> In one short Hour a lasting Fame I'd raise,
> And BURLINGTON should smile upon my Lays.   (17–26)

It is not entirely clear who is doing the bowing, Pope or his muses; they are for a moment antically confused, and the subservient muses emancipated. Even a "halfhearted" tryst lasting only an hour would provide Masters with sufficiently ecstatic inspiration to enable her to write above herself, to achieve the power of strong and stately verse, to move up the socio-poetic scale by "just Degrees." We have only minimally to probe the metaphors of inspiration offered here to recognize the erotic dynamics of this hypothetical exchange: the orgasmic nature of Masters's "panting" reception of Pope's genius, the phallic totem that her invigorated verse would become through this act of homage, of becoming a man in relation to the master, and so of becoming capable of "stately" and "strong" – masculine, monumental – literary production. Still "glowing" from this imaginary encounter with a master of the pen, Masters imagines that such a ravishment wrought upon her by Popean genius would confer lasting fame. Being ravished by the master's text means empowerment for the unknown female poet.

Ironically, however, these lines also reveal that Pope's own genius depends upon the servitude of Muses and Graces. Pope is waited upon by a retinue of classical feminine figures, serving him as Masters hopes to be served by his masculine genius. Ironically, Pope was, among other things, a master of the recycling of couplets, both his own and other people's, and his debts to women writers in particular have tended to go unpaid.[96] One of the effects of these laboring poets' tributes to Pope is to remind us of his privileged status as a man of leisure in addition to his privileged place within literary history as a poet of genius, and a master of intertextual appropriation.

Masters's "To Burlington" both reproduces the plebeian poet's crisis of confidence under the eye of patronage – "To me the tuneful Art did ne'er belong; / Why should I then protract an erring Song?" (27–8) – and declares somewhat sarcastically the material necessity of writing:

> Yet when a *British Peer* has deign'd to shed
> His gen'rous Favours on my worthless Head;
> Silent shall I receive the welcome Boon?
> No; 'tis a Crime to take and not to own.   (29–32)

We should not forget that writing for these poets had a particularly clear economic function. Besides serving potentially as a site of cultural resistance, their poetry was a commodity they could exchange for minimal material relief from poverty. If Masters's ravishment by Pope's texts and her pleasurable plundering of their resources were to succeed sufficiently, she might look forward to continued patronage by the great in the form of generous subscriptions. "To Burlington" concludes with an apology for her inadequacy as a poet at the same time that it praises her subscribers as infinitely desirable:

> The Honour yet above the Gift I place,
> When such high names my humble Volume grace,
> So much distinguish'd by the Voice of Fame,
> That ev'ry Author would the Sanction claim.   (33–6)

Self-deprecation coupled with unabashed self-aggrandizement: the contradictory status of Masters within her text as a poet more pursued by fame than driven to pursue it represents a common tendency within working women's verse. With such patronage, who could ask for anything more? Yet clientage produces its own forms of anxiety, not least the fear that one would need to be Pope to deserve such benevolent patronage.

Where Mary Leapor has entered the literary-historical record, she has usually entered it as an imitator of Pope.[97] When she pays him direct homage, as in "On the Death of a justly admir'd Author," she characterizes his poems as a preserve of ravishing imagination and rapturous sensuous beauty accessible to rustic readers, so that his death has deprived them of a continuous source of pleasurable self-improvement.[98] Even the displaced eroticism of reading can and should be put to good use by the uncultivated country-dweller, in Leapor's scheme: no ravishment without a return in terms of rational understanding:

> For his bright Lines are by their Lustre known,
> Ev'n *Homer* shines with Beauties not his own:
> Unpolish'd Souls, like *Codrus* or like mine,
> Fill'd with Ideas that but dimly shine,
> Read o'er the Charms of his instructive Pen,
> And taste of Raptures never known till then.
>
> . . .
>
> Ev'n we condemn'd at distance to admire,
> Bewail the Hopes that with our Guide expire:
> Ah! who shall now our rustick Thoughts refine,
> And to grave Sense and solid Learning join
> Wit ever sparkling, and the Sweets of Rhyme?
> Farewel, ye Themes, which none but he can sing.   (23–40)

The more chaste language of Leapor's tribute nevertheless contains a brief reminiscence of Masters's rapacity when praising the pleasures of Pope's texts. What his poetry offered the uneducated rustic was a rapturous encounter with the "instructive Pen," the pleasures of intellection in discourse. Pope repaid the rural reader with a more "refined" version of herself, newly awakened to literary possibility among Pope's aestheticized "sylvan Scenes" (41). A class-conscious critique of this veneration of Pope's refinements might insist on the depoliticizing function of such a rapprochement with middle-class culture. To take these plebeian poets at their word, however, acquaintance with the pleasures of high literary texts enables them to take pleasure in their own intellectual powers, representing a form of critical empowerment rather than cultural acquiescence.

A more self-effacing act of homage to Pope than Elizabeth Bentley's brief "On Reading Mr. Pope's Poems. 1786" would be hard to find.[99] Bentley pronounces herself inadequate to "pay her debt" to Pope, abashed by his "native elegance" and the fact that he brought English poetry to its "full perfection." Pope's greatness escapes her pen; Bentley's littleness is all:

> GREAT Pope! was ever verse compar'd with thine?
> Did ever genius so conspicuous shine?
> In ev'ry page sublime, throughout the whole
> Thou hast display'd a great and noble soul;
> With native elegance express'd each thought,
> And poetry to full perfection brought.
> To praise thy sense and judgment, heav'nly Bard!
> It is for my poor pen a task too hard.
> Ages unborn shall pay the debt of fame
> Due to thy works and thy illustrious name.

The image of Bentley's "poor pen," rough and weak as well as penurious, laboring to pay her debt to Pope's sublimity, marks a difference, an incommensurability between them that can barely be broached, let alone supplemented. The tropes of rapturous exchange have faded, become residual like so much in Bentley's not quite plebeian discourse. Yet this poem is the second poem in her first volume, still an opening gambit, a poem positionally of some importance. It would seem that Bentley feels she *must* acknowledge Pope in order to come to terms with her public. We may well be left with the impression that it was through reading the master of sound in sense – and perhaps other women's poems to him – that Bentley learned to express her lack by means of those struggling yet accomplished monosyllables.[100]

The clearest instance of plebeian homage to Pope's poetic influence transformed into rapturous appropriation also occurs late in the century, in Ann Yearsley's "Written On A Visit" (1787).[101] "Written On A Visit" both pays homage to the excitement of Pope's poetry and discloses the mixed effects of his reputation as inimitable genius and Absolute Subject of English literary history on later poets. The point about visiting Twickenham for Yearsley is to feel the rapture Pope felt there, to have a sapphic tryst with his ecstatic muse. She cannot be confident, however, that such creative pleasures will materialize. It is the anxiety of the literary day-tripper, hoping against hope that on this occasion rapturous inspiration will commence the usually arduous work of poetry, and not the anxiety of influence *per se* that generates the poem:

> DELIGHTFUL Twick'nham! may a rustic hail
>   Thy leafy shades, where Pope in rapture stray'd,
> Clasp young-ey'd Ecstasy amid the vale,
>   And soar, full-pinion'd, with the buoyant maid?

Ah! no, I droop! her fav'rite Bard she mourns;
　　Yet Twick'nham, shall thy groves assist my song;
For while, with grateful love my bosom burns,
　　Soft Zephyr bears the artless strain along.   (1–8)

Pope's muse is indisposed by mourning, the poet herself "droops," and cannot mount in flight. There is only that distinctly erotically tinged interjection "Ah!" – a moment of ecstatic possibility immediately displaced into tamer and more "artless" and "grateful" verse than had been hoped for but which is at least flowing easily. The visit to Twickenham initially lacks a certain intensity of rapture but seems to offer a workable compromise.

　　Like all optimistic travellers, Lactilla the milkwoman is hoping to escape temporarily from distress at home into beauty and exotic insularity – a world apart. To Lactilla's mind, Twickenham served Pope well as a retreat from public criticism, and so will serve her as a retreat from everyday hardship. At Twickenham lambs seem unthreatened by slaughter, all is pastoral tranquillity without labor, hunger, or sorrow. Some unspecified friendship has made the journey from Bristol possible and now bolsters her confidence. After eight stanzas roving "Through Maro's peaceful haunt' (9), Lactilla's "native Genius soars with conscious Pride" (32). Turning Pope into the English Virgil heightens the distinction between them, between Pope's classicism and Yearsley's "native Genius," but it also mythologizes Pope into an author by whom he must also have felt overdetermined if not overawed:

See, Maro points the vast, the spacious way,
　　Where strong Idea may on Rapture spring:
I mount! – Wild Ardour shall ungovern'd stray;
　　Nor dare the mimic pedant clip my wing.

Rule! what art *thou*? Thy limits I disown!
　　Can thy weak law the swelling thought confine?
Snatch glowing Transport from her kindred zone,
　　And fix her melting on thy frozen line?

　　　　　　　. . .

Yet, Precept! shall thy richest store be mine,
　　When soft'ning pleasure would invade my breast;
To thee my struggling spirit shall resign;
　　On thy cold bosom will I sink to rest.

Farewel, ye groves! and when the friendly moon
　　Tempts each fair sister o'er the vernal green,
Oh, may each lovely maid reflect how soon
　　Lactilla saw, and sighing left the scene.   (33–52)

The Monthly Review, in praising Yearsley's second volume as highly as her first, and venturing to claim, "that the justness of the observation, *Poeta nascitur, non fit*, was never more powerfully exemplified than by herself," nevertheless finds it necessary to criticize her "not unfrequent" obscurity.[102] These stanzas compress many incompletely articulated possibilities of desire for rapture and imaginative transport, and perhaps even liberation in a more political sense, through that disdaining of "Rule" which covers power relations as well as aesthetic conventions. But Lactilla's "Wild Ardour," her anarchic pleasure in poetical inspiration after Pope's example, is abruptly curbed by the invocation of "Precept." The final two stanzas represent a rather chilly resignation to the rule of precept, a denial of pleasure, almost a death-wish for Lactilla's imaginative aspirations.

Somehow Pope's groves, though particularly tempting to female poets, turn out not to be so hospitable to Lactilla after all. Her wild ardor is short-lived, her wistful self-exclusion from the scene, we must assume, eternal. Why does Lactilla come, see, and so soon, "sighing," depart from Twickenham? Curiously, it is not so much Pope's style or subject-matter but the pleasurable, even eroticized nature of his representation of inspiration that appeals to Lactilla. He can explicitly take pleasure in intellection, with "strong Idea" mounting "Rapture" and soaring, just as Lactilla does, disdaining limits, ignoring what is "proper." Perhaps it is this dangerous enjoyment of the improper that causes Lactilla to hail precept so suddenly. She needs to have it both ways, soaring beyond the rules, yet returning to mine or feed on the "rich store" of precepts before she gets "too carried away," letting herself be "invaded" by "soft'ning pleasure." The heavy sexual charge here is unusual in Yearsley's verse. It is almost as if Lactilla were not speaking metaphorically of aesthetic pleasure but describing the fear of being overwhelmed by physical desire – like the milkmaids she describes in the poem *Clifton Hill* who must dissemble their desire for fear of "shame." The imitation of Pope's wild ardor cannot be sustained because it represents a form of erotic transgression for the milkwoman-poet; if she pleasures herself too much, she will move beyond the saving bounds of propriety, which is a luxury that, as a poet, Pope can afford and Lactilla cannot. For someone as socially vulnerable as Yearsley, going "beyond the pale" in political or sexual innuendo was especially to be feared, and "Written On A Visit" reproduces these anxieties in a palimpsest of prohibited aesthetic and erotic desires.

But what is it precisely that Lactilla "sees" at Twickenham that sends her home? Perhaps what she sees, or rather, recognizes is that Twickenham cannot mean for her what it meant for Pope. Twickenham was the retreat he could afford on the proceeds of his extremely lucrative translation of Homer, a sign of his wealth and reputation. And there is a difference between the liberties that a financially secure poet with many powerful friends can take in verse and the liberties that a Lactilla can afford. Not Pope's inimitable genius, but the relatively genteel safety of his position, metonymized by Twickenham's luxuriant groves, marks that difference.

Rather than being silenced by her un-Popean, plebeian female subjectivity, however, Yearsley dispenses with the Popean mythos and goes on to write increasingly political, radical republican, and protofeminist verse. Her soaring flights no longer take her high above Twickenham's pastoral groves but disclose the scenes of rural labor, social protest, and popular insurrection that distinguish the 1790s as a historical moment in which, once again, as in the 1640s and 1650s, lower-class women in Britain could be seen and heard making history from below.

The most aesthetically successful plebeian supplements to the bard are those that, like Masters's and Yearsley's, plunder Pope's text for their ravishing example and then leave his corpus behind, paying homage to it but being empowered by it. At their most successful, these working-class women's acts of transference on to Pope's texts document their refusal to be silenced by either Pope's and other male writers' continued reproduction of contemporary commonplaces about women or their own consequent exclusion from the literary establishment. In spite of the rapturous praise of Pope's textuality that distinguishes these approaches to a common poetic precursor, this production of supplements represents something of a quiet mutiny in the history of women's writing in Britain. And the bounty at stake is a plebeian protofeminist poetic aesthetic, the appropriation of Her Master's Voice.

Chapter 2

The resignation of Mary Collier: some problems in feminist literary history

THO' She pretends not to the Genius of Mr. DUCK, nor hopes to be taken Notice of by the Great, yet her Friends are of Opinion that the Novelty of a *Washer-Woman*'s turning poetess, will procure her some Readers.

    (Advertisement to the first edition of *The Woman's Labour* [1739])

It should be clear that *working class* women's oppression poses the key theoretical problem here; for unlike women's subordination in feudal society or within the bourgeoisie, it cannot be related to male control of property.[1]

    (Brenner and Ramas, "Rethinking Women's Oppression")

Mary Collier appears to have been the first published laboring-class woman poet in England. So far as we know, the publication of her poems brought her little remuneration and no escape from her work as a laundress, housekeeper, and occasional field hand in West Sussex and Hampshire. Her most important poem, *The Woman's Labour: An Epistle To Mr. Stephen Duck* (1739), is beginning to receive some scholarly attention, but until recently she was a poet almost entirely forgotten by literary history.[2] *The Woman's Labour* is an important text for at least three reasons. First, the poem's appearance as early as 1739 suggests that English laboring- or working-class feminism has a history that predates its usual association with the nineteenth century. Second, the poem demonstrates that a plebeian poet such as Collier can take aesthetic advantage of her distance from the dominant literary culture by ostensibly filling a familiar vessel – the georgic, the neoclassical epistle – with strong new content. And in so doing, she can challenge some of the sexual and socio-political assumptions of the very culture from which she has so skillfully appropriated her aesthetic materials. Finally, the poem articulates an emergent working-class consciousness with an emergent feminist critique of the misogynist tendencies embedded in that consciousness.

The Woman's Labour directly redresses traditional historical silences regarding laboring women's oppression; the triple burden of wage labor, housework, and childcare;[3] and the gender ideology that places women illusively outside both material production and language. Collier thus rewrites the georgic more radically than Stephen Duck had done in *The Thresher's Labour* (1736); she definitively alters traditional maps of eighteenth-century literary history. At the same time, there are significant limits to the radical potential of this and other poems by Collier which must be addressed if we are to understand such women's histories in a nuanced way, alert to the often limiting material and social exigencies of their situations. When the woman in question is herself a writer, we can begin by examining the way she figures herself as a writing subject, for the self-who-writes is socially constructed.

In *The Woman's Labour* Collier locates herself quite clearly in relation to the act of writing as well as in relation to the social space from which her writing emerges. At the point of departure for her speculative flight on the prehistoric origins of sexual relations, Collier figures herself as follows:

> Oft have I thought as on my Bed I lay,
> Eas'd from the tiresome Labours of the Day.[4]   (11–12)

Poor women, taken collectively, may have little time to sleep or dream, as we shall see, but the poet inscribes herself here as conceiving her arguments for verse in repeated moments of meditation that border on dream-work. The source of Collier's productivity as a poet is also the source of her "purity," as well as her "peace" of mind: her relatively exceptional status as a single woman, without children.[5] Despite the poverty that so often accompanied life as a single woman in this period, her working life is more circumscribed, her waking hours are less restricted than those of the married majority of her class, the women on whose behalf she writes *The Woman's Labour*. She works only a double (wage labor, housework), not a triple shift. That is presumably the difference that counts for her, that separates her from other working women: her literacy, her talent, her desire to devote her leisure time to books and writing are in a sense supererogatory. If she had a husband and children to tend, her literariness would be effectively cancelled in advance. Such was not the case with Yearsley, who, by the time of her discovery in 1784, had borne seven children, of whom six had survived.[6] But Yearsley appears to be the exception here. For Collier, as for a significant number of other, particularly lower-class, women writers, the single life was seen as crucial to the liberty of literary production.

The one form of "labor" omitted from Collier's poem is the "labor" of human reproduction as childbirth. In place of the labor of birth, Collier gives us a textualization of women's work as social and material, but not exclusively or primarily biological, reproduction. This she can write about knowledgeably, and link with her literary endeavors. Such general social and cultural work is the compensatory prerogative of the spinster, reputedly always with time on her hands, available for child-minding or night-nursing or more public good causes.[7]

If Collier's talents might have been wasted without leisure, her leisure would certainly have been unrewarding to her without education. Not that she received much; as she writes in "Some Remarks of the Author's Life," her "poor, but honest" parents taught her to read when "very Young." But she was never sent to school; at some unspecified time she learned to write "to assist" her memory (p. iii, p. iv). Throughout her life, she claims, reading books and composing verses have been her chief, if not her only, recreation. In "An Epistolary Answer To an Exciseman, Who doubted her being the Author of the Washerwoman's Labour,"[8] Collier asserts that women's inferior education is the basis of their social subordination, and not merely an effect of it. This poem represents her example of a genre that seems to have been obligatory for laboring-class and many female poets of the period, the poetical self-authentification statement, and as such it serves as a welcome autobiographical moment in an otherwise self-effacing *œuvre*. Collier closes this text with a mock admission of female idiocy, from which she hopes the exciseman can protect himself, concluding:

> Tho' if we Education had
>   Which Justly is our due,
> I doubt not, many of our Sex
>   Might fairly vie with you.   (41–4)

This challenge combines confidence in her sex with a plea for women's education. It is a challenge that assumes education to be an unbiased equalizer between the sexes, something that women have been unjustly denied, and can safely possess; the question of misogyny within traditional erudition itself is not addressed.

Such an assumption marks a limit to the radical potential of Collier's writing; her utopian impulses tend to manifest themselves in an assumed faith in a higher authority that will be capable of rectifying injustices sometime in the future. Here it is education, elsewhere in her work religion or the monarchy. A certain deferral of desire for radical social transformation can read much like a conservative resignation to the status quo, though such a reading would be neither very historically accurate nor responsive to the sexual and social nuances of Collier's texts. So also with Collier's aesthetic achievement. Her subtle innovations and breaks with convention, her skillful appropriation of stock neoclassicism and occasional verse forms, may not seem very daring to modern readers.

The Woman's Labour, like Collier's other poems, challenges our institution-alized critical and aesthetic criteria as working-class poetry is likely to do.[9] We run up against some hard questions about how we define and allocate "literary value," about the intractable importance of political criteria in our evaluative judgments, about whether or not the establishment of a female (or feminist?) counter-canon is a sufficient or even desirable project for feminist criticism to pursue.[10] If one project of a feminist literary history might be not only to rediscover women's texts that have been forgotten or devalued by the practices and priorities of canon formation, but also to establish a critical and political feminist discourse within which to reach such texts, then it is necessary continually to historicize our own discourse of feminism by learning to recognize its continuities and discontinuities with earlier instances of resistance to oppression. Collier's writing, particularly *The Woman's Labour*, represents an instance of resistance to oppression both gendered and class-based. If elsewhere in her *œuvre* we confront discontinuities between the analytical categories of much twentieth-century feminism and Collier's own categories, in this poem the continuities seem more powerful.

Reading *The Woman's Labour*

To read *The Woman's Labour* is inevitably to confront what crucial determinants class and gender are in any textual production.

> No Learning ever was bestow'd on me;
> My Life was always spent in Drudgery:
> And not alone; alas! with Grief I find,
> It is the Portion of poor Woman-kind. (7–10)

The weighing of class allegiance and female identity is present early in the poem in that ambiguous phrase "poor Woman-kind." Worthy of pity as a sex or remarkable for their poverty? Are only impoverished women being addressed, because other women have their marriage "portions" to insulate them from drudgery? We may begin by reading according to the code of "pity," keeping sexual difference to the fore. But without stating anything polemically, Collier manages to convey as the poem unfolds that this is a class issue rather than simply an issue of sexual difference, as a middle-class woman writer would most probably have expressed it. There is an unbridgeable gap between the women of the landowning and employing classes, "our Ladies" (159), and "ourselves." The lot of "*poor* Woman-kind" is her theme, and it is one of the themes given least literary treatment in English up to 1739 and for some time afterwards (Defoe notwithstanding). At a crucial moment slightly more than halfway through the poem, Collier's protest against the laboring man's lack of sympathy with or even comprehension of the nature and extent of "women's work" is supplemented by an equally effective critique of the hard-nosed middle-class mistress for whom poor women "char" – do the laundry, polish the pewter, scour the "Pots, Kettles, Sauce-pans, Skillets . . . / Skimmers and Ladles, and such Trumpery, / Brought in to make complete our Slavery" (210–12). Like Dryden, at moments of high feeling Collier employs the emphatic triplet, which, given her subject-matter, often has the added effect of a sense of labors prolonged, of the rhythms of work as regulated by the sun's movements being violated, all too regularly.

Over against the undeniable hardships and indignities of laboring men's lives, Collier repeatedly asserts the equally never-ending and futile contribution of working-women's labor:

> So the industrious Bees do hourly strive
> To bring their Loads of Honey to the Hive;
> Their sordid Owners always reap the Gains,
> And poorly recompense their Toil and Pains.   (243–46)

The ambiguity of "sordid Owners" here deserves comment, for it is where Collier's protofeminism coincides with her critique of property and class power. Surely (land)"Owners" ought to spring to mind first, so solidly grounded is the text in class consciousness. But a lingering association of women's lot with thankless drudgery may carry from the poem's opening and come to rest here as well. The laboring-class woman is doubly (dis)possessed, her body and her labor owned, but neither acknowledged nor appreciated, by employer and father or husband. Yet it is the hold of gender oppression within the laboring classes that Collier's text sets out to pry loose. Her poem evidences an implicit optimism about redress and improvement where relations between the sexes are concerned. In this, she may be seen to be participating in the discourses of a wider social context in which the debates about middle- and upper-class gender equality and women's fitness for "public" work seem to have been a keen focus of intellectual energy in 1739.[11] Class relations, by contrast, remain insuperably in place in Collier's text, criticized as unjust, but not challenged as historically subject to change through political action.

Collier secures her claim to historical truth by means of an appeal to empirical facts, right down to the crucial matter of women's inadequate wages:

> And after all our Toil and Labour past,
> Six-pence or Eight-pence pays us off at last;
> For all our Pains, no Prospect can we see
> Attend us, but *Old Age* and *Poverty*.   (198–201)

Subsequent research by social historians confirms Collier's testimony.[12] Collier does not stress the sexual differential signalized by the difference between men's and women's wages, but working men and women would be bound to recognize in her "Six-pence or Eight-pence" an allusion to the higher, though still inadequate, wage of a male laborer. How this difference may have functioned to divide the working class, thus effectively diminishing its revolutionary potential, remains a matter of debate.[13] But Collier, by quietly reminding us of the material facts of working-women's exploitation, also adds a dimension to our understanding of Stephen Duck's scornful attitude towards women workers in *The Thresher's Labour*, the text that most immediately provoked her into writing. For the wage differential, as a sign of women's symbolic expendability within the work force, might have varied effects in particular historical circumstances. Yet its general function, symbolically, is always to distinguish men from women as agents of material and social (re)production within a class, thus investing this distinction with those residues of power and antagonism that characterize class relations in the society as a whole.

The articulation of protofeminist and laboring-class consciousness in *The Woman's Labour* is not a matter of ostensible content alone. Collier's textual strategies open up questions of aesthetic criteria in a challenging way. Two features of the poem particularly demand an historically informed and theoretically conscious reading if they are not be be undervalued or inadequately understood: the status of *The Woman's Labour* as an epistolary reply to Duck's version of plebeian georgic, and Collier's use of what may seem like rather hackneyed high literary troping. Is Collier's poem in some sense a mere supplementary appendage to Duck's? Does she fail to invent a suitably oppositional discourse of plebeian female – poor woman's – georgic?

It is true that Collier stakes her text on class solidarity with Duck, despite their differences regarding women's contributions to productive labor. We know from "Some Remarks" that she admired Duck and got his poems by heart, but that she fancied "he had been too Severe on the Female Sex." Less personal pique than the desire to speak out on behalf of the women of her class, to "call," as she puts it, "an Army of Amazons to vindicate the injured Sex" (p. iv), generated *The Woman's Labour*. In the annals of English plebeian literature, Duck's trajectory as a farm laborer patronized as a poetical prodigy by royalty, given place and pension, and encouraged to enter the clerisy – a social rise that ends enigmatically in suicide – represents laboring-class deracination in an extreme form. Duck had made his mark on the literary scene by mocking the leisured conventions of English pastoral and georgic verse, while dramatizing the experience of agricultural labor as *lived*. Scything during the hay harvest becomes an epic competition not entirely innocent of Homeric as well as Virgilian overtones:

> And now the Field, design'd to try our Might,
> At length appears, and meets our longing Sight.
> The Grass and Ground we view with careful Eyes,
> To see which way the best Advantage lies;
> And, Hero-like, each claims the foremost Place.
> At first our Labour seems a sportive Race:
> With rapid Force our sharpen'd Blades we drive,

> Strain ev'ry Nerve, and Blow for Blow we give.
> All strive to vanquish, tho' the Victor gains
> No other Glory, but the greatest pains.[14]   (110–19)

As Raymond Williams has shown, the vigorous colloquial triumph of *The Thresher's Labour* is followed, ironically, by traditional "high-literary" pastoral rhetoric: "When sooty Pease we thresh" becomes "Of blissful Groves I sing, and flow'ry Plains: / Ye Sylvan Nymphs, assist my rural strains."[15] Nevertheless, in *The Thresher's Labour* Duck puts the labor "back" into pastoral verse.[16]

In addition to celebrating the dignity of male labor, *The Thresher's Labour* villifies greedy landlords as well as poking fun at talkative female laborers who treat their occasional employment in the fields as a form of recreation:

> Our Master comes, and at his Heels a Throng
> Of prattling Females, arm'd with Rake and Prong;
> Prepar'd, whilst he is here, to make his Hay;
> Or, if he turns his Back, prepar'd to play:
> But here, or gone, sure of this Comfort still;
> Here's Company, so they may chat their Fill.
> Ah! were their Hands so active as their Tongues,
> How nimbly then would move the Rakes and Prongs!   (162–9)

Indeed, Duck goes so far as to imply that talking is women's chief activity, apart from cooking, child-minding, and keeping hard-working but exhausted husbands on their toes. Structurally, *The Thresher's Labour* obliges us to spot the analogy between the epic heroism of the men's competitive scything and the bathos of the women's conversation, which Duck strains to make competitive as well as noisy and nonsensical. After dinner, the female hay-makers continue to sit on the ground and "chat." The traditional tropes of women's irrational, garrulous behavior, and their inability to "talk sense" while trying to outdo one another in "meaningless" gossip, are obvious enough. But Duck takes a further step of interest to post-Lacanian feminism; he represents women as, metaphorically and temporarily at least, outside the symbolic order of language altogether.

> All talk at once; but seeming all to fear,
> That what they speak, the rest will hardly hear;
> Till by degrees so high their Notes they strain,
> A Stander by can nought distinguish plain.
> So loud's their Speech, and so confus'd their Noise,
> Scarce puzzled ECHO can return the Voice.
> Yet, spite of this, they bravely all go on;
> Each scorns to be, or seem to be, outdone.   (176–83)

Echo, an Ovidian figure for the relative speechlessness with which we are confronted in the "ready-madeness" of language, our imprisonment within a language that can only operate *through* a subject but cannot be operated autonomously *by* the subject, is significantly female. Thus Duck casually evokes the longstanding classical association of femininity and exclusion from language-as-power. But these women stand outside even Echo's relation to language; so confused and confusing is their loud noise that it is incapable of recuperation even by a sympathetic female ear. The implication is that what Echo cannot reproduce is not language at all. Duck's inability to understand the hay-makers is a declaration of his linguistic and cultural superiority, his belonging to a realm of "sense" and meaning that laboring men inhabit, but from which their women are excluded.

Thus Duck helps perpetuate the ideological exclusion of his fellow countrywomen from both productive labor and language, at the same time as he transforms the bourgeois pastoral prospect into a worked landscape. It is hardly surprising, then, that when the "thresher poet" is answered by the "washer-woman of Petersfield," she should take Duck's refusal to "see" women's agricultural labor as, in fact, productive, to be a violation of class loyalty rather than chivalry, good manners, or even good sense.[17] One of her characteristic strategies of refutation turns upon quoting Duck's text in the light of previous pastoral refusals to recognize the contributions of labor to the picturesqueness of the countryside. Where Duck had written of the hay harvest, thus cavalierly cancelling the female hay-makers' sweat and toil,

> Next Day the Cocks appear in equal Rows   (202)

Collier counters with:

> [We] nimbly turn our Hay upon the Plain;
> Nay, rake and prow it in, the Case is clear;
> Or how should Cocks in equal Rows appear?   (60–62)

By scorning his female fellow workers, Duck has done violence to their shared occlusion from the bourgeois pastoral prospect. By selectively quoting from Duck's poem, Collier hurls Duck's jibes at his female fellow workers back in his face. By apostrophizing Duck in her opening lines, and using the same couplet form and narrative structure as he does, Collier poetically apprentices herself to Duck, whose plebeian verse has inspired as well as provoked her own:

> IMMORTAL Bard! thou Fav'rite of the Nine!
> Enrich'd by Peers, advanc'd by CAROLINE!
> Deign to look down on One that's poor and low,
> Remembring you yourself was lately so;
> Accept these Lines: Alas! what can you have
> From her, who ever was, and's still a Slave?   (1–6)

Collier makes the couplet form seem flexible and accommodating, not constraining. With Duck, she helps to constitute the discourse of plebeian georgic by incorporating rural idioms and grammar as well as the subject-matter of work experienced, not observed.

Comparable with her use of her immediate male model is Collier's appropriation of such high-literary tropes as the classical allusion. If Duck relies upon the myth of Sisyphus to convey the working man's ceaseless and ultimately futile round of labor, Collier, as if to fix her image as a washer-woman forever in our minds, invokes Danaus's daughters with their bottomless tubs to fill:[18]

> While you to *Sysiphus* yourselves compare,
> With *Danaus' Daughters* we may claim a Share;
> For while *he* labours hard against the Hill,
> Bottomless Tubs of Water *they* must fill.   (239–42)

For the eighteenth-century poet, classical allusions are stock-in-trade; always in stock, as it were; the very stuff of which verses are made. One proves one's competence to compose, recite, write, publish, and have read, verses by acquiring this stock of and in popular neoclassicism. Both Duck and Collier understandably appropriate the classical figures most easily allied with labor; it would seem that they perceived there to be a certain useful congruence between the representation of manual and agricultural work as lived experience in the texts of antiquity and their own. We need not dismiss the engagement with high literary culture as evidence of opportunism or of failed aesthetic invention. There is a sense in which the plebeian classical allusion proposes a reinterpretation of the classical source as having provided a more immediate apprehension of agrarian labor than most literate English people of Collier's time routinely experienced themselves, or than could be conveyed by the classical allusions of privileged georgic. Collier appropriates the myth of Danaus's daughters in order to assert laboring-class women's value, in the only literary terms that would carry in this historical moment, within such a marginal text.

The polemical edge of Collier's text depends not so much on our previous knowledge of Duck's poem, but on the ways Collier, as a *voleuse de langue*, dismantles and reconstitutes Duck's contemptuous dismissal of female labor through selective quotation within her own text. There is no pretense of either solitary individuality or original genius in Collier's aesthetic; she has adopted a form of dialogue in order to engage in combative persuasion, and so her poem discloses what post-Romantic texts so often deliberately mystify, the necesssary intertextuality of all literary enterprise.[19] Without "belaboring" the point, we should also recognize that Duck's own poem, like so many eighteenth-century texts from Pope's satires to the rival novels of Richardson and Fielding, was implicitly intertextual as well, engaging the whole leisured

pastoral tradition in order to challenge it: "No Fountains murmur here, no
Lambkins play, / No Linnets warble, and no Fields look gay; / 'Tis all a
gloomy, melancholy Scene, / Fit only to provoke the Muse's Spleen" (58–61).
The difference is that Collier's text addresses Duck's poem specifically and
explicitly; Collier does not assume a reified tradition of either misogynist
satire or patrician georgic. Her text is thus more immediately and polemically
intertextual than his.

It might seem that Duck's traditional description of his fellow countrywomen as incapable of working hard or speaking sense, though more than
capable of generating noise, would undermine Collier's project, despite her
skillful intertextual maneuvers. But Collier engages in a strategy invaluable
for any form of ideology critique; she attempts to account for Duck's
prejudices as the products of an historical process that is by no means
inevitable. Adapting the neoclassical commonplace of a mythical Golden Age
to protofeminist ends, she speculates that there must have been a more just
relation between the sexes at an earlier moment in history: the origin of
woman, if divine, could not prove an instance of slavery. There must of
necessity have been some historical degeneration from that happy state, so
justly designed, in order for human society to have arrived at its present
arrangement of female slavery and male arrogance and ingratitude:

> Our first Extraction from a Mass refin'd,
> Could never be for Slavery design'd;
> Till Time and Custom by degrees destroy'd
> That happy State our Sex at first enjoy'd.   (13–16)

Historically speaking, then, familiarity bred contempt. Men ceased to honor
or praise women as these erotically charged relations grew stalely "customary" over time. By degrees women were degraded to their current status as
slaves and drudges. Thus men are not the enemies of women, though they
may "enslave" them, but fellow subjects in the realm of physical and historical
exigency, also subject to the deformations wrought by living-in-time and
being bound by social custom. The forces of deformation may be the same for
both sexes, but their effects are clearly asymmetrical, affecting men and
women differently. Collier's project is one of radical defamiliarization.[20]

Collier's method for making Duck's assumptions about female unproduc-
tiveness and mindless garrulity seem strange is a simple one. She speaks out
against them:

> For none but *Turks*, that ever I could find,
> Have Mutes to serve them, or did e'er deny
> Their Slaves, at Work, to chat it merrily.[21]
> Since you have Liberty to speak your mind,
> And are to talk, as well as we, inclin'd,

> Why should you thus repine, because that we,
> Like you, enjoy that pleasing Liberty?
> What! would you lord it quite, and take away
> The only Privilege our Sex enjoy?   (66–74)

If the politics of a simple "speaking out" on behalf of women's rights seems a little problematical today,[22] we must remember that, for Collier, Duck's dismissal of women's work and women's "noise" warranted just such a direct contradiction. Following in the rationalist tradition of earlier feminists like Astell, Collier writes from the following premise: if a woman addresses the public by writing rationally and eloquently, she *may* be read, and her audience's consciousness altered accordingly. With such a premise in mind, Collier points to an obvious but often "forgotten" detail about our material history as a species:

> And as from us their Being they derive,
> They back again should all due Homage give.   (23–24)

To claim that all men owe allegiance to women as to their mothers is to gesture towards the deliberately hyperbolical, a gesture that is the rhetorical opposite of the later rationalist appeal to liberty. Thus Collier prepares the ground for her plain speaking by archly reminding us of reproductive history: women give birth to men, not the other way around. Women's "extraction" from some divinely created substance is a myth; there is more than one way to narrate the "beginnings" of human history. Men, invariably indebted to women for their being, should give women their "due Homage," not implicitly try to claim the power of "extraction" for themselves alone. Men should not claim, against history and biological necessity, their own self-making, but honor women for it. Unfortunately, their reluctance to pay such homage is understandable within patriarchal social relations; to do so would violate the tradition of female subordination. But Collier's calling attention to the empirical evidence of reproduction, the womb-as-workshop, nevertheless requires some recognition of the prejudicial nature of gender ideology. Collier thus sets out to refute Duck's representation of women as outside material and linguistic production through a powerful combination of personal testimony and reportage.

The central historical subtext of *The Woman's Labour*, and the site of its most telling political intervention, is a theme that both feminist activists and feminist scholars have made all too familiar, that of the triple burden of working women − wage labor, housekeeping, and childcare. This is what gives thematic unity to Collier's narrative, whether the central activity of a passage be hay-making, brewing beer, reaping, gleaning, or washing, and it is also what gives nearly unbearable unity to working-class women's experience historically. Collier's case for women's apparently endless duties, so few of which Duck seems to have noticed, hinges on the difficult necessity of combining child-minding with agricultural work for meagre wages or a portion of the gleanings:

> To get a Living we so willing are,
> Our tender Babes into the Field we bear,
> And wrap them in our Cloaths to keep them warm,
> While round about we gather up the Corn;
> And often unto them our Course do bend,
> To keep them safe, that nothing them offend.   (93–98)

This "divided care" during a day of gleaning might provide a significant portion of the family income. Following Arthur Young, Ivy Pinchbeck reports that "In either case, whether a women's time was spent in working for wages [including reaping, in some districts, though it remained "men's work" in others] or in gleaning, it was generally assumed at the end of the eighteenth century, that the yearly rent of the labourer's cottage was paid by the harvest labours of his wife and children."[23] And this "divided care" during the day is compounded by the evening's cooking, housekeeping, and childcare. Collier's working women belong to cottager families, for whom housekeeping might well include keeping pigs and other livestock as well as working a small garden: "*Bacon* and *Dumpling* in the Pot we boil, / Our Beds we make, our Swine we feed the while" (79–80). As Pinchbeck notes, such female contributions to domestic economy were necessary to supplement inadequate wages, but were rapidly disappearing by the later decades of the eighteenth century.[24] Duck and his mates may dream of work at night, but their women hardly have time to sleep, it seems:

> You sup, and go to Bed without delay,
> And rest yourselves till the ensuing Day;
> While we, alas! but little Sleep can have,
> Because our froward at Children cry and rave;
> Yet, without fail, soon as Day-light doth spring,
> We in the Field again our Work begin,
> And there, with all our Strength, our Toil renew,
> Till *Titan*'s golden Rays have dry'd the Dew;
> Then home we go unto our Children dear,
> Dress, feed and bring them to the Field with care.   (111–20)

So much "care" suggests another way of understanding the female "prattling" to which Duck objects: such gatherings for gossip and other forms of exchange are an expression of community among these rural women, for whom there are so few opportunities for recreation and amusement.[25] In a sense these women have become the custodians of the oral tradition to which their relative exclusion from print culture has increasingly relegated them.

Could it be that what Duck cannot (bear to) hear in the women's exchanges is the therapeutic venting of suppressed female resentment against a harsh regimen?

It has been traditional to assume that, while the Stephen Ducks apply themselves to books in the hope of "improvement" through education, their wives are stranded in incomprehension and hostility towards what seems like mere self-indulgence and time-wasting. Before the vogue of the thresher-poet, who among the laboring classes could expect to profit from poetry? The anonymous biographer of Duck in an early pirated edition of his poems claims that Duck received little encouragement in his studies from his wife, who could not see their point and scolded him for neglecting his work.[26] Duck's "incomprehension" in the face of the hay-makers' chatter could be read as a resentful trace of a conflict over literary and intellectual ambition enacted within marriages like his, in a social context in which the composition of verses seems to promise little material relief, or indeed any compensation of a sort an uneducated wife would be likely to appreciate.[27] But, as Morag Shiach has noticed, we have reason to be suspicious of the characterization of Duck's wife handed down uncritically from one (male) commentator to another, and in the face of some contrary testimony: "It may be that his wife is here used as a condensation of the stupidity and lack of education assumed to attach to her class: Stephen's exceptional nature being constructed in opposition to his wife's."[28] The search for an autobiographical trace in Duck's scornful representation of female laborers may be misguided, but the grounding of his representation in gender ideology and in the cultural differences brought about by its perpetuation seems indisputable.

The agricultural year provides another context for Collier's insistence on historical fact. In Stephen Duck's agricultural year, winter can be dismissed with a single line. But Collier saves her best effects of physical sensation and atmosphere for winter, as if to imply that women go men one better even in this: washing, polishing, and brewing provide a seasonless round of work. The vivid simplicity of her evocation also puts certain passages of James Thomson's *Winter* in a new light by lending them a certain class-specificity.[29] Thomson's berating of the rich for their inhumanity to the poor, already clearly readable as the discourse of a disembodied, disinterested observer rather than a participant in the labor and hardships being described, becomes freshly grounded as the production of a privileged, leisured observer, however sympathetic to those whom his writing represents, and who after Duck and Collier can be seen as capable of self-representation. Rising before dawn in winter, regardless of the weather, Collier's women leave their sleeping men and trudge to the house of local gentry:

> When to the House we come where we should go,
> How to get in, alas! we do not know:
> The Maid quite tir'd with Work the Day before,

> O'ercome with Sleep; we standing at the Door
> Oppress'd with Cold, and often call in vain,
> E're to our Work we can Admittance gain:
> But when from Wind and Weather we get in,
> Briskly with Courage we our Work begin;
> Heaps of fine Linen we before us view,
> Whereon to lay our Strength and Patience too;
> Cambricks and Muslins, which our Ladies wear,
> Laces and Edgings, costly, fine, and rare,
> Which must be wash'd with utmost Skill and Care;
>
> . . .
>
> Now we drive on, resolv'd our Strength to try,
> And what we can, we do most willingly;
> Until with Heat and Work, 'tis often known,
> Not only Sweat, but Blood runs trickling down
> Our Wrists and Fingers; still our Work demands
> The constant Action of our lab'ring Hands.   (149–87)

The extremes of cold and heat, of hostile weather and frantic domestic industry, always working against time, against the sun's rise, because there is always too much to be done, are features that powerfully evoke a winter of labor. The Virgilian topos of "Now we drive on, resolv'd our Strength to try," addresses the washing as if it were an epic contest, the women's strength against the task at hand, and not, we notice, the women against each other, as in Duck's description of male competition in scything. And it is labor that requires not merely sweat, but blood.

James Thomson's winter is a season of vast and awful extremes that often mark the limit or the end of labor, mankind defeated by the elements, suffering helplessly. The reason "Why the lone widow and her orphans pined / In starving solitude" while luxury strained "her low thought / To form unreal wants" (1056–59), Thomson tells us, is that such class division within seasonality is natural: "The storms of wintry time will quickly pass, / And one unbounded Spring encircle all" (1068–69). Collier's representation of domestic labor radically undermines such religio-political "consolation." Thomson's olympian pastoralism, his rapid shifting from the social indictment of poverty to the invocation of nature's grand design, time, and eternity, reveals its ideological limits when read with and against Collier's vindication of women's collective industry.

Patronage and conservatism

As we have seen, Collier closes *The Woman's Labour* on a note of resignation, not vindication:

> So the industrious Bees do hourly strive
> To bring their Loads of Honey to the Hive;
> Their sordid Owners always reap the Gains,
> And poorly recompense their Toil and Pains.   (243–46)

For the laboring woman, as for bees (another Virgilian gesture), history is already unjustly determined, at the level of class at least. How unjustly determined, within sexual and familial relations, is a question Collier leaves to her audience.

But if Collier offers us no radical program for change in the poem's conclusion, she nevertheless insists on the historical and empirical acknowledgment of what her text has made painfully visible. *The Woman's Labour* is, in part, a demand for a history in which women can be seen to participate. Collier's neoclassicism should be understood as operating similarly in aesthetic terms, a compromise achieved within the literary and social status quo that grants the writer some imaginative compensation while allowing her to articulate some trenchant social criticism.

If this seems a disappointingly conservative conclusion, we should keep in mind that Collier, like Duck and other plebeian poets, had reason to feel resigned to the fact that her talents were not so much rewarded as exploited by patrons and audiences, whose consciences could be soothed by promoting exceptional ability among the industrious poor. There is a conservative function to the patronage by élites of members of the poor, as examples of extraordinary genius. One might speak of this function as a version of Barthes's "inoculation," in which a small dose of ideological contradiction, in the guise of some localized injustice or form of "unpleasantness" that arouses indignation, is injected into the social body, neutralizing the threat of an epidemic of social change.[30] In this sense, the declaration of Collier's generalized patrons, in the "Advertisement" to the "New Edition" of her *Poems*, "that had her genius been cultivated, she would have ranked with the greatest poets of this kingdom,"[31] should be read against the material conditions of patronage of *The Woman's Labour* as Collier describes them in "Some Remarks": ". . . at length I comply'd to have it done at my own charge, I lost nothing, neither did I gain much, others run away with the profit" (p. iv).

Collier's patrons' declaration, which simultaneously celebrates and regrets the phenomenon of uncultivated genius, evades the question of the conditions of such cultivation. There is no suggestion that talents like Collier's be encouraged or educated in the future. Nor is a revolution in aesthetics, which would acknowledge the value of laboring-class poetry as such, being proposed. Collier is of literary interest, we must assume, precisely because her genius "remains uncultivated" – she represents the undereducated writer as an object of pathos, not an indictment of social injustice or an enticement to social revolution. The pressure of egalitarian impulses in the discourses of revolution and abolitionism of the 1780s strain this precept of permanent pathos and inferiority to its limit in the case of More's patronage of Yearsley. For Collier, it is enough to have one's exceptional status recognized in however limited a way, to be content with "mere" unlettered prodigiousness, itself something of an emancipatory novelty in 1739 or 1762.

Thus Collier's apparent resignation to an unchanging social order, that can at best be modified in local and temporary ways to render the oppressed some compensation, stands as a figure for her own poetical production. Resigned to class oppression, if not to gender oppression within her class, she offers in *The Woman's Labour* a provisional corrective. Such a gesture eases the burden of plebeian history by subjecting its cultural effects to a certain sardonic scrutiny. Her poetry is not without critical social content, as we have seen, but her protests remain carefully circumscribed and localized rather than becoming radically programmatic. Historically, she accepts her lot, though textually she seeks to argue against the conditions of oppression. By publishing verse at all, she addresses primarily an élite readership, but she never offers to confuse their class with hers, or to become one of them through the act of writing. Her stance of uncultivated genius preserves her class-specificity while securing for her an audience.

We have seen in *The Woman's Labour*, then, that though Collier constructs a class-conscious account of an oppressed "poor Woman-kind," her stance in relation to political and social authority is vexed, both resistant and resigned. This is even more true of her *œuvre* as a whole.

Whether the topic be education, marriage, royal dynasticism, or Scriptural history, Collier tends to couple moral reformism with a certain amiable accommodationism, or compliance with the will of the fathers. Thus, when men become kind and virtuous husbands, though not before, women will prefer marriage to spinsterhood.[32] Kings should be militantly strong, if not explicitly expansionist, in the name of protestant liberty; royal couples should set the pattern of domestic virtue for their peoples.[33] And women's interests can best be served by a humble commitment to fulfilling God's will, for which they will be rewarded.[34] In a sense, then, despite the fact that she speaks on behalf of women like herself, Collier usually writes in a way that is rhetorically "male-identified," written for a projected audience in which men predominate. This orientation is supported by the limited evidence we have of her relations with patrons. The nine Petersfield residents attesting to her authenticity in the signed statement of September 21, 1739 are all men.[35] The respective numbers of male (102) and female (62) subscribers listed in her 1762 *Poems, on Several Occasions* also support this sense of Collier's projected audience. It is as if the fathers' law superseded and circumscribed any feminist speaking, permitting Collier access to the public on the condition that radically different female desires and recommendations not be featured too prominently in her work.

The paradigmatic text for this strategy is *The Three Wise Sentences, from the First Book of Esdras, Chap. III and IV*, published with, and conservative ballast to, *The Woman's Labour*, encoding an insistent subtext of plebeian female consolation in the Word: the displacement of self for the greater good, the displacement of Woman for the glory of the Father, keeper of Truth. Though *The Woman's Labour* may be Collier's most important poem in literary-historical as well as protofeminist terms, *The Three Wise Sentences* is in at least one way more typical of her collected *Poems* of 1762. In this text, the discourse of "Woman," historically and philosophically conceived, is examined for its ideological contradictions only to find itself subsumed within metaphysical, and specifically religious, discourse. This textual maneuver characterizes well Collier's frequent retreats from the potentially radical implications of her subject-matter. The poem begins in the court of Darius, King of Persia, where three favorite youths decide to amuse the king by competing with one another in answering the question, "What, in their Judgments, did in Strength excel / All other Things" (17–18). The first offers "wine," the second, "the king," and the third – Zorobabel – "women – except that God's truth is stronger." Zorobabel's is the winning answer, and as a reward, Zorobabel is granted a wish; ever selfless, the youth asks Darius to fulfill his promise to rebuild Jerusalem, which Darius promptly does. Why did Collier choose to versify this apocryphal text? At the request of a gentlewoman whom she was nursing, Collier tells us in "Some Remarks": "she and her Friends persuaded me to make Verses on the Wise Sentences, which I did on such Nights as I waited on her" (p. iv). A composition to please the ladies, then, Collier's poem discursively elaborates their power and importance – through the "words" of Zorobabel, a handsome young hero of Judaeo-Christian history, we might add – only to displace these topics for a sermon and a vision of a renovated Jerusalem.

This text helps to indicate the possible functions of religious discourse for Collier and her patrons. Collier represents in this piece of writing a social subjectivity most immediately tailored for her employers' consumption, and it is one in which piety is central. Women's strength is no sooner celebrated – in terms of their production and reproduction, their desirability and influence – than divine knowledge and power are invoked as greater through the logics of divine causality and purity. We can see in this reworking of Esdras on the history and theory of gender relations parallels to Collier's similar resort to Golden Age commonplace and Christian myth in the much more purportedly feminist *Woman's Labour*. Zorobabel's winning answer contains the following shift from women's power in giving birth to men to the imperial sovereignty of divine "Truth":

> The greatest Heroes that the World can know,
> To *Women* their Original must owe;

. . .

The Glory and the Praise of Men they are,
And make the Garments which they daily wear:
Nay, without *Women*, Men can't be at all,
But soon the Species would to Ruin fall.

. . .

In Toil and Labour hard he spends the Day,
To gather Wealth, that so he may provide
Treasure to bring unto his dearest Bride:
While other boldly, with a Sword in Hand,
Will cross the Seas, and wander on the Land;

. . .

How great then HE, by whose divine Command,
All Things at first were made, Earth, Sea, and Land!
Strong is the *Truth*, who did create all Things;

. . .

Not only strong, but good beyond compare;

. . .

Whatever Thing is virtuous, good, and great,
In *Truth* we find it perfect and complete:
Then prais'd be *Truth* to all Eternity,
In whom alone is Strength and Majesty!   (132–235)

This is exultant piety indeed, capable of consoling the convalescent or soothing a solitary sleeper. It is also a displacement of the discourse of "Woman" as agent of both production and reproduction, indeed also as chief subject of history. Displaced first, we notice, by "man" in his accumulative and imperialist mode, industrious at home or "wandering" armed abroad in search of "Booty" (164) to bestow upon the woman at home. "Woman" is thus transposed from material producer to consumer. This shift happens within vaguely historical syntactic progression: woman's power to give birth and make garments within a "primitive" domestic economy is displaced by her implicitly more "modern" ability to influence the worker and the warrior to exert themselves on her behalf. According to the poem's logic, how much stronger, then, must be the divine agent who created woman! Collier's broaching of socio-sexual injustice here is tentative and highly mediated: Zorobabel as "feminist man," championing women before a male audience; Collier herself "merely" versifying a text from the fathers for a pious female patron. But even this tentative broaching is soon abandoned for conventional pieties about the "strength" of women's influence and the comfort to be had in the Father's One Truth.

E. P. Thompson has described the function of working-class religion, particularly Methodism and evangelicalism, in the latter part of the eighteenth century as "the chiliasm of despair."[36] Against this interpretation of the function of working-class religion in the period as essentially conservative, H. J. Perkin has argued that the structure of Dissenting religious groups provided the working-class movement with valuable strategies for oppositional organization.[37] For Collier, neither a Nonconformist nor an enthusiast, not the hope of spectacular salvation but the certainty of divine truth is invested with desire. In her *œuvre* the radical possibilities of a discourse of "Woman" are occluded, the question of female subjectivity itself displaced in the name of piety. Her resignation here takes the form of self-displacement as well as self-denial. Rather than pitch hopes on a radical transformation of social relations, apparently unthinkable in 1739, Collier defers her expectation of a joyous Jerusalem until eternity.

For Mary Collier, then, compliance with paternalist authority is legitimated by patriarchal "Truth." Men as individuals may be queried and challenged, but the Father's Word and the fathers' laws demand submission. Religious discourse subsumes further potentially radical investigation of woman, or women, or plebeian female subjectivity. Collier's resignation of her critical tune for the harmonies of metaphysical truth may represent a form of chiliastic impulse in Thompson's sense. But hers is not the chiliasm of despair; it is, rather, the cautious displacement of utopian impulses onto a desirous metaphysics, if not quite a metaphysics of desire.

When, late in her career, Collier comes to pay homage to Stephen Duck in an elegy, faith in religious authority implicitly sustains her in continued poverty, in the social difference of her fate from Duck's. She mourns her male predecessor as a social wonder – "That wond'rous Man in whom alone did join / A Thresher, Poet, Courtier, and Divine" (5–6).[38] The price of his poetic success and consequent social rise, however, is his peace of mind, that possession so celebrated by Collier in "Some Remarks" as attainable in a pious and impoverished single life:

> How doubly Blest couldst thou have kept with thee,
> The sweet companion of thy Poverty?
> That true content and inward peace of mind,
> Which in thy humble Cottage thou didst find.
> Which oft doth to the poor and mean retreat
> But seldom dwells among the Rich, or Great.
> The want of wit thy pleasure turnd to pain,
> Thy Life a Burthen, and thy Death a Stain.   (19–26)

Collier equates Duck's suicide directly if ambiguously with his social trajectory. In straining after "wit," Duck turned his poetic labors and his life from pleasures into pain. But was this elusive wit a literary quality, the class-specific requirement of his new discursive situation as a clergyman, a middle-class professional? Or was it rather the practical "mother-wit" that would have enabled him to keep his poor man's peace of mind in spite of his social rise? Collier remains oblique; "wit" here serves as a stress-point in her critique of Duck's career. It is not entirely clear from her poem how she thought Duck came to fail and fall into melancholy, but somewhere we must posit a loss of faith that resulted in a death that is a "Stain," a wounding of his reputation, a sin, a blot upon the historical record. And it is not apparent what Collier makes of the possibility of any laboring poet surviving a deracination like Duck's, but for her there is no hope of happiness imaginable without religious faith of the sort that enables those who live in "humble Cottages" to maintain that "true content and inward peace of mind" so rare among the privileged, and so crucial to the social incorporation of the disenfranchised.

In Collier's *œuvre*, questions of class and gender are so strikingly articulated, shown to be working both with and against one another, that even in this act of elegiac homage Collier would seem to remember at some level her original quarrel with Duck. The final lines of "An Elegy Upon Stephen Duck" consist of an ironical reworking of Duck's own simile of female hay-makers reacting to a storm like a flock of birds in *The Thresher's Labour*. Duck's melancholy comes upon him, in Collier's text, as "naturally" as the women hush up and take cover from the rain in Duck's poem. This intertext from *The Thresher's Labour* follows immediately upon the Echo passage previously quoted:

> Meanwhile the changing Sky begins to lour,
> And hollow Winds proclaim a sudden Show'r:
> The tattling Crowd can scarce their Garments gain,
> Before descends the thick impetuous Rain;
> Their noisy Prattle all at once is done,
> And to the Hedge they soon for Shelter run.
>
> THUS have I seen, on a bright Summer's Day,
> On some green Brake, a Flock of Sparrows play;
> From Twig to Twig, from Bush to Bush they fly;
> And with continu'd Chirping fill the Sky:
> But, on a sudden, if a Storm appears,
> Their chirping Noise no longer dins your Ears:
> They fly for Shelter to the thickest Bush;
> There silent sit, and All at once is hush.   (184–97)

Collier revises Duck as follows:

> So have I Seen in a fair Summers Morn,
> Bright Phoebus's Beams the Hills and Dales adorn,
> With Flow'rs and Shrubs their fragrant Sweets display,
> And Warbling Birds foretell a Chearfull Day:

> When on a Sudden some dark Clouds arise,
> Obscures the Sun and overspreads the Skies;
> The Birds are Silent, plants contract their bloom,
> The Glorious Day ends in a dismal gloom.   (27–34)

What are we to make of this ambiguous homage, partly irreverent, partly impertinent, partly obsessive? Duck's "Glorious Day" of literary success and upward social mobility is here neatly "clouded" in the very terms Duck had used to poke fun at and abruptly dismiss his female fellow workers as garrulous, idle, and silly. Even late in her career, Collier continues to be mindful of the example of Duck, who so far as we know never replied to her epistle, though he did subscribe to Mary Leapor's poems. Her text of elegiac homage to him represents a complex configuration of admiration for his success, a desire for class solidarity, and feminist indignation at his prejudices against her sex. Like her contemporaries who pay homage to Pope, Collier praises Duck outright as her single most important poetic influence, while cleverly turning his gender prejudices against him in a gesture which only those readers who know Duck's work as well as she does will recognize. For only they will be fit to judge his achievement fairly, without the class prejudice that Collier understands all too well.

To rise socially by means of the pen, as Duck did, is to embrace deracination, with all of its ambiguous and sometimes destructive consequences. And in the absence of a working-class movement (though the presence of one offers no guarantee of opportunities for intellectual work), the prospect of education or a literary livelihood without a radical deracination like Duck's remains unthinkable. Thus Collier's texts reproduce the ideological contradictions of her situation. Her position on the margins of a literary establishment that can tolerate unlettered genius as a novel commodity permits considerable textual resistance but not open rebellion.

We have seen how skillfully Collier situates her poetry within available genres and conventions while transforming these materials in the interests of a protofeminist and laboring-class social critique: "speaking out" in combative dialogue, making use of female ventriloquism and intertextuality, investing a religiously informed, prophetic future with desire, insisting upon the historical and empirical details of plebeian Englishwomen's experience as a class and as a sex. Coming to terms with Mary Collier's achievement requires a thorough reassessment of our own historically constructed conceptions of literary history, poetic value, and agency. That Collier was able to combine resignation to continued servitude with sufficient literary ambition to reformulate the plebeian georgic mode in the service of laboring women may strike us as paradoxical, but that sense of paradox marks the difference of our historical moment from hers. In the vigor and wit and forceful arguments of Collier's verse lies strong evidence for reconstructing, from the available traces, a plebeian female subjectivity and sense of historical agency in this period that are socially subject and politically subjugated, but by no means incapable of resistance. As Collier's Hannah says of her God in *First Samuel Versified*:

> From abject State can raise unto a Throne,
> The Earth with all its Kingdoms are his own;

so might we say of Collier's poetry, its reclamation of the handmaid's voice for eighteenth-century print culture.

Chapter 3

An English Sappho brilliant, young and dead? Mary Leapor laughs at the fathers

But no Englishwoman ever wrote verses worthy of being twice read, who had deviated from virtue.

(*Blackwood's Magazine* [March, 1837], p. 408)

Sappho, Justified, either way

(Ann Yearsley, MS. note in a copy of *Poems, on Several Occasions* [1785])

Mary Leapor's texts have evidently appealed to a predominantly male literary establishment, for various critics and editors seem to have taken a peculiar pleasure in discovering them, only to have them be forgotten and subsequently rediscovered again and again. Under the auspices of John Watts, Samuel Richardson, and Isaac Hawkins Browne, her works were collected and published posthumously by subscription in 1748 and 1751.[1] There follows notice or selected republication of her poems by Christopher Smart in *The Midwife* (1750), by the *Monthly Review* (1749 and 1751), by John Duncombe in *The Feminead* (1754), by George Colman and Bonnell Thornton in *Poems by Eminent Ladies* (1755), by *The Lady's Poetical Magazine* (1782), by the *Gentleman's Magazine* (1784), by Alexander Dyce in *Specimens of British Poetesses* (1827), by *Blackwood's Magazine* (1837), by Frederic Rowton in *The Female Poets of Great Britain* (1848), and, most recently, by Roger Lonsdale in *The New Oxford Book of Eighteenth Century Verse* (1984) and *Eighteenth Century Women Poets: An Oxford Anthology* (1989). The writer in *Blackwood's* comments:

> Mary Barber was the wife of a shopkeeper in Dublin, and Mary Leapor a cook, but neither of them had so much of the *mens divinior* as might have been expected from their occupation. Molly makes Phillis, a country maid, reject the addresses of Sylvanus, a courtier, in favour of Corydon, on the ground of good eating. The lines are savoury.
>
> "Not this will lure me, for I'd have you know,
> This night to feast with Corydon I go;
> Then beef and colewarts, beans and bacon too,

78

> And the plum-pudding of delicious hue,
> Sweet-spiced cakes, and apple-pies good store,
> Deck the brown board – and who can wish for more?"[2]

Thus is Leapor claimed for the province of wholesome sentiments and homely virtues, at the same time that she is cleared of any imputation of zealous religiosity – by 1837, the distinguishing mark, it would seem, of a lower-class imagination. Collier's *mens divinior*, and not her protofeminist polemic or laboring-class testimony, has survived as the chief feature of plebeian verse, after those intervening decades of working-class evangelicalism characterized by Thompson as a displacement of utopian political desires: the chiliasm of despair. *Blackwood's* Leapor is homely, virtuous, and yet capable of arousing a gustatory pleasure that generates poetical excitement. About this poetical excitement, all her discoverers seem to agree. But not all would stress a homely domesticity as the source of that excitement.

Mary Leapor was born on February 26, 1722 at Marston St. Lawrence in Northamptonshire while her father, Philip Leapor, was gardener to Sir John Blencowe (1642–1726), former Member of Parliament for Brackley, Baron of the Exchequer, Justice of Common Pleas, and Justice of the King's Bench. Five years later, after Blencowe's death, Philip Leapor moved to nearby Brackley with his wife and only daughter and established a nursery. Leapor may have attended the village school or she may have learned to read and write at home, taught by her father and mother who appear to have been literate; her verses were at least initially encouraged by her mother, who was at first pleased with her ten- or eleven-year-old daughter's rhymes, but tried to urge her towards some more profitable employment as she grew older. We know from a copy of the first volume of Leapor's poems, still in the library at Weston and inscribed "Once Kitchen maid at Weston," that Leapor went into service as a cookmaid at Weston Hall, not far from Brackley, the house of Susannah Jennens, daughter of Sir John Blencowe. Her poetry arguably bears traces of an embarrassing dismissal from service, followed by a return to Brackley to keep house for her widowed father. Leapor's mother was buried about five years before the poet's burial on November 14, 1746.[3] Only her father lived to see the publication of her work and gain something from the subscriptions.

Daughter of a nurseryman, Leapor employs precise and evocative language to describe rural plenitude in terms of its horticultural specificity. One of her most often anthologized poems, "The Month of August," makes good use of her father's fruit trees:

> In vain you tempt me while our Orchard bears
> Long-keeping Russets, lovely Cath'rine Pears,
> Pearmains and Codlings, wheaten Plumbs enough,
> And the black Damsons load the bending Bough.   (23–6)

In this pastoral dialogue between Sylvanus, a courtier, and Phillis, a country maid, Phillis rejects Sylvanus's offer of rank and genteel comforts in favor of the rustic tastes her father's farm and the swain Corydon can satisfy. Few pastoral females answer back their elevated suitors as confidently and richly as Phillis: Leapor's language constructs for both farmers and plants a relatively democratic freedom to be found in agricultural gardening, gardening for use, and in so doing, Phillis's replies give working farm life a definite edge over the constraints of aristocratic ornamentation, gardening for show, with its implications of feudal mastery and subjugation:

> No Pruning-knives our fertile Branches teaze,
> While yours must grow but as their Masters please.
> The grateful Trees our Mercy well repay,
> And rain us Bushels at the rising Day.   (27–30)

For Leapor's characters here, Edenic plenitude outdoes mere wealth and rank. Sylvanus is silenced by Phillis's refusal of his desire to provide handsomely for her, and Phillis has the last word:

> Let *Phillis* ne'er, ah never let her rove
> From her first Virtue and her humble Grove.
> Go seek some Nymph that equals your Degree,
> And leave Content and *Corydon* for me.   (73–6)

This may seem a quintessentially "pastoral" move in one sense, in that country life represents a "simple" contentment not to be found at court, but the idiom of class serves to aestheticize a life of humble tenantry in its difference from the courtly and its continued resistance to it, not in the end to elevate it by absorbing it into upper-class gentility through the discovery of high birth or the making of an elevating marriage.

Leapor is a poet worthy of critical attention for aesthetic reasons that go beyond the interesting ways in which her texts are marked by considerations of class and gender. The beauty of Leapor's verse lies often in its rich linguistic textures, its lively rhythms, and its specificity of natural detail. Though she sometimes sounds like Pope, Swift, Gay, and other eighteenth-century poets in her descriptions, she often slips in words from quite different idioms and notices things that they do not. "On Winter," for example, contains both a vivid evocation of the physical sensations of outdoor labor in cold weather and some arch reflection on the relation between neoclassical concepts of poetic inspiration and the realities of the English climate to which they remain somewhat alien even after generations of "domestication":

> Poor daggled *Urs'la* stalks from Cow to Cow,
> Who to her Sighs return a mournful Low;
> While their full Udders her broad Hands assail,

And her sharp Nose hangs dropping o'er the Pail.
With Garments trickling like a shallow Spring,
And his wet Locks all twisted in a String,
Afflicted *Cymon* waddles through the Mire,
And rails at *Win'fred* creeping o'er the Fire.
   Say gentle Muses, say, is this a Time
To sport with Poesy and laugh in Rhyme;
While the chill'd Blood, that hath forgot to glide,
Steals through its Channels in a lazy Tide:
And how can *Phoebus*, who the Muse refines,
Smooth the dull Numbers when he seldom shines.   (27–40)

Ironically, it is the same "unrefined" muse of the rural plebeian poet who gives us such a fresh portrait of "daggled" Ursula, muck-spattered among her cows. Thus Leapor, writing as "Mira," her usual persona, makes skillful aesthetic use of her vantage-point rather closer to the mire of georgic and pastoral materials than most eighteenth-century poets were accustomed to getting.

Although readers of Leapor may tend to agree that she succeeds most brilliantly in aesthetic terms by challenging some of the traditional assumptions of such popular eighteenth-century genres as the pastoral dialogue and the country-house poem – as in "The Month of August" and *Crumble-Hall*, respectively – there may be little consensus when Leapor's protofeminism and the possibility of what I will call her sapphic textuality are broached. More sharply and thoroughly than any other plebeian poet of the period, Leapor mounts a critique of the manifold injustices perpetuated by men against women. Filial and familial affections seem strained to their utmost in such texts as *The Cruel Parent* and *The Unhappy Father*.[4] In "An Essay on Woman" from her second volume, Leapor borrows Popean cadences, parallelism, and antithesis in the interests of a very un-Popean demystification of what it means to be Pope's idealized "softer man":

WOMAN – a pleasing, but a short-liv'd Flow'r,
Too soft for Business, and too weak for Pow'r:
A Wife in Bondage, or neglected Maid;
Despis'd, if ugly; if she's fair – betray'd.
'Tis Wealth alone inspires ev'ry Grace,
And calls the Raptures to her plenteous Face.
What Numbers for those charming Features pine,
If blooming Acres round her Temples twine?

    . . .

Tho' Nature arm'd us for the growing Ill,
With fraudful Cunning, and a headstrong Will;

> Yet, with ten thousand Follies to her Charge,
> Unhappy Woman's but a Slave at large.   (1–60)

Abruptly, Belinda's dressing-table from the first canto of the *Rape of the Lock* is stripped of its glamor and mystery, and the crude material base of Belinda's power of attraction is exposed: the "magic" wrought by the sylphs is merely the desirability of wealth, politely disguised. An heiress's plenty will be read in her face; indeed, lovers may not be able to see her features for the superimposed topographical map of her estates she carries there. In "An Essay on Woman," if not for the first time in English literature – we may think of Farquhar's use of the topos in *The Beaux Stratagem*, for instance – but with peculiar effectiveness, the feminized landscape of so much English verse literally *becomes* the beauty in question.

In Leapor's work, not only does marriage begin to seem an impossible institution from a woman's point of view, but women's historical situation is regretted so roundly that the bounds of good-humored satire seem stretched, to say the least. The poems of Leapor's most often anthologized, poems such as "The Month of August," quoted by the *Blackwood's* writer, come from her first volume; the poems most energetically critical of contemporary sexual relations appear in her second, from which few poems have been reprinted. And those few do not include the second "Mira to Octavia," more obviously hostile towards marriage than the first volume's poem of that title; the proudly separatist *Complaining Daphne. A Pastoral*; or such acerbic ripostes to the whole tradition of misogynist verse as the "Essay on Woman," cited above, and "Man the Monarch."

By sapphic textuality I mean to designate both a critical and an affirmative poetic movement within Leapor's texts. From the critique of contemporary sexual relations, of the heterosexual contract and the institutions of marriage and the family as oppressive to women, an alternative green world of female affection is generated. As we have seen, such alternatives to heterosexual obligation, particularly when they involve literary production, are in this period frequently written under the sign of Sappho. Sappho is synonymous with transgressive female erotic and literary exchange. And the oppressiveness of heterosexual institutions in Leapor's verse necessitates some imaginary alternative or release, generates a powerful investment in "sapphic" relations between women: transgressive of patriarchal authority and heterosexual obligation, highly charged in terms of affect, constituted through writing despite the criticism or indifference of the male literary establishment. Leapor's poetry lends itself to, even invites, a reading sensitive to the possibility of a sapphic or lesbian alternative to heterosexual hegemony. To inhabit imaginatively her pastoral green world of female outlaws, escapees from heterosexuality, we must in some sense become "sapphic" readers, alert to erotic possibilities unthinkable within the heterosexual contract and its endless replication of binary sexual difference, with "men" and "women" the only conceivable sexual agents, forever coupled in relations of dominance and subjection.[5] If the study of the socially marginal in terms of class supplements our traditionally restricted versions of history as written from above, from within a hegemonic framework, it is also the case that:

the deviant, whilst being socially marginal, is culturally central: that in studying the deviant, we are studying the dominant order itself, approaching it through its worst fears and nightmares, approaching it through that which it has to outlaw.[6]

In order to do justice to the specificities of Leapor's *œuvre*, then, we should address the question of her relation to Sappho and to a sapphic tradition of transgressive textuality as well as her innovations within traditional poetic genres. And in so doing, we will come to read the dominant culture of Leapor's historical moment in new ways, by reading against the grain of its surfaces, looking for what it has suppressed.

The "sapphic" muse

Leapor's most obvious poetical debt is to Pope, but in a poem from her first volume, "An Hymn to the Morning," she also compares her verse with Sappho's and finds it wanting:

II.
Mira to *Aurora* sings,
While the Lark exulting springs
High in Air – and tunes her Throat
To a soft and merry Note;
The Goldfinch and the Linnet join:
Hail *Aurora*, Nymph divine.

. . .

IV.
May this artless Praise be thine,
Soft *Clione* half divine.
See her snowy Hand she waves,
Silent stand her waiting Slaves;
And while they guard the Silver Reins,
She wanders lonely o'er the Plains.

V.
See those Cheeks of beauteous Dye,
Lovely as the dawning Sky,
Innocence that ne'er beguiles
Lips that wear eternal Smiles:

Beauties to the rest unknown,
Shine in her and her alone.

VI.

Now the Rivers smoother flow,
Now the op'ning Roses glow,
The Woodbine twines her odorous Charms
Round the Oaks supporting Arms:
Lilies paint the dewy Ground,
And *Ambrosia* breathes around.

VII.

Come, ye Gales that fan the Spring;
Zephyr, with thy downy Wing,
Gently waft to *Mira*'s Breast
Health, Content, and balmy Rest.
Far, O far from hence remain
Sorrow, Care, and sickly Pain.

VIII.

Thus sung *Mira* to her Lyre,
Till the idle Numbers tire:
Ah! *Sappho* sweeter sings, I cry,
And the Spiteful Rocks reply,
(Responsive to the jarring Strings)
Sweeter – *Sappho* sweeter sings.

These verses are hardly sapphic in any technical sense. Indeed the reference to Sappho in the last stanza may seem to come out of nowhere. But there is a clear, anguished interplay between Leapor's usual figuring of herself as "Mira" and the direct intrusion of the poetical "I" who cries out that she has failed to equal Sappho; there is a difference between the explicitly poeticized persona and the more autobiographical, though still highly conventional "I" that the relation to Sappho crystallizes. Leapor's poetry is marked not only by a self-conscious difference from the productions of the literary establishment: the difference that renders "Mira" both "merely" a humble, rustic versifier and someone "mired" in the mud and hardships of a laboring life – the muses' "mirror" on what cannot be seen from the usual literary vantage-point of leisured comfort and urbanity. There is also a difference within Leapor's texts that we could identify as a quandary over the "sapphic question" posed for the reader by this invocation of Sappho: the extent to which Leapor's writing represents female eroticism as transgressive, situates it in relation to sapphic textuality, and exposes the necessary construction of such alternative desires within as well as against the very terms of heterosexual propriety from which they are generated.

"An Hymn to the Morning" is in one sense a poem about thwarted poetic ambition. Singing the beauties of the morning offers keen poetic pleasure, but that pleasure dissipates with the recognition that Mira's performance is merely "idle," a form of amusement and of summoning the muse, that cannot hope to measure up to any tradition of poetic greatness, even a female one, and that in any case constitutes an "idle" passing of time bound to be found reprehensible in a world of labor. Sappho may represent no more than a superior female poet, an obvious point of comparison for an aspiring woman of letters, but, as we have seen, Sappho's name also functions in this period as a sign of transgressive female desire. If we read "An Hymn to the Morning" in the light of Mira's yearning to match Sappho in poetical sweet-ness, her technical rivalry with the Lesbian muse – and, more contentiously, her rivalry with Sappho as a wooer of women, her technical rivalry with the lesbian lover – the eroticism of Leapor's textuality becomes distinctly notice-able, though it remains safely mediated by conventional landscape cathexis. The female personifications of neoclassical verse take on a certain aura as objects of desire: Aurora herself, the goddess of the morning; Clione, a descendant of Clio, the muse of history, or human action in time, here rendered only half divine in the person of a local nymph whose beauty rep-licates, in a way that can be desired, the aesthetic beauties of the morning. To write a hymn to the morning allows one to praise the "snowy Hands," "Cheeks . . . Lovely as the dawning Sky," "Lips that wear eternal Smiles," and "Beauties to the rest unknown" – an explicitly erotic blazon – while remaining within the boundaries of neoclassical natural description. The woodbine may twine herself round the supporting oak in what seems a tradi-tional topos for heterosexual union, but the only pronouns or other gendered parts of speech in the text are feminine. In this largely feminized landscape, Mira feels inspired and safe; she asks only that the elements sustain her there by bringing continued "Health, Content, and balmy Rest," that she may never return to the "Sorrow, Care, and sickly Pain" from which she has (poetically) escaped.

What Leapor would have known of Sappho's verse and reputation can only be conjectured. She may well have known Pope's version of Ovid's *Sapho to Phaon* – Sappho the passionate but tormented lover, once a lover of women but now rejected by a young man – for her library contained among its "sixteen or seventeen single Volumes" "Part of Mr. *Pope*'s Works, *Dryden*'s Fables," and "Some Volumes of Plays, &c."[7] The recovery of Sappho for eighteenth-century audiences[8] depended heavily on translations of Longinus and of Boileau's *Traité du Sublime* as well as translations of Sappho's odes and fragments from the Greek.[9] The most widely disseminated view of Sappho was probably Addison's in the *Spectator*, and it encapsulates both ten-dencies towards which Leapor's invocation of Sappho points: towards poeti-cal and aesthetic excitement and towards something so erotic, or erotic in such a way, as to be "dangerous," though the precise dangers thus engendered must of course not be articulated in order to protect the susceptible reader:

> She is called by Ancient Authors the Tenth Muse; and by *Plutarch* is compared to *Cacus* the Son of *Vulcan*, who breathed out nothing but Flame. I do not know, by the Character that is given of her Works, whether it is not for the Benefit of Mankind that they are lost. They were filled with such bewitching Tenderness and Rapture, that it might have been dangerous to have given them a Reading.[10]

The premise of "An Hymn to the Morning" is that Mira has not only "read" Sappho but internalized the sweetness of her lyre as a haunting standard of comparison. "Mira"'s decorum guards against Leapor's "I" breaking into a fully-fledged sapphic discourse – except for that "cry," which signals implicit failure as well as comparison: the poetry of Mira would be a sapphic production, but it is doomed never to equal the dangerous rupture with mid-eighteenth-century English propriety that such explicitly feminized "Tenderness and Rapture" would constitute. The fragmentary status of Sappho's texts, forever suggestive, never to be exhausted of possible meanings, does not diminish, but rather heightens her symbolic power as a "dangerous" muse. And although there is no direct acknowledgment within Leapor's *œuvre* of an engagement with the work of Katherine Philips, one of a number of poets described as the "English Sappho,"[11] we can trace within their texts similar preoccupations, especially the connection between criticism of the institution of marriage and the cultivation of erotically charged female friendships.

Leapor grounds her critique of heterosexuality in the predatory and tyrannical nature of men's desire for and subjugation of women. Unlike Collier, who attributes "female slavery" to a general degenerative tendency in history, to which both men and women are subject, and which oppresses both sexes though not symmetrically or equally, Leapor attributes it to men's desire for power. Because Man was "greedy of Pow'r," he envied the greater sexual asymmetry in other, "lesser" species, which seemed to him to bespeak an unqualified male dominance. Happy in his tyranny over the animal kingdom, he could not bear to share power with Woman, and so seized it by ridiculing her into insignificance. Woman's Edenic body was her downfall, for it made her both powerless to resist Man's oppression and threatening to his precarious sense of superiority, which was put in jeopardy when he noticed that male birds had more splendid plumage than females:

> When our Grandsire nam'd the feather'd Kind,
> Pond'ring their Natures in his careful Mind,
> 'Twas then, if on our Author we rely,
> He view'd his Consort with an envious Eye;
> Greedy of Pow'r, he hugg'd the tott'ring Throne;

> Pleased with Homage, and would reign alone;
> And, better to secure his doubtful Rule,
> Roll'd his wise Eye-balls, and pronounc'd her *Fool*.
> The regal Blood to distant Ages runs:
> Sires, Brothers, Husbands, and commanding Sons,
> The Sceptre claim; and ev'ry Cottage brings
> A long Succession of Domestic Kings.   ("Man the Monarch," 54–65)

For Leapor, this history of domestic despotism is the empirical proof that romantic myths of heterosexual love are insidiously deceptive. "The Temple of Love," a parody of the dream vision of classical and medieval poetry – a topos which Leapor may have known best through Pope's *Temple of Fame* – represents heterosexual attraction as a promise of future bliss bleakly dismantled within the text. As an implied narrative of ruined maidenhood, with the "wealthy Swain" taking advantage of the "blooming Damsel" (36) by ceremoniously giving her gifts but not marrying her, the poem adheres to official eighteenth-century precepts. But nowhere in the text are we reassured that a mere wedding ceremony would avert the catastrophe that ensues after the feast of love; and Leapor's poems on marriage itself are no less disaffected than this exposure of the ruined maiden's fate:

> Then rush'd Suspicion through the lofty Gate,
> With heart-sick Loathing led by ghastly Hate;
> And foaming Rage, to close the horrid Band,
> With a drawn Poniard in her shaking Hand.
> Now like an Earthquake shook the reeling Frame,
> The Lamps extinguish in a purple Flame:
> One universal Groan was heard, and then
> The Cries of Women and the Voice of Men:
> Some roar out Vengeance, some for Mercy call;
> And Shrieks and Tumult fill the dreadful Hall.   (55–64)

The "temple of love" emblematizes an idolizing of heterosexual desire that is mutually destructive for men and women, but promises women only disillusionment and annihilation: men at least have the pleasures of pursuit and momentary possession of women's bodies and their goods – a fleeting triumph of appropriation, of the seizure of property. The telling difference between the two "Mira to Octavia" poems is the latter's greater emphasis upon the purely instrumental, monetary advantage to be gained by a husband in marrying a woman of means, a predatory regime against which only passionate female friendship can provide any kind of bulwark. The first "Mira to Octavia" concludes playfully:

> In spite of all romantick Poets sing;
> This Gold, my Dearest, is an useful thing:

. . .

> But if there's none but *Florio* that will do,
> Write Ballads both, and you may thrive – Adieu.   (62–69)

The second poem of this title, however, overrides the first poem's jocular caution – not to marry even for love, unless there are sufficient means – by proposing that any marriage will be likely to end in the unhappiness and oppression of the bride. Spinsterhood is explicitly advocated; Leapor even reassures her audience that she is neither a "Rebel to your *Hymen*'s Law" nor "Foe to Man" (148–50), as if we were bound to accuse her of man-hating when she argues:

> And shall *Octavia* prostitute her Store,
> To buy a Tyrant with the tempting Ore?
> Besides, I fear your Shackles will be found
> Too dearly purchas'd with a thousand Pound.
>
> Then be the charming Mistress of thy Gold;
> While young, admir'd; and rev'renc'd, when you're Old.   (154–59)

There are verbal echoes here of Pope's praise of Martha Blount in *Epistle to a Lady* and of Clarissa's speech to Belinda in the *Rape of the Lock*, but where Pope explicitly advocates marriage for women, Leapor reverses his advice. Although Pope's good friend Martha was herself a spinster, in order to eulogize her Pope represents her in *To a Lady* as an exemplary wife and mother; a spinster cannot be represented as exemplary within his prescriptions for proper female behavior. Yet Pope also admits that Martha Blount is saved (implicitly, by her spinsterhood) from a tyrannical husband greedy for control of her property; her property-less state proves a blessing in disguise since she is thus "deny'd the Pelf / That buys your sex a Tyrant o'er itself" (287–88). Ironically, Pope's praise of Martha Blount conveys simultaneously that the ideal female virtues are wifely and maternal, but that the ideal female condition is spinsterhood. Leapor, contrary to her own former protest that she writes not as a rebel to "*Hymen*'s Law," writes here to challenge the hegemony of romantic love and marriage. A woman of property can only maintain her liberty – and her happiness – if she refuses to buy a "Tyrant o'er [her]self." And a woman without property, a laboring woman, is unlikely to find happiness at any price except for brief moments of solace in the manner of "complaining Daphne" and Mira herself. We are reminded by the silences in Leapor's texts that the pursuit of happiness as an enabling myth, in terms of official precept accessible to women through romantic love and marriage, remains in this period largely a privilege of bourgeois male subjects. For women and the lower classes, unhappiness is to be endured, not abandoned, even for the pursuit of imaginary alternatives.

Perhaps Leapor's most technically successful intervention against the heterosexist mythologizing of marriage among the upper classes is *The Mistaken Lover*, in some sense a perverse rewriting of Swift's *The Lady's Dressing Room*.[12] Leapor's Strephon could be read as having overcome his disillusionment with female bodies and their excremental functions sufficiently to marry a Celia who shits. As soon as Strephon has won possession of Celia and her fortune, he loses "interest" – both the excitement of pursuit, and imaginary economic speculation on future gain. As a wife Celia is condemned to loneliness, boredom, and the negation of her own desires and possible agency. The sporting terseness of Swiftian couplets is here deployed to savage the decorum of loveless gentry marriages of (in)convenience rather than English policies regarding Ireland or corruption in Sir Robert Walpole's administration:

> 'Twas half a Year – It might be more,
> Since *Celia* brought her shining Store,
> Five thousand Pounds of Sterling clear,
> To bless the Mansion of her Dear.
>
> Some tell us Wives their Beauties lose,
> When they have spoil'd their bridal Shoes:
> Some learned Casuists make it clear,
> A Wife might please for half a Year:
> And others say, her Charms will hold
> As long as the suspended Gold;
> But that her Bloom is soon decay'd,
> And wither'd when her Fortune's paid.   (53–64)

The rule of the fathers renders Strephon, even as a negligent husband, the legal dictator of his wife's future, and he lays down the law of civil decorum as follows: once there was romance between them, as a courting couple,

> "But now, my Dearest, as you see
> "In mutual Hatred we agree,
> "Methinks 'tis better we retreat,
> "Each Party to a distant Seat;
> "And tho' we value each the other,
> "Just as one Rush regards another:
> "Yet let us often send to hear,
> "If Health attend the absent Dear:
> "And tho' each other we would shun,
> "As Debtors do a hateful Dun:
> "(Nor mind the crossing of a Street)
> "Yet let's be civil when we meet,
> "And live in short like courtly Friends:
> "They part – and thus the Story ends.   (167–80)

The end of the story between courtiers and between husband and wife means the end of intrigue, of "plotting" in the conventional and technical senses, and the end of desire, the narrative motor. For Leapor, perhaps the cruellest aspect of male desire is its capricious and self-serving brevity.

Leapor's most explicitly separatist poem, in which the mutability of male desire is villified, and the only refuge is to be found in female affection, is a pastoral to end all heterosexual complaints, *Complaining Daphne. A Pastoral.* Abandoned by Cynthio, Daphne strives to control her passion and remorse, but only in recalling her mother's early love for her and the warnings she received at her mother's knee about men's predatory natures can she steel herself to resolution. During the hottest part of the day, Daphne and her mother would rest from weeding or hay-making by sitting in the shade, and her mother would tell (anti)romantic tales about the perils of heterosexual entanglement:

> Long Tales she told, to kill the tedious Hour;
> Of lovely Maids to early Ruin led,
> Who once were harmless as the Flocks they fed;
> Of some induc'd with gaudy Knights to roam
> From their dear Parents, and their blissful Home;
> Till, each deserted by her changing Friend,
> The pageant Wretches met a woful End.
> And still howe'er the mournful Tale began,
> She always ended – *Child, beware of Man.*   (91–99)

Daphne's response to this remembrance is to pledge obedience to her mother's memory by forgetting Cynthio and embracing her sister shepherdesses. In a triumph of renunciation of heterosexual closure in marriage, the poem ends with a celebration of the tranquillity and harmony to be found when women choose to live only for each other, in a feminine pastoral paradise, a sapphic idyll:

> Yes, sacred Shade! you shall Obedience find;
> I'll banish *Cynthio* from my sickly Mind.
> Come, sweet Content, and long-desired Rest!
> Two welcome Strangers! to my aking Breast:
> Purl on, ye Streams! ye Flow'rets, smile again!
> Your chearful *Daphne* shall no more complain:
> Haste, *Philomela*, with thy charming Lay,
> And tune thy Chorals to the falling Day:
> Ye Sylvan Sisters! come; ye gentle Dames,
> Whose tender Souls are spotless as your Names!
> Henceforth shall *Daphne* only live for you;
> Content – and bid the lordly Race Adieu;

See the clear Streams in gentler Murmurs flow,
And fresher Gales from od'rous Mountains blow.
Now the charm'd Tempest from my Bosom flies:
Sweet Slumber seizes on my willing Eyes.

Ye Winds, no more I ask the tempting Swain:
Go fan the Sweets of yonder flow'ry Plain.   (100–17)

Leapor's only available language for reproducing the elusive pleasures of this idyll is the language of sleep, the bliss of sleep after the turn in a dangerous fever. Not boredom, the sleep of dullness, but peace and a return to the pleasurable, maternally guarded safety of childhood are to be found here. This Daphne too, it would seem, takes her pleasure primarily by escaping – from hot-eyed, masculine embraces and the torments of subsequent abandonment.

To read these rejections of the fugitive pleasures of heterosexuality as a puritanical rejection of the body and its appetites would be to occlude the sensuousness of Leapor's verse, its appeals to visual and gustatory pleasures. The traditional designation of pastoral as a safe and suitable genre for female poets provides an excuse for pastoral veneration of female bodies in such poems as "An Hymn to the Morning," as we have seen. In "Man the Monarch," the conventions of heterosexual blazon are doubly ironized as an historical liability as well as an imprisoning ideology, a legacy of Edenic myth. Speculating on the origins of gender relations, Leapor rewrites Genesis in order to explain Man's "despotic Sway" (5). Unlike Collier's mythical Golden Age, which begins with the sexes ostensibly enjoying mutual harmony until custom stales affection, Leapor's begins with Man, "insolently vain" (7), tyrannizing over the animals, whom Heaven allows to escape into remote places like caves, oceans, and the sky. Faced with such a scene, "But where! ah! where, shall helpless Woman fly?" (23). Woman, the daughter of a complacent Mother Nature pleased with her own handiwork, is told simply to "live, and reign" (29), until the moment of an ambiguous "now," simultaneously mythico-historical and contemporary with the scene of reading, when Mother Nature realizes her mistake: "Beholds a *Wretch*, whom she design'd a *Queen*, / And weeps that e'er she form'd the weak Machine" (30–33).

In a passage of complex irony, Leapor mocks the traditional anatomization of female beauty to be found in love lyrics by men while pointing out how inappropriate to domestic drudgery such a notion of femininity is:

In vain she boasts her Lip of scarlet Dyes,
Cheeks like the Morning, and far-beaming Eyes;
Her Neck refulgent – fair and feeble Arms,
A Set of useless and neglected Charms.
She suffers Hardship with afflictive Moans:
Small Tasks of Labour suit her slender Bones.

Beneath a Load her weary Shoulders yield,
Nor can her Fingers grasp the sounding Shield;
She sees and trembles at approaching Harms,
And Fear and Grief destroy her fading Charms.
Then her pale Lips no pearly Teeth disclose,
And Time's rude Sickle cuts the yielding Rose.
Thus wretched Woman's short-liv'd Merit dies:
In vain to Wisdom's sacred Help she flies;
Or sparkling Wit but lends a feeble Aid:
'Tis all Delirium from a wrinkled Maid.   (34–49)

Idealized femininity remains ambiguous in Leapor's texts, subject to demystification as oppressive, yet returned to again and again, obsessively. Women's bodies often figure in Leapor's verse as objects preyed upon by time and cruelly devalued by social custom as time passes. Indeed the description of female beauty and the regretful chronicling of decay are usually linked in Leapor's work. This combination may seem reminiscent of Swift's preoccupation with decaying bodies as specifically female bodies, as if the idealization of femininity made bodily functions and mortality more textually grotesque than their representation by means of a male body could ever do.

But unlike Swift, who renders the decaying body outrageously grotesque, Leapor avoids satirical inventories of bodily decay in favor of brief allusions. And those brief allusions interweave from poem to poem to form a network of sisterly advice and consolation. At moments of extremity, women may openly comfort one another sensuously and passionately. In "Colinetta," the poetical heroine delivers her last verses from her deathbed on Lydia's lap (Leapor's *œuvre* is replete with premonitions and prefigurations of her own premature death): "On *Lydia*'s Lap pale *Colinetta* lay; / . . . At last reviv'd, on *Lydia*'s Neck she hung, / And like the Swan expiring thus she sung" (14–22).

Unlike Pope, Leapor does not find aging beauties necessarily either ludicrous or contemptible, though derision and contempt are the options socially on offer. Rather, with a sympathy that may seem older than her years, in a poem like *Dorinda at her Glass* – the ambitious poem that opens her first volume and foregrounds metaphors of mirroring – Leapor recommends comforting, not chastising, the body as it ages. The mirror, which allegorically betokens female vanity and keeps Dorinda a slave to arduous rituals that in time are doomed to fail, will be supplanted in this poem by Dorinda's advice to her sisters not to fight time.

More generally in Leapor's *œuvre*, the mirror that Mira's verse represents offers to supplement a female audience's collective imaginary sense of themselves in the hope of displacing such damaging and constraining self-representations. Coquettes and belles need not be ridiculous when time gains the upper hand in their struggle to maintain their desirability as a means to power. For Pope:

> Beauties, like Tyrants, old and friendless grown,
> Yet hate Repose, and dread to be alone,
> Worn out in public, weary ev'ry eye,
> Nor leave one sigh behind them when they die.
>
> . . .
>
> Still round and round the Ghosts of Beauty glide,
> And haunt the places where their Honour dy'd.
>
> (*Epistle to a Lady*, 227–42)

For Leapor, it seems possible to face age with dignity by accommodating oneself to small bodily comforts rather than the theatrical staging of beauty. Her advice is both sartorial:

> Let *Isabel* unload her aking Head
> Of twisted Papers, and of binding Lead;
> Let sage *Augusta* now, without a Frown,
> Strip those gay Ribbands from her aged Crown;
> Change the lac'd Slipper of delicious Hue
> For a warm Stocking, and an easy Shoe;   (88–93)

and philosophical:

> Hear this, ye fair Ones, that survive your Charms,
> Nor reach at Folly with your aged Arms;
> Thus *Pope* has sung, thus let *Dorinda* sing;
> "Virtue, brave Boys, – 'tis Virtue makes a King:"
> Why not a Queen? fair Virtue is the same
> In the rough Hero, and the smiling Dame:
> *Dorinda*'s Soul her Beauties shall pursue,
> Tho' late I see her, and embrace her too:
> Come, ye blest Graces, that are sure to please,
> The Smile of Friendship, and the careless Ease;
> The Breast of Candour, the relenting Ear,
> The Hand of Bounty, and the Heart sincere:
> May these the Twilight of my Days attend,
> And may that Ev'ning never want a Friend
> To smooth my Passage to the silent Gloom,
> And give a Tear to grace the mournful Tomb.   (120–35)

Rejecting any sexually based or gender-specific distinction between masculine and feminine virtues, Leapor equates the sexes morally in order to distinguish them on the grounds of affective economy. In an historical moment when a woman's "honor" was primarily sexually construed, to claim that virtue is the same in the "rough Hero" and the "smiling Dame" is a bold claim, certainly more radical in its implications that Pope's notion of ideal women as softer men, or even a logically possible counter-notion of men's needing to become more like women in order to become "fully human." And again we find the nexus of beauty's decay and female friendship easing the prospect of "friendless" death in a world where men only befriend women for their beauty. Where "beauty" is not a weapon in marriage-market or marital conflict, its loss matters relatively little. On her deathbed, Leapor's Dorinda hopes to be comforted by, not a husband, lover, father, brother, or child, but by a "Friend," which in the context of this poem "by" a woman on behalf of her sex, will almost certainly strike us as designating a female friend.

From what we know of Leapor's experience of patronage, female friendship was crucial to her literary enterprise. Her short and "blameless" life, so free from scandal that one of her patrons, at least, commented that her character "was such as would have been ornamental in a much higher Sphere, to which in all Probability, if it had pleased God to spare her Life, her own Merit would have raised her,"[13] seems to have been devoted entirely to her parents, one childhood friend figured in the *Essay on Friendship* as Fidelia (39–45), a circle of young women whom Leapor possibly met at Weston Hall,[14] and Bridget Freemantle, foremost among her female patrons, who appears in Leapor's verses as Artemisia. As a clergyman's daughter, Freemantle seems to have been well-bred without ostentation; as a spinster whose father had died twenty-six years before, and who lived with her widowed mother, she was sympathetic to Leapor's poverty and obscurity. According to Richard Greene, the name Artemisia "refers to a ruler of Rhodes known for having fostered the arts."[15] Appropriate as this reference is for a patron, I would suggest that the name might well contain another allusion to a better-known classical figure – Artemis, virgin goddess of the hunt, through whom the name "Artemisia" would point towards both militant, if not amazonian, singleness and the cult of unfettered female friendship. Most importantly, Freemantle, living in a nearby village with her ailing mother, seems to have had time and inclination to take an active interest in Leapor's writing and to visit her frequently, as described in such poems as "To Artemisia. Dr. King's Invitation to Bellvill: Imitated." She even supplied Leapor with some family memorabilia, "an old manuscript Pastoral of Mr. *Newton*'s, in Blank Verse" which Leapor liked so much she rhymed parts of it and insisted upon acknowledging Newton in her published volumes; this Mr. Newton was probably Bridget Freemantle's maternal grandfather.[16]

As a patron, Freemantle seems to have been both devoted to promoting

Leapor's career and sensitive to her feelings. Her anonymous account of Leapor in the second volume strikes one by its self-effacement and absence of class prejudice, though it is by no means innocent of class distinctions. Freemantle goes so far as to worry whether her interest in Leapor might prove something of an annoyance to a young woman of the servant class, a cookmaid, who, sometime after her mother's death in 1742 and probably in the first six months of 1745, when she was dismissed from service,[17] kept house for her father without anyone to assist her. After proposing a subscription edition of her poems to Leapor, that she might be able to buy more time in which to write (presumably by hiring a servant), Freemantle indulges herself by calling often to observe Leapor's progress in composing new verses:

My expressing some Fear of being troublesome in coming so frequently, occasioned a great Variety of Invitations, both in Verse and Prose; which I could seldom resist: And indeed her whole Behaviour to me was so extremely good-natur'd and obliging, that I must have been the most ungrateful Person in the World, if I had not endeavour'd to make some Return.

From this Time to that of her Death, few Days pass'd in which I did not either see or hear from her; for she gave me the Pleasure of seeing all her Poems as soon as they were finish'd. And though I never was extremely fond of Poetry, and don't pretend to be a Judge of it, there was something so peculiarly pleasing to my Taste in almost every thing she wrote, that I could not but be infinitely pleas'd with such a Correspondent.

Nor did I admire her in her Poetical Capacity only; but the more I was acquainted with her, the more I saw Reason to esteem her for those virtuous Principles, and that Goodness of Heart and Temper, which so visibly appeared in her; and I was so far from thinking it a Condescension to cultivate an Acquaintance with a Person in her Station, that I rather esteem'd it an Honour to be call'd a Friend to one in whom there appear'd such a true Greatness of Soul as with me far outweigh'd all the Advantages of Birth and Fortune. Nor did I think it possible for any body that was as well acquainted with her as myself, to consider her as a mean Person.[18]

In the case of Leapor and Freemantle, it would seem that we have an example of female alliance across class lines that succeeded where More's patronage of Yearsley failed: in the cultivation of a strong friendship that allowed each woman access to the other's sensitivities. There is also, of course, no question of a possible literary rivalry between patron and protégée, since Freemantle does not even "pretend" to critical, yet alone creative, abilities. And Leapor's premature death put an end to the alliance before it had to stand the test of time – and of possible conflicts over the eventual financial arrangements that publication by subscription was likely to induce.

If the addresses to Artemisia and her female acquaintance tend to be chaste gestures of friendship and sisterly solidarity:

> TO *Artemisia*. – 'Tis to her we sing,
> For her once more we touch the sounding String.
> 'Tis not to *Cythera*'s Reign nor *Cupid*'s Fires,
> But sacred Friendship that our Muse inspires.
> A Theme that suits *Æmilia*'s pleasing Tongue:
> So to the Fair Ones I devote my Song   (*Essay on Friendship*, 1–6)

usually represented within Mira's humble surroundings:

> IF *Artemisia*'s Soul can dwell
> Four Hours in a tiny Cell,
> (To give that Space of Bliss to me)
> I wait my Happiness at three.
>   ("To Artemisia. Dr. King's Invitation to Bellvill: Imitated," 1–4)

Leapor's sisterly strain is sometimes vexed by betrayal on the part of other female would-be friends and patrons. Sometimes the bored frivolity of leisured women leads them to seek out Mira's most recent literary productions for their own amusement – one of the liabilities of her "discovery":

> Yet some Impertinence pursues me still;
> And so I fear it ever must, and will.
> So soft *Pappilia* o'er the Table bends
> With her small Circle of insipid Friends;
> Who wink, and stretch, and rub their drowsy Eyes,
> While o'er their Heads Imperial Dulness flies.
> "What can we do? We cannot stir for Show'rs:
> "Or what invent, to kill the irksome Hours?
> "Why, run to *Leapor*'s, fetch that idle Play:
> "'Twill serve to laugh at all the live-long Day."
>
> Preferment great! To beat one's weary Brains,
> To find Diversion only when it rains!
>   (*An Epistle to Artemisia. On Fame*, 167–78)

The dunce-like dullness of the idle female gentry offends Leapor as much as Artemisia's cultivation pleases her. Such torpid inactivity of mind in a body rendered idle by the weather is crucially linked to the desire for cruel amusement at the socially humbler, and more industrious, Mira's expense.

In "The Disappointment" from volume II, the "Half-promised" receipt of cast-off clothing from the artful but thoughtless Sophronia tantalizes Mira into visions of sartorial grandeur, only to have such visions dashed by Sophronia's forgetfulness:

WHEN you, *Sophronia*, did my Sense beguile
With your Half-promise, and consenting Smile;
What Shadows swam before these dazled Eyes!
Fans, Lace, and Ribbands, in bright Order rise:
Me thought these Limbs your silken Favours found,
And thro' streight Entries brush'd the rustling Gown;
While the gay Vestment of delicious Hue
Sung thro' the Isle, and whistled in the Pew.
Then, who its Wearer, by her Form shall tell:
No longer *Mira*, but a shining Belle.
Such Phantoms fill'd these giddy Brains of mine;
Such golden Dreams on *Mira*'s Temples shine;
Till stern Experience bid her Servant rise,
And Disappointment rubb'd my drowsy Eyes.
Do thou, *Sophronia*, now thy Arts give o'er,
Thy little Arts; for *Mira*'s Thoughts no more
Shall after your imagin'd Favours run,
Your still-born Gifts, that ne'er behold the Sun.   (1–18)

As J. Jean Hecht has shown, "When servants were engaged, they were frequently granted the right to the 'cast clothes' of the master or mistress as a regular perquisite."[19] For female servants, this perquisite most often accompanied upper-servant status; the lady's maid in particular might have "a sumptuous wardrobe of her own" (Hecht, p. 122). The cookmaid, however, was lowest in rank among female servants. For Mira, Sophronia's gift of a silk dress is an exceptional offer, not the rule. "Me thought these Limbs your silken Favours found, / And thro' streight Entries brush'd the rustling Gown": Mira's imagination, stirred by Sophronia's "little Arts" of exciting desire, projects the cookmaid-poet, all "limbs," eager to feel silk against arms and legs, into Sophronia's cast-off gown, and into a new intimacy with the superior Sophronia and her "silken Favours." Thus gloriously dressed, Mira brushes and rustles her way into the primary public arena of the respectable female poor in an English village, the parish church, whose "streight Entry," like Bunyan's wicket gate, is easier of access for the humble poor than the rich or vainly aspiring. Mira's history of straitened circumstances and strait-laced piety competes with her newly awakened vanity and sensuality in these lines, until "stern Experience" gets the upper hand, forcing Mira to recognize that nothing has changed, that disappointment is eminent, and that Sophronia is as untrustworthy and forgetful of her subordinates as ever, her "Favours" merely imaginary, her "Gifts" "still-born."

It is tempting to read the poem that follows "The Disappointment" – "The Consolation" – as a response to such class-specific vicissitudes. In "The Consolation" Leapor returns to her preoccupation with death and funerary arrangements, this time anticipating Gray in presenting a humble, rustic grave as the equal of any queen's because death is the great leveller, the final social transformation in which class will cease to matter. Leapor will have none of the literary tradition of marble monuments, so often meretricious in their grandeur,

> But the plain Stone with Chizel form'd,
> But rudely shapen and adorn'd;
> Inscrib'd with – "*Natus Anno Dom*'
> "Here lies *Mary* in this Tomb."
> And there's no odds, that I can spy,
> 'Twixt *Mary* Queen of *Scots* and *I.*
> So Poets, so shall Critics fall,
> Cits, Wits, and Courtiers, Kings and all,
> Hands that wrote or held a Flail,
> Tongues that us'd to sooth or rail;
> Rivals there no more contend,
> And there Ambition finds an End.   (25–36)

Despite her attachment to upper-class female patrons and her related protests against women's slavery within the family and marriage, Leapor is a poet of class consciousness as well.

Here, though more implicitly than Collier, Leapor links her own situation with Stephen Duck's – he whose hands both wrote and held the thresher's flail. She does not mention him by name, but as Hannah More's memory of him in 1784 testifies, his status as a plebeian poetical genius functions as an eighteenth-century paradigm. It is interesting to note that Duck subscribed to Leapor's first volume. But he remains embedded in her poetical text not as a deracinated thresher-clergyman, the "Rever. Mr. Stephen Duck," subscriber, but as forever the paradoxical thresher-poet whose hands could both labor and write when inspired by the rustic muse.

In a letter included in her second volume, which concerns the publication of her poems, Leapor goes so far as to deny that Duck's "situation" – his status as a laboring poet, hence a "curiosity" – was crucial to his literary popularity, given that he had obtained Queen Caroline's favor:

concerning *Stephen Duck*, I am of Opinion, that it was not his Situation, but the Royal Favour, which gained the Country over to his Side; and therefore I think it needless to paint the Life of a Person, who depends more upon the Curiosity of the World, than its Good-nature. Besides, the seeing myself described in Print would give me the same Uneasiness as being stared at. For this Reason, whenever my Verses shall appear amongst the Public, I hope they will excuse the Author in this Particular.[20]

Here Leapor's gender- and class-specific modesty, her embarrassment at the thought of being offered to the public as a curiosity, contributes to the ideological occlusion of Duck's class position – and her own – as inextricably bound up with their literary reception in the period by royalty and the middle classes alike. Within her poems Leapor appears to be striving for an idealized aesthetic ground of equivalence between her work and the texts of such poetic exemplars as Sappho, Pope, and Swift. The patronage of Bridget Freemantle apparently supported and reinforced this desire. But Leapor's poems also exhibit signs of struggle between a class allegiance that could not be merely taken for granted, and the upwardly mobile tendency of literary imitation in the period. Although Leapor herself may not have been able or willing to see the inevitability of a middle-class public's interest in the laboring-class "prodigy" as such, her texts remain testaments to the very dynamic of literary success and social subordination that she would have preferred to repudiate.

Despite, therefore, the frequent conjuncture between sapphic feeling, Popean or Swiftian imitation, and a certain upwardly mobile ambition in Leapor's verse – to be intimate with the world of fine ladies established most thoroughly as poetical terrain by Pope, to be as aesthetically successful a poet of "the feminine" as he was, and to be capable of Swiftian demystification of idealized femininity, as well – Leapor does not write as such a lady but as an intimate outsider: as a domestic servant, in short, for whom the cast-off silk dress remains both desirable and risible. The dangers represented by Leapor's sapphic muse are thus as much social as sexual: if sisterly alliances, affective and professional, can be formed across class lines, not only families and class hierarchies but the male literary establishment might be threatened by their social effects.

Patronage and patronizing relations

To focus exclusively on the implications of Leapor's sapphic muse or the importance placed on female friendship in her work would be to misread the social context in which her discovery and publication took place. Like Collier's, Leapor's subscription lists contain the names of more men (505) than women (277), though in the list accompanying her second (and arguably, more protofeminist) volume, women (173) outnumber men (111). The proposals for her subscription may have been drawn up by Garrick;[21] Samuel Richardson, Christopher Smart, Isaac Hawkins Browne, John Duncombe, John Watts, and James Roberts were involved in the publication and promotion of her work;[22] as late as 1784, the *Gentleman's Magazine* quoted a line from "Colinetta" as particularly evocative;[23] and as late as 1791, William Cowper cited Leapor's poems as significantly exceptional examples of "strong natural genius."[24] For all Bridget Freemantle's devotion, and apparent success at interesting her friends in Leapor's work, it was still necessary for her to approach important men of letters if Leapor were to be launched as a literary discovery.

Ironically, literary critics and men of letters are represented with suspicion and hostility in Leapor's verse. She writes as if only sycophants and charlatans have come within her ken, either refusing to criticize helpfully for fear of offending, or refusing to read her work at all out of sheer class and gender prejudice. The pressure of composing quickly causes Leapor to lose confidence in her ability not to write like a hack; she seeks help from "Vido," who offers only vacuous praise, implying that he too has been so contaminated by the Grub-street ethos that he possesses no judgment or taste:

> "Pray, *Vido*, look on these: Methinks they smell
> "Too much of *Grub-street*: That myself can tell."
> "Not so indeed, they're easy and polite.
> "And can you bear 'em?"
> "I could read till Night."
>
> (*An Epistle to Artemisia. On Fame*, 127–30)

The situation of the plebeian female poet at the hands of male critics is most vigorously dramatized in Leapor's "Minutius. Artemisia. A Dialogue." At the request of the female patron, Mira's poems are scrutinized by the pedantic "Minutius," though they are not "read." Artemisia has hopes of the critic's appreciating both the form and content of her protégée's verse, but the microscopically inclined Minutius cannot get beyond Mira's unschooled handwriting and punctuation. Artemisia declares, "That you should mark, – was my Intention, / Her Thought, her Language, and Invention" (49–50). Minutius's comments display his socio-sexual prejudices rather than his critical acumen:

> Minutius.
> He! he! – Are these the Verses then?
> She wrote 'em with a filthy Pen.
> As I'm a Gentleman, I vow
> I never saw the like till now:
> There's not a Stop throughout the Song;
> Or, if there is, 'tis planted wrong:
> The hideous Scrawl offends my Sight:
> But how should she know how to write
> 'Tis time to lay all Science by,
> If such as she must versify.   (37–46)

And "lay all Science by" is just what Minutius proceeds to do, proving himself so incapable of a critical judgment, or even of a reading of the verses in question, that we must query his reputation as a man of letters. By contrast, Leapor's poetical talents come off well in this production. We must leave the poem feeling that a new literary era, in which pompous literary bores will be replaced by witty and unprejudiced writers and readers, has been initiated. This democratization of the literary scene, with its implicit feminism couched as a feminization, is a brave gesture on Leapor's part, especially given her dependence on the goodwill of certain literary gentlemen.

Despite these overt criticisms of the quasi-scientific club of gentlemen-critics, Leapor's poetry seems to have pleased that club, and to have gone on pleasing it, right through Roger Lonsdale's recent recuperation. This formal agility or air of openness, "ease," and pleasantry, that must be seen to be duplicitous if we are to foreground the radical possibilities of Leapor's texts, extends to the social space of her own class origins and her family as well, the space from which she situates her writing as a scene of conflict.

Although, like Collier and Yearsley, she seems to have received at home the rudiments of an education and even initial encouragement, so long as writing verses was perceived as a childish pastime, once her writing promised to distract her from "more profitable Employment," it was discouraged. These details are to be found in Freemantle's epistolary account. She reports being told by Leapor's father that Mary (or Molly):

was always fond of reading every thing that came in her way, as soon as she was capable of it; and that when she had learnt to write tolerably, which, as he remembers, was at about ten or eleven Years old, She would often be scribbling, and sometimes in Rhyme; which her Mother was at first pleas'd with: But finding this Humour increase upon her as she grew up, when she thought her capable of more profitable Employment, she endeavour'd to break her of it; and that he likewise, having no Taste for Poetry, and not imagining it could ever be any Advantage to her, join'd in the same Design: But finding it impossible to alter her natural Inclination, he had of late desisted, and left her more at Liberty. . . . she always chose to spend her leisure Hours in Writing and Reading . . . insomuch that some of the Neighbours that observ'd it, expressed their Concern, lest the Girl should over-study herself, and be mopish.[25]

The disturbing possibilities suggested by that phrase "endeavour'd to break her of it" are many; Leapor's strength of will in proving to her parents that "it [was] impossible to alter her natural Inclination" must have been positively formidable. The neighborly concern of those who cannot understand a literary disposition is ruthlessly satirized in Leapor's *An Epistle to Artemisia. On Fame*:

> *Parthenia* cries, "Why, *Mira*, you are dull,
> "And ever musing, till you crack your Skull;
> "Still poking o'er your What-d'ye-call – your Muse:
> "But pr'ythee, *Mira*, when dost clean thy Shoes?"
> Then comes *Sophronia*, like a barb'rous *Turk*:

"You thoughtless Baggage, when d'ye mind your Work?
"Still o'er a Table leans your bending Neck:
"Your Head will grow prepost'rous, like a Peck.
"Go, ply your Needle: You might earn your Bread;
"Or who must feed you when your Father's dead?"
She sobbing answers, "Sure, I need not come
"To you for Lectures; I have store at home.
"What can I do?"
                    " – Not scribble."
                              " – But I will."
"Then get thee packing – and be aukward still."   (149–62)

Here Pope's refusal to stop writing, despite the advice of friends, in the *First Satire of the Second Book of Horace*[26] enables Leapor's defiance, and perhaps her dismissal from service. According to this poem at least, her willful scribbling caused her to be sent packing from her sojourn in the great world at Weston Hall, back to her father's house, just as Pope's writing advertised his sticking close to home at Twickenham, in the light of his disaffection from court and ministry, rather than sojourning in London. This passage also vividly summarizes the objections to writing as an employment for members of the laboring classes expressed so frequently in the eighteenth-century discourse on patronage. The fact that here the uneducated make colloquial objections lightens the tone considerably, though the potential power of a "store" of parental "Lectures" at home forbidding composition lingers ominously. The Turkish prejudice is deployed, as usual, to suggest an alien form of tyranny intruding itself on native domestic peace; if only these people would leave Mira alone with her muse! But Mira's bookishness contradicts the cleanliness, neatness, and industry with which the respectable poor were expected to identify, and which were clearly demanded of domestic servants. As Mr. Leapor confided to Bridget Freemantle, the possible utility or material "Advantage" to be gained by writing poetry rarely if ever entered the heads of the poor, or their employers. Only by plying her needle and minding the work of the gentleman's kitchen and the cottager's household could a Mary Leapor normally expect to earn her bread, and so keep the need for parish relief at bay. A certain class consciousness would seem to be unavoidable given these conditions. But Leapor's texts posit a familial struggle as well.

Leapor's tragedy, *The Unhappy Father*, which she once described as "a Piece I most value,"[27] disrupts the privileged atmosphere of a gentleman's country house by disclosing the seething rivalries and resentments that threaten to pull apart the propertied patriarchal household, still feudal in its extended network of kin and servants but bourgeois in its claustrophobic centering on a single figure: Dycarbus, the landowner-patriarch. Dycarbus is complacently intoxicated by the "royal" good looks of his offspring:

> When round my plenteous Table I behold
> My lovely Daughter, with her noble Spouse;
> And next to them my two majestic Sons,
> Who look as tho' they were of royal Lineage,
> And born to give obedient Kingdoms Law;
> Methinks I flourish like the spreading Vine,
> Whose curling Branches are with Clusters hung,
> That draw their Juices from its friendly Stem. (I.iii. 4–11)

But he is nevertheless willful in his disposition of their affective lives:

> 'Tis true, *Eustathius* is giv'n to Storms,
>
> . . .
>
> These little jars, that shake the Stream of Peace,
> And vex the Spirits of these angry Lovers,
> A Father's Care must dissipate, and join
> These adverse Winds in one united Blast:
> With him I've met Success; and over her
> I claim th' Authority of paternal Power. (I.iii. 12–20)

Dycarbus's fumbling interventions between rival brothers and cousins in love with the same women will nearly empty the stage by the play's conclusion.

More tellingly, the poem *The Cruel Parent* presents an iconography of paternal despotism and daughterly humiliation scarcely to be met with elsewhere in eighteenth-century verse. Celia is held prisoner by her father Lysegus, we know not why: implicit in his cruelty may be a suggestion that she once disobeyed him, but all that the text reveals is that her very existence is abhorrent to him. No mention of a mother is made. The poem is not only Gothic in its gloomy quasi-medieval furnishings but also in its designation of extreme emotions as seemingly groundless and inexplicable, as givens posited for their terrifying effects. Lysegus unlocks Celia's prison, only to silence her plea for mercy with a punitive lecture:

> But see *Lysegus*, her relentless Sire,
> Whose Eye-balls sparkl'd with disdainful Ire;
> His potent Hand the sounding Locks obey,
> With grating Noise the horrid Gates gave way:
> Then prostrate at his Feet the Damsel lay.
>
> . . .
>
> And am – Oh am I – by my Parent curs'd;
> Of all my Woes the deepest and the worst:
> She said – *Lysegus* answer'd in a Rage,
> Hence vile Disturber of my luckless Age:
> Think not by Tears this stubborn Heart to win,

Nor jar my Senses with thy hateful Din:
Go learn of Vagrants (fit Companions) go,
Their Arts of Stealing and their Whine of Woe.
Yet when before the Gate of Pride you stand,
And crave your Morsel at the Porter's hand;
May some stern Slave present the coming Prize,
Thrown to the Dogs before thy longing Eyes:
He ceas'd – but *Celia* views no more the Sun.   (61–94)

Such an effective patriarch is he, his words embodying his will as Law, that his daughter falls dead at his feet.

The cultural precedents for representations of the cruelty of patriarchal oppression available to Leapor are many. In "The Temple of Love" Leapor describes herself reading *Jane Shore* (4) before going to bed to dream horrifically. There is little reason to seek autobiographical causes for Leapor's protofeminist protests. She does, however, situate her writing as necessitating the defiance of her parents', and later, her employers' will. For Leapor, then, the scene of writing itself is a site of resistance to a culture organized round productive labor, defined as "not writing," in which patriarchal relations govern servants within households like daughters within nuclear families. Bridget Freemantle's account represents Mr. Leapor as saying that after years of struggling to break Leapor of her writing habit, he had "desisted, and left her more at Liberty": ironically, an image of freedom as unchaining that fits uncomfortably with Leapor's poetical scenarios of cruel paternal restriction, if not actual imprisonment, as in *The Cruel Parent*. And according to Freemantle, Leapor's deathbed request was that the subscription scheme be carried out for the benefit of her father; is there not some bleak poetic justice in Leapor's writing, against which her father had argued and lectured, contributing to the greater ease of his old age? It may be taken as a generous gesture of filial devotion, to be sure, but Leapor's texts point to a more complex subjective negotiation, in which the daughter proves, by dying *and* earning, the legitimacy of her defiance of her father's will and his limited opinion of her abilities. Freemantle writes, reporting one of Leapor's deathbed conversations:

". . . – I find I am going. – I always lov'd my Father; but I feel it now more than "ever. – He is growing into Years. – My Heart bleeds to see the Concern he is in; and "it would be the utmost Satisfaction to me, if I could hope any thing of mine could "contribute to his comfortable subsistence in his old Age.[28]

In the light of Leapor's harrowing narratives of heterosexual attachment gone awry, as in "The Temple of Love," and family feeling deformed by familial conflict, as in *The Unhappy Father* and *The Cruel Parent*, it is possible to read into this last wish a peculiar kind of vindication. If we are to take this speech as accurate reportage within the conventions of deathbed narratives, is there not something a little remarkable in Leapor's assuring her friend and patron that she has always loved her father, though never so much as now, when she is dying? And the work that he had tried to prevent will now, ironically, endow his old age, even afford him a comfortable subsistence: this work which was viewed as such unprofitable employment. We can imagine that Mr. Leapor wept at his daughter's death, and that her posthumously published poems might have given him some moments of uneasiness, if he read them.

Perhaps the cultural difficulty of this material is partly responsible for Leapor's reliance on the trope of the dream vision as a framing device. So often her poems begin with Mira drowsing, Mira falling into a trance from which she is eventually awakened at a moment of unrepresentable violence or other textual rapture:

> Amid these Scenes beneath a Maple Shade,
> Sat careless *Mira* on her Elbow laid,
> While frolick Fancy led the usual Train
> Of gaudy Phantoms through her cheated Brain:
> Till Slumber seiz'd upon her thoughtful Breast,
> And the still Spirits sunk in balmy Rest:
> But while her Eyes had bid the World farewel,
> Thus *Mira* dream'd, and thus her Dreams we tell;
> A seeming Nymph, like those of *Dian*'s Train,
> Came swiftly tripping o'er the flow'ry Plain
>
> ("The Moral Vision," 7–16)

> WHEN lonely Night compos'd the drowsy Mind,
> And hush'd the Bosom of the weary Hind,
> Pleas'd with plain Nature and with simple Life,
> I read the Scenes of *Shore*'s deluded Wife,
> Till my faint Spirits sought the silent Bed,
> And on its Pillow drop'd my aking Head;
> Then Fancy ever to her *Mira* kind,
> Prepar'd her Phantoms for the roving Mind
>
> ("The Temple of Love," 1–8)

> 'TWAS when the Sun had his swift Progress made,
> And left his Empire to the Queen of Shade;
> Bright *Cynthia* too, with her refulgent Train,
> Shot their pale Lustre o'er the dewy Plain:
> Sat lonely *Mira* with her Head reclin'd,
> And mourn'd the Sorrows of her helpless Kind:
>
> . . .

> Till too much Thought the aking Heart oppress'd.
> And *Mira*'s Eye-lids clos'd in silent Rest:
> Then active Fancy, with her airy Train,
> Compos'd the Substance of the ensuing Dream.
>
> (*The Cruel Parent*, 1–16)

These opening meditations are often followed by a sudden rude awakening, when the ensuing scene would be too violent or disturbing for graphic representation:

> Then with pale Cheeks and with a ghastly Stare,
> Peep'd o'er her Shoulder hollow-ey'd Despair;
> Whose Hand extended bore a bleeding Heart,
> And Death behind her shook his threat'ning Dart:
> These Forms with Horror fill'd my aking Breast,
> And from my Eye-lids drove the Balm of Rest:
> I woke and found old Night her Course had run,
> And left her Empire to the rising Sun;
>
> ("The Temple of Love," 85–92)

> *Lysegus*, mourn thy Cruelty and Pride:
> From the fair Court of Equity I came,
> Call'd by thy Sins, and Conscience is my Name:
>
> . . .
>
> With *Celia*'s Name I arm the dreadful Blow:
> He said and struck – the visionary Dart
> Sought the dark Bottom of *Lysegus*' Heart:
> He fell – and falling rais'd a fearful Cry;
> Then *Mira* 'woke, and found the Morning Sky.
>
> (*The Cruel Parent*, 113–23)

Leapor's dream visions may remind us of Collier's meditations in bed, for they both situate their writing as emerging from their all-too-rare moments of leisure. Both seem to find in the meditation that borders on dream-work a necessary poetic license for their criticism of the dominant order. The border between waking consciousness and unconscious, traditionally "prophetic" revelation, serves them as a fertile territory for writing against the grain of ordinary experience and ideological assumption. The difference between Collier's and Leapor's use of the trope of the dream vision is also significant: Collier represents herself naturalistically as a tired worker, Leapor pastorally, her trances indicative of a writerly interest in the traditional rhyming of "mind" with a body "reclined," and in the topos of the dream vision as such. Where Collier strains against poetic convention in order to make a strong empirical case, Leapor embraces the topos as a sign of the high literary tradition to which she wishes her work to be assimilated, in spite of its protofeminism and its wit at the expense of the fathers.

Reading *Crumble-Hall*

As should by now be clear, Leapor's is in no sense a one-poem *œuvre*. Although Mary Collier can be said to have written nothing so important or innovative again after *The Woman's Labour*, Mary Leapor's two volumes contain numerous poems of aesthetic interest and accomplishment. Nevertheless, there is a case to be made for her poem *Crumble-Hall* as a representative text whose literary-historical neglect has been unfortunate, if unsurprising. *Crumble-Hall* shows off Leapor's abilities as a comic and satiric writer on an ambitious scale; it represents a significant transformation of the genre of the country-house poem, so crucial in the fabrication and consequent reproduction of a propertied eighteenth-century political consensus; and it effectively condenses many of Leapor's characteristic textual maneuvers, from her strategic appropriation of poetical rhetoric recognizable as Pope's or Swift's or Gay's, to her foregrounding of class and gender as important textual determinants. *Crumble-Hall* is that rare artifact: a class-conscious plebeian country-house poem that undeniably mocks and seeks to demystify the values of the gentry, whose social power in large part depends upon the deference – and the continued exploitable subservience – of servants and laborers. Leapor's poem opens up long-closed doors and back stairways, lets light into the servants' hall, shakes things up in a literary genre that traditionally works by assuring us that the world is best organized according to ancient custom and ceremony. Pope had mocked particular country houses and their owners for failing to fulfill their pact with England's glorious agrarian past; Alastair Fowler cites earlier examples of this critical tendency in the genre.[29] But both Pope and these earlier poets nevertheless seek to preserve the country-house ideal. Leapor leaves us wondering how a literary audience could have tolerated such evidently self-serving exaggeration for so long.

Traditionally, the country-house poem serves as a panegyric to its owners and their way of life. This is as true of its first instance as of its better-known later examples. Recent feminist scholarship has proposed that the English country-house poem was invented by a woman, Aemilia Lanyer, though male poets did not follow her line with it.[30] As Raymond Williams has shown, the representation of a deceptively "natural" landscape and, less often, of a worked and working country, means a disposition of that prospect "according to a point of view," the proprietary point of view: "If we ask, finally, who the genius of the place may be, we find that he is its owner, its proprietor, its improver" (Williams, p. 123). In *The Description of Cooke-ham* from *Salve Devs Rex Ivdaeorvm*,[31] Lanyer thanks a female genius of the place, Margaret Clifford, Dowager Countess of Cumberland, "From whose desires did spring this worke of Grace" (12), for commissioning this poem and supporting the poet generously during its composition. The house itself is represented as enabling divine verse – "Where princely Palace will'd me to indite, / The sacred Storie of the Soules delight" (5–6), but most of the poem is devoted to the surrounding grounds and woods, instinct with the presence of Christ and his apostles, including Margaret Clifford herself, and her daughter Anne, Countess of Dorset. This combination of panegyric and devotional verse, with its emphasis on description of the country as a spiritualized green world in which women move freely rather than of the country house, sign of aristocratic honor and legitimation of aristocratic property, tends not to be pursued by later male country-house poets, but such a green world returns emphatically at the end of *Crumble-Hall*.

The flippant tone of much of Leapor's poem, however, marks her difference from Lanyer and from the genre as a whole (with the exception of Marvell's *Upon Appleton House* and particular moments in Pope's *Epistle to Burlington*) at least until Gray's "On Lord Holland's Seat" of 1768. Leapor's *Crumble-Hall* sets out at once to mock the pretensions to grandeur of a gentry class scarcely removed from their servants and laborers in terms of education and culture, and to mock the poetic sycophancy that would write *Crumble-Hall* as a traditional panegyric in spite of these incongruities. To some extent, Leapor's ironic stance as commentator on gentry pretensions prefigures Crabbe's in *The Borough* and in the posthumous tale, *Silford Hall*. In the former, the young attorney Swallow makes crude use of traditional hospitality to stimulate profitable litigation over disputed property, while in the latter, the poor schoolmaster's son, Peter Perkin, glimpses the romance of the great world when he is shown the genteel furnishings of Silford Hall – the happiest, most memorable event of his life:

> How vast that Mansion, sure for monarch plann'd,
> The rooms so many, and yet each so grand, –
> Millions of books in one large hall were found,
> And glorious pictures every room around;
>
> . . .
>
> He told of park and wood, of sun and shade,
> And how the lake below the lawn was made:
> He spake of feasting such as never boy,
> Taught in his school, was fated to enjoy –
> Of ladies' maids as ladies' selves who dress'd,
> And her, his friend, distinguish'd from the rest,
> By grandeur in her look, and state that she possess'd.
> He pass'd not one; his grateful mind o'erflow'd
> With sense of all he felt, and they bestow'd.[32]   (720–34)

Peter's inflated sense of the happiness made possible by wealth is undercut both by his own naiveté and the kind housekeeper's comments. Like Leapor, Crabbe represents the grandeur of the country house as subtly fractured from within by class antagonisms, but his narratorial perspective remains outside and his tone, unlike Leapor's, is distinctly moralizing rather than playful.

The opening of *Crumble-Hall* mockingly anatomizes the reverent traditionalism typical of the country-house poem. Crumble-Hall, we are told, has served as a repository of hospitality since Anglo-Saxon times; it has a noble past; no one has ever left it hungry. Inexorably, we are led to laugh at the sheer conventionality of country-house sentiment, designed to arouse feelings of loyalty throughout the social scale by means of the nostalgic projection of a past of shared wealth and plenty. This conventional summoning of a history of genteel largesse turns into a riot of comically conspicuous consumption that wastes resources in order to satisfy human greed:

> That *Crumble-Hall*, whose hospitable Door
> Has fed the Stranger, and reliev'd the Poor;
> Whose *Gothic* Towers, and whose rusty Spires,
> Were known of old to Knights, and hungry Squires.
> There Powder'd Beef, and Warden-Pies, were found;
> And Pudden dwelt within her spacious Bound:
> Pork, Peas, and Bacon (good old *English* Fare!),
> With tainted Ven'son, and with hunted Hare:
> With humming Beer her Vats were wont to flow,
> And ruddy *Nectar* in her Vaults to glow.
> Here came the Wights, who battled for Renown,
> The sable Frier, and the russet Clown:
> The loaded Tables sent a sav'ry Gale,
> And the brown Bowls were crown'd with simp'ring Ale;
> While the Guests ravag'd on the smoking Store,
> Till their stretch'd Girdles would contain no more.
>
>   Of this rude Palace might a Poet sing
> From cold *December* to returning Spring.   (13–30)

Throughout the poem there is an ironical movement between the old tropes of country-house praise and less exalted disclosures: the venison is tainted, the vulnerable hare has been hunted to death to provide meat for this already groaning table, the guests gorge themselves until they are grossly bloated. Of such an establishment, the poet writes, it might be possible to sing for – at least three or four months, a bathetic deflation. But this seasonal specificity also implies that a poet might well try to seek shelter during these particularly inhospitable months by singing for supper at the gentry's table. There is something self-mocking about the very inevitability of the country-house poem in a culture in which poor poets are paid to praise their social oppressors. Thus we are alerted to the possibility of socially critical digs, jibes, and disclosures in *Crumble-Hall*.

Sometimes the limitations of a plebeian woman's education can be turned to good use, if what is generated is the very close – and critical – reading of a few inspiring texts. As with Mary Collier's intertextual relation to Duck, so also with Leapor's Popean intertextuality: the critical appropriation of a poem that seems to express some of the prejudices of the dominant culture can be radically productive. Leapor's imitation of Pope's style in the service of quite different values is particularly concentrated and effective in *Crumble-Hall*. She seizes upon the *Epistle to Burlington*, Pope's most sustained effort in the country-house mode, but goes beyond his criticism of landowning wasteful-ness and conspicuous consumption, for Pope confines himself to criticizing only the wealthiest and highest ranking landlords. The gentry, the middling sort, and the select few "good stewards" among the aristocracy, such as Pope's friends Burlington[33] and Bathurst, are redeemed, and the country-house ideal upheld. Leapor, while echoing Pope and frequently reminding us of his satirical outbursts in *To Burlington* against such figures of excess as Timon, forces us to re-read Pope's poem through the lens of her own, and so to reread it in a different, more democratic and gender-conscious way. Whereas with Pope we must toil up Timon's monumental garden terraces to greet the host:

> My Lord advances with majestic mien,
> Smit with the mighty pleasure, to be seen:
> But soft – by regular approach – not yet –
> First thro' the length of yon hot Terrace sweat,
> And when up ten steep slopes you've dragged your thighs,
> Just at his Study-door he'll bless your Eyes[34]   (127–32)

with Leapor a sense of cramped quarters and inconvenient architecture predominates; the gentry and squirearchy appear to rule their parish and neighborhood without question, but theirs is a rule far removed from the opulence or national (perhaps prime-ministerial) significance of Timon's villa:

> Shall we proceed? – Yes, if you'll break the Wall:
> If not, return, and tread once more the Hall.
> Up ten Stone Steps now please to drag your Toes,
> And a brick Passage will succeed to those.
> Here the strong Doors were aptly fram'd to hold
> Sir *Wary*'s Person, and Sir *Wary*'s Gold.   (84–89)

Pope's condemnation of aristocratic self-display on a Timonesque scale may now seem a limited protest, perhaps even an instance of Barthesian inocu-lation: attack a particularly offensive example of an accepted general practice, and the whole socio-political structure is obscurely strengthened. From Mira's perspective, even Crumble-Hall is a show place, the local center of birth, wealth, and history – figured ironically in the bulky person and fortune of that shrewd self-preservationist, Sir Wary. And Crumble-Hall should rank, in Pope's terms, with those ludicrous buildings impossible to beautify according to the tenets of Burlington's Palladianism; it is, quite literally, Pope's "some patch'd dog-hole ek'd with ends of wall" (31), an unfashionable monument to the gentry's conservatism.[35] For Mira, however, Crumble-Hall, be it ever so humble, represents the site of privilege and class exploitation.

This confrontation takes at least two forms: a critique of the gentry for failing to make use of their privileges in improving ways, and an exposure of the suppressed narratives of traditional high-literary country-house poetry – the servants' "quarter." Pope rails against Timon as a Philistine who possesses an expensive library for the sake of its commodity value; he is a connoisseur of printers and bindings, not of the contents of books:

> His Study! with what Authors is it stor'd?
> In Books, not Authors, curious is my Lord;
> To all their dated Backs he turns you round,
> These Aldus printed, those Du Suëil has bound.
> Lo some are Vellom, and the rest as good
> For all his Lordship knows, but they are Wood.
> For Locke or Milton 'tis in vain to look,
> These shelves admit not any modern book.   (133–40)

If Pope's is the sneering protest of the contemporary author who will find no patron in this rich man, Leapor's exposure of philistinism has a more radical edge. The issue in *Crumble-Hall* is not fine bindings versus intellectual enlightenment, but the fact of books being possessed in the greatest quantity by those who have plenty of leisure, but who do not read them, when there are others too poor to own many books and without much time for study, who nevertheless cannot get enough to read. This is the burden of over-worked Mira's commentary on Biron's library, in which he has the audacity to sleep. (Leapor, we should recall, possessed all of sixteen or seventeen volumes to which she could turn in her few moments of "unprofitable employment," though at Weston Hall there was a substantial library to which it is likely she enjoyed some access.[36])

> Here *Biron* sleeps, with Books encircled round;
> And him you'd guess a Student most profound.
> Not so – in Form the dusty Volumes stand:
> There's few that wear the Mark of *Biron*'s Hand.   (90–93)

This vignette might pass as a not very caustic comment on genteel idleness if we were not immediately confronted in the poem with a reminder of Mira's situation within the text and within the social space of Crumble-Hall. Mira's

"place" is not among these neglected books, despite the overt literary consciousness manifest in the poem "she" is producing. With the library, we have
come to the end of civilization within the house and are now to be plunged
into the servants' quarters, Mira's "proper" domain, however badly her
fingers may itch to inscribe marginalia in Biron's unmarked volumes. Mira's
proper sphere may not be quite the realm of "Old Shoes, and Sheep-ticks bred
in Stacks of Wool; / Grey *Dobbin*'s Gears, and Drenching-Horns enow; /
Wheel-spokes – the Irons of a tatter'd Plough" (99–101) – the furnishings of
plebeian georgics in the manner of Duck and Collier. But neither is she to
venture freely into the beautiful prospect that can be only glimpsed from the
cramped, airless rooms at the top of the house, so often disposed as servants
quarters:

> From hence the Muse precipitant is hurl'd,
> And drags down *Mira* to the nether World.   (107–08)

Mira's proper sphere is the site of domestic production itself within the
household, the network of kitchens, pantries, sculleries, outbuildings, cottages, and kitchen gardens that supply Crumble-Hall with produce and labor.
The danger in this text is that Mira might get above herself, put on airs, show
too much familiarity with the beauty of leisured prospects and the freedom of
the countryside: write like a traditional country-house poet, in short. From
that possibility, that treacherous attraction to the aestheticizing language of
pastoral, Mira's "precipitant" muse is precipitously hurled. The "precipitant"
muse is getting ahead of herself, acceding to a pastoral freedom from which
she is socially barred. The distinctive status of *Crumble-Hall* depends upon this
exclusion, which necessitates a reversal in traditional generic procedure made
explicit when Mira announces that she will represent for us the "menial
Train" (110), the domestics and fieldworkers of the estate, before the gardens
and groves: "Its Groves anon – its People first we sing" (111).

Crumble-Hall gives us forty-two lines of description of the lower orders
that populate this "nether World," yet the chief innovation and interest of
Leapor's poem do not lie in her supplying, within this self-contained section,
what other country-house poems have omitted. Rather, there is a diffusion of
the servant's perspective throughout the text that this temporarily exclusive
focus on the servants' quarters only encapsulates. The incongruous disclosures
that undermine Crumble-Hall's pretensions to awesome gentility earlier in
the poem include the spider spinning high above the hall, whose web is safe
because it lies beyond the reach of any broom (46–47); the "timeless" heraldic
device that needs to be refurbished once a year (48–51); the mice which run
safely through passages so dark that no one can see them clearly (52–55); the
refusal to elaborate descriptions of the shining china bowls and tapestry that
decorate the parlor, when merely noting their existence will suffice (68–71);
and the observation that the subject of an historical painting looks distinctly

like a member of the lower orders herself – "And, like a Milk-wench, glares the royal Maid" (79). What connects these incongruous disclosures is the perspective from which they emerge: the perspective of the female servant, responsible for cleanliness, sheen, and decorative order in the household. If Timon's Villa were possessed of spiders, mice, and artifacts that required constant tending, a male guest like Pope would not be likely to remark upon them. And more elevated members of the household at Crumble-Hall would most likely dwell not on these "menial" but material questions of domestic maintenance but on the symbolic meaning of objects compelling to gentry families, such as heraldic insignia, with its genealogical significance, and the provenance of valuable collectables like china, wall-hangings, and oil paintings, features of the house to which Mira alludes but neglects to describe.

Mira's servant's-eye view of this establishment is particularized as a female servant's vantage-point in another way as well: in terms of a psycho-sexual dynamic that inflects the gender-specific division of labor. The entrance hall of Crumble-Hall features old and intricate wood carvings which lend a carnivalesque yet sinister air to the house's history and resonate disturbingly with Leapor's examination of patriarchal despotism in other texts. Her sparing use of the Augustan emphatic triplet, after Dryden, strikes strangely here, giving force to this image of a cruel history of gender and family relations so casually lived with as mere customary decoration:

> Strange Forms above, present themselves to View;
> Some Mouths that grin, some smile, and some that spew.
> Here a soft Maid or Infant seems to cry:
> Here stares a Tyrant, with distorted Eye:
> The Roof – no *Cyclops* e'er could reach so high.   (39–43)

The text rushes breathlessly past this image of domestic tyranny, but there it is. And its significance is amplified by one of Leapor's most complex and problematical vignettes within her description of the house's "menial Train."

Ursula and Roger – a mock-georgic couple, as Margaret Doody notes[37] – occupy twenty-six vividly satirical lines and so in some sense come to stand in for their employers, who seem relatively unrepresented in the text. Thus Leapor turns the tables on the traditional country-house strategy of celebrating ownership while suppressing labor by leaving it unrepresented. The owners of Crumble-Hall remain indistinctly drawn, but two servants lay out a lower-class version of the domestic drama which we might have expected from such gentry based on Leapor's treatment of upper-class domestic relations elsewhere in her *œuvre*. Indeed Leapor pushes the nonrepresentation of proprietorship so far that Ursula herself appears to have forgotten that she has employers, or that she labors for any master other than her husband Roger. If, with Ursula, we forget the country-house framework in which this passage is embedded, the character seems to be a satire on a prosperous cottager's wife who is a slave to romance, unlike Collier's cottagers living on the verge of poverty and hunger. Ironically, however, Ursula and Roger's prosperity implicitly depends on the country house whose owners Ursula's obsessive focus on her husband occludes. Like the owners of country houses as traditionally represented, Ursula concentrates all drama and ceremony within her immediate domestic situation, to the exclusion of its relations of production. Her putative employers are as tangential to her self-representation as she would be to theirs, if this were a conventional country-house poem. Thus an ironical equivalence is established between property and labor in the country-house domain; each is represented as excluding the other symbolically while remaining materially dependent upon it. Ursula is as trapped by a domestic ideology that foregrounds romance and marriage to the exclusion of other social relations, including her own servitude, as any middle-class mistress capable of forgetting the labor of the servants who make her domestic idyll possible.

Ursula's lament exposes, from the perspective of the laboring classes, the bankruptcy of romantic gender ideology and the wretchedness of a dependent female subjectivity constructed within marriage under the sign of the "helpmate." While her exhausted husband Roger, "o'erstuff'd" with beef, cabbage, and dumplings, sleeps at the table and the dogs bark and howl, Ursula laments her fate until the kettle boils:

> "Ah! *Roger*, Ah!" the mournful Maiden cries:
> "Is wretched *Urs'la* then your Care no more,
> "That, while I sigh, thus you can sleep and snore?
> "Ingrateful *Roger*! wilt thou leave me now?
> "For you these Furrows mark my fading Brow:
> "For you my Pigs resign their Morning Due:
> "My hungry Chickens lose their Meat for you:
> "And, was it not, Ah! was it not for thee,
> "No goodly Pottage would be dress'd by me.
> "For thee these Hands wind up the whirling Jack,
> "Or place the Spit across the sloping Rack.
> "I baste the Mutton with a chearful Heart,
> "Because I know my *Roger* will have Part."
>
>   Thus she – But now her Dish-kettle began
> To boil and blubber with the foaming Bran.
> The greasy Apron round her Hips she ties,
> And to each Plate the scalding Clout applies:
> The purging Bath each glowing Dish refines,
> And once again the polish'd Pewter shines.   (137–55)

Ursula gives voice to an important ideological problematic whose resonances persist well into our own historical moment: the question of the "bourgeoisification" of working-class ideas about sexuality, marriage, and the family. For Ursula, domestic labor and household production have ceased to have any meaning apart from the expression of marital devotion they supposedly signify. Unlike Collier's wives, Ursula does not "work," she "sighs" while her husband sleeps, wishing he would wake up and show her some affection. At an historical moment when landed middle-class women were beginning to withdraw from production within the household economy and leaving even domestic tasks increasingly to the care of servants, when farmer's wives were beginning not to manage their stock or their dairies themselves, but to hire dairymaids, and when leisured domesticity itself was beginning to be seen as a sufficient occupation for women who could afford it, Ursula reproduces this identification with leisured domesticity at an ideological level. She thereby trivializes her work − keeping livestock, gardening, cooking, washing-up, housekeeping − by transforming these activities into mere epiphenomena of wifely devotion. The whole structure of employers and servants falls away, leaving only the heterosexual couple. One would think that the gargantuan meals Ursula prepares were destined for Roger's table alone, rather than for the gentry at Crumble-Hall, until the last line of her lament: "Because I know my *Roger* will have Part." In a household economy in which Ursula, and not her mistress, is primarily in charge of the cooking, it is possible for her to ensure that her husband will have "part" of every dish, if only after "the quality" have eaten their fill. Obsessively, Ursula invests in a conjugal romance in which Roger's labor, or his dinner, leaves him apparently too exhausted to participate. The life of physical labor minimizes the deployment of affective energies within the household, according to this satiric scheme; emotional work becomes another form of women's work, radically separated from public activity and confined within the household, only to be devalued there as "mere" domesticity, not something in which working men can be expected to engage.

Whether this domestic dysfunction is meant to be seen as confined to the workers at Crumble-Hall cannot be decided; Leapor's class-specific focus gives us the domestic drama of Ursula and Roger rather than the drama of the house's owners. This is the burden of Leapor's plebeian transformation of the country-house poem. For the gentry's marital difficulties, that more familiar tale, we have numerous other sources for citation in Leapor's work, especially *The Mistaken Lover*. There is thus no reason to assume that Leapor endorses the ideology of romantic-love-in-marriage as unproblematical for upper-class women, while satirizing only its peculiar inappropriateness for women of the laboring classes. The laboring situation of Ursula and Roger does, however, render the contradictions of romantic ideology, and its powerfully imaginary status as ideology, particularly obvious.

The disjunction between Ursula's romantic expectations and the circumstances in which she finds herself as a working man's wife and domestic laborer also dramatizes at a strikingly early historical moment what Michèle Barrett, following Mark Poster, characterizes as "a struggle between the familial ideology of the emergent bourgeoisie and the practices of other classes."[38] Barrett acknowledges Poster's argument that "the bourgeois conception of the family has become dominant – that, in fact, the imposition of the bourgeois family onto the working class is 'one of the unwritten aspects of the political success of bourgeois democracy'" (Barrett, pp. 203–04; Poster, p. 196), but she maintains a useful distinction between familial ideology and actual working-class practices that Leapor's poem also articulates:

At an ideological level the bourgeoisie has certainly secured a hegemonic definition of family life: as 'naturally' based on close kinship, as properly organized through a male breadwinner with financially dependent wife and children, and as a haven of privacy beyond the public realm of commerce and industry. To a large extent this familial ideology has been accepted by the industrial working class and indeed has proved effective as motivation for male wage labour and the male 'family'-wage demand. Yet there is a disjunction between the pervasiveness of this ideology (from about the mid-nineteenth century onwards) and the actual household structure of the proletariat in which it exists. Few working-class households have historically been organized around dependence on a male 'breadwinning' wage and the earnings of other family members have usually been essential to maintain the household. . . . Families are enmeshed in and responsive to the ideology of 'the family' as well as engaged in reproducing it. . . . The point I am emphasizing here is that we can make a distinction between the construction of gender within *families*, and the social construction of gender within an *ideology of familialism*, and we can conclude that the latter formulation is the more accurate one.   (Barrett, pp. 204–06)

Thus a good half century before industrialization makes possible the new "industrial working class," and some decades before the American and French revolutions, we find inscribed in Leapor's text the preconditions for the eventual dominance of bourgeois familial ideology. Frustrated romantic wife and exhausted, perhaps indifferent, husband who loves his creature comforts: the agrarian servants and laborers Ursula and Roger represent the soon-to-be hegemonic contradictions of gender ideology fundamental to the bourgeois family, especially the particular construction of female subjectivity effected by this cultural production. The fact that they seem to be a childless couple might then be read as accentuating the power of familial ideology to interpellate individual subjects at the deepest level of unconscious self-identification, regardless of their "real" circumstances.

  These satirical characters may constitute a complex form of ideology critique, but they also exemplify Leapor's skill at appropriating high literary modes of representation. Ursula is drawn as sharply as any of Swift's or Pope's characters, and the last six lines of the passage, her kitchen rites, can stand with Pope's brilliantly squalid mock-epic games in Book II of the *Dunciad* as a parody of Augustan periphrasis in the service of "menial" contemporary materials. Most suggestively, these lines closely follow the last six lines of Gay's "Thursday: Or, The Spell" which stand as an epigraph to this book's introduction. But where Gay gives us Hobnelia's swoon at Lubberkin's return as farce, the gratification of her desire through Lubberkin's willingness to "give her a green gown," to make their liaison public through pregnancy, as low comedy, Leapor represents the consequences of such romantic enthrall-ment as both bathetic and pathetic. The mock-heroic mode of Ursula's kitchen rites seems meant to restore us to comic stability after the absurd but painfully self-righteous masochism of her lament.

Leapor's satire thus spares neither her own class nor women as complicit with their own oppression. Is it not possible, however, that Leapor's satire here succeeds too well in displacing "responsibility" or agency for ideological interpellation onto these lower-class characters, so that the containers of ideology become the object of satire, and not the ideology itself? Or, to put it another way, does she not end up recycling traditional classist and misogynis-tic conventions of representation as part of her satiric apparatus? At what point does Leapor's satire cease to be critical of ideology and help perpetuate instead the very stereotypes of class- and gender-specific subjectivity that her texts also work to destabilize or render untenable? If we had some evidence of contemporary critical reception of this poem, such a determination might be easier, but the evidence is not forthcoming. I would suggest that the narrative, or rather the ideological, excess generated by Ursula's lament, in the context of *Crumble-Hall* as an anti-country-house poem, prevents any easy recuperation of this character in the service of such ideological consolidation. We would have to read Ursula and Roger entirely outside the contexts of the poem and Leapor's *œuvre* to conclude "Servants are just like that!" or "Isn't that just like a woman!" or "How silly of the lower classes to behave in such a way!" To read the vignette out of context might be to construct such a conservatively recuperative reading, but we should remember the country-house conventions in which Ursula and Roger are embedded. As with the proprieties and proprietors of Crumble-Hall, so with its servants, who are neither outside ideology nor uncontaminated by the country-house ethos. If we also keep both class and gender in play as possible textual determinants, and refuse to read the passage outside the larger "text" of Leapor's literary production – the whole apparatus of her self-representation and her patron-ized presentation to the public – then the evidence for her typically critical stance and frequently demystificatory procedures may encourage us to resist a recuperative reading.

Leapor's demystification of the country household as social institution and as literary trope does not end with her satire on gender ideology, however. The poem concludes with a long-deferred escape into those pastoral groves surrounding Crumble-Hall – a briefly glimpsed alternative, even utopian, domain of leisure and freedom. But even here the landscape exists primarily as a site of conflict; the country house can no longer serve as a locus of social harmony or of harmony between human interests and a more complex ecology. The green world of the grove is no sooner escaped into than it is rent by shrieks, for like so many landlords bent on the "improvement" of an estate, Crumble-Hall's owners are felling their timber, in this case for the minor ostentation of a new parlor:[39]

> But, hark! what Scream the wond'ring Ear invades!
> The *Dryads* howling for their threaten'd Shades:
> Round the dear Grove each Nymph distracted flies
> (Tho' not discover'd but with Poet's Eyes):
> And shall those Shades, where *Philomela*'s Strain
> Has oft to Slumber lull'd the hapless Swain;
> Where Turtles us'd to clasp their silken Wings;
> Whose rev'rend Oaks have known a hundred Springs;
> Shall these ignobly from their Roots be torn,
> And perish shameful, as the abject Thorn;
> While the slow Carr bears off their aged Limbs,
> To clear the way for Slopes, and modern Whims;
> Where banish'd Nature leaves a barren Gloom,
> And aukward Art supplies the vacant Room?
> Yet (or the Muse for Vengeance calls in vain)
> The injur'd Nymphs shall haunt the ravag'd Plain:
> Strange Sounds and Forms shall teaze the gloomy Green;
> And Fairy-Elves by *Urs'la* shall be seen:
> Their new-built Parlour shall with Echoes ring:
> And in their Hall shall doleful Crickets sing.   (165–84)

Here Leapor's appropriation of neoclassical tropes with a sapphic tendency takes on new significance in the advocacy of a "green" politics of ecological conservation. The female pastoral idyll that offers at least a partial alternative to the miseries and confinement of marriage is enabled by the very wildness of the forest, as opposed to the worked garden or field. And the forest accommodates the exhausted swain as well; it represents not so much a separatist idyll as a realm of general liberty, of release from social constraints and relief from social oppression. With an intertextual flourish, Leapor reverses the praise that Pope had offered Burlington for his use of the forest in the service of building, commerce, and imperial exploits; for Pope, those who follow Burlington's example as improving stewards of their land are those:

> Whose rising Forests, not for pride or show,
> But future Buildings, future Navies grow:
> Let his plantations stretch from down to down,
> First shade a Country, and then raise a Town.   (187–90)

But for Leapor the grove represents the only site of social ventilation on the estate and should not be sacrificed for mere aggrandizement of the country house. "Improvement" and "progress" are thus subjected to ironical scrutiny at the same time that a more natural economy than the present, "improving" one and an ecological consciousness are recommended. *Crumble-Hall* is a country-house poem that advocates the containment, not the expansion, of the country house: its radical removal from the scene may be as yet unthinkable but its demystification is complete.

Of the plebeian female poets of the period, Mary Leapor possesses the most writerly *œuvre*. Hers is also the body of work most easily assimilable to what we commonly describe today as "radical feminism," with its polemics against patriarchy, male violence, and heterosexist containments of economies of desire. Paradoxically, then, Leapor represents some of the most easily recuperable and some of the most difficult and unexpected possibilities of emergent eighteenth-century feminism. Leapor's contemporary readers would appear not to have read her as radically as some feminist readers may now wish to do. What most delights the traditional literary critic may well prevent him from recognizing what feminist readers might be most interested to discover. That Mary Leapor, a gardener's daughter and a domestic servant, should have had her work published at all, even posthumously, may still seem to us in the late twentieth century little short of miraculous. That too tells us something about the appeal of the unlikely, the curious, the peculiarly marginal, in this period of expanding literary markets. Perhaps Leapor's relative subordination of issues of class consciousness to issues of gender oppression will prove the most easily assimilable aspect of her work; it is also, I would argue, in the U.S. context at least, the least radical, in the strict sense of constituting an uprooting of fixed assumptions, of what is historically and structurally, though differently constituted in different times and places, always already there.

Chapter 4

The complex contradictions of Ann Yearsley: working-class writer, bourgeois subject?

Thus desperately I reason'd, madly talk'd –
Thus horrid as I was, of rugged growth,
More savage than the nightly-prowling wolf;
She feels what Nature taught; I, wilder far,
Oppos'd her dictates –   (*Night. To Stella*, 189–93)

Her downright Country Innocence even to Clownishness and
Rusticity, had something in it, that at this time Captivated him more
than all the Allurements of Wit, Humour, Gayety, High Blood, and
Higher Pride.[1]

(on Lactilla, the "warming-pan" prince's nurse, in
The Amours of Messalina [1689])

Of all the plebeian female poets of the eighteenth century, Ann Cromarty Yearsley, the "milkwoman of Bristol," most repays detailed historical study. Her sizeable *œuvre*, competence across genres, and varied contemporary critical reception give her a strong claim on literary importance as traditionally understood. We can also trace the development of her ideas in relation to political and social events, her increasing radicalization during the French revolution and its English reception, and her enigmatic but perhaps suggestive silence after 1796. Though she wrote at least one play, *Earl Goodwin*, and published a novel, *The Royal Captives*,[2] poetry remained Yearsley's primary medium from her first volume in 1785 to her last in 1796. Jill Rubenstein is quite right to say that it is by her poetry she must be judged.[3] Yearsley's poetical production is best represented by her three major collections of verse, which fall suspiciously conveniently into three phases of development, and by a minor volume, *Stanzas of Woe*[4] and a number of singly issued occasional poems, usually of urgently topical significance. If *Poems, on Several Occasions* (1785) documents her first grateful and often self-deprecating experience of patronage through the direct philanthropy of Hannah More and Elizabeth Montagu, her *Poems, on Various Subjects* (1787)

Published by Alexr. Hogg at the Kings Arms No. 16 Paternoster Row, Jan 1. 1787.

Lowry sculp.

ANN YEARSLEY,
The Bristol Milk Woman & Poetess.

provides ample testimony of her quick and bitter disillusionment with the servility of such clientage and her obsessive desire for self-vindication. Exchanging her exacting female patrons for relative economic independence and the rather distant generosity of Frederick Hervey, Earl of Bristol and Bishop of Derry, Yearsley in this second volume becomes simultaneously aesthetically bolder and more socially criticial. Able at last to quit her duties as the Clifton milkwoman for those of running a circulating library near Bristol Hotwells, in the 1790s Yearsley produced accomplished verse that situates her somewhere uneasily between civic poet and social dissident. *The Rural Lyre* (1796),[5] the rarest of her volumes and arguably the most interesting, marks the end of her literary production – a return to obscurity all too common among laboring-class "discoveries" of the period.[6]

The years from 1785 to 1796: Yearsley's historical moment, unlike Collier's or Leapor's, was in its last years a potentially revolutionary moment for England. Increasingly in Yearsley's *œuvre* we are confronted with striking, and for her eventually disabling, contradictions. The 1790s was a decade when general liberation almost became thinkable, in the wake of the American and French revolutions. Thinkable, perhaps, but not practicable: the American distance between political independence and social egalitarianism has been richly documented by Cathy Davidson in her study of the politics of reading publics in this period. Arguing that élite censure of the sentimental, picaresque, and Gothic novels of the new Republic, many of them by women, was particularly vehement "because the novel was established here in the wake of the Revolution, at a time when disturbing questions (witness the Constitutional debates) about the limits of liberty and the role of authority in a republic were very much at issue," Davidson demonstrates how the gaps between republican rhetoric and the realities of gender, class, and race oppression were often uncomfortably exposed in the early American novel, which appealed to a dangerously wide readership, including minimally educated working women and men.[7] As Davidson notes, "Liberalism, far from mandating a revolutionary restructuring of society, merely opens the way for a different social hegemony with its own possibilities for oppression and exploitation" (Davidson, p. 217). And thus reaction marked the decade at least as distinctly as did revolutionary possibility, on both sides of the Atlantic:

In the United States . . . the late 1790s saw the passage of the Alien and Sedition Acts, arguably the most extensive legislative abrogation of civil liberties in American history, and, in England, the same decade witnessed the State Trials of 1793 and 1794, the prosecution of *The Rights of Man*, and the "Twin Acts" against "treasonable practices" and "seditious meetings," all of which had their effect on the literary enterprise of the era.   (Davidson, p. 219)

The intensity with which counter-revolutionary rhetoric was deployed in England during the 1790s would suggest the presence of what was, at the time, judged to be ominous social unrest, fuelled by the dissemination of radical ideas. John Porteous, the Bishop of London, writes to Hannah More early in the decade, "With respect to Paine's book, the first impression was seized by government, and the circulation of it stopped as much as possible, but still many copies have got abroad, and as I am just informed, have done much mischief."[8] The sort of mischief he was dreading included food riots and laborers' claims to social justice and a "levelling" of political power. As the Bishop had complained to Hannah More in 1791, "The Birmingham riot was an unfortunate thing. I do not love any thing so like the savages and the Poissards of France. The mob may sometimes *think* right, but they always *act* wrong. I am certainly extremely sorry to see them take the administration of justice into their own hands."[9] We find More herself struggling simultaneously with her monarchist and Protestant sympathies; when she thanks Horace Walpole for his edifying "strictures" on the "French distractions," she shudders at what such popular upheavals and seizures of power portend:

These people seem to be tending to the only two deeper evils, than those in which they are at present involved; for I can figure to myself no greater mischiefs than despotism and popery, except anarchy and atheism. I could find in my heart to forgive Louis Quatorze all the spite I owe him, if he could know that the throne of the grand monarque has been overturned by fisherwomen![10]

Hence, we must assume, More's investment in her explicitly depoliticizing Cheap Repository tracts[11] and her plans for Sunday Schools in which the laboring poor would learn piety, self-abnegation, and gratitude towards their betters.

Her tract *The Sunday School* dramatizes, in order to disarm, the sort of criticism of this project More expected from the propertied classes. Farmer Hoskins, reluctant to subscribe to Mrs. Jones's school, protests, "Of all the foolish inventions, and new-fangled devices to ruin the country, that of teaching the poor to read is the very worst." Mrs. Jones replies, for More, "And I, farmer, think that to teach good principles to the lower classes is the most likely way to save the country. Now in order to this we must teach them to read."[12]

But this is clearly a different kind of "uplifting" project from More's patronage of Yearsley. More's schools are designed to provide a course of instruction that will fit her pupils "for servants," nothing more; writing in 1801, she allows "of no writing for the poor."[13] To cultivate anything but "habits of industry and piety"[14] among the laboring classes had become, for More, after her experience with Yearsley and more than a decade of revolutionary ferment and conservative stratagem, sheer folly. In 1821 she writes, with bemusement and irony, "Our poor are now to be made scholars and philosophers. I am not the champion of ignorance, but I own I am alarmed at the violence of the contrast."[15]

The situation of the plebeian writer during periods of popular uprising is surely a complex one. More's undisguised contempt for French "fisher-women" casts an odd light on her previous patronage of "the milkwoman of Bristol." As Moira Ferguson remarks, "Unlike her contemporary, Mary Wollstonecraft, [Yearsley] left no followers, for she was not seen in her lifetime as a political thinker . . . She had the stuff of radical leadership and radical thought, but circumstances and geography obscured that potential and caused her to be relegated to the status of a curiosity, the cohesiveness of her ideas ignored."[16] Yearsley did not, apparently, officially align herself with any of Bristol's radical movements. Within such a context of political isolation, particularly, we should not be surprised at the conventionality of Yearsley's verse, but rather at the occasional boldness of it, its frequent explicit differences-from-itself that attempt to project alternatives beyond the officially sanctioned and the normatively "real." Yearsley's texts struggle to produce the conditions of possibility of ideological (and political) change.

The most insistent strain to emerge and become gradually radicalized in Yearsley's verse is an historically significant political conflict that manifests itself in a struggle for dominance within her aesthetic and her subjectivity. Yearsley rarely fails to locate herself firmly within the social space of the marginal, laboring woman writer – poor, plebeian, and deficient in education and culture. Indeed, she has been critically chastised for this class- and gender-conscious autobiographical tendency.[17] But working within and against the grain of this location within social space is another sort of authorial consciousness: the striving for a literary freedom from social and sexual constraints through the establishment of a sovereign subject, a self-constituting and imperial "I" who takes a rarefied but emancipatory pleasure in the imagination and in aesthetic production. This is not quite the "I" of the Wordsworthian egotistical sublime, as Keats would have it, for the "I" of Yearsley's verse is a site traversed by struggles and desires unknown to the privileged man and the future Poet Laureate. But there is in Yearsley's poems something akin to Wordsworth's command of a landscape and wish to be reabsorbed into its greenly animate prospects and its natural forces of wind and water, that bespeak a power greater than any human power. In a more theoretical sense, the "I" of both her verse and Wordsworth's is the sign of the sovereign subject of ideology, the post-revolutionary bourgeois subject whose sense of identity is peculiarly affirmed and perpetuated through reading and writing.[18]

The dilemma reproduced in Yearsley's texts is that of the laboring writer outside social movements in which working-class intellectuals and artists might find a place. As should be borne out by what follows, here my argument differs significantly from Mary Waldron's in "Ann Yearsley and the Clifton Records" with respect to Yearsley's class location, and indeed to how one determines the class specificity of historical subjects generally. Yearsley's class identification is complex and often contradictory, not least because her writing, as a sign of cultivation and upward mobility, established her as different from many women of the laboring class – different because capable of public self-representation through writing. To assume that this literary–class identification must necessarily put in question, or even displace, Yearsley's laboring origins as well as her class status after marriage, as Waldron argues, requires that one rely on reductive notion of working-class consciousness, effectively denying the laborer any capacity for knowledge outside her immediate circumstances (in Yearsley's case, knowledge of "abstract" financial matters), or for self-contradiction, class pride, social snobbery, or irreverence towards rank that is not in some way connected to her not being a member of the laboring classes at all, but "really" being middle class, and so, in her individual social antagonisms, more comprehensible to the twentieth-century researcher. To write verse at all, for Yearsley, is to enact a certain imaginary emancipation from social exigency, to take upon herself the illusory freedoms of the bourgeois subject while remaining critical of historical developments from which her class and gender cause her increasingly to dissent, in a moment when plebeian political articulation has become possible in ways unthinkable for a Mary Collier.[19] The development of radicalism as a political language can be seen as parallel with this shift in Yearsley's discourse:

Radicalism as a set of ideas emerged independently of class, but part of the story of the years between 1760 and 1848 is of the emergence of class as a political force and of the way in which radicalism was divided and appropriated as an ideology by both working and middle classes.[20]

Perhaps paradoxically, Yearsley emerges as a self-constituting sovereign subject at the very moment of inscribing herself poetically as "Lactilla," a plebeian craftswoman, a "savage" inspired by the rustic and laboring muse.

The "savage" muse

In "On Mrs. Montagu" Yearsley both characterizes Lactilla, the savage, and anticipates willy-nilly the new Romantic landscape poetry, dramatizing a certain reciprocity between nature and mind in the very moment of its incompletion. This text enacts the failure of ecstatic visionary moments to translate themselves serviceably into textual artifacts, but preserves something of the fervor and prophetic promise of those moments:

> Oft as I trod my native wilds alone,
> Strong gusts of thought wou'd rise, but rise to die;

The portals of the swelling soul, ne'er op'd
By liberal converse, rude ideas strove
Awhile for vent, but found it not, and died.
Thus rust the Mind's best powers. Yon starry orbs,
Majestic ocean, flowery vales, gay groves,
Eye-wasting lawns, and Heaven-attempting hills,
Which bound th' horizon, and which curb the view;
All those, with beauteous imagery, awak'd
My ravish'd soul to extacy untaught,
To all the transport the rapt sense can bear;
But all expir'd, for want of powers to speak;
All perish'd in the mind as soon as born,
Eras'd more quick than cyphers on the shore,
O'er which the cruel waves, unheedful, roll.

   Such timid rapture as young ⋆EDWIN seiz'd,
When his lone footsteps on the Sage obtrude,
Whose noble precept charm'd his wond'ring ear,
Such rapture fill'd ⋆LACTILLA's vacant soul,
When the bright Moralist, in softness drest,
Opes all the glorie of the mental world,
Deigns to direct the infant thought, to prune
The budding sentiment, uprear the stalk
Of feeble fancy, bid idea live,
Woo the abstracted spirit from its cares,
And gently guide her to the scenes of peace.
Mine was that balm, and mine the grateful heart,
Which breathes its thanks in rough, but timid strains.   (51–79)

    ⋆See the Minstrel.
    ⋆The Author.[21]

Lactilla the "savage" appears more clearly in what reads much like a
companion piece addressed to "Stella" (Hannah More) and containing
Yearsley's defence for "overpraising" her new great friends and patrons,
especially, we must assume, More and Montagu:

EXCUSE me, STELLA, sunk in humble state,
With more than needful awe I view the great;
No glossy diction e'er can aid the thought,
First stamp'd in ignorance, with error fraught.
My friends I've prais'd – they stood in heavenly guise
When first I saw them, and my mental eyes
Shall in that heavenly rapture view them still,
For mine's a stubborn and a savage will;

No customs, manners, or soft arts I boast,
On my rough soul your nicest rules are lost;
Yet shall unpolish'd gratitude be mine,
While STELLA deigns to nurse the spark divine.
A savage pleads – let e'en her errors move,
And your forgiving Spirit melt in love.

. . .

Blest in dispensing! gentle STELLA, hear
My only, short, but pity-moving prayer,
That thy great soul may spare the rustic Muse,
Whom Science ever scorn'd, and errors still abuse.[22]   (1–24)

Thus Yearsley insists upon her difference from her patrons in class, education, and culture, while thanking them for their support and soliciting their future favors. "Rude ideas" and "extacy untaught" come to the unlettered poet as she goes about her work or finds herself with occasional moments for contemplation in splendid rural solitude. That is how Yearsley describes her daily journeys selling milk – in the manner of the loco-descriptive "prospect" poem in *Clifton Hill* (1785). She nowhere mystifies her own genius, but writes as if such poetical inspiration were common and "natural." In a poem in her second volume, "To Mr. ★ ★ ★ ★, An Unlettered Poet, On Genius Un-improved," Yearsley boldly proposes that those without education may even be more naturally susceptible to ecstatic inspiration than the learned, a judgment with which Edward Young might tentatively have concurred:

Deep in the soul live ever tuneful springs,
Waiting the touch of Ecstacy, which strikes
Most pow'rful on defenceless, untaught Minds;
Then, in soft unison, the trembling strings
All move in one direction. Then the soul
Sails on Idea, and would eager dart
Thro' yon ethereal way; restless awhile,
Again she sinks to sublunary joy.[23]   (49–56)

Such visionary "transports," however, being all "the rapt sense can bear," will vanish without trace unless the means of expression are provided. These remain vague in Yearsley's formulation: "powers to speak." As she hints at them in the rest of the passage from the poem to "Stella," they seem a combination of recognition, encouragement, material support, and access to publication, all of which More and Montagu have provided. And if her gratitude strikes More as unseemly, Yearsley argues, that offers but a further opportunity for More's pity and benevolence to manifest themselves by not judging her protégée's lack of decorum too harshly. There may even be the faintest semblance of an ironical threat in the phrase, "For mine's a stubborn and a savage will": Yearsley may be exceedingly grateful but will not be bullied.

Thus from her appearance in print, the "savage" Lactilla is a proud, sometimes bold, sometimes comical but never cringing or obsequious presence. And Yearsley's use of blank verse – in its rhythms, modulations of conversational and high-philosophical tone, and sense of perpetually striving, exhilarated, even ecstatic linguistic inadequacy – links her with the aesthetic innovations of the poets of the next generation. Yearsley should not be read dismissively as a derivative poet.[24] Though for the eighteenth-century poet, of course, to be derivative in some sense is necessary in order to be a poet at all.

The argument for literary-historical anticipation is an important one in Yearsley's case, but is at best a problematical argument in theoretical terms. What of Yearsley's sources? We know from the first passage above that she knew James Beattie's *The Minstrel: Or, The Progress Of Genius* (1771 and 1774). This poem on the development of the bardic imagination "in a rude and illiterate age,"[25] among scenes of pastoral tranquillity and wildness, contains in its second book an encounter between the young bard-to-be, Edwin, and the world-weary Sage, who tempers Edwin's naiveté and ignorant fancy with sobering lessons from history and philosophy. "The mind untaught / Is a dark waste, where fiends and tempests howl," muses the Sage; Edwin, "Enraptur'd by the hermit's strain," "Proceeds the path of Science to explore":

> And now, expanded to the beams of truth,
> New energies and charms unknown before,
> His mind discloses.[26]

Thus through education the "savage" muse is tamed, and the mind's best powers are thoroughly rust-proofed. Appropriately, Beattie dedicated his poems of 1777, including both books of *The Minstrel*, to Elizabeth Montagu, who functions explicitly in Yearsley's poem as Lactilla's Sage – a "bright Moralist, in softness drest." The uncouth female bard figures the inspiration of Montagu's learning and useful precepts directly, in female dress, not as mediated through a mythical male Sage. For Yearsley, as for Beattie, Montagu represents disinterested charity and intelligent patronage; like the generous Muses in Beattie's poem, the figure of Montagu scorns making a name for herself in the great world by promoting worldly poets. Montagu's delights, like the delights of the generous Muses, "are with the village-train, / Whom Nature's laws and Nature's charms engage."[27] Thus in the act of invoking a poetical precedent – *The Minstrel* – Yearsley assures us once again of Lactilla's village-simple status. It is as if she were implicitly pressing a more authentic claim to "rude and illiterate" bardhood than Beattie's Edwin, a mere high literary creation, could ever muster. Yearsley characteristically makes use of such instances of intertextuality to class- and gender-specific political ends.

Our records of Yearsley's earliest reading bear out this tendency to play on her audience's class-specific expectations, to her own advantage. In the first flush of "discovery," More writes to Montagu:

I asked who were her favorite Authors? Among the Heathens, said She, I have met with no such Composition as Virgil's Georgics." How I stared! besides the choice was so *professional*. Of English Poets her favorites are Milton and Dr. Young, the latter she said had an ardour and boldness in his Imagination that was very delightful to her.[28]

In that ambiguous *"professional"* lies the key to Yearsley's prodigiousness in the polite world's eyes. The *Georgics* is precisely the text that a cow-keeping, pig-feeding poet ought to revere, but that More and her friends would have presumed inaccessible, even in English, to someone with as little formal education as Yearsley: her brother taught her to write, she had never been to school. So a translation of the *Georgics* is not only a "professional" choice in that it represents some of the labors of a country life, a milkwoman's text; it is also the choice that a professional writer of georgic or working-country verse would be expected to offer in this period, the formative poem from classical literature for the writers who come after Pope and no longer aspire *en bloc* to writing the great English epic. Yearsley has packaged herself with a sophistication and taste unanticipated by More.

The unlikelihood of such genius existing at all is its best testimony to authenticity and singular brilliance. In her "Prefatory Letter," More explains Yearsley's apparent facility with classical allusions in such a way as to undermine the mystique of a "gentleman's" education at the same time that she dramatizes for us with understated, yet almost Dickensian poignancy, Yearsley's desire for knowledge: "When I expressed to her my surprise at two or three classical allusions in one of her Poems, and inquired how she came by them, she said she had taken them from little ordinary prints which hung in a shop-window."[29] From the "Prefatory Letter," we also learn that of Milton and Young, Yearsley had read only *Paradise Lost* and the *Night Thoughts*; of Pope, only *Eloisa to Abelard*; of Shakespeare, a few plays; of Dryden, Spenser, Thomson, and Prior she had never even heard. What was most pleasing to Montagu and More, it seems, was the influence of the Scriptures on Yearsley's work.[30] Early in their acquaintance, More determined to provide Yearsley with improving books: "I will get Ossian for her. As she has never read Dryden I have given her his Tales, and the most decent of the Metamorphoses."[31] (What good use Yearsley made of the latter we shall see in *Addressed To Ignorance. Occasioned by a Gentleman's desiring the Author never to assume a Knowledge of the Ancients* from her second volume.)

Throughout the period of their joint patronage, until the moment of the break, More's and Montagu's letters record what they take to be the civilizing of Yearsley – at the same time that they continue to delight in her quaint genius, confining her rhetorically to a state of permanent pathos and inferiority as "a Milker of Cows, and a feeder of Hogs, who has never even *seen* a Dictionary."[32] After four months acquaintance, More fancies that Yearsley the poet is beginning to sound positively genteel:

I cannot help troubling you dear Madam with a new production of Lactilla; which I am the more impatient you shou'd see because it betrays totally new Talents, for I think You will agree with me that there is in it, wit, ease and pleasantry; and what sounds quite ridiculous the Poem appears to me to have the tone of good Company, and a gentility that is wonderful in a Milker of Cows, and a feeder of Hogs.[33]

Yearsley's new poem "betrays" new talents in at least two ways: the new gentility of her writing is simultaneously disclosed within it and abruptly curtailed by the persistent pressures of her social situation. This contradictory desire to improve the tone of Lactilla's verse while keeping Yearsley the milkwoman firmly in her place is the crucial ideological contradiction upon which More and Montagu's alliance with Yearsley founders.

We can grasp something of this contradictory ideological positioning, and something of its critical edge, by examining two of the most ambitious and successful poems in Yearsley's *Poems, on Several Occasions*. The first, *Clifton Hill. Written in January 1785*, Yearsley's loco-descriptive "prospect" poem, consists of a remarkable transformation of Lactilla's scene of labor as a milkwoman into a high literary landscape that nevertheless preserves the traces of its working-class origins in its confrontational shifting of perspectives. *Clifton Hill* presents us with a feminized and socialized landscape significantly different from the view from Denham's *Cooper's Hill*, Pope's *Windsor-Forest*, Dyer's *Grongar Hill*, or the more contemporary georgic landscapes of Cowper and Crabbe. Set in the dead of winter, and not in the usual summer of the travelling spectator looking for meaningful prospects – and from which Thomson's *Seasons* were an innovative departure – *Clifton Hill* commemorates the sights of a Bristol topographical feature – but not by way of a rural critique of the great world or courtly and urban centers of power in the manner of Denham, Pope, and Dyer. The English loco-descriptive paradigm initially distinguishes the rural prospect from London, in that the former provides a necessary view of moral improvement for the latter, only to collapse the two prospects together as "the nation" in a patriotic conclusion, usually involving, as a unifying force, the confluence of country-side and capital in imperial British commerce. This tendency persists at least as late as Crabbe's *The Village* (1783), in which strident criticism of the privileged classes and their sentimental notions of rural simplicity is offset by patriotic compliments offered to the family of Crabbe's aristocratic patron, born to rule – though wisely, the poet cautions, tempered by poetical advice "from below." Even where the pleasures of rural retirement are chosen over the lures of court and city, as in Dyer's *Grongar Hill* (1726), the spectator-subject's perspective remains a leisured and confident one: the gentry's poet is master of all he surveys, and he often surveys his prospects from a reclining position: "Now, even now, my Joys run high, / As on the Mountain's Turf I lie" (154–55).[34]

Yearsley, whose prospects and poetical perspective are anything but leisured, neither views Clifton Hill as remote from the great world politically and morally, nor does she use the local landscape to make political points about the nation as a whole. Thus commerce enters *Clifton Hill* by way of sailors returning to their Bristol families from dangerous voyages and celebrating with "clumsy music" their "rough delight" (191). This is commerce perceived from the laborer's, not the politician's point of view, though Yearsley's position in relation to the plebeian culture of the sailors seems ambiguous. The sailors' music is "clumsy" and their delight "rough" in its vernacularity, its difference from the sensibility of the literate laborer whose powers of literary articulation set her apart from much of the class for whom she speaks and out of whose situation she writes.

For Yearsley, Clifton Hill is a site of personal and local historical significance, fraught with sexual and social conflict, yet beautiful in its residual wildness, its geographical elevation, and its emancipatory effect upon the memory and the imagination. Needless to say, the English loco-descriptive paradigm is a masculine one, in which the sovereign subject of the text's ideology participates in public life with a gentleman's confident reserve, and a gentleman's superior knowledge of likely prospects, both local and national, in matters of property, politics, commerce, and war. Yearsley's prospect poem substitutes protofeminist for conventionally masculine "subjects" in both senses: the dominant consciousness of the poem is always a feminine one, though not so much a unified "self" as a scattering of fragmentary female perspectives. Far from being at odds with the natural world, or seeking to dominate or exploit it in accordance with eighteenth-century notions of progress and empire associated with the prospect poem, these female subjects find consolation and safety in the "inhuman" world of natural forces. And the discursive passages on social and political matters address specifically sexual politics, especially the victimization of young women of fashion whose tragic stories are as well known to the "remote" Lactilla as we might expect from the resident of a rising spa town.

The "I" of *Clifton Hill* is a migratory one, fusing itself with a variety of perspectives both human and animal. But Yearsley grounds her text periodically in Lactilla's situation as a working woman for whom, as for Mary Collier's women, winter brings no cessation of labor; cows must be milked and milk sold door-to-door in the harshest weather:

> . . . half sunk in snow,
> LACTILLA, shivering, tends her fav'rite cow. (19–20)

Labor continues, but eros is displaced; it is too cold to go courting, and both the swain and the nymph are "Alike insensible to soft desire" (17) because of the hardships involved in keeping alive. Thus "Love seeks a milder zone" (19) but for Yearsley the whole landscape becomes cathected. Abandoning the "vulgar dissonance" of the returned sailors' music, and making a virtue of her rural isolation, Lactilla addresses the unpopulated scene of Clifton Hill with ardor:

> Yours be the vulgar dissonance, while I
> Cross the low stream, and stretch the ardent eye,
> O'er Nature's wilds; 'tis peace, 'tis joy serene,
> The thought as pure as calm the vernal scene.
> Ah, lovely meads! my bosom lighter grows,
> Shakes off her huge oppressive weight of woes,
> And swells in guiltless rapture; ever hail,
> The tufted grove, and the low-winding vale!   (192–99)

At the same time, Yearsley furnishes the milkwoman Lactilla who writes verses with a certain knowing detachment from the youthful swains and milkmaids for whom the return of spring will bring renewed sensual desire. Yearsley reverses the terms of the, for us, familiar Freudian dynamic of sublimation. The "ruddy swain"'s ardor, inspired by burgeoning vegetation and spring gales, begins as an inarticulate poetical impulse but lack of education requires that it manifest itself in the pursuit of sexual pleasure:

> The ruddy swain now stalks along the vale,
> And snuffs fresh ardour from the flying gale;
> The landscape rushes on his untaught mind,
> Strong raptures rise, but raptures undefin'd;
> He louder whistles, stretches o'er the green,
> By screaming milk-maids, not unheeded, seen;
> The downcast look ne'er fixes on the swain,
> They dread his eye, retire and gaze again.
> 'Tis mighty Love –   (45–53)

There follows a brief discourse on the differences between plebeian and polite rituals of courtship and sexual practice. The analysis of "high romantic rules" that encourage well-bred female repression of desire is fresh and revealing. This theme, the internalized codes by which middle- and upper-class women are led into romantic martyrdom, is fully adumbrated later in the poem through the tale of the mad Louisa. By contrast, poor countrywomen play a more conscious, though not necessarily less oppressive, game of postponing the admission of their own desire – and the likelihood of pregnancy – until their reputations have been secured by a promise of marriage. (More claims that Yearsley's family married her off against her inclinations because her husband, John Yearsley, had an estate of "near *Six pounds a year.*"[35] As we have seen, such an income might easily be lost, and dependence upon wage labor meant a precarious existence, especially in winter when there was no work. Not much can be gleaned about John Yearsley or their marriage, except that they married in 1774. A "Gentleman, residing on Clifton-Hill" described him as a man "of no vice, but of very little capacity."[36] He seems curiously absent from Yearsley's published work.)

>   – Ye blooming maids, beware,
> Nor the lone thicket with a lover dare.
> No high romantic rules of honour bind
> The timid virgin of the rural kind;
> No conquest of the passions e'er was taught,
> No meed e'er given them for the vanquish'd thought.
> To sacrifice, to govern, to restrain,
> Or to extinguish, or to hug the pain,
> Was never theirs; instead, the fear of shame
> Proves a strong bulwark, and secures their fame;
> Shielded by this, they flout, reject, deny,
> With mock disdain put the fond lover by;
> Unreal scorn, stern looks, affected pride,
> Awe the poor swain, and save the trembling bride.   (53–66)

All this the contemplative Lactilla appears to have put behind her; she merely reports, from an ironical distance, these anthropological observations to an audience for whom they will seem novel curiosities. Lactilla's own libidinal investment lies in the emancipatory prospect offered by the landscape itself, and her ability to narrate the daily progresses necessitated by her labor.

Reading *Clifton Hill*, we may think of John Clare, whose autobiography seems at points to represent something similar to Yearsley's capacity for diffuse cathexis of the natural world in which she labors and writes. As Clare describes his early experience of intense imaginative production, the rhythms of work required that he make regular journeys through his neighborhood, during which he would keep boredom and superstitious fears at bay by composing tales of soldiering and romance, casting himself as the hero. This imaginary activity would not only make the time pass more pleasurably, but would sometimes become entirely preoccupying: "& my mind would be so bent on the reverys sometimes that I have often got to the town unawares & felt a sort of disappointment in not being able to finish my story." These imaginative exercises, Clare speculates, may have been the source of his poetry:

I know not what made me write poetry but these journeys & my toiling in the fields by myself gave me such a habit for thinking that I never forgot it & always

mutterd & talkd to myself afterwards I have often felt ashamed at being overheard
by people that overtook me it made my thoughts so active that they became troublesome to me in company & I felt the most happy to be alone

  with such merry company I heard the black & brown beetle sing their evening
song with rapture.[37]

In *Clifton Hill* we find Yearsley approaching the same pitch of excitement as
her toilsome journeys give rise to poetry:

> As o'er the upland hills I take my way,
> My eyes in transport boundless scenes survey   (67–68)

and as she identifies herself as a human friend to her animal neighbors, not as
the foe they have learned to fear. Of the flocks of sheep ekeing out an existence
on scanty upland fare, she writes:

> Some bask, some bound, nor terrors ever know,
> Save from the human form, their only foe.
> Ye bleating innocents! dispel your fears,
> My woe-struck soul in all your troubles shares;
> 'Tis but LACTILLA – fly not from the green:
> Long have I shar'd with you this guiltless scene.
> 'Tis mine to wander o'er the dewy lawn,
> And mark the pallid streak of early dawn.   (104–11)

The poet as solitary wanderer is not a new phenomenon; we have only to
recall Milton's *Penseroso* to be assured of that. But Yearsley's aestheticization
of her labor, as not, in fact, labor, but a constant source of natural
inspiration, is. From Lactilla's tending of her cow to the vending of milk on
Clifton Hill, we are prevented from reading this poem as having been written
by a non-laboring appreciator of landscape. Duck and Collier made their
labor itself a fit subject for poetry; in this text, Yearsley suppresses hers into a
mere grounding for her poetical trekking over Clifton Hill, as Clare claims he
did in his forced marches as a boy.

  For both Clare and Yearsley there is something desirable, and a little
precious, about a rural upbringing and a life of agrarian labor. Their physical
hardships, in the context of enclosure, urbanization, and early industrialization, can seem comparatively slight, their labor relatively unalienated:
journeying through the countryside becomes almost a dream of freedom and
childish indulgence, its purpose subordinate to its pleasures. As Clare writes
his autobiography, the country of his boyhood has already largely disappeared
into agricultural "improvements" to survive only as a nostalgic dream: "I
lovd the lonely nooks in the fields & woods & my favourite spots had lasting
places in my memory that bough that when a schoolboy screened my head

before enclosure destroyed them."[38] Like Clare, Yearsley is grateful to her local landscape for making her a country poet, for poetry in turn helps make her labor bearable. At the same time, she identifies with those denizens of the countryside who are most at the mercy of their human foes and masters: Clifton Hill may be aesthetically, as well as topographically, uplifting but it remains a scene of struggle. The melancholy of Clare's phrase about enclosure, his profound sorrow at what the new more heavily capitalized agriculture would bring, coupled with that other form of melancholy – his fears of peculiarity and madness – eventually conspire in his confinement in an asylum. Playing upon Yearsley's failure to publish anything after 1796, a number of commentators have suggested that she too meets a melancholy end, perhaps prefigured here in her lonely travels among the guiltless but doomed sheep and other half-wild and wild creatures. Sometime before her death in 1806, perhaps after the death of her husband in 1803, Yearsley retired to Melksham in Wiltshire. As an inhabitant of that village reported, "Ann Yearsley was never seen, except when she took her solitary walk, in the dusk of the evening."[39] Even the meticulous J. M. S. Tompkins accepts the solitary walks as "convincing and characteristic."[40]

Ironically, the finely tuned sensibility of the poor country(wo)man that can thrill to the song of the black and brown beetle, the boundings of sheep, and the mole's "nicely-pointed ear" (175), may find itself increasingly excluded from human society. Even as early as her first volume of verse, Yearsley's exposure of the violence with which men treat the animal world – and the implied connection between this violence and female victimization – may be seen as a critical stance nearly impossible to maintain in individualist isolation. Thus Yearsley's criticism of oppressive and repressive modes of social being ends in anti-social being. The cathected landscape and the "solitary walk," once the means of social strength, in the end absorb her totally.

But there is no more than an intimation of this melancholic alienation from human society in the text of *Clifton Hill*. For every act of violence in the poem, there are, elsewhere, small restorative and defiant gestures of community being made. The violent swain outrages by his "savagery" in a most un-Yearsleyan sense when he shoots "The beauteous red-breast, tender in her frame, / Whose murder marks the fool with treble shame" (23–24). In return, Lactilla heaps curses on his head. But when the invalid young woman of fashion seeks a cure at the Hotwells, she need not fear the roughness of the countryside nor the wind off the Bristol Channel; both will conspire to do her good:

> The breezy air,
> To the wild hills invites the languid fair:
> Fear not the western gale, thou tim'rous maid,
> Nor dread its blast shall thy soft form invade;

> Tho' cool and strong the quick'ning breezes blow,
> And meet thy panting breath, 'twill quickly grow
> More strong.   (130–36)

Thus the great world comes to Clifton Hill, apparently as much a scene of affectation and fashionable feminine weakness as London itself. Briefly waxing as prescriptive as Hannah More does in *Strictures On The Modern System Of Female Education* (1799), Yearsley discourses on female "INDO-LENCE" as a form of internalized repression and self-imposed martyrdom, "Death of true pleasure, source of real pain!" (143). The cure? "Keen exercise shall brace the fainting soul, / And bid her slacken'd powers more vigorous roll' (144–45). But immediately Lactilla feels she must vindicate herself from the charge that this is absurdly inappropriate, because plebeian, advice: "Blame not my rustic lay, nor think me rude" (146). A depersonalized, though personified, Fashion is the cause of female woes. Here Yearsley signalizes by "fashion" what we would call the social construction of femininity, especially as deployed in the maintenance of patriarchal family structures and concomitant female subordination. In their desire to please within these terms, women cultivate an unnatural, yielding softness that leads to masochism and often ends tragically. Yearsley's criticism presents, in miniature, the arguments developed later at some length by More and, more radically, by Mary Wollstonecraft in the *Vindication of the Rights of Woman* (1792), though readers of Swift will recall his offering precisely the same advice to Stella much earlier in the century. To be fashion's slave is to seek a more violent tyranny still – for death is never far behind such unnatural behavior:

> Your high-born maid,
> Whom fashion guides, in youth's first bloom shall fade;
> She seeks the cause, th' effect would fain elude,
> By Death's o'erstretching stride too close pursu'd,
> She faints within his icy grasp, yet stares,
> And wonders why the Tyrant yet appears –
> Abrupt – so soon – Thine, Fashion is the crime,
> Fell Dissipation does the work of time.   (148–55)

Confusedly repressing all energies not explicitly directed at romantically enslaving men (and, in particular, a husband) women of fashion literally dress to kill – themselves. Though men, it seems, continue to offer sufficient encouragement.

This brief discourse on the wrongs of female education mediates between two other, more dramatic, moments of focused female subjectivity, both of them tragic but both heroically restorative of something we might call a female community. Far from being at odds with the natural world, or seeking only to repress, dominate, or exploit it, these female subjects find consolation and safety in the "inhuman" world of natural forces. *Clifton Hill* is in one sense a memorial to Yearsley's mother, who had died the previous winter, when the whole family nearly starved, and who lies buried in Clifton Churchyard. But the text, as well as being a text of loss and mourning, is also a text of reparation through memory: Yearsley's mother is restored to her as a figure of wisdom and power crucial to her own development as a poet – and, more surprisingly – crucial to her sanity, her refusal of a disintegration into madness that afflicts the other chief female presence in the poem, the outcast Louisa, whom "No Mother's bosom ... befriends" (213). In a sense the landscape of Clifton Hill can be cathected by the poet because of the occasions it provides for re-membering: for moments of communion with her mother's buried body, and for reactivation of early memories of her mother's strength. *Clifton Hill* thus represents a feminized landscape in the primal and psycho-analytical, as well as the thematic, sense.

The passage in which Yearsley surveys Clifton Churchyard and recalls her many visits there with her mother, rhetorically dwelling on her disbelief that her mother could be dead, may strike us as a trifle stilted. Yearsley seems aware of the difficulty she is having with this material; she is so worried about it that she anticipates a rich and philistine audience's complete rejection of her mourning. The "proud Croesean crew," she fears, "light, cruel, vain, / Whose deeds have never swell'd the Muses' strain, / Whose bosoms others sorrows ne'er assail, / Who hear, unheeding, Misery's bitter tale," will call for satire at this point, incapable of comprehending a poor woman's grief. Lactilla's muse defies them and "pursues her flight" (93–98), but the anticipa-tion of class hostility has left its mark upon the text. For the laboring poet, not even the most profoundly painful experiences can be imaginatively projected into the public sphere without risking middle-cass contempt, and that favored refuge of the privileged, élitist satire.

Yearsley's mother's grave, beside the "neat dome" of Clifton Church, is the first site contemplated on this topographical journey. The briefest description gives way to an elegiac meditation verging on the distraught and the linguistically inadequate:

> Dead! can it be? 'twas here we frequent stray'd,
> And these sad records mournfully survey'd.
> I mark'd the verse, the skulls her eye invite,
> Whilst my young bosom shudder'd with affright!
> My heart recoil'd, and shun'd the loathsome view;
> "Start not, my child, each human thought subdue,
> She calmly said; this fate shall once be thine,
> My woes pronounce that it shall first be mine."
> Abash'd, I caught the awful truths she sung,

And on her firm resolves one moment hung;
Vain boast – my bulwark tumbles to the deep,
Amaz'd – alone I climb the craggy steep;
My shrieking soul deserted, sullen views
The depths below, and Hope's fond strains refuse;
I listen'd not – She louder struck the lyre,
And love divine, and moral truths conspire.   (77–92)

"Conspire" to keep the daughter alive and to make her a poet, we must assume, or else, why those frequent treks to the churchyard with its "sad records?" Morbidity or strength of character – which more compels the mother to invite the daughter to contemplate death? We know from Gray's *Elegy* that headstones served as a repository for the popular verse of the poor – here, tags from the Scriptures, homilies, and moral precepts, rather than the ribaldry or political boisterousness of ballads. And Clare writes of a gardener who spent his Sundays travelling up to 10 miles to read the epitaphs in church-yards "& get those he liked best by heart," for he had few books.[41] While Yearsley "marks" the "verse," her mother is drawn to the funereal graphics – the skulls that make Yearsley shudder. Is this because her mother cannot read? The Clifton correspondent to *The Gentleman's Magazine* reported that Yearsley told him it was her mother who first aroused her passion for books, borrowing them from *"her betters."*[42] Presumably her mother can read but not write; her literacy is such that she can appreciate books and deliver philosophical precepts but not fix them in verses of her own. Questions of motive aside, the mother's philosophizing strikes the daughter as poetical: a song, accompanied by the lyre; pious and morally uplifting poetry. And despite the breakdown of syntax, of linguistic articulation in the moment of confrontation with death – her own, her mother's, that will deprive Yearsley of her source of strength – the mother's poetry effects a sufficiently powerful conspiracy to bring the daughter through, capable of remembering.

Perhaps Yearsley's uncertainty about the effect of her grief on readers far removed from the wretched deathbeds of the poor can be traced to a certain ambivalence she feels about her own engagement with poetry – and apparent distance from religion. Early in her acquaintance with More, Yearsley distinguishes her mother's piety from her own seeking of solace in verse, implying that within herself there is a certain moral failure – of belief, of noble resignation. As More reports their conversation, Yearsley describes herself as both apologetic (guilty?) regarding her lack of her mother's religious confidence and yet somehow defiant: she has more imagination and education than her mother had. Her mother's daughter, yet different, impious; and a poor poet, about to receive the patronage of a famously pious woman, bravely (defiantly?) confessing her doubts:

> tho' she never allowed herself to look into a book till her work was done, and her children asleep, yet in those moments She found that reading & writing cou'd allay hunger, and subdue calamity. She told me it wou'd look like Affectation were She to describe the tranquility of her Spirit, and her entire self-possession when famine and death stared her in the face. I told her I envied the State of her Mind; don't envy me Ma'am she reply'd, for I have great doubts as to my Motives; I am afraid my Mind is rather *hardened* than *subdued*. It is a calm temper and a lively Imagination which support [me] rather than the religious confidence which my dear Mother had. I have too much imagination to have a proper delight in serious books; I read them, but not with proper delight." (I give you her own words.)[43]

Unlike Collier, Yearsley invests little in a desirous metaphysics, nor does she attempt to please her patron by making piety central to her literary project. She will be her mother's daughter, not her mother. Yet the "calm temper" and the "lively imagination" that support her in extremity are inscribed in *Clifton Hill* as traceable to her mother's influence. Without those early days of bookish intimacy between mother and daughter, and without the powerfully remembered figure of the mother in the present, Yearsley implies, she might be as mad as the unfortunate Louisa. In a world of violence, class hostility, and female victimization, to be motherless and a woman is to be mere wreckage in the storm.

The story of Louisa, a German fugitive who lived for three years under a haystack and refused to enter a house because, she claimed, "Trouble and misery dwell in houses, and there is no happiness but in liberty and fresh air,"[44] gives Yearsley occasion for rewriting Pope's characterization of Eloisa polemically, praising female charity, and exploring states of psychic disintegration and distraction. According to a note to line 207, this fugitive Louisa "once confessed, in a lucid interval, that she had escaped from a Convent, in which she had been confined by her father, on refusing a marriage of his proposing, her affections being engaged to another man." Unlike the victims of fashionable female indolence, who die early, Louisa lives through an affective progression of passion, paternal tyranny, abandonment, confinement, escape, and physical hardship that culminates in madness. Like Pope, Yearsley dwells on the Gothic oppressiveness of Louisa's convent, the tortures of remembered passion and a future likely to be empty of any emotion except despair. But, unlike Pope, Yearsley does not treat this sensational dilemma as the necessary consequence of a female abandonment to passion, to irrational femininity. Rather, the tale of Louisa becomes an object-lesson from which Yearsley hopes new, less oppressive, and less antifeminist laws concerning women's relations to paternal authority will stem. Addressing the anonymous female friend who "to LOUISA's shed of misery came," and who "gently drew her from the beating storm" (223–25), Yearsley demands that the friend (who is likely to be "Stella," Hannah More) try, if she can, to defend the providence that can permit such a tragedy, and, more polemically, testify against the "human laws" that are immediately responsible for it:

> Stand forth – defend, for well thou canst, the cause
> Of Heaven, and justify its rigid laws;
> Yet own that human laws are harshly given,
> When they extend beyond the will of Heaven.
> Say, can thy pen for that hard duty plead,
> By which the meek and helpless maid's decreed
> To dire seclusion? Snatch'd from guiltless joys,
> To where corroding grief the frame destroys;
> Monastic glooms, which active virtue cramp,
> Where horrid silence chills the vital lamp;
> Slowly and faint the languid pulses beat,
> And the chill'd heart forgets its genial heat;
> The dim sunk eye, with hopeless glance, explores
> The solemn aisles, and death-denouncing doors,
> Ne'er to be past again. –   (226–40)

To be immured in a convent, to the Protestant Yearsley, is to be buried alive, to be condemned to bear all the signs of premature death, like the victims of fashion – yet more prematurely still, in the best of health – and at the whim of a cruel father who would maliciously prevent the "guiltless joys" of love to foster his own interest. Thus the horrifically thrilling Gothic furnishings of "dire confinement" are not merely exploited for sentimental or psychological effect, but put to critical use in a challenge to patriarchalism within the family and the law.

In mounting such an argument in verse, Yearsley goes beyond soliciting the friend's testimony, even beyond pleading Louisa's case herself: the poet gradually identifies with the tragic female subject so that her distraction becomes dramatized for us from within. Legalistic discourse gives way to the discourses of eroticism and unreason. The coordinates by which Yearsley makes her way to this merger with a disintegrating rational subjectivity are memory and poverty. The only pleasure left to the confined Louisa, as to Pope's Eloisa before her, is the memory of a once-possible erotic fulfillment that the present and future harshly deny:[45]

> 'Tis momentary bliss, 'tis rapture high,
> The heart o'erflows, and all is extacy.
> MEMORY! I charge thee yet preserve the shade.   (246–48)

But the poet's authority to enjoin Louisa's memory to insulate her by giving her remembered pleasure is limited. Lactilla begins to plead with memory instead and to employ the language of bankruptcy and poverty in order to convey Louisa's desperate situation. Louisa becomes comparable in her misery with Yearsley's experience of deprivation and near-starvation, her hopelessness the emotional state which only Yearsley's reading and writing could alleviate "when famine and death stared her in the face":

> – Ah! turn not yet
> Thou wretched bankrupt, that must soon forget
> This farewel draught of joy: lo! Fancy dies,
> E'en the thin phantom of past pleasure flies.
> Thought sinks in real woe; too poor to give
> Her present bliss, she bids the future live;
> The spirit soon quits that fond clasp, for see,
> The future offers finish'd misery.   (252–59)

The expectation of delivery, which presumably sustains all those "too poor to give" their "present bliss," and may have fuelled Yearsley's literary endeavors, cannot be maintained in Louisa's circumstances. The halting rhythm of the penultimate line mimes the faltering of Louisa's future hopes. Escape she must, or die of confinement. But the cost of escape is overwhelming guilt – at broken vows, at the transgression of religious as well as parental authority. And such excessive guilt takes its toll in a manner remarkably similar to that of fashionable indolence: the subject is broken by it, her frame as well as her mind wracked by repression and submerged, internalized conflict. Unable to challenge the institutions and social practices that are destroying her, she can destroy only herself:

> Too late to these mild shores the mourner came,
> For now the guilt of flight o'erwhelms her frame:
> Her broken vows in wild disorder roll,
> And stick like serpents in her trembling soul;
> THOUGHT, what art thou? of thee she boasts no more,
> O'erwhelm'd, thou dy'st amid the wilder roar
> Of lawless anarchy, which sweeps the soul,
> Whilst her drown'd faculties like pebbles roll,
> Unloos'd, uptorn, by whirlwinds of despair,
> Each well-taught moral now dissolves in air;
> Dishevel'd, lo! her beauteous tresses fly,
> And the wild glance now fills the staring eye;
> The balls, fierce glaring in their orbits move,
> Bright spheres, where beam'd the sparkling fires of Love,[46]
> Now roam for objects which once fill'd her mind,
> Ah! long-lost objects they must never find.
> Ill starr'd LOUISA! Memory, 'tis a strain,

Which fills my soul with sympathetic pain.
Remembrance, hence, give thy vain struggles o'er,
Nor swell the line with forms that live no more.   (277–96)

Certain kinds of modern critical theory could recuperate Louisa's madness as a political gesture, as a higher form of freedom than any available to her within the hyper-rational social and ideological spaces of the period. The anti-psychiatry movement, the work of Michel Foucault, and Gilles Deleuze and Félix Guattari's *Anti-Oedipus: Capitalism and Schizophrenia* in different ways endorse this experience of psychic disintegration and "schizo ego-loss" as potentially liberating – hence the need for clinical and state practices of confinement and "cure."[47] There is, to be sure, something libidinally charged about Louisa's embodying of "lawless anarchy" as Yearsley represents it. There is a subtext of voyeuristic pleasure to be derived from Louisa's dishevelled hair and roving eyes; her wild tresses can only be "beauteous" to some spectator's eye. The brilliantly conveyed pain of her "drown'd faculties like pebbles" uptorn by some powerful undersea current is inseparable from the more familiar spectacle of her passionate abandonment. Louisa's body has been conventionally eroticized as well as wracked by abandonment, her own abandonment to passion, and her lover's abandonment of her to the overpowering forces of unreason and the law. And Yearsley's use of "lawless anarchy" here suggests a perverse triumph over the law that first sought to punish and confine Louisa for "guiltless pleasures."

The ostensible direction of the passage, however, is towards a final view of the pathos of Louisa's situation and a certain equivalence between it and the poet's, both pained by memories of the lost and the dead. Louisa's longing for her lover merges with Yearsley's longing for her mother; the powerful functioning of memory itself provokes the poet's "sympathetic pain." The final couplet of *Clifton Hill* is thus a banishing of "remembrance," a laying to rest of the text's own self-declared impetus, so that both poetical commemoration during the topographical journey and the work of mourning may come to an end. The motherless woman seems doomed to suffer madly in the "vain struggles" of painful remembering. The woman who has recently lost her mother rationally commands remembrance and her own hitherto compulsive writing to stop troubling her, having displaced something of her pain onto the hopelessly doomed figure of the mad woman.

There may be something symptomatic, then, in Yearsley's silence regarding Louisa's eventual fate. Ironically, the narrative of Louisa in Thompson's biography of More suggests that the "real" Louisa lived in her haystack more congenially at peace with the natural world than even Yearsley's persona Lactilla is shown to do. This narrative is replete with tropes of romantic heroism, but offers itself prosaically as fact. Louisa seems to have been the recipient of female charity from her arrival in England, but of a traditionalist and rather unstructured sort. She is first sent to St. Peter's Hospital, Bristol, then released, whereupon she returns to her beloved haystack, whereupon several local women subscribe and buy it for her! When given money, she places it at the doors of houses; when given trinkets, she hangs them from the trees. We cannot help but regret More's more modern and institutional intervention, therefore. Thompson comments that the More sisters "With their customary activity and philanthropy ... immediately exerted themselves in behalf of the unhappy creature, and had her removed to Mr. Henderson's lunatick asylum at Hanham," accompanied by a large subscription which Hannah More continued to administer until Louisa's death. Yet Louisa is shown to be so happy in her wild abandonment out of doors, that More's re-confining her, even to Richard Henderson's asylum, seems a misguided gesture at best. John Wesley may have considered Henderson "the best physician of lunatics in England,"[48] but Thompson's version of Louisa's story ends darkly: nineteen years later (December 19, 1800), Louisa dies in Guy's Hospital, London, a final repository for the incurable.[49] There is a revealing silence surrounding Yearsley's version of the tale of Louisa, a silence marking an ideological limit, a contradiction that cannot be broached. Yearsley is caught between wishing to endorse More's charity (in Louisa's case as in her own) and being unable to conceptualize an unreason indifferent to physical hardship so long as a certain relative freedom of the countryside is provided. Yet this last is precisely "Lactilla's" solace – indeed, her significance – except that she is not mad, and, if her poetry succeeds, she may not have to endure such physical hardships forever. For Yearsley, the expectation of delivery mitigates immediate pain. For Louisa there can be no delivery, but the traces of voluntary action she leaves behind indicate that her primitive open-air refuge is as close to a realized desire as she can imagine.

Thus Yearsley's text is divided, incompletely articulate about its most radical possibilities. We must set the implicit endorsement of Louisa's "living rough" over and against More's deployment of the repressively paternalist practices of the new rehabilitative psychiatry, practices no less repressively benevolent, in the interests of patriarchal forms of social control, because deployed by a woman. In the light of Yearsley's failure to write such an endorsement, and her conflation of her own misery with Louisa's in spite of obvious differences, Yearsley's narrative of Louisa may be more polemically protofeminist than Pope's representation of Eloisa, but both suffer from a certain political enervation when it comes to conceiving of radical alternatives to conventional practice. And neither permits the heroine herself to construct from the pathos of her situation any realizable desire, any liveable alternative.

Less contradictory and ambitious in scope, and more centrally critical of the ideology of gender within its narrower focus, is Yearsley's poem on reading Horace Walpole's *The Castle of Otranto*. Such narratives as Louisa's –

narratives of the threatened or actual disintegration of the female subject, and its abandonment to anarchic feeling and inarticulate despair – we may designate historically as "Gothic," and so rooted in the period of sentimentalism and – usually masculine – literary melancholy. But for Yearsley, reading Gothic fantasy as packaged by and for the polite world in Walpole's *Castle of Otranto*, reveals amusing, if rather juvenile, tendencies in the bourgeois imagination, and, more seriously, a distinct antifeminism, as well as predictable class prejudices. The poem of Yearsley's to which More refers in her letter to Montagu of December 7, 1784, and which she praises for its "wit, ease and pleasantry" and – what she can scarcely credit – its "tone of good Company," is most likely to be *To The Honourable H–E W–E, On Reading The Castle of Otranto. December, 1784.* In it, Yearsley puts her new "politesse" to complicated uses, ironically threatening a less than docile or obsequious gratitude for her tutelage by the privileged, and stealing the tone of good company in order to mock its pathetic fancies and resolute misogyny. The playfully critical edge to Yearsley's fluent ventriloquizing of upper-class "wit, ease and pleasantry" More appears to have missed, but it is not likely that less class-bound readers will. With *Clifton Hill*, this is one of the most ambitious and successful of Yearsley's early poems.

An eighteenth-century instance of reader-response criticism, as well as an interesting case of wittily subversive intertextuality, *On Reading The Castle of Otranto* announces itself as by "BIANCA's Pen": Yearsley has relocated Lactilla's rusticity in the servant Bianca of Walpole's novel.

> TO praise thee, WALPOLE, asks a pen divine,
>   And common sense to me is hardly given,
> BIANCA's Pen now owns the daring line,
>   And who expects *her* muse should drop from Heaven.   (1–4)

Even such mock humility and self-deprecation mute any possibility of Yearsley's rudely debunking the mystique of Walpole's Gothic fiction. But there is a persistent subtext of the poet's not being taken in by Walpole's fashionable thrills and chills mechanisms, though she enjoys them as diverting fictions, up to a point. That "point" is Walpole's conventional conflation of lower-class and female mindlessness in the "prate" of Bianca, who mixes "Noise and Nonsense" in a way distinctly reminiscent of Duck's hay-makers. Yearsley briefly regrets that Walpole's "happier talents" never appear in his characterization of Bianca; then, switching subjects abruptly, she hastily assures us that not only women love empty tattle – there are men as well who mimic giddy females: ". . . for mimic fools, / Who boast *thy* sex, BIANCA's foibles wear" (11–12). Ironically, of course, Walpole has himself "mimicked" Bianca successfully in order to represent her at all. From the poem's beginning, then, there is a suggestion that Walpole is as deeply silly as his silliest female characters, or else he wouldn't have been able to make them so,

compounded by a hint that Walpole's female readers–admirers have been
deceiving him by playing up to his expectations in ways that please him, but
conceal the devastating potential of female wit. Thus, "Supreme in prate shall
woman ever sit, / While Wisdom smiles to hear the senseless squall" (13–14) –
and not a moment longer! If women ever decide not to elicit male smiles by
being silly, there may come an end to the "senseless squall," which will be
replaced by – feminist irony? We should recall what Walpole himself wrote in
his preface regarding the domestics in *The Castle of Otranto*:

Some persons may perhaps think the characters of the domestics too little serious for
the general cast of the story; but besides their opposition to the principal personages,
the art of the author is very observable in his conduct of the subalterns. They discover
many passages essential to the story, which could not be well brought to light but by
their naivetè and simplicity: In particular, the womanish terror and foibles of *Bianca*,
in the last chapter, conduce essentially towards advancing the catastrophe.[50]

From the first, Walpole touts the utility of Bianca's "womanish terror and
foibles" in bringing the horrendous truth of the narrative to light. Yearsley's
Bianca is merely ironically fulfilling Walpole's wishes, then, when in her
bumbling naiveté she reveals a few truths about the social implications of
Walpole's fiction.

As a reader, Yearsley's Bianca displays the empathetic subjectivism of much
reader-response criticism; she identifies naively with the passions and struggles
of the main characters: "The horrid helmet strikes my soul unbid, / And with
thy CONRAD, lo! BIANCA dies" (19–20). Manfred's perplexity particularly
arouses her sympathy and elicits high praise for Walpole's skill as a writer:

> By all the joys which treasur'd virtues yield,
>   I fell thy agonies in WALPOLE's line;
> Love, pride, revenge, by turns maintain the field,
>   And hourly tortures rend my heart for thine.   (29–32)

As we might expect, what Yearsley most values about the pleasures of such
absorbing texts is their power to "beguile" a reader's "real woe." Fictive
diversions allow readers to neglect their own sorrow while imagining
someone else's; for a time, present unhappiness is displaced by imaginative
excitement. That expert mimic, Fancy, is a "kind inventress" whose designs
have a soothing, emancipatory effect:

> The kind inventress dries the streaming tear,
>   The deep-resounding groan shall faintly die,
> The sigh shall sicken ere it meet the air,
>   And Sorrow's dismal troop affrighted fly.   (65–68)

But from what kind of woe is Yearsley's Bianca seeking solace? Ironically,
from a certain oppressive silencing stemming from Walpole's text and from

the class category "men of power" embodied by Manfred and by Walpole himself. Bianca has dared to move from an analysis of Walpole's female characters to a critique of his "images of women" as antifeminist propaganda – and then abruptly censored herself with a veiled threat – or a flirtatious ploy? – about concealed female "omnipotence":

> MATILDA! ah, how soft thy yielding mind,
>   When hard obedience cleaves thy timid heart!
> How nobly strong, when love and virtue join'd
>   To melt thy soul and take a lover's part!
>
> Ah, rigid duties, which two souls divide!
>   Whose iron talons rend the panting breast!
> Pluck the dear image from the widow'd side,
>   Where Love had lull'd its every care to rest.
>
> HYPOLITA! fond, passive to excess,
>   Her low submission suits not souls like mine;
> BIANCA might have lov'd her MANFRED less,
>   Not offer'd less at great Religion's shrine.
>
> Implicit Faith, all hail! Imperial man
>   Exacts submission; reason we resign;
> Against our senses we adopt the plan
>   Which Reverence, Fear, and Folly think divine.
>
> But be it so, BIANCA ne'er shall prate,
>   Nor ISABELLA's equal powers reveal;
> You MANFREDS boast your power, and prize your state;
>   We ladies our omnipotence conceal.
>
> But, Oh! then strange-inventing WALPOLE guide,
>   Ah! guide me thro' thy subterranean isles,
> Ope the trap-door where all thy powers reside,
>   And mimic Fancy real woe beguiles.   (41–64)

In the first two stanzas of this passage Yearsley employs a double-edged rhetoric that recalls simultaneously the action of Walpole's plot and the psychological ramifications of these horrific incidents. Matilda is not only "cleaved" or "rent" emotionally by her father's tyrannical will which would forbid her to love Theodore, his rival for the Otranto estates – her father literally rends her breast with a dagger, thinking she is Isabella, the girl he would rather kill than allow to marry someone other than himself. So the dagger Manfred plunges into Matilda, mistaking her for Isabella, is a bald displacement of the overweening desire to rape Isabella which has dogged him since his son Conrad's – Isabella's fiancé's – bizarre death. The "hard obedience" and "iron talons" that lethally inscribe themselves on Matilda's body represent quite literally the father's prohibition of female desire and his sadistic insistence upon realizing his own, which is almost always instrumental to patriarchal succession, tied to property, titles, and power, rather than an anarchic desire for erotic pleasure for its own sake.

With the introduction of Hippolita, Manfred's long-suffering wife, Yearsley's Bianca abandons polite ambiguities for forthright criticism of Walpole's antifeminism. Hippolita's "fondness" for Manfred is a form of foolishness, her passivity and "low submission" are excessive and antipathetic, to Bianca's mind. Hippolita is even willing to agree to a divorce, against her religion and her better judgment, if Manfred wishes it – a form of submission Bianca will not brook. The lines "BIANCA might have lov'd her MANFRED less, / Not offer'd less at great Religion's shrine" demand some unpacking. In one sense, Bianca would show herself to love Manfred less than Hippolita does by refusing to agree to a divorce, and this would result in, *de facto*, a more pious gesture than Hippolita's mere submission to her husband's will. More radically, Yearsley's Bianca is espousing the position that to disobey one's husband on religious grounds may be a positively more pious and morally correct thing to do than to obey him. In this sense, Hippolita's mere obedience to Manfred's will could not be less pious, indeed is impious and "low" – not meek but base. Bianca goes on to attack mindless submission to religion as well as to male desire: both forms of authority require an uncritical obedience based on the belief that "all is for the best," a belief that is unreasonable because it contradicts women's interests and goes against both reason and the empirical evidence of the senses. Female submission to masculine authority is thus represented as a plan designed by men, not God: "Imperial man / Exacts submission" and women assent out of a confusion of "Reverence, Fear, and Folly" that they assume to be a sign of divine providence, of some eternal master plan. This is a daring challenge to the ideology of female subordination as perpetrated by both church and state – but it is no sooner voiced than retracted, or covered, as an example of Bianca's prating, a form of poetical raillery. And similarly, the claim that Isabella possesses "equal powers" – of prating? Or of reasoning? And equal to whose? To those of the men of Walpole's narrative or to those of men at large? – is presented only negatively, as something that will not be revealed here. This rhetorical suppression of female "omnipotence" is thus at least doubly ironical, suggestive of an infinite regress of meaning in which women's historical subjugation, mythical omnipotence, and potential equality become progressively indecipherable, even unthinkable, notions.

Yearsley's text offers an inchoate resistance to those conservative tendencies within the available ideological range that would keep women subordinate while taunting them about their supposed superhuman powers (of desire, of sexual pleasure, of prating). But although the "idea" of female equality had been theoretically thinkable in philosophical and radical sectarian discourse in

England since the seventeenth century, in 1785 it remains inarticulable as practicable social theory or as theorized social practice. Yearsley's text narrates the difficulty of thinking ideological change at the very moment that this gap, this yawning abyss of regressive unthinkability, signalizes an ideological shift in the making.

Faced with such an impasse, Bianca seeks solace in escapist literature like Walpole's: "But, Oh! then strange-inventing WALPOLE guide, / Ah! guide me thro' thy subterranean isles." If overturning bourgeois misogyny is as impossible as it seems, these lines imply, than one might as well explore the furthest reaches of that inimical ideology, especially its fantastic and unconscious dimensions. And it is in its mapping of subterranean horrors, its striving for potent and novel effects, that Walpole's Gothicism seems to Yearsley most transparently juvenile, if not absurd. This is where Yearsley's attention shifts from Walpole's text to Walpole's friendship with Hannah More, and the bond of polite society represented by that friendship, from which Yearsley, as "Bianca," is excluded. The poem's concluding stanzas caution "Stella" about trusting herself to "this noble Sorcerer" Walpole (85) who may torment and even kill her if she should visit him at home. In short, as a woman, she would be at Walpole's mercy; as an aristocrat he would show her middle-class niceness no sympathy. If Stella were to prove herself the sort of reader really impressed by Walpole's textual terrors, there would be little hope of saving her from a discourse of grotesque bathos:

> Trust not his art, for should he stop thy breath,
>   And good ALPHONSO's ghost unbidden rise;
> He'd vanish, leave thee in the jaws of death,
>   And quite forget to close thy aching eyes. (89–92)

This is doubtless the sort of "pleasantry" More so effusively praises in her letter to Montagu. Yearsley here covertly projects a scene of flirtation between Walpole and More which turns perverse, as he abandons her to die of fright – or is the state of staring, aching-eyed, rather one of sleepless tedium generated by one of his Gothic conjurings? Again, Yearsley as Bianca draws attention to her boldness in order to mute it, wittily and politely:

> But is BIANCA safe in this slow vale?
>   For should his Goblins stretch their dusky wing,
> Would they not bruise me for this saucy tale,
>   Would they not pinch me for the truths I sing? (93–96)

The only refuge from the terrors of Walpole's text and from his authorial rage should he learn that "Bianca" has "call'd him names" (97), is sleep; ironically, the only power greater than Walpole's belongs to Morpheus: "To thee, Oh, balmy God! I'm all resign'd, / To thee e'en WALPOLE's wand resigns its power"

(107–08). If the supposedly sophisticated tensions of Walpole's narrative collapse in sleep, as does civilization, overcome by Dulness at the end of Pope's *Dunciad*, the joke is surely on those who regard Gothic fiction as genuinely terrifying – or important. In writing this poem, Yearsley has acceded to a certain discourse of witty raillery without being impressed by the intellectual powers of such a formidable arbiter of taste as Horace Walpole. To mimic gentility without being taken in by it, to trade in the aesthetic currency of the polite world while ironically undercutting its pretensions to superior knowledge and understanding – these are the achievements of the best of Yearsley's *Poems, on Several Occasions*.

There are, therefore, at least two sides to Lactilla's "savagery": her deliberate rusticity, with its capacity for a cathected relation to the natural world; and her shrewd laborer's wit that discloses aspects of middle- and upper-class culture not commonly on offer from the "major" writers of the period, who usually belong precisely to these classes. In this latter sense, Yearsley may remind us of another poor eighteenth-century prodigy whose peculiar vantage-point between the high and the low, between aristocratic dissolution and the squalor of the urban poor, disrupts the familiarity of middle-class territory. Convinced that he was the son of Lady Macclesfield, and shaped by that conviction, Richard Savage, with his poverty, his talent, and his resentments as narrated by Johnson, sheds a useful light upon Yearsley's sometimes impudently, sometimes resentfully "savage" muse:

The Insolence and Resentment of which he is accused, were not easily to be avoided by a great Mind, irritated by perpetual Hardships and constrained hourly to return the Spurns of Contempt, and repress the Insolence of Prosperity; and Vanity surely may be readily pardoned in him, to whom Life afforded no other Comforts than barren Praises, and the Consciousness of deserving them.

Those are no proper Judges of his Conduct who have slumber'd away their Time on the Down of Plenty, nor will a wise Man easily presume to say, 'Had I been in *Savage*'s Condition, I should have lived, or written, better than *Savage*.'[51]

We should remember, if tempted to regret Yearsley's obstreperousness in her relations with More, what "Insolence of Prosperity" More must have embodied for her protégée. Yearsley aestheticizes her labor in *Clifton Hill* by writing as if she were on holiday. When not teaching or occupied in philanthropic work, Hannah More did freely ramble the countryside with her sisters, turning a working landscape into a scene of leisured pleasure – one reason, perhaps, why she so carefully copied out the manuscript of *Clifton Hill*. As More puts it in a letter to her sister, in the year of Yearsley's "discovery," there was a need for middle-class young women like themselves to keep generating "discoveries" of a recreational kind: "I hope you have been clever and industrious enough to discover some new little retired delightful spots for our gypsey frolics." Roberts adds a sympathetic footnote:

This alludes to those rural rambles which formed their chief amusements during the holidays, when, furnished with their work-bags stored with provisions and books, they passed a few hours in the enjoyment of the open air, and the delightful scenery of the Clifton Rocks, King's Weston, &c.[52]

This privileged, bookish freedom, so fiercely desired by poets like Yearsley, Duck, and Clare, and so often denied them by history, is precisely the source of pleasure most taken for granted by "insolent prosperity." More's cottage at Cowslip Green, purchased during More's patronage of Yearsley and so perceived by the latter as perhaps purchased with her subscription money, and suitably thatched and picturesque but fitted up comfortably enough for More, whose health was delicate, signifies a concomitant privilege provocative of class antagonism: More's uncomprehending aestheticization of "poverty," as defined by her middle-class means relative to those of her very wealthy friends, and her romanticization of her deliberate experiments in "privation." Writing to Montagu in 1789, More seems to have learned nothing from her acquaintance with Yearsley that could remotely be called progressive class consciousness: "You great folks shou'd now and then condescend to visit us little ones, that you may see how many things one can do without; one day of real, actual privation is worth fifty descriptions in a Book."[53] If More had been able to understand the complex subjectivity produced by Yearsley's experience of and attempt to articulate a lifetime of "real, actual privation," she would not have been so easily offended by Yearsley's challenge to her charitable authority.

At the height of their alliance, it seemed to Yearsley that she had learned a great deal from More, not least how to see through some of the misprisions of class itself that inflect class conflict, including the assumption that class subjects cannot change. Wishing to emulate her patron, Yearsley hopes to translate her previously untutored "savage virtues" into an affective economy akin to More's "social love." Significantly, Yearsley can only conceive of the encounter as a "choice" between two forms of class-specific behavior: "once that, now this." The demystification and enlightenment are all on one side, in the form of criticism of laboring-class unreflective stricture and inarticulacy of feeling: "the iron lore" and "savage virtues of untutor'd minds":

> STELLA, how strong thy gentle argument!
> By thee convinc'd, I scorn the iron lore,
> The savage virtues of untutor'd minds:
> In thy mild rhetoric dwells a social love

Beyond my wild conceptions, optics false!
Thro' which I falsely judg'd of polish'd life.

(Night. To Stella, 199–204)

Lactilla so admires Stella's generosity, her admirable disinterestedness in promoting those with unlettered aspirations, that the poet inspired by the savage muse reproaches herself for her earlier suspicion of upper-class charity and offers herself to be made over according to More's values:

> This is the sullen curse of surly souls,
> To disbelieve the virtues which they feel not.
> Ah, STELLA! I'm a convert; thou hast tun'd
> My rusting powers to the bright strain of joy.   (205–08)

After such ecstatic gratitude, Yearsley's break with More may seem inexplicable. But her willing suspension of disbelief in More's disinterestedness was clearly taxed by developments in their alliance that Yearsley's class position and the complex subjectivity produced by it caused her to struggle against.

Which is to say that the material process of writing, the linguistic transactions that writing involves, can permit a certain access to the theoretical space from which criticism, and new ideological possibilities, can emerge. To the extent that Yearsley figures herself within her text as Lactilla, patronized plebeian writer and rustic savage, she generates a space from which working-class criticism of bourgeois culture can be (incompletely) articulated. Whatever Ann Yearsley, historical subject, may have desired in the way of material improvements and upward mobility, her poetical discourse as such politically positions itself as laboring class, marginal, critical, increasingly inspired by the more radically levelling elements of bourgeois republican ideology.

Despite, or rather because of, its boldness and critical edge, Yearsley's first volume was received enthusiastically. Not only did *Poems, on Several Occasions* go through four editions, but *The Monthly Review* found in her best work "a genius of no common bent, and a fancy pregnant with those images which give to poetry its most captivating power," going on to praise the signs of struggle that were present in the work:

On the whole, these Poems present us with a very striking picture of a vigorous and aspiring genius, struggling with its own feelings. We see an ardent mind exerting itself to throw off every incumbrance that oppresses it, and to burst from the cloud that obscures its lustre.[54]

The struggle for liberty metaphorically reproduced here within the safely "aesthetic" space of the imagination suggests just how unevenly ideology can develop on, say, the philosophico-aesthetic and political fronts. Yearsley could be publicly praised for trying to emancipate herself imaginatively at the very moment when the question of upward mobility through access to her subscription money was so hotly contested. We should note that *The Monthly Review* would give comparable notice to her second volume in 1787 and to her novel in 1795, and that *The Critical Review* praised her work as well, evidence of keen critical reception.[55]

Ironically, Yearsley comes to see More's ideas about patronage not as class amelioration through the promoting of individual "exceptions," but as yet another instance of deliberately oppressive incumbrance, another cloud that would obscure the luster of an emergent poetical reputation. Their alliance provides a social text particularly rich in what cannot be adequately subsumed or explained away under the heading of "historical ironies," but that strike one nevertheless as ironical. As Yearsley writes in her "Narrative"defense, one of More's final reproaches turned on the question of Yearsley's "savagery," so that the poet's own self-characterization became a weapon in her patron's mouth:

Miss More appeared to be greatly moved, and told me imperiously, that I was "a savage" – that "my veracity agreed with my other virtues" – that I had "a reprobate mind, and was a bad woman." – I replied, "that her accusations could never make me a bad woman – that she descended in calling me a savage, nor would she have had the temerity to do it, had I not given myself that name!"[56]

Lactilla could not effectively control the contexts of her own reception; few writers, especially marginal writers, can. But the struggle between More and Yearsley indicates the degree to which Yearsley attempted to control the context of her own production within middle-class culture, and in so doing, endorsed resistance and not assimilation.

The pleasures of the text – with a vengeance

A few details of Yearsley's relation with More and Montagu have already been given, but the foundering of their literary alliance possesses implications of a more than anecdotal kind. Particular coordinates of the impasse so quickly reached in their relationship demand close scrutiny if we are to read Yearsley's subsequent volumes of verse in nuanced ways and avoid replicating More's well-intended but destructive patronage of Yearsley in our historical recuperation of her texts. The existing accounts of their quarrel are fiercely partisan, with the exception of that left by Joseph Cottle, who attempts fair-mindedness:

Here was a strong-minded, illiterate woman on one side, impressed with a conviction of the justice of her cause; and further stimulated by a deep consciousness of the importance of success to herself and family; and on the other side, a refined mind, delicately alive to the least approximation to indecorum, and not unreasonably, requiring deference and conciliation. Could such incongruous materials coalesce? Without extraneous testimony, the presumption is, that Ann Yearsley's suit, on this occasion, was urged with a zeal approaching to impetuosity, and expressed, not in that measured language which propriety, undeniably, would have dictated; and any deficiency in which, could not fail to offend her polished and powerful patroness.[57]

The occasion was Yearsley's request, after supper at More's house, that certain modifications be made in the deed of trust More had caused to be drawn up: that she, Yearsley, be admitted as joint trustee with More and Montagu, that her subscription money be secured for her children to claim equal shares when they reached twenty-one, and that she be given the interest on it without restrictions. These will undoubtedly seem to us reasonable desires on Yearsley's part, and indeed her defense of herself in the "Narrative" addressed to her "Noble and Generous Subscribers" is both eloquent and convincing. But in this historical moment, such temerity on the part of a protégée and a social inferior More could not countenance: More felt she was being accused of bad management and self-interest. When More responded haughtily to Yearsley's queries about the disposition of the trust, Yearsley's suspicions that she might have been taken advantage of by her patrons were no doubt confirmed. The money in question amounted to some £350, invested by More in the funds – the "Five Per Cents" – which would yield interest of about £18 a year. More had advanced Yearsley £28.14s "to cloathe her family and furnish her House," and pay off some debts, as it turned out; More was, we should remember, mainly interested in making Yearsley comfortable without removing her from her station. But so much money as £350 – and with subsequent editions, it came to more than £600 – seemed to Yearsley to promise a more radical mending of her family's circumstances than could be brought about by More's careful doling out of small sums here and there.[58]

There were other charges as well; all Yearsley's suspicions regarding the middle class were rekindled by More's refusal even to consider that her paternalist arrangements might not have been for the best. Aggrieved, More writes to Montagu:

Her other charges against me are, that I have spoilt her verses by my corrections, and that she will write another book directly to show I was of no use to her; that I have ruined her reputation by the Preface which is full of falsehoods; that it was the height of insult and barbarity to tell that she was poor, and a Milkwoman. – . . . I have spent above 8 months entirely in this business, I have written above a thousand pages on her subject and with your generous concurrence have got near five hundred pounds; I believe it will be more, for I am preparing for a second Edition, and am trying to get the husband a place, I do not see her of which she is very glad, as she says I am such a

Tyrant; I hear she wears very fine Gauze Bonnets, long lappets, gold Pins etc. Is such a Woman to be trusted with the poor Children's Money?[59]

In another letter More adds, "She tells every body my envy of her makes me miserable, and that I cannot bear her superiority."[60] It would seem that Yearsley feels acutely the difference between the class-specificity of her own self-representation as Lactilla, and More's exploitation of the pathos of her situation. We might go so far as to say that Yearsley repudiates what in More's public promotion of her verse could be read as class stigma, and that she ventures to suggest the possibility of a class-free aesthetic interest for her texts, lest that stigma render her verse unreadable. We would thus do Yearsley an injustice to read her only as "a working-class woman poet" in an unproblematically tokenizing way, for that was something she seems to have predicted, and protested against. And yet the very notion of a class-free aesthetic in this period is inextricable from the assumption of a certain gentility inherent in poetic practice. In a sense Yearsley is offended because her aspirations to gentility – one might just as well say her aspirations to poetic practice as such – have been repudiated by her patron.

Since Yearsley's case has been represented thus far largely through More's reportage, some further evidence should be adduced. The manuscripts of Yearsley's *Poems, on Several Occasions* and of other poems that were not published in that volume were never returned to her. More was moved enough to say, in a fit of pique, that they had been left at the printer's, and then that they had been burned.[61] In a letter to More, which survives only in More's transcription of it in a letter to Montagu, Yearsley accuses More of patronizing her from motives of "vanity" rather than "humanity" or "a disinterested desire to serve" her. Yearsley's style is certainly forthright. As she admits in her "Narrative," she cannot hope to mime successfully the polite "manner of speaking" (or not speaking) about money, a subject too fraught and anxious-making to be casually broached: "As to the manner of speaking, I fear I shall always err in that, as I have not been accustomed to your rules of polished life."[62] Her unpublished representation of her own case to More includes the following assessments of this crisis of patronage:

"You tax me with ingratitude, for why? You found me poor yet proud, if it can be "called pride to feel too much humbled by certain obligations, and above submitting "to servility. You helped to place me in the public Eye; my success you think beyond "my abilities, and purely arising from your protection; but granting this to your "Vanity, surely mine does not *soar*, in thinking the singularity of my situation wou'd "have secured me some success . . . I cannot think it ingratitude to disown as obli- "gation a proceeding which must render me and my children your poor dependents "for ever. I have trusted more to your *probity* than the event justifies. You have led "me to sign a Settlement which defrauds me of my right, and makes it ever received "your peculiar gift. Your bankruptcy or death may lose it for ever, and let me ask "you Miss More what security You have ever given my children whereby they may "prove their claim?[63]

In a world of traditional aristocratic patronage and clientage, such anxiety about "rights" and "bankruptcy" and the legal proving of claims, even when projected into the future, would be unthinkable. Yearsley here stands as a fully conscious, bourgeois head of the family, and bourgeois writer. Were Yearsley and More aristocratic, neither would fuss about money; were Yearsley a client to More's patronage in the traditional sense, she would have accepted her allowance without complaint. More herself has established a business arrangement between them, but not fully recognizing Yearsley's access to the discourse of "rights," or her grasp of investment procedures, is shocked to be challenged on the grounds that she herself has chosen. Cottle sums up More's likely reaction to this discovery thus:

Both parties meant well, but from the constitution of the human mind, it was hardly possible for one who had greatly obliged another (and the recipient, in subordinate station) to experience the least opposition, in an arrangement, deemed by the principal, expedient, without experiencing, at least an uncomfortable feeling. The thought, from the power of association, would almost necessarily arise in Hannah More's mind; "Ann Yearsley, you are at present decently apparelled, but without my patronage, you would now be serving hogs, or be weighed down with a milk pail, and do you oppose any disposition I and Mrs. Montague may think proper to make!"[64]

Eventually the trust is resigned, Yearsley gains control of the principal and a new patron presents himself. More scoffs:

Did I tell you, that Lord Bristol had given her fifty Pounds? how suitable the Patron to the Protégée . . .[65]

In the light of More's and Yearsley's difficulties, it is hardly surprising that More's replacement should have been an aristocrat, evidently disinclined to worry about settlements in the first place. Both the nobleman and the knowledgeable laboring woman find community through an imagined tradition of happy coexistence in which bourgeois legality and business negotiations have little place. What gifts her new patron gives her, Yearsley is free to manage as an independent (bourgeois) agent whose little estate cannot threaten his (vast) privileges. Thus begins a new era in Yearsley's career during which her obligations to Frederick Augustus Hervey, Earl of Bristol and Bishop of Derry, encourage a freer poetical discourse and eventually such material improvements as the apprenticeship of her son William to an engraver and her establishment of the circulating library. More was no doubt referring to Hervey's reputation as a free-thinker and womanizer – as a disgrace to the church, in short – when suggesting that Yearsley and he deserved each other. An unconventional clergyman he seems to have been, known for his "great liberality," and preferring Italy to England.[66] But the *D.N.B.* describes his insight into Irish politics and his endeavors towards agricultural, architectural, and parochial improvements in Ireland as admirable.[67] In her dedications, Yearsley herself stresses, respectively, his "liberality of soul," his "active Virtue" and "exalted Sentiments," and his "talents," "genius," and "exalted virtues."[68] In the dedicatory epistle to *The Rural Lyre*, perhaps by 1796 sufficiently well-read to be echoing Johnson's famous letter to Chesterfield, she gives the most complete description of their relations:

Ten years are now elapsed, since in my cottage I was honoured by the presence of your Lordship. Through the cloud which then covered my confused spirit you had the goodness to discern an impatient desire for attainments so remote from my humble station, that by many they were deemed unnecessary, by most superfluous; and though by some a share of discrimination was allowed me, yet mental accomplishments were considered as incompatible with my laborious employment. This, my Lord, was not your opinion. You inspired me with hope, encouraged me to persevere, and enabled me to divide my domestic cares with the pleasures of meditation. Your Lordship immediately left England. In this long interval, whilst cheered by your instruction, animated by your sentiments, delighted with your elegant language, and supported by a reliance on your protection, I became less fearful of general approbation.

(*The Rural Lyre*, pp. vi–vii)

Hervey also appears to have stood sponsor for one of Yearsley's children, a son named Frederick who died soon after the christening.[69]

Under his aegis, the texts that make up *Poems, on Various Subjects* (1787) demonstrate Yearsley's attempts at self-vindication in the wake of the More controversy, pronounce sharper social criticism than she had previously dared to write, and sometimes display dazzlingly successful aesthetic experiments. But Yearsley also engaged in a continued counter-offensive against More which did not go unnoticed. Upon the publication of *Poems, on Various Subjects*, More writes to Horace Walpole, pointing out how "curious" it is that Yearsley has prefixed to this new volume More's original "Prefatory Letter" and the "scurrility" of the autobiographical "Narrative":

Do, dear Sir, join me in sincere compassion, without one atom of resentment (for that I solemnly protest is the state of my mind towards her) for a human heart of such unaccountable depravity, as to harbour such deep malice for two years, though she has gained her point, and the money is settled to her wish. If I wanted to punish an enemy, it should be by fastening on him the trouble of constantly hating some-body.[70]

But the quarrel with More seems to have become enlarged into social typicality in Yearsley's mind; More has ceased to represent a single instance of an insensitive middle-class patron and come to stand for the prejudices of a whole class. More, though not invoked by name in the texts of the poems, hovers over the volume by virtue of the prefixed material, and it is impossible not to connect her with passages in which a partial, class-blinkered view of social relations is pilloried.

   This exposure of "optics dim" we can cite as an historical prefiguration of the term "ideology:"

> YOU, who thro' optics dim, so falsely view
> This wond'rous maze of things, and rend a part
> From the well-order'd whole, to fit your sense
> Low, groveling, and confin'd; say from what source
> Spring your all-wise opinions?
>> ("To those who accuse the Author of Ingratitude," 1–5)

These metaphors of blinkered views may remind us of the first epistle of Pope's *Essay on Man*. But Pope presents a theory of "partial views" – both limited and interested – in order to insist that they are a "human" failing, rather than a class-specific phenomenon. Here Pope emphasizes the philosophical concept of empirical limits to human reason: "Say first, of God above, or Man below, / What can we reason, but from what we know?" (17–18) in contradistinction to divine omniscience: "'No ('tis reply'd) the first Almighty Cause / 'Acts not by Partial, but by gen'ral laws" (145–46).[71] Where Pope rhetorically asks human beings in general if they can comprehend God's cosmos, implying that only the extremely arrogant would presume to, he goes on to claim that he has successfully explained, from the outside, what was only apparently mysterious, the workings of the individual psyche. For Yearsley, however, it is the psyche as socially subject, even her own subjectivity, however familiar, which remains most powerfully incomprehensible.

   Yearsley's view of the workings of ideology is thus more socialized and more politically grounded than Pope's. The components of the particular form of imaginary relation that Yearsley is attacking have a class-specific charge, through one that could be deployed to criticize working- as well as middle-class conservatism:

> A wish to share the false, tho' public din,
> In which the popular, not virtuous, live;
> A fear of being singular, which claims
> A fortitude of mind you ne'er could boast;

A love of base detraction, when the charm
Sits on a flowing tongue, and willing moves
Upon its darling topic. These are yours.
But were the stedfast adamantine pow'rs
Of Principle unmov'd? Fantastic group!
Spread wide your arms, and turn yon flaming Sun
From his most fair direction; dash the stars
With Earth's poor pebbles, and ask the World's great Sire,
Why, in Creation's system, HE dare fix
More orbs than your weak sense shall e'er discern?
Then scan the feelings of Lactilla's soul.   (34–48)

The desire for social homogeneity is revealed as not only falsifying in its convenient oversimplifications but also as actively coercive. The class-specific demands of homogeneity coerce by excluding as "marginal" any tendencies within the social body towards a radical heterogeneity – of which Yearsley's "singularity" might prove an instance. The appeal to a divine patriarch whose plenitude has resulted in a heterogeneity of "orbs" – both eyes and worlds, perspectives and social realities – is thus couched as an ironical affront to a homogeneous complacency ("How *dare* He create conflict rather than consensus!"). Then the appeal is personalized, with the emphasis falling once more on the lived – Lactilla's feelings are posed as a proper object for the scanning gaze of the complacent conformist who despises and fears singularity ("Only *look* and you will understand something of alterity!"). The rationale of this last appeal is presumably one of the premises from which "Lactilla" continues to write – a certain confidence in the persuasive sympathy to be generated by the fearless exposure of self-representations, however "singular," to a potentially alien gaze.

This is the limit of Yearsley's critique of ideology, homogeneity, and hierarchy. It does not translate explicitly into a republican politics, or even into an "organized" political position among the available movements of her day. Yet this limit, paradoxically, may also make Yearsley's texts peculiarly, politically readable. The politics of Yearsley's textuality, the play of signification within her texts, their contradictions and gaps, may seem mysteriously less circumscribed by history because she did not align herself with a specific political movement. And yet several poems in this second collection mount bold and complex attacks on particular social phenomena. Most effectively, Yearsley exposes the patriarchal bias perpetuated by certain readings of the Scriptures, and the prohibitions on women's and workers' appropriation of high literary culture. *On Jephthah's Vow, Taken In A Literal Sense* draws a startlingly literal connection between the patriarchalism of Old Testament texts and the oppressiveness of patriarchy, the rule of the fathers. *On Jephthah's Vow* makes a very precise move from the rule of the father *per se* to the sacrifice of the daughter, enabled by an expedient notion of God-the-Father as like the father, the sovereign subject of familial and social relations.

As in Judges 11, Jephthah bargains with his God in order to win a victory over Ammon. In Judges 11:31, he explicitly promises to sacrifice "whatsoever cometh forth of the doors of my house to meet me, when I return in peace," having triumphed over the Ammonites, but Yearsley leaves this unspoken. She assumes that we will know only too well that it is Jephthah's daughter who comes out "To meet him with timbrels and wild dances" (Judges 11:34) and that she is his only child. A certain Miltonic influence may be detected in the poem's opening lines, which are urgently interrogative – and remain unanswered because they treat of those finally unknowable quantities: the psychology of vows of sacrifice and the likelihood of a self-critical biblical hermeneutics:[72]

> WHAT sudden impulse rushes thro' the mind,
> And gives that momentary wild resolve
> Which seals the binding vow? Alas, poor man!
> Blind to a dark futurity, yet rash
> To mad extreme; why thus, with impious soul,
> Throw up to Heav'n the edict of thy will;
> Erase humility, and madly call
> Events thy own, which may be born in woe?
>
> Or what sad wretch dare lift th' accusing eye
> To an insulted Deity, when torn
> By dire effect, recoiling Nature feels
> Those horrors he with loud presumption claim'd?
>
> O, Jephthah! the soft bosom melts for thee.   (1–13)

Rather than attack the rule of the father/warrior, Yearsley sympathetically dramatizes his situation. Without directly answering the questions "Why make such a vow?" and "Who would dare blame God afterward for first putting such an idea into his head?" the poem makes Jephthah's case comprehensible in terms of the desire for victory over a hated enemy and the martial inspiration which religious zeal can provide: "Israel's hero feels / Fresh inspiration from his ill tim'd faith" (22–23). Throughout the text there is a tension between the enigmatic, potentially bloodthirsty Old Testament god – who must have authorized such blood to be shed in his name, both on the battlefield and at the altar – and Yearsley's projected deity who is too grand and unlike human patriarchs even to be comprehensible to them.

This tension opens a gap between Jephthah's faith in the divine justification for his daughter's murder, though he is horrified by it, and the possibility that no god could conceivably approve such an atrocity. Thus Jephthah and other men are acting on their own – against "Nature" and human compassion as

well as against reason. Like Blake, Yearsley puts in question from the
Christian point of view the patriarchal discourse of such biblical texts: how
could such a god be "ours"? Is Jephthah's story perhaps included because he
gets things wrong, dares to bargain with God and so suffers for it, in the flesh
of his daughter, if not in his own? If this were the "true" reading, then the Old
Testament would be a self-reflexive, self-critical text, portraying patriarchs
not as models of faith but as foolish and inhuman fathers, whose example we
are to repudiate, in spite of their victories and their unquestioning faith. This
would indeed be a radical recuperation of the Scriptures.

   And for the central portion of the poem, in which Jephthah and his
daughter confront one another on his return in triumph to Mizpeh, it seems
that we are to read the biblical story sympathetically in this way, attending to
the horror of the unforeseen consequences of Jephthah's foolish vow. Yearsley's narrative here reads almost cinematically, again perhaps informed by
Miltonic technique. The meeting of father and daughter seems to take place in
slow motion, sending a sequence of shocks through the whole affective
register of filial attachment, until the unthinkable is broached calmly and with
terrible resolution:

> He holds her from him; and with looks of woe,
> In which the pangs of Pity, Love, and Death,
> Alternately appear. He murmurs loud
> Against assiduous Duty; wildly asks,
> Why *She*, the first, to welcome Jephthah home?
>
>   Alas! the question freezes; these are sounds
> Stern and unusual to her list'ning ear,
> Which oft had hung on accents breath'd in love.
> She stands amaz'd: her sire, with sighs, exclaims,
> "Oh, thou hast brought me low! my soul desponds,
> For I have pledg'd thee to the Lord of Hosts,
> A victim to my conquest and ambition;
> Yes, thou must die: the registers of Heav'n
> Are ope'd, nor dare I trifle with my God."
>
>   The blush in haste forsook her lovely cheek
> At the too rigid sentence: yet resign'd
> To all a father ow'd, or Heav'n would ask,
> She meekly cry'd, "Thy will was ever mine.[73]
> An off'ring chearful on the altar laid,
> This frame shall soon consume; my soul to God
> Shall fly with speed; yet will I slowly rove
> O'er yon high mountain, till the moon hath spent
> Two portions of her light. Ye Virgins, come!
> Let soft notes the fatal vow deplore,

Without accusing Jephthah!" On she goes,
Leaving her father fix'd in speechless grief.   (61–86)

The text of Judges 11 leaves us to bemoan this pious virgin's fate but does not
explicitly tell us whether Jephthah is right to fulfill his part of the bargain so
unquestioningly – so meekly, yet so surely. The biblical chapter closes by
informing us that "it was a custom in Israel, *That* the daughters of Israel went
yearly to lament the daughter of Jephthah the Gileadite four days in a year"
(Judges 11:39–40). For fathers, daughters are dispensable; only the women of
the tribe continue to mourn them. In fact it is Jephthah's daughter's virginity,
her not knowing *man*, that causes the women of Israel to mourn. God
presumably approves the sacrifice.

   This is where Yearsley's rewriting of the biblical text diverges sharply from
the King James version. While the alter blazes, "bigots dare pronounce / The
sacrifice acceptable to Heaven" (92–93). The poet erupts in outrage, addresses
the biblical patriarchs – and by extension, her supposed Christian audience –
vehemently condemning the whole notion of bargaining with a god, and the
notion of a god who would accept such sacrifices as the Scriptures record –
infants and virgins:

>   Hence, dupes! nor make a Moloch of your God.
> Tear not your Infants from the tender breast,
> Nor throw your Virgins to consuming fires.
> He asks it not; and say, what boasting fool,
> To great Omnipotence a debt can owe?
> Or owing, can repay it? Would'st thou dare
> Barter upon equality! Oh, man!
> Thy notion of a Deity is poor,
> Contracted, curb'd, within a narrow space,
> Which must on finite rest. Hark! Jephthah groans!
> And 'tis the groan of horror. Virgins, sigh
> For the fair victim: vain the melting tear!
> She's gone, while Jewish records hold the vow
> To future ages, penn'd with cruel pride.   (94–107)

We must imagine for ourselves Jephthah's "horror," grief, and remorse, in
order to recognize and repudiate the nature of the savagery here being
recommended in the name of religious faith. Orthodox readings of the
Scriptures, but behind them the Old Testament writers themselves, are thus
precisely situated in Yearsley's poem as the producers of a tyrannical rule of
the fathers, which they insidiously justify by means of recourse to a deity at
least as bloodthirsty and tyrannical as they themselves are: an Absolute Subject
constituted by and dependent on their patriarchal subjectivity, and cast in the
image of their own desire.

Women and children are not the only victims of this reign of terror. The slaughter of the Ammonites, the prize for which Jephthah's daughter is exchanged, is so thorough as practically to constitute genocide. Yearsley does not dwell on this aspect of Old Testament savagery, merely representing it with a brief but shocking image of the cruelty of Jephthah's men in victory, who literally seek to "stamp out" the last vestiges of the Ammonites:

> . . . Jephthah returns
> With vict'ry nodding on his gaudy plume;
> While his exulting troops, with ruthless foot,
> Press out the soul, yet quiv'ring on the lip
> Of Ammon's sons, disfigur'd in the dust.   (32–36)

The structure of Yearsley's poem implies that war, in this case "holy war," has transformed Jephthah and generated new forms of violence, for war is a law unto itself. But the atrocity of Jephthah's sacrifice of his daughter – itself only one instance in a familial reign of terror – explains only too well why there are also war, genocide, and the legitimation of these through the concept of an absolutist God capable of condoning such practices.

In Yearsley's reading of the Scriptures, the cruel pride of the Old Testament fathers produces the records by which we justify our own cruelty, interpreting their words as an exculpation of our own tyrannical impulses. The concluding lines of *On Jephthah's Vow* ring ominously because both Yearsley's contemporaries and we are the "future ages" towards whom this legacy has been directed through centuries of orthodox, and cruelly patriarchal, interpretations. Yearsley's text is not an abstract philosophical polemic against patriarchy as a theory, but a powerful dramatization of the less-than-disinterested brutality of its praxis.

Interestingly, the preservation of sacred territory in an ideological rather than literal sense provides the occasion for one of Yearsley's most original and accomplished poems. *Addressed To Ignorance, Occasioned by a Gentlemen's desiring the Author never to assume a Knowledge of the Ancients* has recently been cited by Margaret Doody as a highly unusual instance of a woman's attempting a poetical charivari – as a social ritual, the "mixture of the celebratory and the violent, enacted by a crowd," and as a literary mode, "the daring dispersal of reality in favour of a crazed version of it."[74] As a literary mode, the charivari produces reversals, subversions, a turning upside-down and mixing up of ordinary social relations, fuelled by libidinous energy and often by specifically female sexual powers. As such, it was not a mode that women poets were encouraged to employ; Doody speculates, "perhaps their contemporaries uneasily felt that if a topic often representing the female powers and sexual unease were seriously invoked by a female, matters would get out of hand" (Doody, p. 130). Doody praises *To Ignorance* as a successfully subversive appropriation of charivari within the "Augustan" tradition of

Ovidian poetical metamorphoses, but concludes that this is "a rather melancholy achievement" in 1787, "as the nature of poetry and ideas of what poetry
should be were about to alter radically" (Doody, p. 131). They were about to
alter in ways that Yearsley herself elsewhere anticipated, as we have seen. If we
congratulate Yearsley primarily on having achieved in verse something called
Augustanism, then *To Ignorance* will be read as a less interesting and important
poem than it might otherwise reveal itself to be.

The premise of *To Ignorance* is Yearsley's having been forbidden to enter
the privileged precincts where classical subjects hold sway. "Assuming a
Knowledge of the Ancients" would signify, in a poor laboring woman, that
she was "getting above herself," "putting on airs." Yearsley counters by
proving that without recourse to a gentlemanly education she possesses "a
Knowledge of the Ancients" sufficient to inform a riotous panorama of
classical allusions. As Doody notes, the poem depends for its basic conceit on
an allusion to Pythagorean metempsychosis, a notion in which Yearsley
delights because of the opportunities it offers for the high and mighty to be
brought "low" as a milkwoman. There follows an almost hallucinatory
pageant of classical figures reborn among the English masses:

> But Zeno, Tibellus, and Socrates grave,
>   In the bodies of wan Garreteers,
> All tatter'd, cold, hungry, by turns sigh and rave
>   At their Publisher's bill of arrears.
>
>   . . .
>
> There's Virgil, the Courtier, with hose out at heel,
>   And Hesiod, quite shoeless his foot;
> Poor Ovid walks shiv'ring, behind a cart-wheel,
>   While Horace cries, "sweep for your soot."
>
> Fair Julia sees Ovid, but passes him near,
>   An old broom o'er her shoulder is thrown;
> Penelope lends to five lovers an ear,
>   Walking on with one sleeve to her gown.
>
> But Helen, the Spartan, stands near Charing-Cross,
>   Long laces and pins doom'd to cry;
> Democritus, Solon, bear baskets of moss,
>   While Pliny sells woodcocks hard by.   (29–52)

The most radical suggestion made by Yearsley's comic appropriation of the
ancients in this way is surely that the subject-matter of the texts of antiquity
cannot be sealed off as an inviolable upper-class preserve. Institutionally, a
classical education was to remain the sign of a well-born and -bred man for
some generations after Yearsley's. But the gradual increase of mass reproduc-

tion of texts and images, and the marketing of cheap editions of books and prints for mass consumption, combined with the commercialization of leisure, had definite effects on the social dissemination of "the classics."[75] We should remember the earliest source of Yearsley's own classical material, so energetically and subversively disported here: too poor to buy books, she took her classical allusions from "little ordinary prints that hung in a shop window." "Little" and "ordinary" – these are commodities designed not for the rich and well-born, but for the industrious common people desirous of "improvement." The ancients cannot be forbidden to the plebeian poet because they are indeed being "reborn" on mass scale, in the form of mass-produced images of themselves.

To Ignorance is more than a feminized reworking of Augustan tropes in another respect as well. Modern history enters the poem in the figure of Voltaire, followed by a move from his secular skepticism to popular violence and political assassination. Yearsley's interest in English peasant uprisings, which looms largest in her play *Earl Goodwin*, is figured here when Wat Tyler, leader of the peasants' revolt of 1381, reappears in Margaret Nicholson, the housemaid who tried to stab George III with a dessert knife during a royal procession in 1787:

> Wat Tyler, in Nicholson, dares a King's life,
>   At St. James's the blow was design'd;
> But Jove lean'd from heaven, and wrested the knife,
> Then in haste lash'd the wings of the wind.   (65–68)

These enigmatic lines are difficult to assess, but the ambiguity of Tyler/ Nicholson's blow being "design'd" "At St. James's," recording both the scene of violence and its object, suggests a possible political register: a blow aimed at St. James's, at the court and the monarch as embodiment of the institution of monarchy. This ambiguity gives way to a most peculiar image of flogging and confinement produced by the ambiguity of "lash'd." What sort of wind has wings? Are we to think of Jove's eagle urged to make a quick getaway after the providential *deus ex machina* that has saved the king's life? Or is Jove binding a "winged wind" – the phoenix of republican liberty? – that would otherwise spread through the land? Yearsley's syntax is too evasive for us to be confident of her referents, but such evasiveness and the retreat into obscure metaphor may themselves be signs of a desire to say something that requires heavy coding, something subject to censorship. Perhaps something to do with popular disaffection recurring through English history, the first time as tragedy, the second time as farce? When turning the world upside-down means taking a dagger, or even a dessert knife, to the king, then charivari has been revealed as having a political, not only a poetical, function.

The next and last stanza helps support this hypothesis, for in it Yearsley "defies" her historical circumstances and low birth, "Allowing herself," as

Doody claims, "a mock-slangy familiarity with the ancients" while also making "a declaration of human equality" (Doody, pp. 130–31):

> Here's Trojan, Athenian, Greek, Frenchman and I,
>   Heav'n knows what I was long ago;
> No matter, thus shielded, this age I defy,
>   And the next cannot wound me, I know.   (69–72)

Margaret Nicholson dared to assault a king because she apparently believed that she was as "royal" as anyone – an almost neo-Pythagorean fantasy of the high-born mistaken for or trapped within the low, as well as a convention of romantic narrative.[76] It would seem that, however carefully coded that image of "lash'd wings" may be as a sign of rebellious aspirations punished or bound, Yearsley is coming close to declaring herself a leveller, a proponent of liberty and equality. This is neither an Augustan theme nor simply a topos from the wild fantasia of charivari. In the course of her witty reclamation of classical allusions, Yearsley also manages to construct a reading of modern history incompletely articulated but suggestive of potentially republican–revolutionary sympathies.

For all her social antagonisms and "struggling spirit," we find Yearsley in this volume also trying to please her audience, and to convey a sense of graceful resignation to her social location akin to Mary Collier's. As J. M. S. Tompkins remarks, it was this will to remain, "however rebelliously, within the 'pale of order'" that brought Yearsley "admonition" but not "rejection" from Richard Polwhele in *The Unsex'd Females* (1798). Because Yearsley was not a thorough follower of Mary Wollstonecraft's "female Libertinism," in which the political advocacy of egalitarian liberty becomes inseparable from sexual license, Polwhele hoped that she could be redeemed.[77]

As a declaration of independence from her discoverer and a vindication of her talents, however, *Poems, on Various Subjects* takes the business of writing seriously. In this volume Yearsley pursues the pleasures of the text with a vengeance, inscribing both her desire for revenge on More and the polite world and her own aspirations towards the freedom to write as she likes. Her most interesting poems in this second collection risk being bold formally as well as argumentatively. But Yearsley is about to go further, towards more pointed political commentary, and will suffer for it. She will also attempt to make a virtue of domesticity, and, in so doing, transform available definitions of the "political" in protofeminist ways.

Domesticating the political and the politics of domesticity

The final phase of Yearsley's career is initiated by a furious burst of litigation and published controversy in which her near-establishment as Bristol's unofficial civic poet – in the wake of her anti-slavery poem[78] and her play linking the heroism of English peasant rebellion, and the sacrifice of a noble woman, with the French revolution – is countermanded through a series of domestic misadventures with a definite class fix. In 1789 during the hay harvest, Yearsley's three sons were horsewhipped by the footman of Levi Eames, the mayor of Bristol, two for playing in the mayor's fields, one for "expostulating" with the footman "in a childish manner." Yearsley pressed charges against the footman but was advised by her lawyer to drop the case, because he justly supposed "her purse not to be *quite* so heavy as Mr. Eames's."[79] One might well think of Godwin's *Caleb Williams*, particularly the following passage:

Hawkins had hitherto carefully avoided, notwithstanding the injuries he had suffered, the attempting to right himself by legal process, being of opinion that law was better adapted for a weapon of tyranny in the hands of the rich, than for a shield to protect the humbler part of the community against their usurpations. In this last instance however he conceived that the offence was so atrocious as to make it impossible that any rank could protect the culprit against the severity of justice. In the sequel he saw reason to applaud himself for his former inactivity in this respect, and to repent that any motive had been strong enough to persuade him into a contrary system.[80]

The following June, as Yearsley was sitting outside her cottage, Eames's groom chased some children, who were not hers, from the by then former mayor's fields. When the children escaped, he turned on Yearsley so violently that she miscarried later that evening. *Stanzas of Woe*, dedicated ironically to Eames, was her only form of protest. But its publication caused her to lose her commission for an ode on the Magdalen Hospital, a misfortune which she attempted to rectify by publishing *The Dispute. Letter to the Public From The Milkwoman*.[81] Moira Ferguson has described Yearsley's public dispute with Eames and his supporters as evidence of Yearsley's radical potential expressed in a class-conscious confrontational politics.[82] Yet these incidents seem to me to represent at best a problematical instance of a lower-class woman with limited resources idealistically attempting to use the legal system and her pen to her advantage, perhaps naively believing that the law would indeed guarantee her rights and grant her justice, another of those illusory freedoms promised by bourgeois ideology and as sacred to the rhetoric of the Glorious Revolution of 1688 as its counterparts "liberty" and "property" – but not, we notice, "equality."

In *Whigs and Hunters*, E. P. Thompson makes some important distinctions between the law as an instrument of class power and the rule of law, to which the ruling class must also conform, thus curbing potentially worse abuses.[83] Yearsley's going to law and publishing her experiences of judicial injustice do represent a lower-class woman's attempt to use her literacy and her know-ledge of the law to resist class domination. To claim that Yearsley ought to have sought retribution by any other means would be historically unsound, according to Thompson. For the law itself was an arena of conflict in the eighteenth century, and not wholly a form of mystification masking class tyranny. The rule of law offers even the poor greater opportunities for liberty and equality than the rule of force. All this Yearsley clearly understood.

Nevertheless, her manner of going to law does not so much suggest a testing of the system on behalf of laboring people like herself as an untheo-rized personal claim. She represents herself not as a milkwoman who is forbidden to pursue justice through the courts because her purse is lighter than her antagonists, but as the milkwoman – the exception to the rule, because of her literary reputation. The circumstances of her second encounter with one of the former mayor of Bristol's servants are truly horrific. When the children the groom is chasing elude him,

his fury immediately turned upon the Author; he treated her in a vulgar opprobrious manner. On her enquiring, and being informed that he was servant to Mr. Eames she withdrew, but being in a state that claims gentler treatment, the shock was too violent: her life was preserved, her Infant expired the same night.[84]

She composed *Stanzas of Woe* from her sickbed, mourning her dead child thus:

> Go to the cheated tygress of the plains,
>   Robb'd of her young she'd scare thy coward soul;
> Maternal agony high in her veins!
>   What pow'r of thine would her fierce wrath controul?
>
> Insolent Tyrant! humble as we are,
>   Our minds are rich with honest truth as thine;
> Bring on thy sons, their value we'll compare,
>   Then – lay thy infant in the grave with mine.   (33–40)

Ferguson is right to say that Yearsley refused to allow herself to be abused as a poor milkwoman, and thus struck a blow against class tyranny. But she also left herself open to charges of melodramatic publicity-seeking through the sensational, heart-rending, entirely personal focus of her public appeal. The problematical nature of women's unfeignedly speaking out "as themselves," as the authentic voice of injured womanhood, is more pronounced in this case than in Collier's, partly because Collier's rational appeal to the empirical evidence of women's work countermands any suggestion of special pleading. Yearsley's anguished poetical demand that Levi Eames lay his infant in the grave with hers is almost too affective. We lose sight of the magistrate in the man. And we lose sight of the political subject whose rights have been so severely violated and then curtailed in the rhetorical flood of uncurbed, unmoderated rage published by this bedridden mother.

It is almost as if Yearsley could not believe that this injustice had happened to her. How dare these civic fathers so abuse Bristol's native genius? Yearsley has leapt ahead of herself in her imaginary emancipatory program, expecting to gain bourgeois freedoms through the still frequently illusory, though not wholly sham, promise of justice under the law that Thompson calls, despite its uses as an instrument of imperialism, "a cultural achievement of universal significance," and "an unqualified human good."[85]

Such sorrow and anger notwithstanding, for the next six years Yearsley attempts to write against the growing tide of reaction that marks the 1790s in England. She expands her subject-matter on several fronts at once, exploring current events abroad, particularly in France, and writing for the first time explicitly about both domestic politics, as in the *Bristol Elegy*, and the politics of domesticity, as in *To Mira, On The Care Of Her Infant*. The allusion to Wat Tyler and Margaret Nicholson in *To Ignorance* will be adumbrated in such poems as "Elegy Sacred To The Memory Of Lord William Russel" and *Prayer and Resignation*. There is much internal evidence in the poems of *The Rural Lyre* to support Tompkins's theory that not only "domestic troubles" but Yearsley's identification with "liberal sentiments" brought her career to a premature halt in 1796, because she "could no longer, in this time of growing reaction, expect a fair hearing."[86]

Nevertheless, Yearsley's is a far from programmatic response to current events. Although *Earl Goodwin*, written in 1789,[87] allusively applauds the early stages of the French revolution as an expression of the will of an oppressed peasantry championed by well-born and educated leaders sympathetic to their plight, the executions of Louis XVI and Marie Antoinette prompt her most direct commentary. As in *A Poem On The Inhumanity Of The Slave-Trade*, there is a certain identification of her domestic sympathies with those she imagines for her fellow victims of history, tyranny, and violence. And at moments Yearsley attempts a sublation of the political into the aestheticized body of nature – not as in her cathected relation to the landscape in her earlier work, but as a substitution for political yearnings gone awry or eternally deferred. In her most Coleridgean moment, Yearsley simultaneously praises the literal inspiration of the breeze and its analogous properties to human feelings of liberty and strength:

> Yet gentle ★Air, unseen and ever felt,
>   To Thee again my invocations rise,
> Ah, let me not in burning fevers melt!
>   But bear at least my spirit thro' the skies.

> ★This Poem was begun the first morn of the Physician's allowing the air to play through the Author's window.   (*Stanzas of Woe*, 101–04)

When we come to her two poems on Louis XVI's execution, written within three weeks of the event, it would seem that liberty resides only in idea and is symbolized in natural forces:

> Ask, ye! where joyous Liberty resorts,
>   In *France*, in *Spain*, or in *Britannia*'s Vale?
> O no! – She only with poor Fancy sports
>   Her richest Dwelling is the passing Gale.
> ("Reflections on the Death of Louis XVI," 25–28)[88]

However much in sympathy she might have been with the earlier moments of revolutionary fervor, she has no taste for royal martyrdom; it suggests entirely too much affinity between this supposedly popular rule and the old absolutist tyranny. For her the execution of Louis represents only another instance of needless bloodshed and the shattering of familial affections.

The same appeals Yearsley offers on behalf of African and native Caribbean families torn apart by the slave trade she uses here to criticize the wrong-headed pursuit of liberty by means of violence and war. We are asked to pity Louis's son and daughter, and the poet asks specially for some "unseen" healing and inspirational "Pow'rs" "To whisper Comfort to his mourning Queen" ("Sequel," 1–24, 50–56). The false pursuit of liberty that ends in tyranny is destructive to the popular "Warriors" as well, who both kill and themselves die as the victims "to fallacious Charms" ("Reflections," 23–24).

When we come to the death of Marie Antoinette in October of the same year, Yearsley's identification with wronged nobility in the image of a devoted wife and mother becomes most obvious. It is not Marie Antoinette's royal status but her vulnerable femininity that Yearsley wishes to champion. We are assured that the queen will triumph over her enemies in some future time when her "Truth" will burst forth, oddly like the phoenix of republican liberty, and its flames will devour everything except the record of that truth: "her spotless Line."[89] As it is, her death represents an horrific rupture in history. One is tempted to conclude that Yearsley has conflated her own recent public victimization as a wife and mother with the French queen's. At the very least, as a figure whose femininity makes her a peculiarly horrifying, or satisfying, spectacle of public execution, depending upon one's political point of view, the queen represents a vexed instance of gender politics playing with and against national politics. Disgusted at the brutality of the execution, Yearsley reads the queen's beauty and helplessness as goodness and innocence:

> O'er her pale Beauties, Hist'ry stands amaz'd,
>   The Pencil trembles as she draws her Lines,
> While MARIE, on whom Crowds with Pleasure gaz'd,
>   On the cold Bosom of her Lord reclines.   (53–56)

The very fact that Marie Antoinette was once an object of pleasurable viewing by the populace, a spectacle of beauty, a sight, makes her murder the more terrible; indeed nearly incapable of historical or poetical representation.

But the focus on French royalty as, first and foremost, a shattered family and not an instrument of monarchical power does not fully encompass Yearsley's response to these events. If the first poem on Louis XVI's death, the "Reflections," ends with a plea for Louis's spirit to forgive his murderers, that they may spare the royal children, the "Sequel" goes further towards envisaging a renewal of France's pursuit of "true" liberty through peace, virtue, and social order. The saving remnant of right-thinking, liberty-desiring Frenchmen, "the brave few of *Gallia*'s moral Sons," must be brought to realize — through a combination of those "Pow'rs" that exceed rational knowledge and the poet's mediation — "That yet some white-wing'd Hour remains behind": again we are given the image of liberty as winged, apocalyptic (59–60). This eventual restoration of true liberty will repair the violent rending of history and the social fabric that murder and martyrdom bring about. That "white-wing'd Hour" will be a moment:

> When Peace and Virtue, thro' the vernal Shade,
>   Shall lead their radiant Images along,
> ORDER fill up the Gulf by Murder made,
>   And martyr'd LOUIS, hear the sacred Song:
>
> That Song, which Virtue and bright Truth inspire
>   The Sons of social Love, shall oft relate;
> While Shades of Pity sweeping o'er the Lyre
> Shall touch the Mem'ry with a Monarch's Fate.   (61–68)

In such a post- but not counter-revolutionary future even the memory of violent martyrdom may be put to use in heroic and tragic songs, the epics of a benighted era. Poets will be undoubtedly crucial in this new reign of "social Love," by the re-use of which term in this new context we would seem to have come a long way with Yearsley from the ideal of disinterestedness first represented by Hannah More's patronage.

Perhaps this second poem on Louis XVI holds a key to understanding the framing of *The Rural Lyre* three years later, in which Yearsley projects herself as an image of "British Liberty" both in the frontispiece and in several poems, most notably her *Brutus. A Fragment*, so strongly reminiscent of Pope's unfinished epic on the same theme that it seems likely she knew of that project from Ruffhead's *Life of Pope*. This volume, her first without an "occasional" or topical title, may have been meant to mark her emergence as a political poet in the bardic sense: the singer of tragic pasts and emancipatory futures whose lyre can both accompany historical struggle and "touch the Mem'ry" with narratives of the fallen. Yearsley would seem to be working towards making herself a poet of moments that are particularly difficult of historical representation, those moments in which occur those unnatural shocks given to history by violent upheavals of the body politic, when "Hist'ry stands amaz'd."

And, as I have suggested, her method of entry into these difficult scenes will be by way of the domestic relations that may seem to have been relegated to the "private sphere" by the sexual division of labor, but so often make themselves visible from a woman's point of view as intrinsic to the workings of the "public" sphere as well – as indeed inseparable from it. "For if the fabric of the so-called public sector is woven of the so-called private, the definition of the private is marked by a public potential, since it *is* the weave, or texture, of public activity. The opposition is thus not merely reversed; it is displaced."[90] Working from the radical republican commonplace that the public order has domestic roots, and that conversely the family may be dangerously disrupted by false public values, Yearsley specifies women's possible contributions to a politics that would transform both domestic and public life by collapsing the distinction between them in the interests of greater democracy and participation.

Yearsley's poetry in this final phase of her career thus simultaneously attempts to domesticate the political by "bringing it home" and to generate, in a more visionary, utopian, and incompletely articulated sense, a radical democratic politics in which domestic relations, hitherto marginal, are at the center. The "politics of domesticity" that I pose here is not entirely symmetrical with that described by Nancy Armstrong in her recent work on the novel, though they are related. I am not arguing, as some feminists do, that women's power within the family and within literary culture in itself constitutes a radical challenge to state power and the dominant culture, nor that female desire represents a hitherto repressed force merely awaiting liberation; on the contrary, as Armstrong, following Foucault, demonstrates, such a separation of spheres according to sexual difference is characteristic of bourgeois culture with its discursively productive eliciting and regulation of desire. However, Yearsley's texts give us, if incompletely, certain intimations of a more radical alternative than the romance of domestic fiction or the figure of the domestic woman. The reconstitution of the subject in opposition to British anti-Jacobinism and imperialism, if its implications were to be worked through, would radically transform political culture, not merely provide its domestic complement or some liberal "feminization" or "humanization" of the modern bourgeois state.[91]

In this respect, Yearsley might be said to anticipate Owenism. Of the available political languages that succeeded the dispersal of radicalism, Owenism comes closest to articulating Yearsley's political vision. As Edward Royle and James Walvin argue:

The most explicit theoretical acceptance of women in a reform movement . . . came with the Owenites, who totally rejected the conventional attitude towards the role and status of women in society. Some indeed, following Owen, rejected conventional marriage itself. Like many utopian thinkers, Owen saw the family as the bastion of conservatism and a socially disuniting hindrance to the coming of his new moral world. The irony is that, in practice, Owenism appealed to women by strengthening the family. The social life at the Halls of Science was designed to attract women, catering for all the family and offering women complete equality with men in the organisation and running of local branch life.[92]

Gareth Stedman Jones remarks upon the inclusion and participation of women within Owenism as connected with the movement's most far-reaching political implications and its anticipation of socialism, its advocacy of "natural and universal equality, human perfectibility, the malleability of social and political institutions," and its rhetoric directed "unambiguously to the future rather than the past":

In place of the wrongs of the 'free born Englishman', in place of a limited vocabulary appropriate to the redress of particular grievances, Owen offered his adherents a universal and historically unencumbered language in which to express their demands and aspirations. It was the form in which the popular movement inherited the rationalist and scientist strand of enlightenment thinking.[93]

The fullest treatment of connections between Owenism, 1790s radicalism, and feminism after Mary Wollstonecraft is provided by Barbara Taylor, who argues for the centrality of radical reconceptions of gender relations and sexual politics for this social movement:

The link between women's emancipation and a general social emancipation which had begun to be forged in the era of democratic revolution now took on a new shape, as a concrete strategy for the creation of a 'Social System' which had the liberation of women as one of its central objects.[94]

Yearsley's texts do not achieve a full articulation of this visionary politics. *The Rural Lyre*, far from being either a seamlessly Jacobin or proto-Owenite manifesto, is fraught with contradictory tendencies to which we would do well to attend.

   Not the least of these contradictions is Yearsley's partial move away from a vocabulary of active class resistance at the very moment when she is striving to articulate a most urgent need for social transformation. This refusal of a class vocabulary for articulating grievances is also characteristic of the discourse of Owenism, which strives to provide an all-encompassing language for advocating total ideological as well as political transformation. As incorporated into the labor movements of the later nineteenth century, however, Owenism becomes articulable with a class-conscious politics.[95]

And coupled with this partial effacement of class activism is a focus on the representation of women that positions Yearsley as closely as she ever comes in her *œuvre* to a bourgeois politics of domesticity in Armstrong's sense, in which women's power to influence public morality from their hearths and nurseries is celebrated, and women's cultural power within literary production is both trivialized and presented as a satisfactory substitute for direct political participation. Such a domestication of the political requires that Yearsley put a victimized woman's body at the center of her poems; this is the trope that links works as various as *Earl Goodwin, Stanzas of Woe*, "An Elegy on Marie Antoinette," *To Mira, On The Care Of Her Infant*, and the *Bristol Elegy*.

Literally representing the figure of woman as embodying politics, women's bodies as sites of political intervention, Yearsley is figured in her last and most radical volume of verse under the sign of British liberty. It is hard not to see in the frontispiece to *The Rural Lyre* a representation of Yearsley herself as both "The British Muse" and *British Liberty*. Since the engraving was executed under the tutelage of A. Scott by her son, William, for whose apprenticeship 100 guineas had been raised, who was named after her beloved brother who taught her to write, and who seems to have been the child most attuned to her cultural interests, the frontispiece was undoubtedly meaningful and important to Yearsley. Tompkins finds the figure of *British Liberty*, mediating between the British nation and its God, reminiscent of Mrs. Siddons,[96] but there is a certain resemblance as well to the other portraits we have of Yearsley. The legend reads: " 'Eternal Jove,' she cried, 'be these thy care.' " Looking rather victimized, British Liberty mediates between Jove and the Britons, delivering them into his care, while attempting to memorialize the heroic exploits of Brutus, the grandson of Aeneas and the legendary founder of Britain. Her right breast is bared, her neoclassical gown is fashionably draped, and her hair is fashionably curled in long locks, but her features are sorrowfully imploring. If we are to read the female poet in the frontispiece, we must read there that the cost of such divinely sanctioned mediation between the ideal of national liberty and the British public is great.

This strenuous notion of the poet's function accounts for the unfinished state of Yearsley's epic on Brutus, which, like Pope's, tries to treat the present and future in terms of an heroic (and prophetic) past, but cannot sustain the work of historical analogy at epic length. Like Pope, Yearsley incorporates material from New World travelers' narratives to characterize the native Britons discovered by Brutus. The colonial encounters fuelling eighteenth-century British imperialism and commerce become representable through historical displacement onto the island of Great Britain itself. The funda-

vide Brutus

Wᵐ Cromartie Yearsley delinᵗ!

A. Smith Sculpᵗ!

"Eternal Jove," she cried, "be these thy care."

mental ideological problematic of imperialism – that the conquest, frequent slaughtering, and enslavement of cultural others are performed in the name of global enlightenment and progress – is displaced in favor of the simultaneous celebration of "native" British liberty and noble savagery: if the Britons were once savages, they were nevertheless possessors of native liberty, so not in need of colonial reformation like other savages. As the goddess Liberty says to Brutus: "my Britons are not slaves: / There lives no conqueror but the man who saves. / Untaught, unpolish'd is the savage mind, / Yet firm in friendship, to affliction kind" (319–22). Like the poems on the deaths of Louis XVI and Marie Antoinette, *Brutus* argues for true liberty as only possible in the absence of civil war; Liberty herself intones: "Let him my blessings never hope to know, / Who sternly bids a brother's blood to flow!" (179–80). Peace at home and war abroad: this is the traditional post-Elizabethan compromise, with the difference that for Yearsley, as for Pope, to establish liberty versus civil war as the primary political problematic requires displacing contemporary European and colonial wars by means of imaginary history, imperial fiction.

Pope's *Brutus* exists mainly as sketches and notes, with an opening six lines of, significantly, blank verse its only finished portion. As a fragment, it invites completion by another hand. Yearsley's *Brutus. A Fragment* is 523 lines long, prefaced by an "Argument" describing the poem's fragmentary status explicitly as an inspiration to future poets to complete this native British epic: "The Author offers this humble specimen as a spark, from whence she wishes a body of fire may arise in the imagination of some more able Poet." Abandoning the original heroic mood for an erotic pastoral closure that is not a closure, but rather an invitation to a new beginning, Yearsley turns from arms to eros through the passionate romance between Brutus and Hermia, an "untutor'd" woodland woman, also of Trojan stock (470). Evident in Yearsley's *Brutus*, then, is an aborted experiment in mode as well as genre.

Indeed one of the curiosities of *The Rural Lyre* is the way in which many of the poems that comprise it reintroduce erotic discourse into Yearsley's *œuvre*, a discourse previously highly and variously mediated, as we have seen, or else conventionally represented in short lyrics that are among Yearsley's least interesting poems, and that I have chosen thus far to ignore. *Brutus* ends abruptly after the tryst and union between the Trojan hero and his beloved in their death, but even that is cast as an eternal erotic conjunction: Brutus "Slept with his Hermia in the grassy tomb" (506). And in a series of epistles written in imitation of the "simplicity of the ancients,"[97] both the male dependence on and discarding of women, and women's shrewd strategies of self-protection, are somewhat tersely investigated. The Consul C. Fannius, for example, expresses both his erotic longing for Nisa and the foolish indulgence and injustice of his adulterous liaison with her; warned off by Fulvia, a wise countrywoman, he breaks free of his attachment, gives his fields to Nisa's husband, and hopes that his example will prove useful to the younger Fannius

Didius. It is as if the typical heterosexual erotic mode and the subject-matter of romantic intrigue were usually inaccessible to Yearsley except through historically distanced narratives, as in *Brutus*, excessive cultural mediation – as in, most pointedly, these Roman epistles – or bleak satire, as in the unhappy marriage and triangle of *Lucy, A Tale For The Ladies*, which teaches a "Hard lesson": "For marriage-rights are very few" (57–58).[98]

Taken all together, the poems of *The Rural Lyre* represent experiments in subject-matter as well as style, and a general improvement in Yearsley's poetical accomplishments as well as a radicalization of her politics.[99] Tompkins is right to praise this collection as presenting "clear evidence of an advance in style and verse as well as substance," but we need not agree with her that Yearsley's use in *The Rural Lyre* of blank verse and the highly formalized couplet "proves also that in these forms she could never overtake her lack of training,"[100] a judgment that implies disabling – and uninteresting – failure on Yearsley's part and suggests that her silence after 1796 might have been poetically justified. Rather, the increasingly uniform accomplishment of Yearsley's verse in this period, coupled with her use of new and provocative materials, ought to make us regret that she appears to have published nothing after *The Rural Lyre*.

Even such a slight poem as "The Indifferent Shepherdess to Colin" possesses some unexpected turns, while perpetuating the genre of the female lyric refusal of love well established by the end of the century, epitomized by a number of Lady Mary Wortley Montagu's "Songs," and well-represented in Elizabeth Hands's corpus. This indifferent shepherdess does not play with or torment her swain by feigning indifference, or by preferring another man. Yearsley's shepherdess is a politically conscious single woman jealous of her "liberty." Here the code of friendship between equals, so longed for since those early poems of Yearsley's first volume, supplants erotic intrigue altogether. This shepherdess is a separatist of sorts, for only by maintaining her distance from amorous men can she maintain her liberty, and hence her right to "tune" the rural lyre:

> For my eternal plan
>   Is to be calm and free.
> Estrang'd from tyrant man
>   I'll keep my liberty.   (29–32)

Increasingly, the networks of power within erotic and domestic relations come into focus in Yearsley's work.

Even where the erotic mode is dominated by political concerns, a certain feminization of traditionally masculine topoi, present in *Clifton Hill*, becomes the distinguishing feature of these last poems; as we have seen, the presence of a victimized woman's body at the center marks many of Yearsley's texts of the 1790s. The *Bristol Elegy* represents a look at domestic politics in another way as well: it is Yearsley's most direct comment on a local event — popular direct action against the reinstitution of the Bristol bridge tolls in 1793, followed by military repression. According to Yearsley, about twenty people were killed and forty wounded for taking down the gates and the toll-board. Two stanzas past the poem's medial point, the carnage of officially instigated reprisal is emblematized by the body of a pregnant young woman stabbed by a soldier with a bayonet and thrown into the river:

> — What fearful scream
> Troubles the air? — Must gentle *woman die?
> Ah! plunge her not beneath the restless stream:
> Behold, assassins! her imploring eye!
>
> Gaze full on its mild beams, and ye shall feel
> Softer emotions than the sword inspires;
> Compassion, love, and sympathy would heal
> Your spirits raging with destructive fire.   (65–72)

*A young woman, within a short time of becoming a mother, found stabbed with a bayonet in the river; supposed to have been thrown in by the soldiery, who opposed the removal of the bodies, some of which drifted down to King's Road.

Presumably the soldiers could have met her imploring look and been melted by it, but they did not or were not. The civic officials who ordered in the troops, however, are meant to read this description and feel ashamed. Yearsley does not push the connection between the toll itself and the armed repression needed to enforce it, nor between the "compassion, love, and sympathy" that would show mercy to the protesters and the magnanimity that would refuse to reintroduce the toll when confronted by popular protest. But her publication of the *Elegy* with an "Advertisement," in which she expresses hope that, like other Bristol poets who have written on "civic" themes, she will be rewarded by the city for this poem, suggests the use of deadpan irony and a deliberate refusal to make the obvious political connections, but to persuade us to make them, throughout. Rubenstein accuses Yearsley of sentimentality here,[101] but I think that such seemingly gratuitous effects as the pregnant woman's corpse are being employed to strengthen a particular argument.

This murdered mother-to-be at once contradicts received images of popular rebels and embodies a new ideal of pacifism. In Yearsley's poem, we are a long way from the counter-revolutionary notion of uprisings induced by incendiary mechanics and male outlaws — disorderly, dissolute, and overwhelmingly terrifying. Instead, the *Bristol Elegy* argues, this legitimate expression of the popular will, supported by respectable citizens of the poorer classes, deserved a fair hearing, not automatic slaughter. This strategy represents another variation on the technique of dramatizing social relations as, above all, familial relations: because she is carrying a child, this woman is not only made excessively vulnerable to the soldier's weapon, but she is prevented from performing a social duty; her murder doubly outrages. Only a doctrine of peaceful social cooperation can assure that human life will not be so recklessly squandered again and again: "Through Peace alone the source of human Joy" (106). The self-effacing heroes of this poem thus emerge as "the respectable body of Quakers, who offered to liquidate any arrears that the bridge-commissioners might demand, to the amount of two thousand pounds." Yearsley tells us this in a note to line 105, which concludes, chillingly, "This offer was refused before the several murders were committed, and accepted afterwards." What a waste of life could, then, have been avoided if the Quakers' peace-making gesture had been initially welcomed by the civic officials.

We should recognize the extent to which Yearsley is endorsing not so much the ethics of popular protest, but rather the conciliatory generosity of the industrious, prosperous – and above all, "respectable" – Quakers (a far cry from the radical Quakers of the 1650s). It would seem that Yearsley's representation of social movements has shifted from a focus on class consciousness, to the extent that such a focus can be discerned in such textual moments as the critique of "optics false" and the allusions to Tyler and Nicholson, and has been refocused on violence and bloodshed in the service of power. As the Genius of England, sounding very much like Yearsley in her guise as "British Liberty," insists elsewhere in *The Rural Lyre*:

The union I commend, is LIBERTY.[102]

Lest between her moving elegies on Louis XVI and Marie Antoinette and this plea for social order – indeed, for peace at all costs – we begin to suspect that Yearsley has crossed over into timorous reaction because of unforeseen developments in France, we should consider her most straightforwardly Whiggish poem, the "Elegy Sacred To The Memory Of Lord William Russel." For this text presents traditional Whiggish liberty both humbled to peasant status and modernized through an effect of historical palimpsest – the contemporary peasant and the aristocratic rebel merge, in solidarity. An advocate of Protestantism and lawful resistance, Russell supported the Exclusion Bill blocking James's accession and was executed in 1683 for his alleged part in the "Rye-house plot" to murder Charles II.[103] In Yearsley's poem, Charles II is frankly condemned for capitulating to French interests in a continuous trance of voluptuous enervation; Yearsley's argument is not that Charles should have been militarily aggressive, but that he should have heeded his subjects and not pledged "fair Albion" to a "Gallic lord" (35). Russell, the young aristocratic rebel of the previous century, who dared defend Protestant liberty against popish absolutism, is recuperated as a model for contemporary peasant disaffection:

Believe me, Russel, when thy tale is told
Beside the peasant's hearth, his children weep:
His fire neglected dies; their blood runs cold;
To their low pallets they in silence creep.

No clamour of the state, no party broil,
Inflames the pensive wand'rer of the vale:
He with his ox by day pursues his toil,
At night sits list'ning to the tragic tale.

Patiently spelling Hist'ry's length'ning page,
Virtues recorded youthful swains inspire –
They feel as Russel did: more softened Age
Drops the mild tear o'er thy distracted sire.

"I had a son," the hoary shepherd cries:
"He lives no more! – my labour's nearly done! – "
By Hist'ry taught, he wipes his tearful eyes;
There Bedford's shade is heard – "I had a son!"

Russel, thy tablet holds him: there I see
The venerable statesman sunk in woe;
With eyes uplifted, on his bended knee,
"One life (he cries), one life, my king bestow!   (49–68)

Yearsley's class perspective gives us a scene quite different from Gray's humble hearths of the poor in his *Elegy*, from which Gray's poor have been banished, of course, since they are dead:

For them no more the blazing hearth shall burn,
Or busy housewife ply her evening care:
No children run to lisp their sire's return,
Or climb his knees the envied kiss to share.   (21–24)

In Yearsley's peasant household, people read – not tracts or homiletic verse, but "Hist'ry"; and not history as in the glorious chronicles of royal dynasticism, but the history of English insurgency. That it is in this case the history of a Protestant martyr is significant; Yearsley's anti-Catholicism is as plain as Hannah More's, though it is less militant. And generational division determines the peasant's reception of historical narrative as surely as it does the actions of the characters represented "as" history. The young feel Russell's rebelliousness, the older people feel for Russell's father, the Earl of Bedford. This moment in the text represents a thematic turn that is also a modal shift.

If there was intertextuality, in the loose sense, working in the resemblance to Gray's *Elegy*, there is prescience in Yearsley's anticipation of Wordsworth's *Michael* here in the shepherd's cry that he has lost his only son. Formal differences pale beside the shift in perspective, brought about in Burns and

Clare as well as Yearsley, that makes the representation of peasant subjects possible, and not merely the representation of peasants as objects of a sympathetic, but "other," gaze. From mournful landscape pastoral, newly politicized as a site of the continuous historical memory of disaffection and rebellion, to the "new" pastoral of peasant subjectivity, Yearsley's poem is strongly transitional. But what marks it as distinctively of its time is the radical edge to that memory of the English revolution as "all about liberty" – and to be regretted only in so far as too much blood was shed. Yearsley's shepherd has lost his son within a context which admits of history, struggle, and state reprisal; we may be moved to speculate that there is more to the resemblance between the son and Russell than mere youthful ardor – perhaps visible disaffection, ruthlessly put down. Wordsworth's Michael has explicitly lost a son to urbanization and "progress," in a moral fable: a son thwarted in his innocent rural ambitions corrupted by the city. Yearsley's scenario is both more open and ambiguous and more political than Wordsworth's.

The dramatic upheavals of the 1790s reproduce themselves irresistibly, in a near crisis of representation in the poem's final stanza:

> Invok'd by Poesy, the yielding shade
> Forbore to torture my dissolving soul;
> Ascending as he flew, the axe display'd –
> Too near the throne – I saw the visage roll.   (85–88)

Having summoned Russell's shade, the poet is too overcome by the revealed scenes not to be "tortured" by them, even "dissolved" in grief. Ever honorable, the ghost takes his leave of the poet, ascending skyward with the dreaded executioner's axe "display'd" for all to fear. Then there is a moment of perfect but tortuous ambiguity in the final line: at once, Russell's shade displays the axe too near the throne (by threatening the king's life in the supposed "Rye-house plot"), and his own beheading is re-enacted. The hypothetically wished-for murder of Charles combines hallucinatorily with the historical execution of Russell. Yearsley herself has got "Too near the throne" not to see something gruesome and symbolic of monarchical authority – that horrid "visage" rolling into history.

After such temerity, what restitution can the socially vulnerable poet make? *Prayer and Resignation* represents Yearsley in her most Collierian mode, but the differences between their deployments of religious verse are significant. Yearsley prays ironically for staunch forbearance at the very moment that she discloses the relations of force which sustain political tyranny and social injustice in the name of divine benediction. Resistance to political dogma and social dictum, resistance to human authority generally, are counterbalanced by a struggle to give herself over to obeying the mysterious workings of the divine will. But if we consider the poem in relation to its title, it seems that the text is not so much a prayer for resignation, though it is this ironically and in part. Rather, the text represents the state of mind, and of public affairs, in which such a prayer has become urgently necessary. Clearly a certain "resignation" is needed to carry oneself with dignity and keep despair at bay during the events to which Yearsley alludes – war with France, bad harvests, famine and scarcity, popular disaffection. In this struggle towards resignation, there is a comparable movement to Wordsworth's *Resolution and Independence*, though the differences suggested by the titles, and the important formal differences, demand that one not push the comparison too far. In its questioning, the poem also anticipates Hardy and is reminiscent of Blake's "Holy Thursday" from *Songs of Experience*. As a sustained feat of rhetoric, *Prayer and Resignation* is unsurpassed in Yearsley's *œuvre*, so I will quote from it at some length:

> O DEITY! Distributor of joy,
>   Whose attributes we vainly strive to know,
> Thou, whom my brethren call to save – destroy,
>   As suits their present hour of bliss or woe!
>
>   . . .
>
> Whether, when call'd for purposes of woe,
>   Thou wilt obey the impious pray'r of man;
> E'en when the ruffian bids Thee aid his blow,
>   That on the heart despoils thy beauteous plan:
>
> Whether, now seated on some radiant throne
>   (A throne to us the utmost bench of power),
> Thou, pitying, bid thy minister make known
>   Our doleful frolics at this trying hour:
>
>   . . .
>
> Whether to-day Thou wear'st an awful frown,
>   Because we eat and sleep on this fair isle;
> And, angry, hurl'st us war and famine down,
>   To call them up at evening with a smile:
>
> Whether all nations be thy care – or we,
>   First in thine estimation wisely live;
> At court, in cottages, so true to Thee,
>   That thy great seal seems stamp'd on laws we give:
>
>   . . .
>
> Whether we may be quiet, or may war
>   As suits our humour, and our public purse;
> Whether on ★★★★★★'s bosom the deep scar
>   Got in a hurly-burly makes him worse;

Or in the sight of angels makes him fair
    (As some avow): or whether we should sit,
Some starving on a stone – some on a chair,
    And humbly pray for WAR and noble PITT:

Or whether we should question Thee, – or fast
    By proclamation; whilst the hungry die
Of this same holy abstinence, – outcast,
    And needing proclamations of supply:

Whether pale Rapine, wand'ring o'er the land
    Hungry and haggard, stung with guilty thirst,
Defile the peasant's hearth at thy command,
    And, ere his babes are fed, be fed the first:

Whether yon noisy Gallicans conspire
    To steal our gold, – or THEE, – or break our laws;
Or merely dance a jig themselves to tire,
    Whilst *wiser we* stand batt'ry in thy cause,

IS NOTHING, SIRE, TO ME – Be where thou wilt,
    I will adore: to Thee my thought shall fly –
But beg, should my poor life by man be spilt,
    Thou will not wear for me one sable sky.

        . . .

Teach me to soothe the fierce; to melt the heart;
    To paint the passions nipping beauty's bloom:
When pensive age is ling'ring to depart,
    Give me to chase black horror from the tomb.

        . . .

For me, I am obedient – whilst I stay,
    My fellow-dreamers thro' the world I'll love;
Nor shall one grieve, can I his griefs allay,
    Much less should earth ensanguin'd fury move.

Be still, ye nations! – Ye but fight to die.
    No trophies deck this path of threescore years,
Worthy the widow's groan, and orphan's cry –
    Your mimic wars Jehovah never hears!

And it were best oblivion should await
    Those crimes at which e'en human thought is chill'd –
Or go, grim warrior! boldly challenge fate,
    Command thy God to mark thy number kill'd!

O Deity! hear not this warrior's voice;
   Be deaf, lest Thou condemn him with a frown –
Or shouldst Thou hear him – mercy be thy choice!
   Think he but murder'd to preserve a crown.

All I commend to Thee! I am but one;
   O'er me the mighty pass; I fear the strong –
But till thy voice comes for me o'er the sun,
   I'll here attune my solitary song.   (1–112)

There is no central vision of "resolution and independence" here, no emblematic spot of time or extended personification of human virtues, but rather interrogation and exhortation. We may be reminded not so much of the Wordsworth of *Resolution and Independence* here as the Wordsworth of the *Ode to Duty*. The "Deity" gives no sign. It is part of Yearsley's pact with her resigned self that he does not need to. As she promises elsewhere in this collection, in "The Rustic's Avowal Of Faith" (with what may, for us, read like a gender-specific polemical inflection):

Can these men explain to my enquiring, my mysterious soul thine eternal beauty? Art Thou known to them, and wilt Thou be a stranger to me? No; I will seek thy footsteps through the universe, I will in the grand features of the world behold my God.

   But the interrogatives to which there are no answers not only culminate in an exhortation of divine mercy, and an affirmation of the poet's post-pastoral, post-Christian, proto-Romantic isolation, her "solitary song" – they also accumulate irony. The capitals in "IS NOTHING, SIRE, TO ME" suggest not so much an excess of certitude as ironical understatement. For these queries that begin with "Whether" are far from trivial; rather, they address the same complex social and political issues we have seen gathering force and meaning in Yearsley's work. The portrait of Britain as a nation is so deliciously double-edged: is British law specifically divinely sanctioned? If not, then from whence does British politico-cultural "superiority," so touted in the context of colonialism and the slave trade, derive? We are back to Thompson's notion of the development of English common law as an "unqualified human good," but only provisionally and ironically. And that business about a throne being, for us, the "utmost bench of power" – hence we imagine that the Deity has one too: this is another of Yearsley's ideology-critical gambits, so that we cannot take any further received wisdom about that deity as simply true – not for the duration of this text anyway. The scorn with which the capitals in "WAR and noble PITT" seem to have been inscribed bursts into open outrage in the doubleness of "holy abstinence" – and we have returned to our first sight of Yearsley offered in More's "Prefatory Letter": the starving laborer-poetess, who keeps herself alive by means of reading and writing, both literally and metaphorically; whose sustenance is her "solitary song."

The energy and intricacy of the prayers needed to bring this poet to a state of calm resignation testify to her profound sense of the social world as a scene of strife not easily reconciled with a notion of providential order. But the points of conflict she cites are not the "timeless" and commonplace ones of disease, disaster, hereditary (and so, unchangeable) distinctions, but rather the historically specific hardships imposed by an economy gearing up for full-scale war with France in spite of, or rather partly because of, the domestic privations and political disaffection of the times. Especially for the poorest, cottageless and "starving on a stone," 1795 was a year of "Scarcity and Alarm," as Hannah More's editor tells us from the relatively safe distance of 1816.[104] Pessimistic, addressing herself to her "fellow-dreamers" who maintain hope of utopian social transformation, but with little hope of ending the war she dreads, Yearsley ends by praying for mercy for the soldiers who will die with murder on their hands. In the light of what has preceded it, the line "Think he but murder'd to preserve a crown" is bitterly ironical, and yet seemingly authentic in its desire to vindicate the hapless soldier, who, like Blake's soldier in "London," will find his "sigh" – of resignation, of his last breath – running "in blood down palace walls" (11–12).[105] The imperative to war comes from elsewhere, from the crown that the soldier is pledged, at all costs, to "preserve." Yearsley's poem produces a domestic and populist view of a period of scarcity and alarm, not from the propertied perspective of those with privileges to lose at the hands of the mob, as in More's *The Riot*, but from below.

Bringing the social consequences of political events so forcefully "home" is a textual strategy that informs many poems in *The Rural Lyre*. But the poem that identifies domestic politics most dramatically as "the politics of domesticity" is *To Mira, On The Care Of Her Infant*, a poem to which we shall return in chapter 7. Crucially, this text also gives us Yearsley's most elaborate theorization of the constitution of the subject, who in the poem is male, and whose subject-constitution is, philosophically speaking, classically bourgeois, presumably owing much to the works of Rousseau, which figured largely in Yearsley's public library. Her catalogue lists translations of the *Confessions* in five volumes and in three, and an *Eloisa* in four volumes, but the primary connections appear to be with the four-volume *Emilius and Sophia, or a New System of Education*, for the latter is what *To Mira* proposes.[106] There is a deliberate refusal of war and indeed of the whole "public" sector of political activity as presently conceived.

With Rousseau, Yearsley deplores the corruptions of modernity; with Wollstonecraft, she seeks to make women's power within the household eventually subversive of an exclusively male sphere of political power. Women's situation does not change except in so far as "women's work" receives a new valuation, at least by women themselves. The prospect of a gradual social transformation brought about by different childrearing and educational practices, akin as a process to what Raymond Williams describes as a "long revolution," and Juliet Mitchell echoes as the "longest revolution,"[107] defuses in Yearsley's text the desire for a radical encounter with the present. Neither the assumed masculinity of Yearsley's typical infant subject nor the question of class relations "after the revolution" is problematized or even addressed.

These ideological contours have an uncannily familiar look. In a certain sense, the limits of Yearsley's historical moment remain ours, and the complexities of her last works, in their politicized yet cautious engagement with public events, retain a peculiar urgency for our times. Her progressive radicalization can be traced historically in some detail, as we have seen, but it was not without its contradictions. The "bourgeoisification" of Ann Yearsley transpired almost transparently against her will, in her complex exchanges with middle- and upper-class people whose prospects had a greater immediate purchase on power/knowledge, whose lives seemed so much freer of material and, possibly, ideological constraint than her own, and who could, if they wished, more freely think, write, and publish the discourse of radical social re-formation than she could afford to do. This is a pardigm more familiar to us than that of Duck's apparently complacent, even eager, but ultimately tragic deracination. Yearsley's is above all an Anglo-American and protofeminist paradigm.

The fact that Ann Yearsley's work has been so little read when it offers such complex political insights and aesthetic pleasures suggests what can so easily be lost to the historical record or the literary canon through our collective "forgetting." And it is this forgetting, this repression of a possible collective memory of human agency in particular political struggles and specific forms of resistance, that Yearsley herself attempted to oppose and that recovering and reading her work may help us overcome, beginning with the terrain of literary and social history.

Chapter 5

Laboring in pastures new: the two Elizabeths

Elizabeth Hands on the pastoral

Reading publics change with literary expectations. The traces left on the historical record by Elizabeth Hands (*fl.* 1798) and Elizabeth Bentley (1767–1839), and the ways their poetry is likely to be read by us now, no longer quite add up. Hands left hardly any mark and Bentley left a number of them, including praise from the poet William Cowper,[1] but Hands's is now arguably the more readable, aesthetically satisfying corpus. Her single volume of verse, *The Death of Amnon. A Poem. With an Appendix: containing Pastorals, and other Poetical Pieces* (1789)[2] may seem a slim claim upon literary-historical importance, but in that volume Hands emerges as a versatile, skillful poet and a sharp social critic. She also satirizes more acutely than anyone else the peculiar situation of the working-class writer in England on the eve of the French revolution. Not since Swift have we seen comical satirical verse of the order of Hands's "A Poem, On the Supposition of an Advertisement appearing in a Morning Paper, of the Publication of a Volume of Poems, by a Servant Maid" and *A Poem, On the Supposition of the Book having been published and read.* And no other plebeian woman poet of the period appears to have engaged the English poetic tradition explicitly with such vigor and skill. If *The Death of Amnon* as a collection seems rather insulated from world-historical events, I would argue that such insulation is deliberate, part of a strategy of constructing a village world immune to the ravages of history, a world of "timeless" village life that had never quite existed and that was rapidly vanishing from the English scene with the last wave of major enclosures, urban migration, and what some historians would call proto-industrialization, the laying of the groundwork economically and socially for the factory labor system of the nineteenth century.[3] Steeped in the English literary tradition yet bold enough to mock it, paying homage to the fathers yet reworking pastoral verse forms in a feminizing way, Hands is almost too successful a ventriloquist for her own good. Handing on the pastoral while

186

querying certain of its conventions, disappearing into parodies of traditional poetic forms, disappointing the reader hungry for autobiographical detail in a self-effacing way, Elizabeth Hands, even on the limited evidence of one volume, could well be the most accomplished comic poet of these plebeian women writers.

In one sense, Hands's single volume of verse and the absence of supplementary documents about her life cast her as peculiarly representative of the elusiveness of the laboring woman poet. If her *œuvre* did not exist, one would have had to invent it. Her representation of the circumstances out of which the poetry of labor most often arises in this period is provocatively transparent; in her verse we can observe both rural inspiration and the cessation of domestic labor making possible the moment of literary composition, ironical reflection on the class determinations of literary reception, and mimetic meditation on the tradition of English verse which she addresses as a gifted alien. There are also historically specific traces of a shift both in popular conceptions of the rural poor in this period and of working-class resistance to those conceptions. Sentimentalism and moralism, on the one hand, and a certain arch compliance with the structures of power and privilege, on the other, both made possible by faith in a higher power and the eventual achievement of justice by religious means: we may not seem to have travelled so very far from Mary Collier's attitudes, but the differences are important.

Reconstructing Elizabeth Hands's life requires some guesswork since no autobiographical or biographical narratives accompany her poems. That she was a domestic servant we know from the two poems on the publication of her verse; that she may have recently retired from service to marriage and motherhood we can infer from "On the Author's Lying-In, August, 1785," in which she mentions a husband and infant daughter; on the other hand, she may have continued as a living-out servant after marriage. In a letter by Henry Sacheverell Homer (1719–91), rector of Birdingbury in Warwickshire, to the Rev. Richard Bisse Riland of Sutton Coldfield, she is identified as Elizabeth Hands "of Bourton," and we learn that "She was a Servt for many years in the family of the late Mr. Huddesford & of Miss Huddesford, of Allesly, his Daughter, the latter of whom speaks of her as a Servant in Terms of the highest commendation."[4] Her volume is dedicated to Bertie Greatheed, Esq. (1759–1826), the dramatist, a member of the local gentry whose mother was a duke's daughter, and who thus plays the dual parts of literary and social mediator for the unknown poet.[5] Hands claims that she owes everything to do with publication to her "particular friends"; her disclaimer of literary and social importance could serve as model of the genre:

THE difficulties which an Author, under my circumstances, has to contend with – born in obscurity, and never emerging beyond the lower stations in life – must have been an insurmountable bar to the publication of the following POEMS, had not the approbation and zeal of some particular friends to serve me, been exerted in a manner which demands my most thankful acknowledgments, and with a success which I had little reason to expect.[6]

What she hopes to gain from Greatheed's imprimatur is some relative freedom from class prejudice, an openminded reading, "the candour, if not the attention of the Public" (A1v). As "Daphne" she had already received some public attention by publishing poems in *Jopson's Coventry Mercury*, and, according to Henry Homer, *The Death of Amnon* at least had been shown to Thomas James, headmaster of Rugby, and gained his approval.[7]

Hands would seem to have considered the long poem *The Death of Amnon* her major work, its length alone demanding that it be valued more highly than anything else she had done. As she has the characters in *A Poem, On the Supposition of the Book having been published and read* remark, the theme of rape in that poem may be its most remarkable feature – "A Rape! interrupted the Captain Bonair, / A delicate theme for a female I swear;" (32–33) – but though the other poems in the volume may give "some little pleasure," "the Murder of Amnon's the longest and best" (40–41). We have already seen how and in what ways the genre of versified Scriptural narrative may have come to appeal to laboring women poets like Hands, Collier, and Yearsley.

What *A Poem, On the Supposition of Publication* adds to our knowledge of the many displacements enacted in Hands's *œuvre* is the extent of her apparent consciousness of such displacement and maneuvering, her implicitly self-critical reflexiveness. The only other poem which the characters in this mock commentary on her verse's projected reception mention is the carnivalesque anti-pastoral and counter-georgic, "Written, originally extempore, on seeing a Mad Heifer run through the Village where the Author lives":

> O law! says young Seagram, I've seen the book, now
> I remember, there's something about a mad cow.
> A mad cow! – ha, ha, ha, ha, return'd half the room;
> What can y' expect better, says Madam Du Bloom?   (88–91)

Thus the textual coordinates that Hands herself provides for mapping our reading in advance are the high seriousness of biblical imitation – *Amnon* – and the bathos of rustic "non-events" that are not so much ridiculous in themselves as subject to ridicule by the polite world.

Hands draws together these tendencies, and these anticipations of genteel dismissal and scorn, in the poem's final lines:

> The Rector reclin'd himself back in his chair,
> And open'd his snuff-box with indolent air;
> This book, says he, (snift, snift) has in the beginning,
> (The ladies give audience to hear his opinion)

Some pieces, I think, that are pretty correct;
A stile elevated you cannot expect:
To some of her equals they may be a treasure,
And country lasses may read 'em with pleasure.
That Amnon, you can't call it poetry neither,
There's no flights of fancy, or imagery either;
You may stile it prosaic, blank-verse at the best;
Some pointed reflections, indeed, are exprest;
The narrative lines are exceedingly poor:
Her Jonadab is a _____ the drawing-room door
Was open'd, the gentlemen came from below,
And gave the discourse a definitive blow.   (94–109)

The rector's pomposity may be familiar enough from previous literary representations, usually by members of the Church of England, sometimes though not always part of an anticlerical or reformist movement. But if this particular parson is any indication of Hands's opinion of the established church, there is no reason why she should not have been a Dissenter, as has been hypothesized, though the evidence is far from conclusive.[8] Ironically, the "pretty correct" pieces "in the beginning" of this book must be the two poems on publication, for they follow *Amnon* and precede the pastorals. No wonder the rector thinks that these poems "may be treasured" by Hands's equals and read with pleasure by "country lasses," for the objects of satire here are the rector's snobbery and his pseudo-critical pretension.

Hands thus sharply prefigures what might be said about her own poetical failings: in *Amnon*, a too-literal translation of the Scriptures, with "pointed reflections" of a subtly sexual–political nature dominating both imagery and narrative; in the other poems, correctness that remains a far cry from an "elevated" style precisely because the writing represents socially an eruption from below. Hands has her revenge on the rector, too; his forever interrupted discourse is marked by a blank in which we must surely be tempted to inscribe irreverence if not profanity, rupturing his decorum as "he" has ruptured the discourse of Hands's texts. The definitive blow given his discourse by the gentlemen's rejoining the ladies stands in for whatever punishment the servant, country lass, or other reader pleased by Hands's verse may feel inclined to bestow on all such critical nay-sayers.

The dominant mode in Hands's volume is pastoral, not georgic, and in this respect her work represents a repastoralization of the countryside and of village life that historically accompanied its politico-economic marginalization. As John Barrell has argued, though the representation of laborious agricultural work continues throughout the century:

The social constraints which influence *how* the poor are represented at work do change, however: in the mid-eighteenth century they work blithely, for work is then a pleasantly social activity; at the end of the century, cheerfully, to reassure us that they do not resent their condition, or blame us for it . . . One could put it another way by saying that the poor are now *blamed* for the thoughtless animal behaviour – drinking and wenching – that the tradition of Gay had happily attributed to them: the poverty of the rural labourer is seen as the squalid consequence of that behaviour, and the poor are then urged to a temperance and industry.[9]

In Hands's work, the image of life among the rural poor is defiantly pleasurable, not resolutely cheerful. Swains, shepherdesses, and milkmaids engage in amorous dalliance, the author herself composes while sitting picturesquely "on a Cock of Hay," and a heat-maddened heifer turns village life temporarily topsy-turvy. Accompanying this partial repastoralization of the plebeian georgic is a consistently moral strain that works both with and against the poems' picturesqueness. The moral discourse is not without a certain class consciousness, though it takes a rather conservative form, arguing that things used to be better than they are, rather than looking to engage with topical, and highly controversial, questions of liberty and natural rights. A distinctive combination of social criticism and nostalgic reflection about the possibilities for erotic harmony among the poor marks "On a Wedding":

> With all marriage articles pen'd on the heart,
>   The parties so sweetly agreed;
> They needed no lawyer, with quibbling art,
>   Or parchment to draw up a deed.
>
> For Love, the first blessing of blessings below,
>   That Heaven to mortals can give,
> Was all the kind shepherdess had to bestow,
>   And all that she wish'd to receive.   (13–20)

Where the lovers feel their vows have been completely internalized, no legal documents are necessary, Hands claims. The affectional body itself becomes the site of self-regulation and the self-discipline imposed by monogamy. Thus Hands writes as if poised between an older tradition of verbal promises that, before the Marriage Act of 1753, constituted legal marriage without involving either church or juridical apparatus, and perhaps a new veneration of an insistence upon monogamy among the propertyless.[10] In a similar vein, set amongst the pastorals is a small, terse poem entitled "Observation":

> LET the vain avaricious with oaths safely bind,
>   Lest either forgetfully rove;
> The band of affection secureth the mind,
>   When the wishes are centered in love.
> If virtue alone is the guide of the will,

> Distrust has no right to be there;
> The swain has no reason to doubt of his skill,
>   And the fair one has nothing to fear.

The emphasis on virtue and on the happiness of the poor being dependent only on their own self-discipline coincides with Barrell's description of the conventions for visual representation of the poor during this period, except that in Hands's poetry this self-discipline is indigenous to plebeian culture, and does not need to be imposed from above. Here the metaphor of labor is given its fullest erotic possibility – and that's not much: the action of binding sheaves becomes, not the legal, contractual binding of marriage settlements, but the affective bonding of minds and desiring bodies in an erotic embrace. Marriage is at once moralized, eroticized, and legally deregulated. Arcadian sentiment regarding a "pre-avaricious" (pre-capitalist?) time when formal church marriages were not required by law and marriage contracts were not customary marks the poem as in one sense conservative. Yet the critique of contractual relations also represents a timely protest against increasing juridical intervention in social and sexual matters, attempts to regulate the lives of the poor in a period of social unrest. We should not read Hands's *œuvre* as purely in keeping with mainstream representations of the cheerful, humble, and virtuous poor, without resentments and without class consciousness. Her return to pastoral represents as well an engagement with defending traditional village values and economies as harmonious in the wake of their disruption by the last phase of eighteenth-century agrarian capitalism (including enclosures), the demographic upheaval that accompanied this phase, and the juridical intervention that attempted to adjudicate the consequences of these socio-economic shifts.

To assert the dignity and independence, not the cheerful gratitude and humility, of rural labor in this period is thus itself something of an act of resistance. In "Contentment," Hands writes:

> While no unwelcome visitants,
>   My solitude invade;
> The monarch is not more secure,
> Than I beneath this shade.   (9–12)

There is no controversial invocation of liberty as such in these lines but rather an illustration of it by means of the literary trope of poetic reclusiveness. Independence equals a green solitude; the true test of British liberty is one's ability to experience rural retirement, if only for a moment's rest from labor. Such "liberty" in the shade puts the worker, the writer, on a level of achieved pleasure equal even to the king's.

As the arrangement of Hands's volume indicates, her positioning of herself as a "servant maid" in two early poems is meant to influence our reading of subsequent ones and to modify our understanding of the long poem *The Death of Amnon* which precedes the "servant maid" verses. Our attention is particularly drawn therein to "Written, originally extempore, on seeing a Mad Heifer run through the Village where the Author lives." This is Hands's chief venture into the mock-heroic mode as well as a memorable anti-pastoral and counter-georgic poem. A subversive animal energy undercuts her other poems' more conventional representations of rural life. Neither amorous shepherdesses and swains nor honest, hardworking field hands can withstand the disruptive pressure of the mad heifer's dash through a decaying village tranquillized almost into eternal sleep. Conventional description of the beauties of a peaceful countryside is rudely interrupted by the cow's intrusion:

> Sudden from th' herd we saw an heifer stray,
> And to our peaceful village bend her way.
> She spurns the ground with madness as she flies,
> And clouds of dust, like autumn mists, arise;
> Then bellows loud: the villagers alarm'd,
> Come rushing forth, with various weapons arm'd:
> Some run with pieces of old broken rakes,
> And some from hedges pluck the rotten stakes;
> Here one in haste, with hand-staff of his flail,
> And there another comes with half a rail;
> Whips, without lashes, sturdy plough-boys bring,
> While clods of dirt and pebbles others fling:
> Voices tumultuous rend the listening ear;
> Stop her – one cries; another – turn her there:
> But furiously she rushes by them all,
> And some huzza, and some, to cursing fall:
> A mother snatch'd her infant off the road,
> Close to the spot of ground where next she trod;
> Camilla walking, trembled and turn'd pale;
> See o'er her gentle heart what fears prevail!
> At last the beast, unable to withstand
> Such force united, leapt into a pond:
> The water quickly cool'd her madden'd rage;
> No more she'll fright our village, I presage.   (5–28)

The stilted voice of official precept which dominates the last line notwithstanding, this is an interesting mock-heroic experiment. Book III of the *Georgics* on livestock and the various epic games and battles of Homer and Virgil, mediated by the English poets that Hands herself cites elsewhere – Shakespeare, Milton, Butler, Prior, Swift, Pope, and Young – stand behind this text but do not fully account for it. Neoclassical imitation of densely packed rhetorical figures, especially chiasmus and zeugma, gives the passage linguistic energy, while the cow's escapade serves as a kind of barometer that measures the villagers' own states of feeling: the men are spoiling for a fight, the women preoccupied with saving their infants or themselves. Camilla's terror verges on the pathological; "what fears" precisely she might have of the runaway cow remain unstated, open to speculation, but her timorousness suggests that she has always something to fear. This is only one of several moments in Hands's *œuvre* that seem undecidable regarding whether a female character should be pitied or seen as deserving of parody, a point to which I shall return.

As an image of rural life, the poem at once insists that nothing worthy of literary representation ever happens in a typical English village and belies that assumption by describing the incident with such virtuosity in the high mock-heroic style that we can read the text as simultaneously neoclassically successful and absurdist. But what of the material conditions of village life in this period, on which, I have been suggesting, Hands implicitly comments? That fact that the thresher, sturdy plough-boys and other villagers eager to do battle with the cow seize "old broken," "rotten," and partial or "half" weapons, including lashless whips, adds to the poem's comic counter-georgic potential. But even if we wish to insist as well that country villages are always tumbledown, always possessed of an abundance of broken or worn-out implements of labor, there is another possibility at work. Rather than being a period-specific image of honest rural industry interrupted in a comic fashion, this poem suggests that the sleepy village atmosphere is far from temporary, and that the state of the rakes, hedges, flails, fences, and whips points ominously towards a general condition of decay and irreparability. Here is a possible intimation of the effects of the capitalization and final marginalization of agricultural work. One could read this bovine comedy as another instance of the poor as determinedly cheerful, here even in their own self-represent-ations. But the descriptions of both ruined implements and the women's terror at a physical threat cast a darker shadow, evidence of a subtle redirection of attention towards the complexity of rural lived experience in the face of studied literary aestheticization or indifference.

This is not to claim for Hands some "authentic" working-class stance unmodified by polite convention; if anything, Hands is among the most literary of our laboring-women poets. In an exercise that closes her volume of verse, "Critical Fragments, on some of the English Poets," Hands demonstrates what an agile ventriloquist of the masculine canon she is:

> MILTON, in pond'rous verse, moves greatly on,
> Weilding his massy theme; with wond'rous strength
> He labours forward.
>
>   SHAKESPEAR gently glides,
> And, like a polish'd mirror, as he passes
> Reflects all nature.

> YOUNG, in thought profound,
> Muses, contemplates, sees, and feels the woes
> That clog the soul; yet with aspiring wing
> Behold him 'rise majestically slow,
> And like an eagle soar, and soar aloft:
>   But SWIFT delights as much to rout
>   I' th' dirt, and then to throw't about.
> POPE sings a soft and sweet harmonious lay,
> So mellow flutes in pleasant concert play.
>   MATT. PRIOR, like an easy horse,
>   Keeps ambling on, ne'er out of course:
> But trotting BUTLER beats him hollow,
> He leads a way that none can follow;
> He dashes on through thick and thin,
> Not for the criticks cares a pin;
> From censure he's receiv'd acquittal,
> And grammar, metre, rhyme submit all.

The absence of anything like an historical sequence in this text suggests the way in which the "English Poets" were likely to be read: as a panoply of styles rather than as a chronology. Hands has also managed to ignore the notion of a patrilinear succession within literary history, the notion of poetic greatness as an inheritance handed down from one strong male author to the next. Breaking up the historical sequence gives Hands a certain demystified access to poetic male precursors whom she can raid and ransack at will, without undue reverence or humility in the face of an authoritative hereditary succession. And so her mimicry is playful, antic, running somewhat counter to common-place critical judgments. It is hard to say which is more unusual, the admiration for Butler so late in the century or the successful capturing of his rhythms. What this exercise implicitly argues for is an unfettered aesthetic, a kind of Butlerian freedom from the fear of censure that would allow the materials of verse to bend themselves freely to the poet's will. Butler's very "inimitability," which the text itself disproves by its recognizable imitation of his style, would seem to be his main attraction for Hands. Here we find what Yearsley's poem on visiting Twickenham also produces, the yearning for a distinctive poetic aesthetic, uncensurable by critics, superior to and so unfetterable by contemporary judgment or taste. Perhaps this is why there are no women poets among Hands's assortment, and no poets who are truly her contemporaries. However literary history may now be seen to have been changing throughout the period, with the possibility of female literary authority, plebeian poetry, and even feminist protest well established by the second half of the eighteenth century, from the perspective of collections of "great English Poets," the canon remains recalcitrantly male and upper- or middle-class. In this sense, Hands's literariness and her self-effacement, her subtle rather than explicit positioning of herself as a critical voice, reinforce one another. It is hardly surprising to find that her poem entitled "Enigma," her contribution to a genre that proffers secret keys or mock-secret keys to the puzzles of poetic authority and poetic masking, turns out to be a poem dedicated to the book.

Thus we should read even her contribution to what may be the most common site of feminist protest in eighteenth-century women's verse, the epistle to another woman, as a highly literary production, though Hands claims no knowledge of the traditions of women's epistolary poetry. And the poem which she quaintly entitles so that we must picture her, "the author," sitting composing verse on a haycock, should be read not so much as autobiographical revelation as an engagement with the tradition of amorous pastoral complaint. "An Epistle" gives us a Belinda burning with longing for her absent Maria, and setting her desire against the heterosexual mainstream:

> Let love-sick nymphs their faithful shepherds prove,
> Maria's friendship's more to me than love;
> When you were here, I smil'd throughout the day,
> No rustic shepherdess was half so gay;
> But now, alas! I can no pleasure know,
> The tedious hours of absence move so slow;
> I secret mourn, not daring to complain,
> Still seeking for relief, but seek in vain.
>
> . . .
>
> When on my couch reclin'd my eyes I close,
> The God of sleep refuses me respose;
> I 'rise half dress'd, and wander to and fro
> Along my room, or to my window go:
> Enraptur'd I behold the moon shine clear,
> While falling waters murmur in my ear;
> My thoughts to you then in a moment fly,
> The moon shines misty, and my raptures die.   (5–36)

The facility with which Belinda equates her boredom with the absence of her woman friend sounds suspiciously like parody – subtle parody, not grossly exaggerated parody. The satirical weight falls on leisured Belinda, with her "painted chair" (21), flower garden, room with a view, house apparently not shared with anyone, and tedious, choreless hours to fill. She is the fanciful self-proclaimed "rustic shepherdess" of earlier aristocratic pastoral, for whom this "role" is theatrical not social. Not women's passionate friendship so much as its place within upper-class culture – and women's removal there from the sites of material production – is being pilloried. As one of our few married plebeian women poets, and the only one to write a poem on her lying-in, Hands writes primarily in support of equitable and affectionate marriages, not female strategies for maintaining independence from men. But a biographical explanation of her affective preferences will not suffice. Her parody of the discourse of amorous epistolary exchanges between women is a literary intervention, and it should be situated within the epistolary tradition of Katherine Philips and her eighteenth-century followers, including Leapor and Hands's Scottish contemporary, Janet Little.

Similarly, we may be encouraged by the title to read "Written while the Author sat on a Cock of Hay" as autobiographical, but the poem itself turns out to be about literary posing, and the enjoyment of literary posing, by the now, in the 1780s, familiar figure of the plebeian female poet:

> FAIR Daphne to the meadow went,
>   To tedd the new mown hay;
>   She went alone,
>   For well 'twas known,
>   No shepherd went that way.
>
>   . . .
>
> The sun that o'er Arabian fields,
>   Bids spicy odours play;
>   By the same pow'r,
>   Doth in an hour,
>   Raise sweetness from the hay.
>
>   . . .
>
> But yet amidst this pleasing scene,
>   Our nymph doth sullen prove;
>   Such things says she,
>   Might pleasure me,
>   If I was not in love.
>
> To cheerful strains I'll not aspire,
>   Since fate that led me here,
>   Forbid my swain,
>   To tread this plain,
>   I'll drop a silent tear.   (1–45)

Once again, the studied quality of Hands's characters directs our reading towards both sympathy and self-parody. So much for the author as pictur-esque countrywoman naively, autobiographically working out her romantic melancholy in verse. Even the "true" country working woman in the volume, the figure of the author, who bears the name Daphne under which Hands published poetry in *Jopson's Coventry Mercury*, is elaborating and working up her feelings in order to enjoy the pleasurable sensations that dwelling on erotic deprivation, on the absence of the other, generates. Village life, experienced by "real" villagers, is itself as much a literary construction as the notion of the humble, rustic poetess pouring out her feelings to a middle-class public of subscribers and other readers.

Hands gives us a complaining Daphne who is frankly compelled to complain, who revels in complaint from some obscure literary-cultural necessity. And Hands produces this self-parodic text under the guise of a spontaneous outpouring, composed in a moment's rest from labor, or at least at a traditional scene of female labor, hay-making. This poem, read in a fully nuanced way, comes close to parodying the entire tradition of plebeian female pastoral and georgic, by drawing attention to its artificiality, its extreme conventionality, which must always be at odds with the notion of the unlettered poetic genius. Hands's verse exposes these contradictions in ways both historically revealing and important for a feminist literary history.

If we may speak of these poetic texts as traversed by contradictory and sometimes incompletely articulated possibilities for the production of new poetic subjectivities, we should attend to certain moments when Hands's language approaches a colloquial register. Particular words in her *œuvre* mark her poetic discourse as heteroglossic, in Bakhtin's sense. For Bakhtin, literary discourses, especially the novel, are privileged spaces in which language can be analyzed as a site of ideological and cultural conflict: "As a result of the work done by all these stratifying forces in language, there are no 'neutral' words and forms – words and forms that can belong to 'no one'; language has been completely taken over, shot through with intentions and accents."[11] If Bakhtin's formulations partially flatten the linguistic struggle within poetry, as opposed to the novel, reading working-class women's verse helps re-accentuate that struggle. When Daphne goes to the meadow to "tedd" the hay (2), and when in "Lob's Courtship" Lob's rejection by the woman of his choice causes him to "shabb" off and say no more (48), we can find in Hands's poetic language intimations of new forms of colloquial expression and class consciousness in verse. To "tedd" means to scatter the hay for drying, to "shabb" off means to slink away (O.E.D.): both words have a colloquial resonance that verges on dialect, owing to Anglo-Saxon rather than latinate roots, and both suggest something of the possibilities for a radical rural poetic language which the discourse of working-women's verse was historically unable to support, except for such brief moments.

As we have seen, Hands's *œuvre* is equally contradictory or intermittent in its engagement of contemporary gender relations. Her emphasis on sexual morality and respectability can be seen to be at odds with her criticisms of increasingly formalized, legally regulated, and property-conscious marriages among the rural poor. Both respectability, combining industriousness with piety, and propriety in marital arrangements became watchwords for the class incorporation or "bourgeoisification" of the laboring population throughout the eighteenth and nineteenth centuries. Where there is little property to speak of, the institution of marriage as a form of property conveyance serves little purpose, and the poor were less likely to pursue legal ratification of their affective and domestic arrangements than the property-owning classes, legal ratification that in any case did little to ensure women's property-owning rights. Thus Hands's protest against "avaricious" marriage contracts carries with it potentially class- and gender-specific criticism, but does not lead to anything as radical as a critique of the institution of marriage itself or the double standard of sexual morality.

What we have instead is a new situating of the pastoral itself that displaces a male shepherd-centered poetics in favor of a female-centered one. Hands's pastorals may look conventional enough at first, with their neoclassical names and rhyming couplets or interlaced stanzaic rhymes. But Hands's female figures not only come to dominate her pastoral landscapes, they also cause awkward, anticlimactic, or witty reversals of traditional pastoral assumptions about romantic love, male desire, and the inevitability of the couple. Taken as a whole, the pastoral sequence operates as a mapping of pastoral conventions and an exposure of both their hyper-conventionality and their irresistible utility in representing rural life. Between the two poles of "Wit and Beauty" and "Absence and Death," the first two poems in the sequence, the poles of desire and loss, Hands's pastorals offer a broad affective range, some interesting sociological commentary, and a dominantly ironic or humorous attitude towards the pastoral itself. Most strikingly, Hands's rustic nymphs have the upper hand with their lovers and within the sequence as a whole. Female, not male, desire is the motor of these pastorals. These shepherdesses are usually so pleased with themselves that they can desire, mourn, or dismiss their suitors with equal spirit. Hands's pastorals testify to her skill in producing comic pleasure and irreverent reversals of generic expectation.

The collection's central pastoral sequence moves from "Wit and Beauty" and "Absence and Death," through various permutations including "Perplexity," to the poem on the author's lying-in, in which gratitude for having survived the labor of giving birth generates the labor of poetic composition:

> My tongue did almost ask for death,
> But thou did'st spare my lab'ring breath,
>   To sing thy future praise.   (4–6)

After such deliverance from the act of delivery itself, the poet promises joyous thanks. By being an exemplary wife and mother, and by schooling her daughter according to godly precept, she hopes to repay the divine generosity that has spared her almost against her will. In undertaking her daughter's religious education, promising to "shepherd" her, the poet ends the sequence by substituting one form of pastoral for another.

Especially where different kinds of pastoral are juxtaposed in the collection, Hands is able to use various kinds of generic interpenetration to good effect. A "public" occasional poem celebrating the royal family on progress to Kew, for example, ends up celebrating romantic constancy, a domestic theme, while the "private" contemplative poem that follows, on "Contentment," becomes informed, as we have seen, by an invocation of royal sovereignty democratized as the liberty of the rural subject. "Written on Their Majesties coming to Kew" turns from loyalist pastoral to a brief object-lesson on domestic constancy without leaving the political entirely behind:

> In Spring's fresh robes the trees are clad,
>   The fields are fair to view;
> And every loyal heart is glad
>   The King is come to Kew.
>
> Ye lovers of inconstancy,
>   Now blush and take a view;
> A bright example you may see,
>   The royal pair at Kew.
>
> May God continue still to give
>   Them pleasures ever new;
> And many summers may they live
>   To reign and visit Kew.   (13–24)

If there is some interesting unease here regarding both inconstant lovers and those whose inconstancy might take a political form, it has been achieved by the briefest of generic interpolations. The public occasional poem becomes the occasion for "private" domestic advice. Indeed, the royal pair become praiseworthy because they appear domestically constant; they deserve loyalty because they set not an heroic or martial but a marital example. And if the royals are domesticated, Hands's rendering of pastoral contentment in the succeeding poem is shot through with an assertion of the political sovereignty of the British subject: it would seem that the privacy represented by rural retreat has also its "public" political dimension.

The political, property-owning dimension of erotic pursuit is similarly disclosed in the song "Phillis to Damon"; there is trouble in the paradise of pastoral when the interpenetration of worldly concerns disrupts pure romance. That is, at least, Phillis's "own" interpretation of why Damon has wooed, only to reject, her; she shifts inexplicably from "not knowing" why she has been slighted to assuming her poverty and his avarice must be responsible:

> REmember, false Damon, how often you've said,
> You lov'd me as well as a man could a maid;
> Though you slight me at last, and I cannot tell why,
> Yet, trust me, I never with sorrow shall die.

In my bosom so tender, your power to prove,
You planted the fair blooming flow'ret of love;
But for its destruction a frown you prepar'd,
To blast at your pleasure the flow'ret you rear'd.

Yet boast not your conquest, tho' from me you part,
Nor think yourself wholly possess'd of my heart;
Your smiles are not summer to melt the cold snow,
And your frowns are not winter, I'd have you to know.

Go seek for a maid that has money in store,
And amuse yourself often in counting it o'er;
Yet, Damon, believe me, your bliss will be small,
If counting your gold and your silver be all.   (1–16)

The confident rhythm of the third stanza, in its defiance and moment of colloquial assertion – "I'd have you to know" – establishes the grounds for Phillis's brief sermon against riches. The rich man always "thinks himself scant" (19), "While the poor that's contented ne'er feels any want" (20). Phillis rounds off her sermon generously, if more than a little self-righteously, by wishing Damon well:

May all pleasures attend you, that treasures can bring,
May you find of your joys a perpetual spring;
Yet I'll envy her not, that has money in store,
Nor think myself wretched, although I am poor.

Perhaps I the truth of some shepherd may prove,
Whose treasure's contentment, whose pleasure is love;
Then I without wealth shall be happy as you,
So Damon, false Damon, for ever adieu.   (25–32)

We are thus left with a choice between believing that Damon has indeed abandoned Phillis for a woman of means, or suspecting that her preaching, in its defensiveness, is rather beside the point, that she must find ways of justifying herself to herself in order to rescue her self-esteem in the face of romantic rejection. Hands's pastorals often raise such questions, leaving the "world" of the pastoral romance itself torn open by apparent intrusions from "outside." However accustomed we may be as readers to the inevitable political and social investments of pastoral, Hands's pastorals stage the conflict between romantic or green retreat and the economic and legal operations of power in a particularly stark way.

Of the named characters in the pastorals, Daphne most consistently mediates pastoral debates, expresses longing, is desired, and eventually, in "On a Wedding," married. Perhaps the moment of most nearly perfect mutual pleasure occurs in a poem simply entitled "A Pastoral" (pages 62–65), in which

Damon, with a little help from Laura, pursues Daphne, who has seemed deaf to his suit on previous occasions but who allows herself to be persuaded to take a walk with him. Typically for Hands, this consent on Daphne's part also means a detour from her previous desire, the rather whimsical determination, on such a beautiful day, to return to his master a runaway sheepdog she has been keeping since "the other day":

> Daphne.
>
> A shepherd's dog has long been gone astray,
> I found him on the green the other day;
> This fav'rite dog, the swain does much lament,
> I'll lead him home, and give the swain content.
>
> Damon.
>
> Why in such haste! the sun, my fair one, see,
> Is yet as high as yonder lofty tree;
> Those verdant meadows, where fresh daisies grow,
> Invite our steps, my Daphne, shall we go?
>
> The maid consented, making no reply;
> What maid could such a small request deny?
> A chrystal stream, in gentle murmurs glides
> Along the valley, and the meads divides;
> Along the banks the verdant alders grow,
> Their branches bending to the stream below;
> The tender leaves that hung on ev'ry spray,
> And hawthorn blossoms shew'd the month was May;
> Flow'rs, of various hue, bedeck'd the shade,
> And there young Damon led the tender maid:
> Her slender waist no gaudy ribband bound,
> But Damon's arm did form a circle round;
> Soft were the whisp'rings of the western gale,
> But with more softness Damon told his tale;
> The pleasing tale the maid in silence heard,
> But in her heart the gentle swain preferr'd;
> Thus o'er one meadow they were quickly gone,
> Yet still by pleasant meadows tempted on,
> How soon the lovers moments pass away,
> How soon, how soon, approach'd the close of day,
> The sun departed, and the plains grew damp,
> And rising Cynthia trimm'd her silver lamp;
> No more the birds to charm the year aspir'd,
> And wand'ring lovers from the plain retir'd;

> The swain ne'er thought to go, his steeds to find,
> The nymph forgot to leave her dog behind.   (47–80)

Provided that Damon (and not the shepherd with the missing dog) is the "gentle swain preferr'd" (70) by Daphne, and provided that Damon is "preferr'd" to his own "pleasing tale," so that he outdoes himself in the pastoral competition, this poem conveys a certain overpowering happiness by means of gentle understatement. In the delicious forgetting of a previous determination a new desire hovers. The wry anticlimax of both characters' neglecting their putative agrarian tasks (though Daphne's suggests flirtation as much as work) restores the working landscape to its "properly" pastoral rather than georgic status. This poem reclaims the pastoral for the rural laborer, however aestheticized by the moment of leisure itself. The country walk, the forgetting of time in a merging with pleasant meadows, comes to stand for the eros of courtship in a particularly concrete way: it is as if the typical pastoral conventions for representing courtship by substituting for its descriptions of landscape, the green world for the world of affect, were being rediscovered and re-enacted by the rural swain and maid themselves.

Such moments are rare in Hands's pastorals. There is more often an overriding sense of pastoral as usually representing a highly conventionalized fictive alternative to the real, and a poem like "A Pastoral" (pages 69–71) discloses this difference ironically. Corydon, a "blithesome swain" (1) only partially grounded in locality by keeping his flock by the river Leam (3), hastens chivalrously to the rescue of the generically named Pastora by offering to walk with her since evening is coming on:

> He said, and took her by the hand;
>   O happy shepherd he!
> Pastora too was pleas'd as well
>   As shepherdess could be.
>
> The swain no longer sought around,
>   His straying ewes to find:
> O happy nymphs that live in plains,
>   Where shepherds are so kind.   (45–52)

Once again, the test of erotic desire is the abandonment of labor, horses and sheep being left to themselves, left to stray or wander errantly like the current of desire itself. But the reflection of the last two lines works in at least two ways, as a cautionary example and as an ironic recognition of the gap between pastoral fiction and a possible real state of affairs in which either indifference or assault might well take the place of this courteous kindness.

Hints of trouble in paradise recur throughout Hands's pastorals, even when courtship and coupling seem relatively unproblematic and desire relatively mutual. In a poem again entitled simply "A Pastoral" (pages 72–73), in which

Daphne and Thirsis, the couple who will marry seven poems later, rest together after hay-making, there is a subtle realignment of point of view that points towards a possible disturbance of mutuality. Both because and in spite of its high moral tone, this poem's shifting of perspective and its relation to subsequent poems, especially "Thirsis and Daphne," interrupt any unproblematic flow of desire or promise of heterosexual bliss:

> As Thirsis and Daphne, upon the new hay
>   Were seated, surveying the plain;
> No guilt in their bosoms their joys to allay,
>   Or give them a moment of pain.
>
> Not Venus, but Virtue had made them her care,
>   She taught them her innocent skill;
> The swain knew no art, but to pleasure the fair
>   That nature had form'd to his will.
>
> Inspired by love, on his pipe he did play;
>   O Virtue! how happy the swain!
> While sweet Robin-red-breast that perch'd on the spray,
>   And Daphne was pleas'd with the strain.
>
> How pleasing the prospect, how cooling the breeze;
>   The sun shone delightfully 'round;
> And apples half ripe, grew so thick on the trees,
>   The boughs almost bent to the ground.
>
> Thus happily seated, by sympathy bound,
>   How pleasing the mutual chain;
> When either is absent, the prospects around
>   Display all their beauties in vain.
>
> They sat till the mist that arose from the brook,
>   Inform'd them the ev'ning was nigh;
> Th' swain shook his head with a languishing look,
>   And 'rose from his seat with a sigh.
>
> His flute he disjointed, and silent a while
>   He gaz'd on his maid with delight;
> Then gave her his hand, she arose with a smile,
>   He kiss'd her, and bid her good night.

An exemplum from a courtesy book on procedures for chaste courtship aimed at would-be pious lovers or a one-sided male fantasy in which Daphne can barely be seen to participate: much depends upon that guilt the lovers are without and those half-ripe apples hanging so heavily. Do they suggest luscious plenitude, an incipient fall into knowledge and betrayal, or a little of both? "Thirsis and Daphne," the third poem following, helps tip the balance away from the assurance of achieved mutual pleasure and towards a reading that would stress some postlapsarian asymmetry of desire. Thirsis declares himself and pleads with Daphne for a "kind" (24) answer; as in the former poem, she merely smiles and remains silent:

> To hear him thus his ardent flame express,
> Poor swain! she pity'd him; what could she less?
> Her love, perhaps, at length may be attain'd,
> By the dear swain that has her pity gain'd.   (35–38)

Establishing a context for "On a Wedding," these Thirsis and Daphne poems work to erode eros as such in favor of sympathy and friendship as a likely basis for marriage. Mutual pleasure seems intermittent at best, in the best pastoral tradition, but the work of compromise involved in social coupling is exposed here, a move rather untypical of canonical male pastoral.

Sometimes coupling is entirely rejected in favor of female independence, a detour nearly unthinkable in traditional pastoral. For Hands, this takes the form of humorous deflation and anticlimax. In "Lob's Courtship" and "The Widower's Courtship," for example, Lob and Roger both make clumsy bids for Nell, who rejects them out of hand. Part of the humor of each poem derives from the half-heartedness of the male suitors' offers, which deserve to be questioned if not rejected on the grounds of a certain lack of intensity. Roger "a doleful widower, / Full eighteen weeks had been" (1–2) when he asks to carry Nell's milking-pail for her, and Lob's desire for a wife comes to him comically in the midst of his cow-keeping, arousing our suspicions about his automatic association of the labor of feeding and nurturance with marriage:

> AS Lob among his cows one day,
> Was filling of their cribs with hay;
> As he to th' crib the hay did carry,
> It came into his head to marry.   (1–4)

Lob declares himself to his chosen Nell by letter, sending her two apples that she "likes better" than the letter, which she throws into the fire without answering. He pursues her in person only when he finds it convenient, "When roads are good, and weather fine" (21) and "The cows were all turn'd out to grass" (31):

> What Nelly! how dost do? says he,
> Come, will you go along with me
> O'er yonder stile, a little way
> Along that close; Nell, what dost say?   (41–44)

Nell's reply could hardly be blunter in its surly colloquialism:

> Me go with you o'er yonder stile?
> Says Nell, indeed I can't a-while;
> So she stept in, and shut the door,
> And he shabb'd off, and said no more.   (45–48)

In Hands's pastoral, women's silence regarding men's questions can be read as their tacit acquiescence in the circuit of courtship. But when women speak their minds, there is little room for ambiguity, and no room for men to answer them back. Nelly's reply to Roger's offer of assistance:

> . . . my milking pail
>   You shall not touch, I vow;
> I've carried it myself before,
>   And I can carry it now   (9–12)

is reinforced by her categorical refusal of his or any other man's affections, leaving him practically speechless:

> A sweetheart I don't want, says Nell,
>   Kind Sir, and if you do,
> Another you may seek, for I
>   Am not the lass for you.
>
> When she had made him this reply,
>   He'd nothing more to say
> But – Nelly, a good night to you,
>   And homeward went his way.   (25–32)

The dash before Roger's abashed, polite goodnight may remind us of the dash marking the interruption of the parson's pompous droning about Hands's *Death of Amnon* earlier in the volume. Discursive break and disruption of male desire to pronounce, control, pass judgment: Hands's bathetic dashes effectively silence male figures who would, it seems, otherwise always be talking.

As for female desire constituted in forms other than tacit acquiescence to male maneuvers or declarations of independence, it exists in its most positive guise in the poems offered by unnamed female narrators, poems of erotic longing expressed as interior monologic debate, as the agonized or amused weighing of choices. "Perplexity" registers the impossibility of untroubled happiness in a world of monogamous heterosexual choice: either "beautiful, witty, and gay" Collin or "kind-hearted" Damon (3–4) may legitimately be loved and lived with, but not both. In the manner of Lady Mary Wortley Montagu's "The Lover," Hands's "The Favourite Swain" reverses the tradition of the masculine blazon and anatomizes the qualifications of a truly desirable lover from a female point of view. For Montagu, these ingredients include command of an upper-class division between public and private affairs that produced those lines about the champagne and chicken which appealed to Byron:

> But when the long hours of Public are past
> And we meet with Champaign and a Chicken at last,
> May every fond Pleasure that hour endear,
> Be banish'd afar both Discretion and Fear,
> Forgetting or scorning the Airs of the Croud
> He may cease to be formal, and I to be proud,
> Till lost in the Joy we confess that we live
> And he may be rude, and yet I may forgive.[12]   (25–32)

When Hands displays her requirements, which may strike us as archly rural in contrast to Montagu's, those requirements turn out to represent a parody of pastoral conventions themselves. Such a swain must scorn "the state" (9) and "the great" (12) as well as "headstrong passion" untempered by virtue and friendship (43–48) – again, a certain tension concerning male "passion" as violence surfaces – know "not how to veil his mind" (14), but be so artful in his artlessness that:

> . . . when he pipes upon the plain,
> He must all approbation gain,
>   In spite of envious pride;
> And force his rival swains to say,
> His matchless skill must bear the sway,
>   It cannot be denied.   (25–30)

The text registers the hyperbolic nature of these qualifications, but insists that no improbable fantasy lover is being described. The female narrator has the pleasure of baiting and then flying in the face of the "envious youths" who "Say such a one was never found, / And all my search is vain" (49–51) by producing her own candidate defiantly:

> Mistaken swains know this my song,
> Does to my Thirsis all belong,
>   For he's my Fav'rite Swain.   (52–54)

This defiant tone also marks the most powerful of the female monologues, "A Song" (pages 117–18):

> YE swains cease to flatter, our hearts to obtain,
> If your persons plead not, what your tongues say is vain;
> Though fickle you call us, believe me you're wrong,
> We're fixt as a rock, as a rock too are strong.

Though sometimes, when suddenly struck with your charms,
We melt into softness, and sink in your arms,
Or breathe a soft sigh, when you from us depart;
That shakes not the purpose that's firm in the heart.

Too vainly ye boast we are easily won;
If on you, as on all, we should smile like the sun,
You laugh in your sleeves, when you from us retire,
And think that we love, when we only admire.

We are not so easily led by the nose,
Though with coxcombs we chatter, and flirt with the beaux;
Yet seldom or never our hearts they command,
Though sometimes through pity we give them our hand.

A tony, a coxcomb, a beau, or a clown,
Well season'd with money, may sometimes go down;
But these in our hearts we can never revere;
The worthy man only can hold a place there.

Suddenly the pastoral world of "swains" opens onto a distinctly urbane array of masculine types, in which the rural "clown" seems as out of place as if he were a character in an eighteenth-century comedy, and the female narratorial voice becomes impressively world-weary in her anatomization of relations between the sexes. The foolish, the conceited, the vain, and the clumsily countrified become equal targets of Hands's irreverent humor, and while "worthy" is never defined positively, it must be constituted through negation of the unreflective male opinions fundamental to the tradition of erotic lyrics and ballads catalogued in the poem itself. Read against some of Dryden's songs, for example, Hands's "Song" critically contradicts assumptions about both gender and class that the high Augustan tradition as usually read never addresses.

If we turn from Hands's pastorals to her version of the popular poetic tribute to Pope, the contradictions between literary sensibility, itself in this period usually read as a sign of class aspiration towards respectability, and a possible poetry of plebeian and feminist protest become acutely visible. Situating herself discursively within her volume as a laboring-class subject who writes, a servant-maid who publishes poems, and hence resists the class and gender-specific constraints that operate within contemporary discourses on rank, Hands nevertheless ventriloquizes a whole set of cultural constraints upon her own subjectivity when she confronts a text from the tradition of great male English poets. Her general comment on Pope in the "Critical Fragments" is similar to the opinions of her female contemporaries; she admires the sweetness and harmony, the ravishing sensuous beauty of his verse. But she is clearer and more precise than they about which of Pope's poems has most influenced her, his *Eloisa to Abelard*. "On reading Pope's Eloiza to Abelard" contains a configuration of ideological contradictions that typifies Hands's predicament as a laboring-woman poet in 1789.

The poem begins by praising the power of Pope's characterization of Eloisa to evoke sympathy and understanding; in this respect it follows previous models of female homage to Pope — praise for his skillful ventriloquism of female desire, passion, and loss, praise for his "writing like a woman" — with the implication that there "is" something subversively feminine about Pope's writing in spite of his occasional antifeminist pronouncements. In Hands's poem, however, this praise is short-lived:

> But when I hear thee unrelenting boast
> Thy tainted virtue, and thy honour lost,
> All sense of pity in my bosom dies,
> And direful tumults of reproaches rise:
> No passions soft, or sadly-pleasing pain,
> But rage and madness in thy bosom reign;
> Ah! must thy Abelard exalted be,
> Above the Maker of himself and thee!
> And darest thou thus explode the wedded dame,
> Disclaim her virtues, and disdain her fame:
> Blush, Eloiza, at a thought so vain,
> Thy face with crimson let confusion stain;
> And while thy bosom glows with guilty fire,
> Let every hope of happiness expire;
> But if again thou would'st my pity move,
> Lament at once thy honour and thy love.   (7–22)

Eloisa's passion is acceptably moving provided it does not cross certain boundaries: Eloisa as the victim of thwarted erotic expectations is an admirable production; Eloisa as sexual outlaw, proclaiming the superiority of her passion for Abelard to chastity, honor, religious faith, and the institution of marriage cannot be brooked. At the moment at which Eloisa declares her independence of God and the Law, shows anger rather than grief, she moves beyond the pale of Hands's tolerance and becomes subject to fierce denunciation. We may be reminded of Richard Polwhele's holding out some hope for Ann Yearsley's recovery from the pernicious principles of Wollstonecraftian liberty and sexual emancipation in *The Unsex'd Females*. Provided the working-class female subject does not go beyond the pale in sexual matters, provided she clings to religious piety and the law, the forces of social reclamation may not abandon her entirely to her own willful, passionate "abandonment."

There is, however, a stress-point in Hands's denunciation of Eloisa's impiety and willful impropriety that connects her reservations about Eloisa's victimization with Mary Collier's complex resignation to continued servitude: a loaded phrase from which we need to unpack a certain socially critical as well as a conservative tendency. It is Eloisa's attack on marriage that most astounds Hands the reader of Pope; "exploding" the sanctity of the "wedded dame," the virtues and good fame that go with marriage, is, for Hands, "a thought so vain." The vanity here must be primarily Eloisa's, contextually speaking; she is vain enough to think that her passion for Abelard and her theoretical objections to the institution of marriage exempt her from dishonor; her passion, as outlawry, must needs be purer in some sense than "mere," because sanctioned, wedded affection. And this audacity on Eloisa's part, this angry flouting of a religious and legal institution, Hands cannot accept. But "exploding" the myth of guaranteed virtue and happiness within marriage for women might be read as a "vain thought" in another way as well. In the context of the tradition of protofeminist criticism of marriage, which was well established by the end of the century, but which had not altered popular conceptions of marriage as a necessary institution, especially for women – indeed, those conceptions seem far from radically altered even today – Hands's "vain thought" might be read as an incompletely articulated, even barely realized, protest against the tyranny of legal institutions as regulators of affectivity and desire. How vain of Eloisa to think she can breach cultural precept singlehandedly, and how vain the attempt to explode the desirability of marriage for women by means of sheer polemic when the only alternative offered is sexual disgrace.

Thus Hands, like Collier, occasionally turns her literary abilities towards poetic imitation of those higher authorities, the great poets and God's Word, and hence towards self-effacement rather than sustained protofeminist challenge. The contradictions that operate within that complex subjectivity, Elizabeth Hands, about whom we still know so little, may seem peculiarly acute because we have only one volume of poems as evidence of her achievement. In it we may discover most strikingly both how difficult it must have been for her to write and publish poetry at all, and what complex delight she must have taken in her subtle shafts, muted protests, and skillful mimicry. The drawing-room crowd who knew of her accomplished parodying of themselves can never have been quite the same again, and for her contemporaries in domestic service, she might well have seemed an exhilarating example of a kind of resistance that the 1790s would render increasingly suspect, the resistance of the literate laborer.

Elizabeth Bentley, the "Norwich maiden"

Such a rightward tendency in the political climate after 1789 may perhaps mark the texts of the other Elizabeth with whom this chapter began, Elizabeth Bentley. The daughter of a cordwainer and a cooper's daughter, Bentley knew poverty but appears never to have gone into service or been employed in any other form of menial labor. Her poetry thus remains marginal to this study, but a few comparisons between her volume of 1791 and Hands's work may tell us something about the specific coordinates of the discourse of plebeian women's verse I have been reconstructing. *Genuine Poetical Compositions, on Various Subjects*[13] establishes Bentley as a talented poet "disadvantageously circumstanced," in Cowper's phrase. For Cowper, this social positioning combined with "genius" places Bentley in a very small tradition; he can think of no poet similarly situated except Mary Leapor. In fact, the preface to Bentley's first collection stresses her lack of education in terms most reminiscent of the "Advertisement" to the "New Edition" of Mary Collier's *Poems*:

Elizabeth Bentley had no education; she read only by accident; but from the moment she did read, she felt in herself a power of imitation, and a faculty of combining imagery, together with a facility of poetical expression, which, with adequate advantages, would have placed her in a situation little inferior to the first in Lyric composition.   (Sig. A1v)

Bentley's editor, the Rev. John Walker of Norwich, writes as one gentleman critic to another, faced with such a female talent; it is assumed that Bentley's readers will be gentlemen, just as her patrons are "Gentlemen of taste and fortune," and Walker even apologizes for preempting this hypothetical male reader's freedom to judge her verse as he sees fit:

An apology is, perhaps, due to the Reader for thus trespassing on his attention, and anticipating his own observations: but those Gentlemen of taste and fortune who have been the liberal patrons of E. Bentley, deemed some introduction not altogether unnecessary; and they have been comprized in a narrow compass, the Writer of them by no means wishing to obtrude his own opinions on others, or ostentatiously to enlarge upon them. He concludes, notwithstanding, with being firm in the hope, that the candid Critic will agree with him, that the Authoress, who is not less respectable for her modest virtues than her superior abilities, has *some* claim to the Choir, and is not the last or meanest in the train who

> "Follow where seraphic Milton led★."
> ★See page 68.

(Sig. A2v–A3r)

Of the individual subscribers to the volume who can be identified by gender, 907 are men and 716 women, not counting those included under "Ladies unknown," a category of "Additional" subscribers appended to the list. The women range from peeresses to local women and include Elizabeth Carter and Hester Chapone.[14] Walker's assumptions about Bentley's readership seem inappropriately one-sided, to say the least, but they also tell us something about the construction of a discourse of critical reviewing in this period which was gendered as masculine in spite, as well as no doubt because, of the proliferation of women's writing in the period.

In this context, the attention to Bentley's "modest virtues" as seeming no less necessary to her literary respectability, her successful imitation of Milton, than her "superior abilities," should come as no surprise. Walker's guidance to the reader involves signalling certain of the pleasures in store – "Let us mention, in particular, the Ode to Chearfulness" (Sig. A1v) – and, of course, marking his own perspicacity as a critic, since he has brought Bentley to our attention:

This is not a place for such an investigation: it may, nevertheless, be transitorily remarked, that the Poems in ten-syllable verse are prosaic, compared with those of a more varied and free measure; and the first superior exertion of her Muse is when she bids it "expand thy gentle wing," in the Ode on a Summer Morning.   (Sig. A2v)

This concatenation evinces in a strikingly literal way both the contemporary emphasis on the cheerful, grateful attitude expected of the poor as recipients of benevolence and the sense that the "unlettered" muse ought to find "freer" verse forms more hospitable than the high-literary pentameter couplet, which was in any case no longer fashionable as it had been in Pope's day. The appeal of the "Ode To Chearfulness" for Walker must lie in its subject-matter, its ideological resonance, because it is far from being one of Bentley's best poems, and is certainly less successful than her "Ode To Pleasure." A final postscript to the preface introduces Bentley's own brief autobiographical statement and testifies to the authenticity of her productions. The preface thus closes with a fixing of Bentley as both humbly cheerful and exceptionally respectable, and a reference forward towards her poem of homage to the great male English poets, "Lines, Addressed As A Tribute Of Gratitude To The Subscribers In General," in which Pope, Gray, Thomson, Shakespeare, and Milton are praised as being vastly beyond her ability to imitate them. The contrast with Hands's humorously parodic "Critical Fragments" could not be clearer, particularly as each is the last poem in its volume:

> WHAT glorious vision charms my wond'ring sight!
>   A Goddess with benignant smile appears;
> Her graceful form, attir'd in robes of light,
>   And in her hand a rural pipe she bears.
>
> 'Tis Gratitude! I know the heav'nly Maid!
>   Whose bosom's with ecstatic feelings fraught;
> Love and respect are in her mien display'd,
>   Her anxious looks express each inmost thought.

Receive, she cries, receive this pipe, and play
    Such sounds as I shall dictate to thine ear;
For lib'ral deeds demand thy noblest lay,
    Such lays as Angels might with pleasure hear.

Spare me, bright Goddess! how shall words impart
    Thy glowing sentiments which fire my breast?
Such shining, gen'rous deeds o'erwhelm my heart
    With transports, ah! too great to be exprest.

O! had I POPE's or GRAY's harmonious lyre,
    O'er Nature's paths with THOMSON could I tread,
Or catch one vivid ray of SHAKESPEAR's fire,
    Or follow where seraphic MILTON led.

Then would my Muse expand her ardent wings,
    And far beyond these nether regions soar;
Drink deeply at Parnassus' hallow'd springs,
    And Fancy's airy heights with ease explore.

Then, led by chearful Hope, unaw'd by Fear,
    I'd bend a constant vot'ry at thy shrine;
Such notes as thou should'st whisper to mine ear,
    Should breathe melodious through the flowing line.

But since unerring Fate's divine decree
    Has fix'd my lot to sing in humbler strain,
I'll sound the simplest shell, content to be
    The last and lowest of the tuneful train.

Under the sign of gratitude, Bentley writes a poem about her inability to write gratefully enough. In order to pipe a properly grateful pastoral, she would have to achieve an imitative sublime, a sublimity of imitation, of which she claims to be incapable. One could read this poem as in part a subliminal refusal of the demands made on plebeian clients by benevolent patrons in this period. The muse of Gratitude may look like a good girl, anxious to please – "Love and respect are in her mien display'd, / Her anxious looks express each inmost thought" – but anxious to please whom? Her respectful demeanor is directed towards the benevolent patrons for whom her thoughts are working overtime in the hope of anticipating their demands, not the poet, with whom she is positively dictatorial: "Receive, she cries, receive this pipe, and play / Such sounds as I shall dictate to thine ear." Only poetry conceived as a form of divine dictation or automatic writing hypothetically pleasurable to the angels would be good enough, apparently, for such a liberally philanthropic audience.

Bentley responds initially to this command with pathos that could be tinged by a certain asperity – "Spare me, bright Goddess!" – but that response quickly devolves into the inexpressibility topos. Like her "poor pen" in "On Reading Mr. Pope's Poems," she lacks the capacity to pay her debts; her muse is ardent but inadequate, incapable of the soaring "transports" of the master poets. Ironically, only if she could give voice to gratitude in their masterfully sublime manner, could she seem sufficiently "chearful" to be readable by a polite audience, neither awed by rank nor choked by fear; only then could the grateful strain flow melodiously as required. But Bentley closes the text by closing off that very possibility, by reinscribing her social difference, her humble status, at the risk of failing to please. Not the pipe of grateful pastoral but the shell, the single inarticulate sound of the found instrument, will be the sign of her poetic production. She signs herself "content" to be the last and lowest of the bards, humble imitator not witty parodist of their distinctive voices.

The two Elizabeths also address other topics in common, including the topical one of monarchy. If Bentley sets herself up as a humorlessly humble follower of the great tradition, we should not be surprised to find her singing a royalist strain more self-consciously patriotic than Hands's. The greater the distance from a plebeian tradition, a speaking on behalf of other plebeian voices in this period, the more comfortable the fit between this poetry ostensibly "from below" and patriotic verse as such, verse in praise of the British state as well as the monarch as a domestic figure. The juxtaposition of poems like "On His Majesty's Happy Recovery. March, 1789," which is remarkably similar to Hands's "Written on Their Majesties coming to Kew," with "On The Bill For Preventing The Exportation Of British Wool. 1788" situates Bentley's loyalist compliment in an imperial and nationalistic rather than domestic context. In this first collection of Bentley's, dominated not by pastoral like Hands's but by odes to abstract qualities or states of mind, the jingoistic strain does not come easily, but by 1821, as we shall see, her modest social rise is accompanied by confident, full-blown celebrations of military victories and imperial expansionism.

If we compare the failures of "On The Bill For Preventing" with the eloquent indignation and powerful argument of her "On The Abolition Of The African Slave-Trade. July, 1789," we may begin to do Bentley's 1791 collection at least rough justice. The georgic project of writing panegyrics to commerce is a feature of eighteenth-century poetry that has not worn well; the risk of bathos is considerable. "On The Bill For Preventing" attempts to equate the policy of not exporting British wool with winning a commercial war against France, and the image produced of Frenchmen cowering at the prospect of hoarded British fleece is a ludicrous one:

> BRITONS! rejoice at your approaching fame,
> Now haughty France shall shudder at your name;

> Your antient grandeur soon restor'd you'll find,
> With commerce 'tis inseparably join'd.
> In future records of this happy land,
> Unmatch'd shall that illustrious aera stand;
> When Britain's Senate, fir'd with noblest zeal,
> Stood forth and acted for their country's weal;
> And gave her sons alone the pow'r to hold
> Their snowy Fleece, more worth than mines of gold:
> The Fleece, their nat'ral right, their greatest boast,
> Their strength, by neighb'ring kingdoms envy'd most;
> From this fam'd period future times shall know
> Those matchless blessings which from commerce flow.   (1–14)

Even coming from a Norwich poet, all too aware of the importance of the wool trade to the local and national economy historically, this opening fails to translate the politics of commerce into an heroic and martial idiom without accident. Even Bentley's command of standard English, usually seamless, more free of colloquialism or dialect than the more strictly laboring poets' language, wavers: "more worth than mines of gold." The effort at patriotic sublimity seems to overtax her linguistic control.

If the poem on the wool trade seems overwrought, "On The Abolition Of The African Slave-Trade" is a distinguished anti-slavery poem, employing many of the features of abolitionist discourse that will be examined in chapter 6, and sustaining an exalted pitch of argumentation for ninety-four lines, which makes it the longest poem in her volume. Bentley employs the common strategy of denouncing slavery as a destruction of familial bonds and an infringement of human freedom, but she also, more clearly than many abolitionist writers, stresses the injustice of slavery as a legal institution and its violation of the slaves' rationality as well as their capacity for feeling and physical suffering:

> Too long the vile reproach has stain'd our land,
> Of arming Cruelty's despotic hand
> With legal pow'r, to render most forlorn
> Th' unhappy men in Afric's regions born;
> To seize and hale them from their native shore,
> Force them to toil and swell their master's store!
> To break the dearest, tend'rest ties of life,
> Rend from the husband's arms the much-lov'd wife!
> Fond parents from their weeping babes to force,
> Viewing the plaintive tear without remorse!
>   . . .
> Are not their species and our own the same?
> In colour only differing, not in name?
> By nature are they not endu'd with pow'rs,

Affections, feelings, sense, and life like ours?
Witness that *man of their despised race,
Whose genius claim'd him an exalted place
Amongst the sons of learning, wit, and fame,
Whose native worth deserves a deathless name;
His heart with ev'ry virtuous passion glow'd,
Bright sense was his, by nature's hand bestow'd;
Which proves – in their uncultur'd minds are sown
The seeds of knowledge equal with our own:
And shall we rob them of the bliss design'd
By Heav'n, the common right of all mankind?
Of liberty, to ev'ry soul most dear?
No! Britons will no more the censure bear;

        . . .

May heav'n–inspir'd Philanthropy increase,
And through each realm spread Liberty and Peace.   (11–94)

    *Ignatius Sancho, an African.

Bentley's fine use of enjambment emphasizes the paradox that slavery as an established form of commerce "arms" Cruelty's despotic tendencies with "legal" power, so that slavery becomes an arena for acting upon, "over there," impulses towards lawless violence that contradict the domestic values supposedly dear to free-born, liberty-loving Britons. The interrogative mode in the section on African humanity should be read, I think, not as a rhetorical dodge but as a moment of legal discourse in which the poet is allowed to pose persuasively analytical questions, as if before a jury. If what follows the dash ("Which proves – ") now seems undeniably racist in its lack of cross-cultural understanding, it should be read in the context of abolitionist arguments which stop short of granting African peoples even the potential for, let alone the achievement of, "culture," or cultural and intellectual accomplishments of any sort. Bentley's vision of global liberty and peace here would seem to work against her earlier endorsement of bellicose nationalism in "On The Bill For Preventing." Ideological contradiction is in this case reproduced in a distinct fracturing of aesthetic achievement.

If Elizabeth Hands carries on the plebeian pastoral tradition but modifies it through her distinctive wit, Elizabeth Bentley lands us back in the world of pre-plebeian pastoral. The pastoral figures in her *œuvre* as a residual series of moments, written from above, under the sign of humble cheerfulness rather than the possibility of resistance implicit in the representation of the dignity, not the humility, of labor:

Man to his daily labour takes his way,
   With sweet contented face and healthful brow;

> That health and peace can all his toils repay,
>> Which exercise and temperance bestow.
>>
>>   ("On A Summer Morning," 13–16)

This was evidently a version of pastoral appealing to Bentley's audience, which included some of the most influential literary figures of her time. If it strikes us now as a comparatively tame or derivative version, less interesting and innovative than Hands's version of pastoral, we might consider that Bentley herself clearly grasped the inevitability of historical vicissitudes, even the in-built obsolescence of historical narratives themselves. In the "Ode To Time, January, 1791," she writes:

> E'en Hist'ry's self, whose deathless page
> Conveys each truth from age to age,
>> At her thou oftimes aim'st a blow;
> She, who thy purpos'd rage defeats,
> As thy rude arm the stroke repeats,
>> More obsolete shall grow.   (19–24)

This is a compelling moment in Bentley's *œuvre* for a number of reasons, not least because it seems to anticipate her own fate within literary-historical narratives up to the present time. The relatively marginal status of Bentley's work in this study is not the consequence of some putatively disinterested aesthetic valuation but a recognition of the social and discursive differences that distinguish her literary production from that of the other poets I have been investigating. She should certainly be read, but not as a poet of the laboring classes.

Chapter 6

Other others: the marginality of cultural difference

These English Songs gravel me to death. – I have not that command of
the language that I have of my native tongue. – In fact, I think that my
ideas are more barren in English than in Scotish.[1]
(Robert Burns, letter to George Thomson)

She does not seem to have preserved any remembrance of the place of
her nativity, or of her parents, excepting the simple circumstance that
her mother *poured out water before the sun at his rising* – in reference, no
doubt, to an ancient African custom.[2]
(Margaretta Matilda Oddell, "Memoir" of Phillis Wheatley)

Mary Collier, Mary Leapor, Ann Yearsley, and Elizabeth Hands may have
been tolerated and even encouraged to flourish on the margins of what the
eighteenth-century English critical establishment defined as literature. Their
otherness in part helped consolidate canonicity, a centralizing set of literary
practices with specific gender, class, and cultural assumptions and interests,
against which their textual production could be seen as curious, exotic, and
ephemeral. But however marginal their writing may have been in terms of
established canons and an emergent literary history, Collier, Leapor, Yearsley, and Hands share a common nationality, at least in the sense of a native
language, with their cultural arbiters. Such is not the case with two further
writers of plebeian women's verse in the period, Janet Little (1759–1813) and
Phillis Wheatley (1753?–84). Historically and culturally, these two remain
more radically excluded from the mainstream than their English
counterparts.

The exoticism of the doubly or triply excluded other has been brilliantly
analyzed, especially in the context of imperialist narratives.[3] As Gayatri
Spivak has argued, across the fractured semiotic field of colonized native cultures, the narrative of imperialism writes itself, installs itself proleptically as
law in a process of "epistemic violence." The cultural effects of this violent
rupture are complex but include the effective silencing of "authentic native"
cultures as such. Spivak concludes:

that "great works" of *literature* cannot easily flourish in the fracture or discontinuity which is covered over by an alien legal system masquerading as law as such, an alien ideology established as only truth, and a set of human sciences busy establishing the "native" as self-consolidating Other ("epistemic violence").[4]

When the fractured semiotic field and the epistemic rupture are brought closer to "home" within the narrative of imperialism – as when the native other is taken to the imperialist capital as a trophy, an exhibition of colonial produce – a domestication of the other is attempted, a blurring of that "self-consolidation" of otherness instituted by colonialist science. To tolerate the other within one's midst requires both a "humanizing" gesture of theoretical inclusion – theological if not legal, formal if not social – and a demand that the other speak only in the alien language, not be able to "answer one back," as Spivak puts it (p. 131), in any "native" language.

If for Spivak the planned epistemic violence of the imperialist project silences the native speaker while constituting her as a "native informant," a potential source of knowledge/power for the imperialist subject, then the displaced native informant as slave or exotic within the European imperialist domestic scene is *forced* to speak. And to speak a reassuring patois: how grateful the servant or slave is to be subject to English imperialism – political, religious, linguistic, cultural, semiotic; how reassuringly subject the native is in producing this speech which is not native but is an imitation of the English word by a native mimic, a form of mimicry and an effect of colonial hybridization.

Homi Bhabha has theorized "hybridity" as *the* culturally specific effect of colonialism – operating within what Spivak calls a fractured semiotic field and producing a discourse that doubles, doubly displaces, and disrupts the self-proclaimed "authoritative" representations of the imperialist power:

If the effect of colonial power is seen to be the *production* of hybridisation rather than the hegemonic command of colonialist authority or the silent repression of native traditions, then an important change of perspective occurs. It reveals the ambivalence at the source of traditional discourses on authority and enables a form of subversion, founded on that uncertainty, that turns the discursive conditions of dominance into the grounds of intervention.

For Bhabha, native mimicry instantiates cultural and political resistance to imperialism, rather than abject capitulation:

To the extent to which discourse is a form of defensive warfare, then mimicry marks those moments of civil disobedience within the discipline of civility: signs of spectacular resistance. When the words of the master become the site of hybridity –

the warlike sign of the native – then we may not only read between the lines, but even seek to change the often coercive reality that they so lucidly contain.[5]

When we turn to the hybrid discourses of Janet Little, "the Scotch milkmaid," and Phillis Wheatley, "Negro Servant to Mr. John Wheatley, of Boston, in New England," as their respective title-pages describe them, we would be wise to read their works with some attention to the specific cultural, linguistic, and national or racial displacements thereby articulated.

The hybridity produced by imperialism, and native mimicry as its distinctive subversive practice, have been historically constituted precisely as disguise, camouflage, protective coloration that changes with the scene of action. They are not transparent, not easily open to a reading by the master or to decoding through a master discourse. Charges of excessive "conventionality" have been brought to bear on Wheatley's texts in particular, as if to diminish the historical and aesthetic importance of her writing by proclaiming *de facto* its derivativeness, conflating its lack of apparent (racial) political consciousness with a conservative refusal of cultural rebellion. But if we attend to the subtleties of Wheatley's verse, the piety, gratitude, and use of Anglographic poetic conventions and the materials of white colonialist culture assume a more complex significance. In Wheatley's texts there is cultural resistance dramatized as deracinated amnesia supplemented by mimicry of the master and mistress, and there is a buried idiom of subversion of authority, an awareness of revolutionary republican and abolitionist consciousness that Wheatley can only intimate but not openly embrace. Read with the nuances of postcolonialist cultural criticism in mind, Janet Little too refuses to be entirely written off as compliant in the face of English cultural imperialism, despite her obvious, and remarkable, mastery of English poetic forms.

This brief study of Little and Wheatley as exorbitantly marginal to the discourse of native Anglographic laboring-class women poets, with whom they share so many other historical and textual coordinates, is in no sense intended as a definitive or final word on either the Scottish or the African American literary scenes. If I deal with Little and Wheatley rather more briefly and tentatively than I do with the English poets, I do so, to borrow a phrase from E. P. Thompson, "not out of chauvinism, but out of respect."[6] It will be for others to challenge and enrich the connections I have attempted to make here between the marginality of English laboring-class women poets writing in their own country and for an audience with whom, formally at least, they shared a language, and the further subjections of plebeian Scottish women and enslaved African women in the context of the English literary establishment, and, more globally, the context of British imperialism.

Janet Little breaks into Scots

The Scots are different from the English; there is little disagreement about this in the later eighteenth century, on both sides of the border. English travelers speak of the Scots as rather primitive and very dirty. The exigencies of their climate and their relative material deprivation require a different standard of hygiene and different domestic technologies which the English label backward and sluttish.[7] Of particular interest to our reading of plebeian female georgic poets is the radical difference between English and Scottish procedures for housework and laundering clothes. All over the British Isles in our period women perform domestic tasks in essentially the same way, using strikingly similar mops, brooms, and brushes – except in Scotland:

Edward Burt, an Englishman who recorded their ways in the 1750's, found that they liked to do as much housework as possible with their feet, including laundry, parsnip and turnip washing, barley grinding, and floor mopping. 'First they spread a wet cloth upon part of the floor; then, with their coats tucked up, they stand upon the cloth and shuffle it backward and forward with their feet; then they go to another part and do the same till they have gone all over the room. After this they wash the cloth, spread it again, and draw it along in all places, by turns, till the whole work is finished. This last operation draws away all the remaining foul water.' Burt adds that when he first saw this floor cleaning method he ordered a mop to be made 'and the girls to be shewn the use of it'. But his efforts were in vain: 'there was no persuading them to change their old methods.'   (Davidson, p. 122)

This employment of the feet carries over into innovative methods of washing and ironing as well; instead of "beetling," or pounding their linen with a bat-like implement called a beetle or a battledore:

In Scotland women washed their laundry by trampling on it with bare feet in tubs of water, much to the astonishment of English visitors who were accustomed to the technique of beetling . . . They normally washed in groups, two women to a tub, supporting themselves with their arms thrown over each other's shoulders, while they danced up and down and sang rousing songs. Foreigners tended to suspect that they washed in this way for lascivious reasons (it was, after all, rather immodest to show so much leg in public). But this was unfair. Scottish women preferred to wash with the full weight of their feet because it was more efficient. It may also have been easier to keep blood circulating in the feet than the hands, especially in winter. For Scottish women washed all the year round, even, as Edward Burt wrote in 1754, 'in the hardest frosty weather, when their legs are red as Blood with the Cold'.

(Davidson, pp. 139–40)

There is a refusal to bow down to the household gods of cleanliness, as it were; life is hard enough for Scottish women without willfully engaging in excessive, back-breaking, and relatively inefficient labor. And the infusion of camaraderie and unexpected physical pleasure into the routines of domestic labor suggests something hedonistic and defiant about Scottish women's relation to housework. Where the danger of collapse into sheer drudgery is greater, north of the border, in a country of greater poverty and hardship than England, the women's resistance to gender-specific drudgery is more pronounced. They may be said to tread their clothes with a certain glee, though they may not shred them rebelliously, with bacchic abandon.

The difference of the Scots from the English does not begin and end with housework. In some remarks on "the Character and Condition of the Scottish Peasantry" prefixed to his life of Robert Burns, James Currie situates Burns for us as a member of a class that enjoyed certain educational advantages unavailable to the English poor:

In the very humblest condition of the Scottish peasants every one can read, and most persons are more or less skilled in writing and arithmetic; and under the disguise of their uncouth appearance, and of their peculiar manners and dialect, a stranger will discover that they possess a curiosity, and have obtained a degree of information corresponding to these acquirements.

These advantages they owe to the legal provision made by the parliament of Scotland in 1646, for the establishment of a school in every parish throughout the kingdom, for the express purpose of educating the poor.[8]

The prejudiced English sense of Scottish "difference" as "uncouthness" combines here with the social historian's desire to account for cultural specificity and the biographer's desire to explain the phenomenon of Burns. What emerges is a eulogy of Scottish popular learning, so that Burns and his contemporaries gain in authenticity what they lose in exceptionality.

The Scottish diffusion of reading and writing in English, however, has a special bearing for our reading of Burns's poetic contemporary and fellow laborer, Janet Little. Born near Ecclefechan in Dumfriesshire, the daughter of parents who "were not in circumstances to afford her more than a common education,"[9] Little became a domestic servant, first with the family of the Rev. Mr. Johnstone and then with Frances Anna Wallace Dunlop of Dunlop, Burns's patron. From Dunlop-house she went to Loudoun Castle, along with Mrs. Dunlop's daughter Susan, Mrs. Henri, who rented the castle for several years after the suicide of the Earl of Loudoun in 1786. Here Little superintended the castle's dairy, a position of considerable responsibility and prestige,[10] and found a patron for her verses in Mrs. Dunlop, who brought her to the notice of Burns. Her collection of poems, *The Poetical Works Of Janet Little*,

The Scotch Milkmaid (1792),[11] dedicated "To The Right Honourable Flora, Countess Of Loudoun," then twelve years old,[12] distinguishes her as a skillful, sometimes daring occasional poet in both standard English and Scots. She is said to have cleared about £50 through this publication, a very respectable showing, and the subscription list, to which Burns contributed, is impressive in its length and social clout.[13]

   Little's close relations with the Dunlop and Henri families, as well as her feudal relation to the young Countess of Loudoun, suggest at once a more intimate connection between the laboring woman and her employers and patrons than we have observed in comparable English situations, and a more abject dependence. Collier's and Hands's employers remain relatively anonymous within their work; Leapor was subject primarily to her father, and indebted to Bridget Freemantle; Yearsley had mainly anonymous customers for her milk business and her library, once relations with More had been severed for the more distant patronage of the Earl of Bristol. But Little's life is intimately bound up with Frances Dunlop's, who employs her as an amanuensis and companion, as well as reading and promoting her verses.[14] The promotion involves cajoling Burns in particular to take notice of Little and edit a few of her poems as if for publication, that Little might establish herself more independently than Mrs. Dunlop's charity would allow:

She says ten guineas would make her as happy as worldly circumstances could do. Is it not a pity of me that can hear this and not copy the man in the *Guardian* or *Spectator*, who set down the article in his pocket-book "How to make a Man happy £10?" Yet I think were her rhymes properly put out, as the phrase is, she might be made happy and indebted to none but herself, since her modest wishes are placed within such humble bounds, and I dare even say there would be some of the collection not unworthy your reading, perhaps honoured with your applause, tho' you well know I have no reason to call you lavish of that . . . I shall send you a few lines she gave me one day lately . . . but to instruct my ignorance and hers too, I will beg you would just write over a verse or two of it, and return me just as a thing should be done for the press; for I have a curiosity to see what that requires.   (Wallace, II, p. 103)

Her desire to promote Little's literary enterprise makes her protective of her protégée, especially when other Scottish poets are mentioned. And the prejudices of gender contribute insidiously to this defensiveness:

So all this week I have done nothing but read Wilson's poems, which Jenny Little brought me, and I am almost sorry I have seen them . . . I fear it will hurt Jenny by comparison, as it has all that masculine advantage over her that your sex generally have over ours on paper.   (Wallace, II, pp. 182–83)[15]

The attitude towards Little's class represented in these passages is distinctively marked by both a greater projection of social distance and laboring-class deference than Bridget Freemantle considered suitable between herself and Mary Leapor, and a closer emotional bonding than More could conceive between herself and Yearsley. Dunlop takes to Little from the first both because she has "ideas above her station," indicative of intelligence and industry, and because her ambitions remain reassuringly class-bound.[16] This is the double-bind of Scottish peasant education and Scottish reverence for industrious application within the working class – a more acute contradiction between potential intellectual attainments and material circumstances than was common in England, and one intimately related to English political, economic, and cultural domination.

The distinctive Scottishness of Little's comparatively feudal relation to her patrons and of her accomplishment in mastering both English and Scots – for it is only the dominant culture that can afford to ignore other languages – is adumbrated by her heightened consciousness of a vocal, hypercritical literary establishment. The critical self-consciousness of Scottish men of letters in this period was a complex phenomenon, produced in part by the Scottish educational regimen, and in part by the dual functions of Edinburgh as national capital and provincial cultural center – seeing itself as a rival to London, yet refusing rivalry, rather as York had done, historically. This self-consciousness was also partly generated by an emergent Scottish nationalism in both politics and letters. That Scottish critics were rigorous, ruthless, and much to be feared is an assumption shared by poets as different as Burns and Byron. Even so rustic a poet as Janet Little apparently felt that she had reason to fear for her works when they were received by those (in)famous men of Edinburgh. The solitary bumbler, Minutius, who fails to come to terms with Leapor's verse, seems a pallid antagonist when compared with the comical, self-serving, but powerful critics envisaged in Little's satire "To My Aunty."

And that a plebeian Scottish woman poet should labor under a greater apprehension of critical disparagement than her English counterparts is testimony to her greater sense of marginality and vulnerability as a literary voice. There is the pressure to prove oneself skillful in two literary languages, as a first obstacle, and the still uneasy relation between English literary culture and Scottish which the poetry of Burns had begun to broach but which in 1792 remained unresolved. Neither previous decades' magisterial mimicry of standard English by Scottish writers nor a totally defiant nationalism, and investment in Scottish dialect verse, was simply available to a Scottish poet of the 1790s. Within the polyglossic field of Anglo–Scottish cultural relations, a certain hybridity, a certain warlike mimicry, was inevitable. And the heteroglossic possibilities of poetic language could be foregrounded by the Scottish poet.[17]

The poetic texts of Janet Little bespeak a national and cultural conflict worked out in a warring of literary languages. Significantly, her *Poetical Works* unfold at first in standard English, then erupt into Scots with the crucial emergence in her text of the figure of Burns as a national poet – and a plebeian genius. But the bilingualism of Burns, and his association of poetic mastery with Scots rather than English, does not fit Little exactly. Burns's Scots poetics, while defiantly nationalist and truculently heteroglossic, mingling fragments of many discourses from the high literary to the plebeian, is not an entirely appropriate vehicle for the distinctively female and protofeminist discourses with which Little is engaged, some of which she continues to pursue in standard English. Neither is Burns an unproblematical exemplar in socio-sexual terms for a female poet. Little's admiration of Burns is tempered by her ironical sense of his rapacious egotism that, like so many manifestations of masculine desire, so often serves itself at the expense of the women it claims to desire, to value, and to represent.[18]

The twenty-fourth in her collection of fifty-four poems, "Given To A Lady Who Asked Me To Write A Poem," is Little's rewriting of literary history to accommodate both herself and Burns as Scottish writers who refuse to be silenced or colonized by Anglographic cultural hegemony. Presumably the demands of improvisational occasional verse "legitimate" the sudden linguistic disruption that occurs when the text shifts from standard English to a mild form of Scottish dialect verse:

> IN royal Anna's golden days,
> Hard was the task to gain the bays:
> Hard was it then the hill to climb;
> Some broke a neck, some lost a limb.
> The vot'ries for poetic fame,
> Got aff decrepit, blind, an' lame:
> Except that little fellow Pope,
> Few ever then got near its top:
> An' Homer's crutches he may thank,
> Or doun the brae he'd got a clank.
>
> Swift, Thomson, Addison, an' Young
> Made Pindus echo to their tongue,
> In hopes to please a learned age;
> But Doctor Johnston (*sic*), in a rage,
> Unto posterity did shew
> Their blunders great, their beauties few.
> But now he's dead, we weel may ken;
> For ilka dunce maun hae a pen,
> To write in hamely, uncouth rhymes;
> An' yet forsooth they please the times.

> A ploughman chiel, Rab Burns his name,
> Pretends to write; an' thinks nae shame
> To souse his sonnets on the court;
> An' what is strange, they praise him for't.
> Even folks, wha're of the highest station,
> Ca' him the glory of our nation.
>
> But what is more surprising still,
> A milkmaid must tak up her quill;
> An' she will write, shame fa' the rabble!
> That thinks to please wi' ilka bawble.   (1–30)

At once we have the mocking of Johnson as self-appointed critical gatekeeper of English poetry, the heroization of Burns, and the self-deprecatory introduction of Little. All modern English poets have been literary-historical cripples, it would seem, needing the crutches of epic translation or Pindaric precedent in order to sally forth into the public arena. Burns breaks conventions both by means of his agrarian peasant stance and his boldness in writing on contemporary topics. He also speaks across class lines and religio-political factions, thus opening things up for other plebeian poets who may hope to address a wide audience:

> Yet Burns, I'm tauld, can write wi' ease,
> An' a' denominations please;
> Can wi' uncommon glee impart
> A usefu' lesson to the heart;
> Can ilka latent thought expose,
> An' Nature trace whare'er she goes:
> Of politics can talk wi' skill,
> Nor dare the critics blame his quill.   (35–42)

As Little writes in "An Epistle To Mr. Robert Burns," which appears some forty-five pages later, "To hear thy song, all ranks desire; / Sae well thou strik'st the dormant lyre" (13–14).

Burns realizes the potential "dormant" within Scottish linguistic capacities at the same time that he "exposes" every "latent thought" of a projected popular reader. And now, gangway! What Burns has begun may prove an unstoppable project – if Little herself can win over this somewhat skeptical, somewhat recalcitrant, definitely prejudiced "popular reader" with a distinct Scottish accent:

> But then a rustic country quean
> To write – was e'er the like o't seen?
> A milk maid poem-books to print;
> Mair fit she wad her dairy tent;
> Or labour at her spinning wheel,

An' do her wark baith swift an' weel.
Frae that she may some profit share,
But winna frae her rhyming ware.
Does she, poor silly thing, pretend
The manners of our age to mend?
Mad as we are, we're wise enough
Still to despise sic paultry stuff.   (43–54)

It would seem that gender prejudice is a stronger barrier to enthusiastic popular reception than mere "chieldom." Women's work is to remain strictly menial and "profitable" in the sense that Mary Leapor's parents intended it: dairy-tending, spinning, done both swiftly and well, to maximize productivity. A Janet Little can expect no financial return on her volume of verse – though, ironically, she did earn one. As for reformist zeal as a motive for publication, the hypothetical Scottish reader scoffs and takes comfort in being able to distinguish between the pleasures of Burns and the possibly emendatory purposes of a Little.

The poem concludes dialogically with a "quoted" speech from a supposed Scottish critic of Little's verse and the "poet's own" reply, ironically in standard English:

"May she wha writes, of wit get mair,
An' a' that read an ample share
Of candour ev'ry fault to screen,
That in her dogg'ral scrawls are seen."

All this and more, a critic said;
I heard and slunk behind the shade:
So much I dread their cruel spite,
My hand still trembles when I write.   (55–62)

The text has closed back on itself in a self-referential and self-deprecatory way, acknowledging its improvisational and inconsequential origins, its inconclusive status. The last line is a joke, the poet not so frightened by critical spite she stops writing, only so frightened her hand trembles as she continues committing this daring offence. Registering the mock-terrors of bilingual marginality, Little legitimates herself as a writer "after Burns," paying homage to him but not enslaved by his aesthetic or his (perhaps too easy?) popularity.

The disruption of the Anglographic text by Scottish dialect verse serves to foreground the degree of skillful mimicry that abounds in Little's English poems. Of particular interest for feminist literary history are the acknowledgment of Lady Mary Wortley Montagu and Elizabeth Rowe as influential precursors, and the appearance, once again, of poems to women, of an affective if not explicitly erotic kind, which bolster the persuasiveness of such texts of female independence from male desire as "From Delia To Alonzo" and "From Flavia To Carlos."

Through the mediation of what we must read, in the light of the foregoing "Given To A Lady Who Asked Me To Write A Poem," as Scottish mimicry of standard English verse, a parodic extended metaphorization of the "star system" within literary history fits uneasily with homage to Montagu and Rowe. "On Reading Lady Mary Montague [*sic*] And Mrs. Rowe's Letters" gives us a Montagu bright as Venus eclipsed, in her turn, by a Rowe brighter than Apollo: "Superior rays obtain'd now the bays, / And MONTAGUE [*sic*] bended the knee" (11–12). Little goes on to find Rowe the preferable exemplar, whose combination of "virtue and wit" must function as a model for whosoever reads her. The final quatrain hypothesizes Rowe's transformative effect on female readers which will in turn cause men to grant Rowe's female imitators pride of place, and cause critics (implicitly male) to cease savaging women's writing and admire it – speechlessly:

> Would ladies pursue, the paths trod by you,
>   And jointly to learning aspire,
> The men soon would yield unto them the field,
>   And critics in silence admire.   (17–20)

There remains some unresolved tension between the hyperbolic metaphors of instauration and the text's concurrence with the triumph of Rowe over Montagu. The poem never specifies possible causes determining which women writers will achieve praise and fame beyond "the gay circle," "mankind," "they," and "Britannia's shore."

Nor is it clear that Little is making a strictly aesthetic judgment and not inadvertently miswriting female literary history. Rowe began publishing in the 1690s, while Montagu's work circulated mainly in manuscript until after her death in 1762. In no sense could Rowe "displace" Montagu's reputation chronologically, and Little's text bespeaks no knowledge of such literary-historical chronology anyway. A tradition of women's writing may have been well established with the middle-class reading public by mid-century, but laboring-class women's poetry does almost nothing explicitly to corroborate the popular reception of that tradition. Little's would seem to be the only poem by a laboring woman paying explicit homage to English women writers, and Little herself may have been reading without much historical knowledge about her predecessors Rowe and Montagu.

Textually, we are supposed to be persuaded simply to accept that Rowe is the "better" writer, a judgment with which even the "vanquished" Montagu is shown to concur. Yet contextually, in the light of Little's *œuvre*, such celebrity itself is ironically undercut by the resilient, virtuosic voice from the cultural margins, speaking of "Britannia's shore" but not for it, by reason of her nationality, her gender, and her class.

Within the bilingual or, after Bakhtin, the polyglossic, text of Little's *Poetical Works*, the parodic function of Scottish mimicry of English, and of Scottish rendering of the vernacular into literary language, is foregrounded. And heteroglossic possibility, that contest of linguistic traces marking the social within texts and words as a site of struggle, thus becomes apparent within each poem, though differently, depending on its relation to the still dominant literary discourse of eighteenth-century standard English.

The four poems that constitute a correspondence with "Nell" shift the question of female literary community culturally closer to home. Though separated by geographical distance, "Nell" and "Jenny" contrive visits and epistolary verses to one another after Jenny leaves Ecclefechan for Loudoun Castle. Like Katherine Philips's Orinda, Lucasia, and Rosania before them, they also exchange vows of undying affection. Their shared pleasures in the past have consisted mainly of meetings in the open air, "in Eccles' peaceful bow'rs" ("Another Epistle To Nell," 5) and in the fields at harvest time: "With joy we would our sickles wield, / . . . None better can that weapon ply" ("To Nell When At Moffat Well," 19–22). Except that their labor claims much of their time and affection – "As time for study is but scarce, / Accept extemporary verse" ("Epistle To Nell, Wrote From Loudoun Castle," 5–6) – the two correspondents project no sense of incongruity between their social situations and their desire for "skill" sufficient for "Parnassus' hill" ("Another Epistle To Nell," 19–20). Nell longs for an "air-balloon" that would convey her to Loudoun so that they could continue their former meetings and talk of poetry, particularly the phenomenon of Burns's success, which implicitly legitimates their own aspirations:

> With you, dear Jenny, I would pass some hours,
> Amongst its shady walks and fragrant bow'rs.
> Of poetry and poets talk by turns,
> And pleas'd make comments on the far-fam'd Burns.
>
> ("Nell's Answer," 25–28)

Self-mockery seals their pact of mutual aspiration and praise: Burns's success has, it would seem, loosed a crowd of would-be rustic poets on the world. But Jenny and Nell's attempts to write are buttressed by their friendship, so that literary fame becomes a secondary consideration. Their verse epistles textualize their mutual desire for companionship, and their poetic aspirations constitute a shared desire for more writing that their mutual reflection in one another's verse perpetuates:

> We'll beat the bushes for the rustic muse,
> Where ev'ry dunce her inspiration sues.
> 'Mongst the vast crowd, let you and I aspire
> To share a little of Apollo's fire.

> If Fortune prove, like Cupid, ever blind,
> We may perhaps some petty favour find;
> But if no more we gain by these our lays,
> We'll please ourselves with one another's praise.
>
> ("Another Epistle To Nell," 25–32)

The choice, we notice, is "Apollo's fire," the code of Rowe's virtue and wit rather than Montagu's discourse written under the sign of Venus, that concatenation of personal beauty and aesthetic achievement in which plain virtue would be out of place. Jenny and Nell write not as beauties but as plain rustics, whom only a "blind" good fortune could rescue from obscurity. And yet their circuit of affect and literary aspiration seems completely satisfying in a way untypical of contemporary heterosexual epistolary discourse, fraught as it is with contention for power.

If the "Jenny and Nell" poems recall faintly the seventeenth-century erotic epistles to women by Katherine Philips, who may well have influenced Mary Leapor's epistles to female friends, the exchanges between heterosexual lovers in Little's English verse recapitulate the intransigence of Leapor's *Complaining Daphne*. Little's male lovers make unconditional demands, strive to dominate the discourse, disclose in their desire for their beloveds an obsession with absolute power and narcissistic self-reflection that would deny and cancel the desires of the other. This self-affirming circuit of male desire is most clearly parodied in "From Philander To Eumenes," in which one friend tries to talk the other into marriage, only to talk himself out of love with women altogether. Beginning with a list of the blessings that a "virtuous wife" (14) can bring to a man, so that male desire is revealed as covetous and entirely egocentric, Philander finishes by declaring his own entrapment in desire, his fear of sexual ecstasy and loss of control, from which reading Eumenes' letter and replying to it have apparently just saved him:

> I find I'm better while your lines I read,
> I'm almost from my Gallic fetters free'd.
> As you alone were partner of my grief,
> Pray now congratulate my quick relief.   (41–44)

Sexual suspicion would appear to be insuperable for both sexes, in Little's scheme. But significantly, only male characters cast their desire in terms of combat, possession, property, and the emotional security to be gained through marriage. When Little's men reject their beloveds, they end by rejecting their own narcissistic hunger for emotional largesse from the other. Little's women write to sustain both independence and desire, Little's men to sustain their sense of their own sovereignty, which requires careful tending. And Burns himself epitomizes this need for constant feminine nurturance and reassurance in Little's "On A Visit To Mr. Burns," in which Burns, having broken an arm in a fall from his horse, is solaced by both wife and female guest, to the exclusion of all other conversation, except praise of his work:

> With beating breast I view'd the bard;
>   All trembling did him greet:
> With sighs bewail'd his fate so hard,
>   Whose notes were ever sweet.   (29–32)

Little's protofeminist impulses thus demand that she engage with literary languages other than Burns's, that she connect her work with existing traditions of English women's writing.

The women to whom Little's men address their affections wish for friendship and resist being persuaded or bullied into marriage. Marriage promises only unhappiness in these epistles; therefore, why renounce the single life, with its occasions for writing and independence, for the closure of marriage? The sensual argument for seizing transient bliss at any price is not allowed to stand. Delia refuses Alonzo's proposal on the grounds that Adam and Eve's bliss, which he would imitate, ended abruptly in their ruin:

> But think, fond youth, how transient was the bliss.
> Scarce had he felt the joys of mutual love,
> Scarce had he once receiv'd th' ambrosial kiss,
> When ah! his darling did his ruin prove!
>
>   . . .
>
> A single life we find replete with joys.
> The matrimonial chain I ever dread.
> A state of celibacy is my choice;
> Therefore Alonzo never can succeed.
>
> ("From Delia To Alonzo," 13–28)

The poem that follows this one in the volume, "From Delia To Alonzo. Who Had Sent Her A Slighting Epistle," represents Alonzo as an arrogant and vengeful, as well as injured, lover. Once again sexual desire is not so much displaced onto a desire for literary fame; rather, each desire establishes and conditions the other. Alonzo, slighted, responds by writing Delia a "slighting" epistle, in which he tries to make her regret her choice of celibacy through his textual prowess. In fact, we must ourselves compose Alonzo's "slighting" epistle from what Delia says about it. The shape of the correspondence itself directs our sympathies by silencing Alonzo and rendering Delia's "coldness" an admirable strategy of self-defense against such a pompous, importunate, and easily angered lover:

> You've been upon Parnassus' top,
> More high than Alexander Pope;
> And wild Arabia's plains you grope

For Phenix rare,
That useful knowledge you may drop,
    While dunces stare.

            . . .

Such eloquence does merit praise;
Deep erudition swells your lays:
You seem the laureate of our days;
            And all the nine,
Your mighty character to raise,
            Do now combine.

'Tis pity, sir, that such as you
Should agriculture's paths pursue,
Or destin'd be to hold the plough
            On the cold plain;
More fit that laurels deck'd the brow
            Of such a swain.

Yet Homer's parts few did commend,
Till death his doleful days did end;
Then seven cities did contend
            A right to claim;
Each vow'd from thence he did descend,
            So great his fame.

Perhaps, sir, in some future age,
Struck with the beauties of your page,
Old Scotia's chieftain may engage
            Your name to raise;
More have they to excite their rage,
            Than Homer's lays.

But I must drop the pond'rous theme,
Lest you my weak attempts should blame;
So sure your title is to fame,
            Who runs may read;
Of such your merits to proclaim
            You have no need.

Know then, that love within my breast,
Has never yet been known to rest;
Nor would I harbour such a guest,
            To give me pain:
I wish you, sir, so much distress'd,
            Soon well again.   (7–66)

Alonzo's great ambition, we must assume, both impresses Delia and strikes
her as pretentious because it is at odds with Alonzo's circumstances. Like
Burns a ploughman poet, Alonzo is not the omnipotent social being he would
need to be to force Delia's hand and the critical establishment's too; but this is
not why Delia rejects him. If anything, it is his humble status coupled with
literary accomplishment that has laid the groundwork of friendship between
them in the first place. Rather, Delia, however ironically, wishes him fame, if
only posthumous fame, since that seems the most likely sort of fame for an
as-yet unknown poet to achieve. But she remains unmoved on the subject of
marriage, or heterosexual love, so that Alonzo's passion appears to be a form
of overweening arrogance on his part: if desire is not mutual, can the lover's
high-handedness be justified? Why should Delia desire Alonzo simply because
he wishes to marry her? A similar strategy is employed in "From Flavia To
Carlos," though their epistolary relation represents an earlier stage of friendship. Attempting scrupulous honesty, Flavia refuses the epistolary conventions of flattery and overstatement; at the risk of offending Carlos, or of being
misread, she declares:

> Know Sir, when friendship does commence,
> All flatt'ry must be spurn'd from thence:
> No real friendship can exist,
> In the disembling flatt'rer's breast.
> What can poor Flavia then bestow,
> But wish you still may better grow?
> Your wit still more and more refine,
> And all the beauties of your min',
> With radient lustre ever shine.   (25–33)

Thus an heroically rational, if faintly ascetic, female sensibility emerges from
these texts of self-declared "celibacy." Such poems establish not instrumental
reason but a protofeminist recognition of women's heightened vulnerability
within the circuit of heterosexual desire.

Little's mimicry of English neoclassical epistolary discourse has a polemical
bent that links her *œuvre* with the separatist tendencies of Leapor's, and more
occasionally, Yearsley's and Masters's work. But the male lovers of these texts
are not villified into figures of folklore as in *Complaining Daphne*'s childhood
stories. Little's heroines do not wish to break off correspondence but to
maintain it, and to continue textualizing desire, rather than embrace the
silencing closure of marriage. The desire to write refuses to be collapsed into a
displacement – figured as some ineffable sensual bliss – when marriage as Law
is represented as the only alternative, a culmination of desire that would
abruptly end it. Within the conventionality of the erotic epistle, Little's
cultural ventriloquism nevertheless allows her to produce poetic heroines of
independent mind, for whom writing itself constitutes and fulfills their desires

in ways otherwise impossible in their historical moment. Such figures are of considerable interest to a feminist literary history. For them, as Linda Kauffman claims, "The writing is the revolution."[19]

If Burns stands at the center of Little's forays into Scottish dialect verse, a figure of national and linguistic authority, a totem of male success achieved across class lines, and so an imitable master text, there are moments in Little's Scots poems that refute phallocentrism in a radically deconstructive way. By turning to figures even more marginal to the literary-critical establishments of Scotland and England than herself, Little gives not voice but textual materiality, even a certain monumentality, to female social texts not easily recuperable by either contemporary literature or criticism, and which foreground the dynamics of gender and class power that exclude and silence the disenfranchised. *A Poem On Contentment. Inscribed To Janet Nicol, A Poor Old Wandering Woman, Who Lives By The Wall At Loudoun And Used Sometimes To Be Visited By The Countess* could stand in distinct contrast to Hannah More's "rescuing" of the fugitive Louisa as described in Yearsley's *Clifton Hill*. It also suggests a potentially different poetic stance in relation to the poor borderer figures of the *Lyrical Ballads* from the one most often adopted by Wordsworth, of inchoate, rather distant social protest coupled with aesthetic recuperation. *On Contentment* works dialogically in at least two senses. First, there is an address, autobiographical and direct, on the part of the poet's "muse" to Janet Nicol, rather disingenuously asking permission to dedicate a "song" to her while already in the process of composing it, followed by a structuring of the verses that directs each stanza to Janet Nicol while describing other characters in the more distant third person. And second, there is an articulation of standard English with Scots throughout the poem, so that the poet both "speaks as herself," an educated bilingual poet, and addresses Janet Nicol more intimately as a friend, fellow Scotswoman and plebeian.

The address to a social inferior is surely significant. Little appears less constrained than other laboring poets by the need to write directly for patrons. And in seeming to choose her own subjects, she decides to represent and address the nearly outcast. There is some evidence that in Scotland women of almost-outcast class did write and publish: Isobel Pagan and possibly, at the end of her life, Jean Adams.[20] So it may be that Little is not benevolently aestheticizing Janet Nicol, turning her into a curious literary object because her own class privilege encourages it. According to Frances Dunlop, Janet Nicol was a "poor half-witted creature that lives at the coal-pit here."[21] Little may be interceding for a woman who was outcast because she could not represent herself adequately, speak for herself with legal or social authority. What is perhaps most interesting about this relation is that rather than stressing a privileged distance between herself and Janet Nicol, Janet Little's muse finds similarity and complicity:

> O JANET, by your kind permission,
> My muse, in tatter'd low condition,
> Would fain attempt, if you'll allow,
> To dedicate a song to you.
> Possess'd of few attractive pow'rs,
> Her case does much resemble yours;
> So lest none else should deign to hear,
> She humbly supplicates your ear.   (1–8)

If the relation between poet and interlocutor here is a narcissistic one, it is presented as mockingly and self-consciously so. The obscure spinster poet and the solitary "wandering woman" both lack an audience; this poem will compensate for that lack by reinscribing the relative absence of social connectedness in Janet Nicol's text as "contentment" – that which the poet most desires for herself, and which is not so often associated with female figures in eighteenth-century writing as are contrivance, distress, seduction, or abandonment.

Because Janet Nicol is irreducibly other, the classically feminine discursive positions of wife and lover cannot be assigned to her. Her otherness becomes approachable only through her difference from such representations as Celia, the unhappy wife, and Delia, the rejected lover. The poet wishes that Janet – and it is at these moments in the text that "Janet" takes on a distinctly autobiographical and self-referential resonance – may never know the miseries of loveless marriage or "ill requited love":

> May stars propitious guard your life
> From all the mis'ries of a wife:
>
>   . . .
>
> O Janet, may you never know
> The pangs that lovers undergo.   (35–48)

The pangs of unrewarded scribbling are the third feminine situation from which Janet Nicol's otherness excludes her; "Cordelia" too suffers for her femininity through the senselessness, and consequently harsh critical reception, of her verses:

> O may you never feel the pain,
> We heedless scribbling fools sustain.   (61–62)

Neither is Janet subject to the delusions of the patriot, the courtier, the coxcomb, or the miser, which also bring unhappiness:

> O Janet, shun the coxing tribe,
> Who barter virtue for a bribe.
>
>   . . .

> The Miser hopes his joys to hold,
>
>   . . .
>
> Thieves, moth and rust, corrupt his rest,
> May all his sorrows be your jest.   (69–78)

Instead, Janet Nicol can only be more directly apprehended through an anatomy of the elements that comprise her contentment, at least as ventrilo-quized by the poet, that other Janet, who can slip so easily from standard English into literary Scots:

> May your old shoes, your staff and plaidy,
> Be always for the journey ready:
> And blithly may ilk neighbour greet you;
> May cakes, and scones, and kibbocks meet you;
> And may they weel ilk pocket cram,
> And in your bottle slip a dram.
> May your wee glass, your pipe and specks,
> Be ay preserv'd frae doleful wrecks.
> May your wee house, baith snug and warm,
> Be safe frae ev'ry rude alarm
>
>   . . .
>
>   Janet farewel, you've lint and tow,
> O keep your rock ay frae the low;
> Tho' turmoils torture land and sea,
> Content may smoke a pipe with thee.   (85–127)

We are left admiring the "simple" pleasures of a wandering woman's existence in all their sharp sensory effects – as cozy, yet exotic, as the pungent scent of pipesmoke outdoors on a chilly afternoon. The details of food, drink, serviceable clothing, and warm shelter may represent comfort, yet they do not signify enclosure and domesticity, but rather the possibility of mobility and freedom – "always for the journey ready." If this anatomization of marginal social being is somewhat sentimental and recuperative in a Words-worthian sense, it is also familiar and concretely particularized in a way that Wordsworth's "peasants" never are. The Scots dialect ruptures into dis-continuities what is in Wordsworth a typically seamless poetic discourse. A certain levelling effect of familiarity, of linguistic commonality, binds the two Janets into a relation of mutually enforcing strength-in-marginality.

Ironically, the guarantor of Janet Nicol's contentment is the 12-year-old Countess of Loudoun: "The little, lovely, blooming fair, / Who makes thy cot and thee her care" (100–01). The precariousness of Janet Nicol's happiness is here admitted. The social obligations of feudalism are only as reliable a means of support for the poor as the characters of lairds and ladies. Janet Nicol is subject to the whims of an aristocratic patron in much the same way as Janet Little is subject to those of the Dunlop and Henri families. Both inhabit a precarious niche that looks increasingly anachronistic in the light of the revolutions in America and France, and particularly in view of the tide of republican sentiment in which Burns himself was caught up, and which nearly put an end to his friendship with Mrs. Dunlop, whose daughter Mrs. Henri had married a royalist partisan. Thus it is not young Flora's noble birth or wealth that guarantees Janet Nicol's security, but rather her exceptional character, her generosity and romantic sympathy, which are at odds with her elevated status and proportionate social power:

> Whose gentle, gen'rous, noble mind,
> Tho' great and rich, can here prove kind;
> Whose footsteps mark her path with peace,
> Whose smile bids ev'ry sorrow cease;
> For age and want, and wo provides
> And over misery presides.
>
>   . . .
>
> Whose rays have found in James and thee,
> The melting charm of misery.
>
>   . . .
>
> Let James and you for Loudon pray,
> Whose charms have lur'd me from my lay.   (102–23)

There is a discordant note in the return here to an official English, the language of royal precept, which ironizes "the melting charm of misery" and Janet Nicol's supposed contentment. Relations of patronage are not adequate to the task of ending "misery," merely capable of sustaining it by offering a few amenities. Indeed it could be said that the language of much needed social protest emerges here, mediated and mitigated by the countess's youth and attractiveness. We cannot dwell comfortably in this text on Janet Nicol's peace of mind but must both sensuously apprehend its otherness and recognize its precariousness within a social field where the almost outcast are no less subject to the operations of power and ideological contradiction than their masters, but rather more abjectly so.

  If we have seen Little drawing upon the critical power of the socially marginal, who remain exorbitant to established literary conventions, but within the discourse of Romanticism will become increasingly conventional- ized figures of more or less explicit social protest, in "To My Aunty" Little capitalizes upon her own linguistic and social marginality. The "Aunty" represents a type of sage, a wise old woman whose "primitive" technology links her with radical sectarian prophets of the past against a pompous, largely male literary-critical establishment. She can both "Unravel dreams" and "truth in mystic terms declare, / Which made us aft wi' wonder stare" (4–6). But a comical tone throughout saves the text from polemic; it is hard to read the Aunty too seriously as a source of countercultural wisdom when the cultural arbiters are themselves so baldly satirized. Little writes of a dream in which her works are published only to be savaged by the critics, a textual strategy which at once disarms criticism and glamorizes the slim volume of verse in which we read:

> My works I thought appear'd in print,
> And were to diff'rent corners sent,
> Whare patrons kind, but scant o' skill,
> Had sign'd my superscription bill.
> Voratious critics by the way,
> Like eagles watching for their prey,
> Soon caught the verse wi' aspect sour,
> An' did ilk feeble thought devour;
> Nor did its humble, helpless state,
> One fraction of their rage abate.
>
> . . .
>
> Will Hasty, in an unco rage,
> Revis'd the volume page by page;
> But aft was deem'd a stupid ass,
> For cens'ring what alone might pass.   (13–34)

To appeal to the Aunty to unravel this dream is to seek an extratextual authority for textual audacity, the legitimation of a literary practice as outside established canons as the Aunty's gift is beyond the pale of eighteenth-century science. Here Little capitalizes on her rustic quaintness, her literary "backwardness," in an appeal to a mock-primitivism that ironizes her achievements while adumbrating their difference from standard English poetry. The question of the emergent conventionality of Scottish dialect verse is scrupulously avoided. Little habitually inscribes her moments of self-representation as eruptions of "real" Scots into her official standard English texts, but the texts remain heteroglossic, neither one thing nor the other. Thus the cultural specificity of English imperialism is articulated with and against an emergent Scottish nationalism. The mimicry of Anglographic conventions serves as a textual ground from which Little can stage departures of a culturally resistant and protofeminist kind.

Slavery and sensibility: Phillis Wheatley within the fracture

The laboring-class women poets we have investigated so far may have invoked the metaphor of slavery to characterize their domestic obligations, their confinement to drudgery; Phillis Wheatley writes literally as a slave. The poetic sensibility of her white counterparts may be produced from within the constraints of servitude and class-based attitudes towards plebeian sub-jugation, but Wheatley's "sensibility" is from the first moment of her poetic enunciation put in question by her status as a slave. Even abolitionist discourse of the period, at the same time as it argues for the emancipation of slaves, is traversed by doubts and hesitations about the slaves' status as "human," and hence discursive, subjects. Wheatley may have found "herself" figured in certain abolitionist texts; she clearly read the Bible as a potentially emancipa-tory document; to a certain extent her writing seems to have been a liberationary gesture. Yet given the terms of the great debates about slavery in the period, abolitionist discourse itself also functioned as a form of discursive constraint upon Wheatley's literary production.

Even as late as 1788, four years after Wheatley's death, such abolitionist poems as Hannah More's *Slavery, A Poem* and Ann Yearsley's *A Poem On The Inhumanity Of The Slave-Trade*[22] represent the black slave as a crudely patched-together figure, a field of contradictions that reveal the workings of ideology, the desire to naturalize and recuperate the other while remaining uneasily alert to the threat of cultural difference. J. M. S. Tompkins suggests that "it must have been in conscious rivalry that [Yearsley] published her poem . . . within a few months of Miss More's *Slavery*."[23] Read as rivals or not, the poems represent quite different takes on the question of abolition. Yearsley writes in blank verse, More in couplets; Yearsley appeals to local authority in Bristol and More to London-based parliamentary and so, ostensibly, national authority. Yearsley heroically dramatizes the native characters Luco and Incilanda, while More presents a rational argument against slavery bolstered by an appeal to religion. Yearsley's vision of an emancipated future is a civic one – Bristol uncorrupted – while More represents the end of slavery not geographically or politically but metaphysic-ally. If Yearsley's poem seems rather overwrought, More's rises to occasional argumentative elegance only to fracture disablingly along ideological lines. Imperial conquest equals pillage, we are told, yet Britain can "give" Africa her rightful liberties; colonialism is rendered brutally suspect, yet we are assured that no natives were killed in the settling of Quaker Pennsylvania. For both poets, slave uprisings represent a crisis of legitimacy comparable with contemporary rebellions against monarchy. Yearsley achieves Miltonic elo-quence in her attack on "Law" and "Custom" in favor of "Heav'n-born Liberty" (15–18):

> . . . Custom, Law,
> Ye blessings, and ye curses of mankind,
> What evils do ye cause? We feel enslav'd,
> Yet move in your direction. Custom, thou

> Wilt preach up filial piety; thy sons
> Will groan, and stare with impudence at Heav'n,
> As if they did abjure the act, where Sin
> Sits full on Inhumanity; the church
> They fill with mouthing, vap'rous sighs and tears,
> Which, like the guileful crocodile's, oft fall,
> Nor fall, but at the cost of human bliss.   (18–28)

But she also recuperates black resistance by refamiliarizing her slave subjects as affectingly domestic, as if that sameness could save them for white audiences, the same strategy that Wheatley herself employs in her brief autobiographical moments:

> "Parental fondness, and the dear returns
> "Of filial tenderness were thine, till torn
> "From the dissolving scene." –   (413–15)

More, however, even as she argues that blacks "have heads to think, and hearts to feel, / And souls to act, with firm, tho' erring zeal" (67–68), falls back on a notion of their cultural difference as savagery:

> Strong, but luxuriant virtues boldly shoot
> From the wild vigour of a savage root.   (73–74)

> Tho' dark and savage, ignorant and blind,
> They claim the common privilege of kind.   (137–38)

And while she insists vehemently that blacks can feel as well as whites, she seems less sanguine about their capacity to reason:

>   Plead not, in reason's palpable abuse,
> Their sense of *feeling callous and obtuse:
> From heads to hearts lies Nature's plain appeal,
> Tho' few can reason, all mankind can feel.   (147–50)
>
>   . . .
>
> *Nothing is more frequent than this cruel and stupid argument, that they do not *feel* the miseries inflicted on them as Europeans would do.

Surely the argument that Africans (like white laborers) might not be able to reason is at least as cruel and stupid an argument? But More does not pursue this line of thought. And thus the abolitionist case that would preserve both liberty and difference begins to undermine itself in Enlightenment terms, collapses rational argument back into a matter of Christian faith that must transcend "mere" rationality, and that forever casts the other as a primitive or childlike being in need of civilizing discipline and the Word.

Whether recuperative, effacing difference, or seeking to preserve difference at the expense of the other's rationality, abolitionist discourse is fraught with inconsistency. Though it offers Wheatley a lever to use in opening up discursive space within white colonial culture, abolitionist discourse is far from offering her a utopian projection of alternatives to her fractured semiotic field and her situation of enslavement.

Similarly, Wheatley's relation to the existing discourse of plebeian poets is a complex and not unambiguous one. Her difference from white laboring-class women writers is figured forward from the frontispiece of her volume of verse, a portrait which at once emphasizes her Africanness as exotically other and decorously domesticates it by means of the discipline of writing. Yet the fact that her *Poems On Various Subjects, Religious And Moral* of 1773[24] was first published in London, not Boston, because subscribers in England – most influentially Selina Hastings, Countess of Huntingdon, to whom the volume is dedicated – were more forthcoming in support of the productions of a "Negro Servant" than were American colonists, may suggest the extent to which an already existing discourse of laboring-women's poetry legitimated Wheatley's writing and made possible its widest dissemination.

In a sense, then, Wheatley's is the limit case of the plebeian female poet working within and against the dominant culture on all fronts, linguistic, cultural, racial, sexual, and socio-political. Her slavery and her sensibility may remain constitutively different from those of her white British counterparts, her exploitation more totalized and extreme. But we can only know these differences in important, and nuanced, ways if we read her in relation to those other discourses, the plebeian and the abolitionist, that helped constitute and condition the reception of her own.

To make a case for Phillis Wheatley's cultural resistance may not now prove so difficult as it would once have done. Although her work has often been criticized as disablingly conventional and derivative, recent studies are marked by the desire to find in her an authentic African American literary foremother. This recuperative desire produces a consequent strategy of reading in the light of the complex problematics of race her work represents. In one sense at least, the dynamics of race consciousness and literary reception have radically shifted since 1784, when Thomas Jefferson could write, reminding us briefly of More writing about Yearsley's plight:

Misery is often the parent of the most affecting touches in poetry. Among the blacks is misery enough, God knows, but no poetry. Love is the peculiar oestrum of the poet. Their love is ardent, but it kindles the senses only, not the imagination. Religion, indeed, has produced a Phyllis Whately [*sic*]; but it could not produce a poet. The compositions published under her name are below the dignity of criticism. The heroes of the Dunciad are to her, as Hercules to the author of that poem.[25]

The crudeness of Jefferson's projection of sensuality without an erotic imaginary onto the ostensible subjectivities of black people may be auto-biographically revealing; and his commentary on the *Dunciad* suggests something of the popular penetration that Pope's Grub Street fantasia may have had in late eighteenth-century America. Pope's smallness, slightness, and physical frailty, in contrast with Hercules's superhuman strength, serve as a touchstone for the absurdity, the grotesqueness of Wheatley's "pretension" to poetic status. It is gratifying to note that Jefferson's prejudices did not go unchallenged in his lifetime.[26] But the contention that American black culture is somehow debilitatingly imitative of white culture is with us still. Not so baldly stated, perhaps, as in 1878, when Jefferson's views were defended in *The North American Review*, with Wheatley characterized thus:

She was a poet very much as "Blind Tom" is a musician, her verses being the merest echo of the common jingle of her day . . . A fatal facility of imitation stands in the way of this interesting race, and we cannot fairly deny that facts give support to the opinion of an inherent mental inferiority . . . To the present hour the negro has contributed nothing to the intellectual resources of man.[27]

Even black scholars intent on recovering a tradition of African American literary achievement have often hesitated to read Wheatley as other than subject to "a fatal facility of imitation." Where neoclassical imitation as such is not denigrated as a literary practice, Wheatley still receives faint praise for failing to develop a more "original" or innovative aesthetic, presumably the primary determinant of poetic greatness:

As I have said, she was not a great poet; but in her way, in her time, and in her locale, she was a fairly good writer of poems generally in imitation of the neoclassical mode made popular by Alexander Pope.[28]

The *Poems* revealed Phillis to be an imitative poet whose work lacked qualities of greatness; but clearly she had written some of the most interesting verse of colonial America.[29]

To have written "some of the most interesting verse of colonial America" is not enough: one must still apologize for Wheatley's reliance on imitation. One of the boldest scholarly vindications of Wheatley's aesthetic to date asserts her relative originality:

Scrutiny of her work will reveal, however, that she was not as derivative of Pope as has been long asserted. In fact, recent scholarship is beginning to detail the extent to which she was not the extensive imitator of anyone.

Yet such a vindication on aesthetic grounds alone cannot be allowed to stand because the political commitments of much black scholarship demand an analysis of a writer's race consciousness as well, and here Wheatley may be defended against previous denigrations – but not entirely vindicated:

Perhaps the most persistent criticism of Phillis Wheatley has been that based on the usually unaesthetic grounds of her chosen subject matter. She did not write enough about blackness, some charge. She is said by others to have been callously indifferent to her contemporary black life generally, and archly above black slave life in particular. So contending, some see her as the progenitor of a posited black American literary tradition of black self-abnegation, black self-loathing. One writer would have it that so powerfully shaping were the unchallenged New England cultural pressures on a haplessly malleable young Phillis that she was compelled to develop into nothing else but a kind of psychologically malformed grotesquery – a black-white, colonial woman poet. There is perhaps some truth in some of these charges, but a greater truth is that Phillis was very much aware of being a black person, however celebrated a personality, in a world dominated numerically and culturally by white persons, and that she wrote of such matters in her volume of poems, in her miscellaneous poems, and in her letters.[30]

The apologetic caution expressed here – "There is perhaps some truth in some of these charges" – prevents a closer and potentially more radical investigation of how the dominant New England "cultural pressures" are both inscribed in and resisted by Wheatley's literary production. Rather than allowing ourselves to feel a disabling revulsion at the grotesque spectacle of a "black-white, colonial woman poet," and to stop there in our exploration of black colonial female subjectivity, we should look again at the articulation of Wheatley's abolitionist consciousness with her potentially subversive mimicry of white Anglographic cultural forms.[31]

Thanks to recent scholarship, Wheatley need never again be read as a writer unworthy of sophisticated formalist or literary-historical analysis, nor a writer oblivious of or indifferent to the brutal injustices of slavery. Nor need we continue to separate these two considerations as antithetically "aesthetic" and "political." The recovery and republication of her letter of February 11, 1774 to the Rev. Samson Occom, the Amerindian preacher, provides powerful evidence of Wheatley's political acuteness regarding the institution of slavery, and her skill in weaving a texture of allusion and allegorical reference that is keenly critical of – and politely sarcastic about – the hypocrisy of white Christian racism. In her letter, written several months after she became a freed woman, Wheatley praises "the glorious Dispensation of civil and religious Liberty, which are so inseparably united, that there is little or no enjoyment of one without the other." Thus the religious conversion of many Africans to Christianity must lead, ironically if inevitably, to their desire for an emancipated civil and political status. This constitutes a radical reading of Christianity on Wheatley's part, a deployment of religious impulses in the direction of progressive social transformation in spite of the injustices of imperialist conquest and slavery. This utopian impulse points towards concrete social and political equality, not religious consolation in heaven. This is the emancipatory tendency in appropriations of Christian doctrine we might usefully connect to the social radicalism of many sects during the English Civil Wars. Wheatley's Christianity is not the Christianity of political quietism and submissive piety. Just as the Israelites were "solicitous for their Freedom from Egyptian slavery," so African slaves, captive but encouraged by New World ideas of divinity and "natural Rights," rightly desire their liberty:

God has implanted a Principle, which we call Love of Freedom; it is impatient of oppression, and pants for Deliverance – and by the Leave of our modern Egyptians I will assert that the same principle lives in us. God grant Deliverance in his own Way and Time, and get him honour upon all those whose Avaraice impels them to countenance and help forward the Calamities of their fellow Creatures. This I desire not for their Hurt, but to convince them of the strange Absurdity of their Conduct whose Words and Actions are so diametrically opposite. How well the cry for Liberty, and the reverse Disposition for the exercise of oppressive power over others agree I humbly think it does not require the penetration of a Philosopher to determine.[32]

Here Wheatley foregrounds the contradiction between republican theory and oppressive practice in the slave trade. The source of this contradiction, she claims, is economic self-interest or avarice. Only greed perpetuates slavery in defiance of the emancipatory possibilities of republicanism. Just as she pushes the sanctities of republican rhetoric to their limit in this letter, so also her poetry foregrounds the contradictions of colonial experience until even the most pious invocation of Christian faith may be read as the site of hybridity – "the warlike sign of the native."

There may well be a threat disguised as ambiguous gratitude in the autobiographical moment of Wheatley's "To the Right Honourable William, Earl of Dartmouth, His Majesty's Principal Secretary of State for North America, &c.":

> Should you, my lord, while you peruse my song,
> Wonder from whence my love of *Freedom* sprung,
> Whence flow these wishes for the common good,
> By feeling hearts alone best understood,
> I, young in life, by seeming cruel fate
> Was snatch'd from *Afric's* fancy'd happy seat:
> What pangs excruciating must molest,
> What sorrows labour in my parent's breast?

Steel'd was that soul and by no misery mov'd
That from a father seiz'd his babe belov'd:
Such, such my case. And can I then but pray
Others may never feel tyrannic sway?   (20–31)

What if the brutality of imperialist conquest so evident in the slave trade were to produce a generation of freedom-loving rebels amongst its ruthlessly transplanted "native informants?" If the experience of tyranny as forcible transplantation and enslavement produces revolutionary aspirations, they are ironically couched in the language of the slave traders and slaveholders themselves, for whom colonial rebellion will soon prove necessary for preserving their commerce, including the slave trade, as a sign of their much-vaunted liberty. The ostensible humility of Wheatley's pose here ("Even I, a lowly African slave, beseech you, Dartmouth, to be a benevolent administrator lest you produce an anti-imperialist, anti-tyrannical rebellion") does indeed become subtly warlike when we address the question of Wheatley as cultural mimic.

For the terms in which Wheatley can couch her advice to the new secretary of state, the terms in which she can formulate her own experience of slavery, are the white man's terms. That first violent rupture of native community, which leads inexorably towards transportation via slaveship and deracination in the New World, can be projected only retrospectively and speculatively: "*seeming* cruel fate," "*Afric's fancy'd* happy seat," "What pangs excruciating *must* molest" [emphasis mine]. Wheatley does not "know" what happened, cannot remember, can only envisage within the master's language what her native prehistory might have been. Except for one detail, which occupies two lines of confident memory and undisputed knowledge, and that is the distinct, reifying brutality and distinctly "unchristian" immunity from compassion that signify the slave-trader as imperial subject: "Steel'd was that soul and by no misery mov'd / That from a father seiz'd his babe belov'd." Of the inhumane instrumentality of the sovereign subject of imperial commerce Wheatley is convinced, and it is a belief reinforced here by an equal conviction of African paternal affection.

As so often in abolitionist discourse, from the anti-slavery poems of Yearsley and More to Harriet Beecher Stowe's *Uncle Tom's Cabin* (1852), the appeal to previously unknowable communities as sites of familial affection attempts to clinch the argument by an act of refamiliarization as refamiliali-zation. Wheatley may not "remember" her father – we have just been led to believe she remembered almost nothing of her life before captivity – but in the Boston of 1772 the notion of paternal affection so rudely violated by the seizure of a child is likely to be read as sympathetic. Here as elsewhere, Wheatley's self-presentation coincides with the representations of slaves' lives manufactured in white, and residually racist, abolitionist discourse. Her self-presentation is often inextricably complicit with the discursive formation in which "freedom" and slavery continue to coexist, and in which "freedom" all too often means the rights of the propertied. Yet this mimicry of a subjectivity recognizable to white readers is explicitly foregrounded in Wheatley's texts as miming, as mimicry — and, as such, it constitutes the grounds for the eventual challenging of the racist formation with which it is deceptively complicit.

Within the fracturing of a semiotic field, Spivak warns, what we are likely to recognize as "great literature" will probably not flourish ("The Rani of Sirmur," p. 130). But the partial erasure and silencing of native cultures wrought by the violence of imperialism may produce strange hybrids. That some profound fracturing of semiotic fields transpires in the Atlantic voyages of eighteenth-century slaveships seems indisputable. We have only to notice that the schooner *Phillis*, owned by Timothy Fitch of Boston, brought Phillis Wheatley to New England to begin to account for some of these discontinuities. The name "Phillis Wheatley" = the slaveship yoked to the white master; a "Christian name" signifying enslavement and a patronymic metonymizing white ownership within the rhetorics of an "extended family."

The cultural amnesia experienced by some transported slaves has been documented, though its interpretation has often been tendentious.[33] Wheatley seems to have suffered from this disarticulation of the memory rather acutely, if we are to believe her nineteenth-century memoirist, Margaretta Matilda Oddell. According to Oddell, the great-grand-niece of Susanna Wheatley, Phillis's mistress, Phillis Wheatley could remember nothing of her previous life before captivity except "the simple circumstance that her mother *poured out water before the sun at his rising* — in reference, no doubt, to an ancient African custom." So she remembers only a stylized glimpse of tribal ritual, her mother propitiating a masculine sun, the "natural" beauty of ritual rendered in a "native" setting. Oddell goes on to speculate that this lack of memories from early childhood might be unusual but does not necessarily indicate a lack of intelligence:

We cannot know at how early a period she was beguiled from the hut of her mother; or how long a time elapsed between her abduction from her first home and her being transferred to the abode of her benevolent mistress, where she must have felt like one awaking from a fearful dream. This interval was, no doubt, a long one; and filled, as it must have been, with various degrees and kinds of suffering, might naturally enough obliterate the recollection of earlier and happier days.[34]

Childishly "beguiled" or, more polemically, violently "seiz'd" as Wheatley puts it in "To Dartmouth": either way, slavery ruptures Wheatley's experience and her semiotic field. But the specific gendering of her memories seems to have much to do with her intended audience: paternal affection for

Dartmouth; maternal ritual, a feminized security, for Susanna Wheatley and her great-grand-niece.

What is perhaps most interesting about this lack of early memories, this lack of knowledge of indigenous cultural formations, is that it foregrounds the implantation of imperialist culture on the deracinated subject. Nowhere is this clearer in Wheatley's *œuvre* than in the production of the poem "On Recollection":

The following was occasioned by being in company with some young ladies of family, when one of them said she did not remember, among all the poetic pieces she had seen, ever to have met with a poem upon RECOLLECTION. The African (so let me call her, for so in fact she is) took the hint, went home to her master's, and soon sent the following.[35]

Thus Wheatley explicitly produces a meditation on memory, the "native" materials of which she lacks, for a white colonial patron. Even her "Recollection" is constituted discursively as a function of imperialism, of its power to bestow education and "culture," of its power to solicit the spontaneous poetic expression of colonized subjectivity. Wheatley thus produces a poem on a subject "never before" encountered by the lady patron, proving her poetic genius and authenticity in the very moment of confirming her writerly status as a dependent – indeed subject – construction of imperial discourse. And what are we to make of her single memory of childhood, so legible to white colonial society as exotically cryptic yet true to type – "in reference, no doubt, to an ancient African custom"? Wheatley, whose recollections have been so violently circumscribed, ironically supplements the lack of a poem on "Recollection" for a slave-owning audience.

What Wheatley took to be the function of her writing within white colonial society is far from clear. But in her poem "On Imagination" the contradiction between writing as aesthetic pleasure and writing as a form of social accommodation to an alien and oppressive culture is disclosed. Elsewhere in her *œuvre*, stashed away in poems ostensibly on other topics, Wheatley figures her relation to writing as ardent, even licentious: like other women poets of the period, and especially those whose pleasures were most restricted by class oppression, Wheatley represents the workings of imagination as erotically charged. She can dare to do so most openly only in brief passages where the context forces other ideas to the fore. Thus, as June Jordan notices, in "To the University of Cambridge, in New-England" it is "an intrinsic ardor" which "bids" Wheatley to write verse: "not to dismiss the extraordinary kindness of the Wheatleys, and not to diminish the wealth of white men's literature with which she found herself quite saturated, but it was none of these extrinsic factors that compelled the labors of her poetry."[36] And in "Thoughts on the Works of Providence," Wheatley's formulation of dream-work renders the unconscious the site of libidinal investment and intellectual freedom:

> Say what is sleep? and dreams how passing strange!
> When action ceases, and ideas range
> Licentious and unbounded o'er the plains.　(85–87)

When writing about "imagination" directly, however, Wheatley's representation is no less erotic but distinctly more constrained. Her poem "On
Imagination" discloses the contradiction between imaginative "freedom" and
the circumstances from which she writes. The discipline of poetic composition, those "silken fetters," keeps her in "soft captivity" that has somehow
displaced – not the poet's historical servitude – but a previous state of
unbounded imaginative freedom:

> Now here, now there, the roving *Fancy* flies,
> Till some lov'd object strikes her wand'ring eyes,
> Whose silken fetters all the senses bind,
> And soft captivity involves the mind.　(9–12)

But why figure the imaginary fixing on an object, the investing of that object
with desire and intellectual engagement ("involves the mind") as a form of
captivity at all? Surely, ironically, we must read back into the poem what has
ostensibly been left out: the situation of servitude from which Wheatley
writes, the slavery within which her sensibility is both produced for public
consumption and held captive, though a comparatively "soft captivity" it
may be: one that allows this slave poetic license.

Wheatley's poetic project may be characterized as one of cultural hybridity
with a vengeance. Her most direct allusions to the injustices of her historical
situation, and those of other Africans, are always offered, as we have seen,
ostensibly in the service of something else: congratulations to university
graduates, praise of a new government official, musings on the imagination.
Interestingly, in a manuscript poem, "An address to the Deist 1767,"
Wheatley writes at the age of fourteen:

> Must Ethiopians be employ'd for you?
> Much I rejoice if any good I do.　(1–2)[37]

The contradiction between her desire to question, if not refuse outright,
conscription into the service of white culture, whether marked by deistical or
missionary zeal, and her acknowledgment that to be of service is also
intellectually gratifying is broached openly here. A comparable gesture of
taking pleasure from the imperialist culture to which she would not be
subjected, against which she obliquely protests, but from whose subjection
there appears to be no escape, occurs in the ambitious long poem *Niobe in
Distress for her Children Slain by Apollo, from Ovid's Metamorphoses, Book VI.
and from a View of the Painting of Mr. Richard Wilson.*[38] A single couplet connects this elaborate venture into neoclassical imitation with Wheatley's brief

mention of her enslavement in "To Dartmouth" where the brutal implacabil-
ity of the slave-trader is set against African paternal love. In the very midst of
proving herself a true poet in eighteenth-century neoclassical terms, Wheatley
represents her poetic heroine in an act of rebellion fuelled by her paternal
inheritance and expressed in the paternal language which Wheatley herself has
been forbidden to speak, from which her own discourse has been forever
ruptured:

> "No reason her imperious temper quells,
> "But all her father in her tongue rebels.   (97–98)

For this impious queen, this daughter of the desiring, vanquished mortal
father, ambition (for her nation, her family) thus articulated succeeds only in
producing a disarticulation – the punitive silencing of Niobe through the
murder of her children. No "reason" moderates her pride, her desire to rule
her people and protest subordination to the gods. And the price of that
rebellion is eternal silence: Niobe is turned to stone.

It is precisely "reason," we must assume, that quells Wheatley's own
temper, that moderates her discourse and decorously channels the "intrinsic
ardor" and "licentious" imagination that drive her to write. And reason is
what Wheatley most decisively must prove she possesses if she is to do "any
good" as an "Ethiopian" employed by white colonialists, serve the interests of
liberty and abolitionism, and write so as to be read as a true poet, thus
disproving the assumptions upon which racial prejudice could be based. As
Henry Louis Gates has so eloquently argued, writing by Africans was crucial
to the eighteenth-century debate over slavery. If an African could write – and
especially an African woman – then Africans should not be enslaved, as
reasonable, fully human beings. Gates concludes that "writing, for these
slaves, was not an activity of mind; rather, it was a commodity which they
were forced to trade for their humanity."[39] Understood thus, Wheatley's
"soft captivity" as a site of literary production becomes an image not so much
of reconciliation and compliance as a sign of hybridity, "the warlike sign of
the native." Out of the imperialist fracture, the ruptured native "tongue,"
comes a mimicry that is more than merely ironical, and far from innocent.

What are we then to make of a poem like "To Maecenas," the poem that
introduces Wheatley's volume to the public and explicitly addresses questions
of patronage, acculturation, and native poetic desire? How could such a
corpus as Wheatley's have been read and not recognized as radically subversive in a cultural climate as skeptical of African writing as eighteenth-
century Boston or Britain? "To Maecenas" makes clear by means of its very
obscurity how Wheatley's mimicry both represents and conceals rebellion,
stages ideological conflict within neoclassical imitation but so obliquely that
those possibilities of heteroglossic resistance can only with difficulty be teased
out.

In "To Maecenas," Wheatley inadvertently reveals Pope's own hybridization, while asking in Popean language for direct access to classical inspiration, like Homer and Virgil. She writes as one who would have Pope's own classical inspiration in spite of the cultural barriers between her and the master texts of Western antiquity. Pope himself is not mentioned in this poem, but his classicized English landscape predominates, and Wheatley addresses Maecenas in conclusion much as Pope addresses Bolingbroke at the close of the *Essay on Man*; we may also think of the last section of *Windsor-Forest* in which Pope envisages global peace as the end of imperialism and slavery:

> As long as *Thames* in streams majestic flows,
> Or *Naiads* in their oozy beds repose,
> While *Phoebus* reigns above the starry train,
> While bright *Aurora* purples o'er the main,
> So long, great Sir, the muse thy praise shall sing,
> So long thy praise shall make *Parnassus* ring:
> Then grant, *Maecenas*, thy paternal rays,
> Hear me propitious, and defend my lays.   (48–55)

The epistolary form, with its implied dialogics, is here neither directed amorously towards a lover nor intertextually towards literary precursors, except for Terence, a fellow African (37–42). Rather, Wheatley indirectly addresses her various lacks as an African female slave poet by invoking the ideal type of the patron, neoclassically speaking: Gaius Cilnius Maecenas, Roman statesman and wealthy patron of Virgil and Horace, a rich man of taste who supports the arts, and the patron to whom Virgil's *Georgics* in particular are dedicated. But so obliquely does Wheatley treat the dynamics of patronage in this text, that readers may well share the confusion of one commentator, who notes that Maecenas refers to Gaius Cilnius, only to add in the same note that Wheatley seems to be addressing not a patron but a fellow poet.[40] The paradox of Wheatley's idealization of relations of patronage is that she must conceive of the ideal patron as a poet, as someone blessed equally by the muses, in order to collapse the class-charged distance between patron and poet into imaginary identification:

> MAECENAS, you, beneath the myrtle shade,
> Read o'er what poets sung, and shepherds play'd.
> What felt those poets but you feel the same?
> Does not your soul possess the sacred flame?
> Their noble strains your equal genius shares
> In softer language, and diviner airs.   (1–6)

The patron is no sooner assured of poetic genius than Wheatley must hanker after it too. As with Yearsley's and Masters's desires for Pope's rapturous inspiration, so also with Wheatley's desire here; if she could rival Maecenas and Virgil in a single page of verse, or at least lay claim to Virgilian inspiration, she too would experience the rapturous ardor of genius, mounting and soaring above her groveling situation:

> O could I rival thine and *Virgil's* page,
> Or claim the *Muses* with the *Mantuan* Sage;
> Soon the same beauties should my mind adorn,
> And the same ardors in my soul should burn:
> Then should my song in bolder notes arise,
> And all my numbers pleasingly surprize;
> But here I sit, and mourn a grov'ling mind,
> That fain would mount, and ride upon the wind.   (23–30)

"Thine and *Virgil's* page": The patron who is himself capable of verse is the patron who does not exploit or feed parasitically upon his protégée. And the greatest praise that Wheatley as a humble protégée can offer is the recognition that her rich and classically educated white male patron, British or colonial, her Maecenas, himself possesses poetic laurels worth stealing:

> While blooming wreaths around thy temples spread,
> I'll snatch a laurel from thine honour'd head,
> While you indulgent smile upon the deed.   (45–47)

Thus a coy Phillis Wheatley represents herself audaciously snatching a token sprig of the bays from one whose abundant supply means that he will indulge her in her theft, her audacious imitation. *Les voleuses de langue*, the thieves of language steal but also fly: Wheatley will mount and soar poetically after all, thanks to the indulgence of rich white patrons. And such is the fate of the poet generically, it would seem. Did not Pope himself do much the same in his poetic inscriptions of his friendships with great noblemen in the *Epistles to Several Persons* or *Moral Essays* and the Horatian imitations? Through Wheatley we can even recognize the relatively unacknowledged hybridity of Pope's neoclassicism, the lacks he too experienced in relation to the texts of antiquity, the etiology of his desire in and for writing.

At what possible moment, then, could such egregious flattery become the "warlike sign of the native?" For Wheatley's hybridity is in one sense at least categorically and politically different from Pope's, as we have seen. If we read Wheatley's obliquities scrupulously enough, but do not force the closure of a single referent or role for Maecenas, then this text too speaks of fracture and inscribes a mimicry far from benign. "As long as *Thames* in streams majestic flows, / Or *Naiads* in their oozy beds repose" (48–49): is this a naturalizing simile, a reflex of ideology that accepts British imperialism as given and eternal, and classical culture as rightfully the sign of imperialist dominance? Or is the end of white colonialist hegemony being implicitly insinuated in that "As long as"? "So long as" the imperial regime remains in place, both the

muse and Wheatley will celebrate Maecenas' bounty. But after that? Here the
Pope of *Windsor-Forest* who predicts a peaceful aftermath to British colonial
rule, with native liberties restored, may have particularly appealed to her. The
language of contracts, of negotiations that are the products of human agency,
subject to revision and change, can be read in the silences surrounding the
eternality of a classicized "nature" entirely foreign to Wheatley, entirely
consciously learned. As she writes succinctly in the much anthologized "On
being brought from Africa to America," "Once I redemption neither sought
nor knew" (4). The cultural amnesia consequent upon deracination has made
possible her absorption of Christianity, and also of a landscape inhabited by
Phoebus and Aurora; but this pre-existing set of native knowledges, however
approachable only as negativity or lack, introduces an element of subversion
into the tightest of Wheatley's literary imitations.

Whether we read Maecenas primarily as a figure for John Wheatley,
paternalist patron, or for Nathaniel, his son, who accompanied Phillis to
England in search of a larger public, or more broadly as a figure for the
collective type of potential subscribers and readers, who, whether they lived
in America or England, were seen by Wheatley as culturally "English," the
material conditions of patronage and clientage are obscured. In the gap created
by this mystification there arises the possibility of a future undetermined by
the majestic Thames, British militarism and commerce, their epiphenome-
non, the slave trade, and the neoclassical mythology with which imperialist
culture legitimates and sometimes obscures its projects. Until that moment,
Wheatley will write, as write she must, and so will continue to find herself
subject to the whims of patrons for whom race-, gender-, and class-consciousness strain the old terms of patronage as intimate friendship beyond recognition.

Robert Hayden begins his *American Journal* with "A Letter from Phillis
Wheatley, *London*, 1773" (to her black female friend Obour Tanner) in which
the crisis of Wheatley's cultural difference from her masters and patrons is
dramatized.[41] Hayden's Phillis writes:

> Today, a little Chimney Sweep,
> his face and hands with soot quite Black,
> staring hard at me, politely asked:
> "Does you, M'lady, sweep chimneys too?"
> I was amused, but dear Nathaniel
> (ever Solicitous) was not.   (45–50)

Which caused Nathaniel Wheatley greater consternation in his solicitude: the
fact that the chimney sweep drew attention to Phillis's color at all ("What
cheek!")? The fact that her color, thus recognized as a possible sign of labor,
might cast both New World visitors as déclassé colonials, the huckster and the
freak, "the Yankee Pedlar / and his Cannibal Mockingbird" (36–37)? Or the

fact that the sweep's liberty of speech and the carnivalesque reversal upon which it depends – a lady who sweeps – indicates a certain possible fluidity of class categories, at least imaginatively speaking, that Phillis finds amusing and Nathaniel unthinkable? How Phillis Wheatley's masters must have dreaded even the dimly apprehended possibility of her laughter, and guarded against it through their solicitude.

June Jordan argues that only Wheatley's status as a slave, a dependant, made the publication of her verse safe and acceptable; that the death of Susanna Wheatley in 1774, in the same year as Phillis's twenty-first birthday, meant that she was free, but also without access to publication. Such is the "difficult miracle" of black poetry in America, Jordan claims, for which Phillis Wheatley's history remains the prototype. For Jordan, the strangeness of Wheatley's presence in the historical record can only be evoked by means of incantation and sermonic repetition: "And it was not natural. And she was the first."[42]

It was certainly not "natural" that a female slave wrote and published "verse" in colonial Boston. For Wheatley, every word represented a contest of cultural forces, the most radical kind of heteroglossia inscribed within the fractured, once polyglossic, semiotic field of African American history. But by working within as well as against the logic of abolitionist discourse, by trading the commodity of writing for her humanity, by pushing revolutionary republican principles to their limit without flouting neoclassical decorums, this slave was able to force a "write of way to Western civility," as Houston Baker calls it.[43]

It could be argued that, of the poets examined in this study, Wheatley represents the extremest case of contextual criticism: one whose work may at first sight seem totally conventional, and this perception changes (if it does change) only in the light of biographical knowledge, here the knowledge that the poet was a black, female slave.[44] I would argue, rather, that the material conditions of a text's production, including such "biographical knowledge" and knowledge of relations of patronage, subscription, publication, and reception are part of the text as such and not "contextual," that is, supplementary or secondary.[45] Particularly in the case of volumes of verse packaged as by "exceptional" figures, as Wheatley's and the collections by the other poets of this study were, such knowledge would be inseparable from the act of reading the poems at all. One would have to posit an ahistorically formalist scene of reading in order for Wheatley's poems to appear stripped of any trace of their conditions of production, and even then some of that biographical knowledge is figured in the poems themselves.

If laboring-class women's poetry published in Britain in the period can be said to constitute a discourse, Wheatley's *Poems* is both related and marginal to it. Read with such texts as Collier's, Leapor's, Yearsley's, Hands's and Little's in mind, Wheatley's *œuvre* becomes a site of resistance where gender oppression specifies but does not comprehend the poet's situation, where gender seems less at stake than race and class in the poet's precarious "soft captivity." Ironically, Wheatley's early death can be attributed directly to those exigencies of gender which her writing tends to ignore. Freed and married to the freedman John Peters at the age of twenty-five, she was dead at thirty-one, worn out by poverty, illness, and childbearing. Read with some attention to the issues raised by postcolonialist criticism, Wheatley's *œuvre* becomes a site not of native or naive servility but of colonial hybridity, in which even the most docile neoclassical allusion, the most pious invocation of Christian faith, may be seen as a warlike sign, as warlike as was possible within this gendered colonial discourse.

Chapter 7

The 1790s and after: revolutions that as yet have no model

What a revolution took place, not only in my train of thoughts, but feelings!

(Mary Wollstonecraft, *The Wrongs of Woman* [1798])[1]

"Revolutionary women" in Britain as impure contradictions

The notion of "revolutionary women" in Britain at the end of the eighteenth century is an impure idealization, a contradiction in terms. Not even the revolutionary potential of British social movements of the 1780s and 1790s could be said to represent an historical rupture, and the revolutionary potential of these years was itself ruthlessly suppressed by arms as well as the persuasive arts. While across the Channel women were reportedly dancing in the streets – and, as Hannah More gloated, "the throne of the grand monarque ha[d] been overturned by fisherwomen!"[2] – British women made different sorts of accommodations to the revolution in France, but accommodate themselves they did.

Women's political pronouncements in the period prompted writers like Richard Polwhele to attack British women's pro-revolutionary, democratic, and feminist desires: "Our unsex'd female writers now instruct, or confuse, us and themselves, in the labyrinth of politics, or turn us wild with Gallic frenzy." Polwhele takes this sentence as his epigraph from T. J. Mathias's poem *The Pursuits of Literature*, a text which he claims has stabilized readers' principles in favor of religious authority, monarchy, and the suppression of the French revolution: "For I can assert, on the best authorities, that many in this country, whose politics and even religion have been long wavering, are now fixed in their principles by 'the Pursuits of Literature'."[3] I shall let Polwhele's sometimes arch polemicism against feminism, liberty, and democracy serve as a shadow text to my own less playful polemicism in favor of these commitments.

That Polwhele published his poem *The Unsex'd Females* in 1798, at the end of a controversial and turbulent decade, suggests that he suffered from a certain residual fearfulness lest a conspiracy of female writers inspired by the revolution in France actually manage to bring about significant social if not political change in Britain. I say "residual" because, by the time he wrote and published the poem, his chief antagonist, Mary Wollstonecraft, was already dead – of complications ensuing upon the birth of her daughter, who would grow up to write *Frankenstein*. *The Unsex'd Females* triumphs over Wollstonecraft's sad fate, reassuring Polwhele and his party that history has triumphed over revolutionary possibility. Perhaps, contrary to Polwhele's hopes, the monstrosity of women's intellectual, social, and political production was to be merely deferred and not interred, not laid with Wollstonecraft in the grave?

Against Wollstonecraft's radical challenge to custom in sexual and political relations, Polwhele sets Hannah More's conservative moralism. Between these two polarities stands a whole host of women of varying degrees of recuperability, including Ann Yearsley, who may not, like Wollstonecraft, have gone absolutely beyond the pale in Polwhele's terms. Wollstonecraft looms as a sinister spectre of radicalism within the text, a woman whose writing serves as a rallying cry for impressionable females shamed by her raillery into imitating her dangerous militancy. Polwhele hyperbolically turns Wollstonecraft's plea for women's rights into female tyranny, a sexual world turned upside down. Implicitly, the end of such a politics for the women in question is an ignominious death; Polwhele plays on his audience's knowledge of Wollstonecraft's "despis'd" love – her unhappy affair with Gilbert Imlay – and her attempted suicide:

> See Wollstonecraft, whom no decorum checks,
> Arise, the intrepid champion of her sex;
> O'er humbled man assert the sovereign claim,
> And sight the timid blush of virgin fame.
> "Go, go (she cries) ye tribes of melting maids,
> "Go, screen your softness in sequester'd shades;
> "With plaintive whispers woo the unconscious grove,
> "And feebly perish, as despis'd ye love.   (63–70)

If any readers missed this allusion to Wollstonecraft's attempt to drown herself by jumping off Putney Bridge into the Thames, Polwhele provides in a footnote fourteen pages later the details of the event, based on Godwin's *Memoirs* of Wollstonecraft.[4] His thesis is that under the influence of ideas from France, British women like Wollstonecraft have unsexed themselves by dispensing with their natural modesty and submissiveness in favor of licentiousness and defiance. "The Amazonian band – the female Quixotes of the new philosophy" (p. 6, n.) have, with Wollstonecraft, transgressed all "natural" female-feeling, especially maternal feeling. As a clergyman, Polwhele connects this new philosophy not with political events and new democratic demands but with the abandonment of religion: "But, burst the ties of religion; and the bands of nature will snap asunder!" (p. 29, n.). His chief example of such burst bonds is Wollstonecraft's attempting suicide when "she was a mother, deserting a poor helpless offspring" (p. 29, n.). Thus his concept of natural feeling is paradoxically revealed to be so fragilely constructed that the doctrines of the Church of England in which Wollstonecraft was brought up are necessary to preserve those natural bands, keep "nature" from exploding into anarchy. Among those infected by Wollstonecraft's example is Yearsley, whose once "natural" verse has become modishly satirical about women's subjection at the same time that she has learned to desire such expensive finery as silk:

> And YEARSLEY, who had warbled, Nature's child,
> Midst twilight dews, her minstrel ditties wild,
> (Tho' soon a wanderer from her meads and milk,
> She long'd to rustle, like her sex, in silk)
> Now stole the modish grin, the sapient sneer.   (99–103)

After speculating in a note on Yearsley's arrogance and ingratitude towards More, Polwhele insists that his "business" with Yearsley "is to recall her, if possible, from her Gallic wanderings – if an appeal to native ingenuousness be not too late; if the fatal example of the Arch-priestess of female Libertinism, have any influence on a mind once stored with the finest moral sentiment" (pp. 19–20). Yearsley's subjectivity thus serves Polwhele as a test case, a potential battleground for winning back the women of Britain to sexual and political conservatism, after the example of More. More's call to her British sisters is predictably angelic:

> "O come (a voice seraphic seems to say)
> "Fly that pale form – come sisters! come away.
> "Come, from those livid limbs withdraw your gaze,
> "Those limbs which Virtue views in mute amaze;
> "Nor deem, that Genius lends a veil, to hide
> "The dire apostate, the fell suicide.   (169–74)

Here again Pope's *Eloisa* glimmers as a source; Polwhele makes More echo the dead or imaginary nun who seeks to persuade Eloisa that a convent life can be calm and satisfying. Eloisa finds the nun's voice compelling but does not abandon her search for a resolution to passion or change her "rebellious heart." More, however, triumphs unequivocally by winning her British sisters to her side of the debate, the side of "repentance" – of female ambition as well as emancipation; More lives, and Wollstonecraft is dead: "She ceas'd; and round their MORE the sister's sigh'd! / Soft on each tongue repentant murmurs died" (203–04). Marking his own antithesis between More and

Wollstonecraft, Polwhele continues, in a note: "Miss Hannah More may justly be esteem'd, as a character, in all points, diametrically opposite to Miss Wollstonecraft; excepting, indeed, her genius and literary attainments" (pp. 35–36). Against the simple dichotomy of Polwhele's antifeminist polemic, I would insist on the insertion of that problematical third term, the other woman. Other in class formation as well as "sensibility," Yearsley deserves more than Polwhele's attempted recuperation, the recuperation that is also a move towards reaction. Arguably, we are still caught in historical contradictions that Wollstonecraft would have understood. Feminism and democracy remain embattled in the 1990s – differently, but embattled nevertheless.

Was there indeed significant coincidence between women's literary production and a radical politics in the 1790s? What does it mean to find Polwhele quoting the poet George Dyer as claiming: "The most sensible women . . . are more uniformly on the side of Liberty, than the other sex – witness a Macaulay, a Wollstonecraft, a Barbauld, a Jebb, a Williams, a Smith" (Polwhele, pp. 16–17, n.)? What became of this revolutionary energy? In particular, what were the effects of this discourse of liberty upon an emergent working-class female subject, for whom neither Wollstonecraft's middle-class feminism nor bourgeois radicalism could be said to be unproblematically appropriate as political languages? What if we attend to Ann Yearsley as well as to Mary Wollstonecraft or a conservative reformist like Hannah More?

Mary Wollstonecraft and Hannah More reconsidered

Both the conservative reaction of More, struggling between monarchist sympathy and chauvinist dislike of French Catholic royalty, and Wollstonecraft's endorsement of the revolution, qualified primarily by her fear that it would not go far enough towards the enfranchisement and emancipation of women, attempt to broach, however inchoately, the practical discontinuity but ideological comparability of radical republicanism and feminism.[5] "Comparability" but not necessarily "compatibility." Wollstonecraft dedicates her *Vindication of the Rights of Woman* to Talleyrand, in the hope that she can persuade him to consider "the rights of woman and national education" as crucial to the revolutionary program:

Let there be then no coercion *established* in society, and the common law of gravity prevailing, the sexes will fall into their proper places . . . [F]or, if women are not permitted to enjoy legitimate rights, they will render both men and themselves vicious to obtain illicit privileges.[6]

For Wollstonecraft the eradication of tyranny from the terrain of social life depends upon the emancipation of women from ignorance and sensuality into rational understanding, political equality, and an equal participation with men in determining political and social practice. Female emancipation is comparable with the republican overthrow of absolutist tyranny, just as women's ignorance, prejudice, and ultimately blind submission to authority are comparable with the weak analytical faculties of soldiers, who are similarly deprived of a systematic rational education: "So that if they have any sense, it is a kind of instinctive glance that catches proportions, and decides with respect to manners, but fails when arguments are to be pursued below the surface, or opinions analysed" (*Vindication*, p. 106). The movement of analogy – women are like soldiers – produces a mock-revelatory recognition – women *like* soldiers – confined mock-modestly to an interrogative footnote: "Why should women be censured with petulant acrimony because they seem to have a passion for a scarlet coat? Has not education placed them more on a level with soldiers than any other class of men?" (*Vindication*, p. 106, n. 1).

Pushing at the limits of ideological possibility within her historical moment, Wollstonecraft frames ironical questions that open up potential articulations beyond what can be argumentatively advanced. Wollstonecraft can broach the matter of female emancipation as being analogously like, and so comparable with, republican emancipation. But she can only archly query whether this "likeness" will plausibly issue in an emancipatory practice that will of necessity run counter to so many common prejudices about women.

Hannah More's conservatism, her evangelizing project that spares neither rich nor poor in its compulsion to exact piety and submission, abhors a revolution but claims that British liberty as traditionally established must be enough. Even in More, rendered by Polwhele as Wollstonecraft's arch-rival, there is a desire for rational female education in the mode of Enlightenment discourse – only to have that desire brought up short by its potential conflict with piety, with the submission to Scriptural and ecclesiastical authority demanded by rigorous religious devotion. More can see the necessary connection between her own intellectual attainments and her relative – and for her sex, exceptional – liberty. As a middle-class spinster, More writes as if she need answer to no man, and as a writer she managed to earn some £30,000.[7] Intellectual application is thus something to be advocated for women; ironically, however, its advocacy makes more glaring than ever how constraining women's social position is:

Serious study serves to harden the mind for more trying conflicts; it lifts the reader from sensation to intellect; it . . . corrects that spirit of trifling which she naturally contracts from the frivolous turn of female conversation, and the petty nature of female employments; it concentrates her attention, assists her in a habit of excluding trivial thoughts, and thus even helps to qualify her for religious pursuits.[8]

The indictment of women's petty employments here threatens to overthrow the appeal to piety. More's disdain for the trivializing functions of domestic femininity nearly erupts in a feminist analysis. If women's education, such as it is, leads to a spirit of trifling and frivolity, then surely women's social situation needs a radical overhaul and not just the addition of periods of serious study? More's advocacy of rational education in the service of religion is fissured by its protofeminist yearning for women to undertake solid intellectual work.

More refuses, however, the connection between women's education and democracy. Traditional British liberty guarantees the rights of the freeborn Englishman; to demand further rights and enfranchisement is to court absurdity. As she makes Jack the Blacksmith declare in *Village Politics* (1792):

What . . . we imitate them? We follow the French! Why they only begun all this mischief at first, in order to be just what *we* are already. Why I'd sooner go to the Negers to get learning, or to the Turks to get religion, than to the French for freedom and happiness.[9]

Far from pursuing the logic of extension and comparability, More savages Enlightenment thinking's "natural progression" from the rights of man to rights for other social groups whose right to rights no longer strikes us as categorically absurd:

The *rights of man* have been discussed, till we are somewhat wearied with the discussion. To these have been opposed with more presumption than prudence *the rights of woman*. It follows according to the natural progression of human things, that the next stage of that irradiation which our enlighteners are pouring in upon us will produce grave descants on the *rights of children*.   (*Strictures*, I, p. 135)

And, we might add, the rights of others, the "Negers" and the "Turks."

More draws her boundaries tighter, excludes categorically more of the populace from her discourse of liberty than does Wollstonecraft. She refuses the logic of comparability, trusting that practical incompatibility between the rights of man and women's emancipation need never even arise. Yet her description of women's confinement to petty employments, with its deleterious intellectual and moral effects, encodes a version of protofeminist critique that, if put into practice, would bring about social transformation. Indeed, More's is the path that the most visible and vocal women of Britain will appear to take for most of the nineteenth century, inscribing within a discourse of piety and domestic virtues a profound indignation at the social articulation of their circumscribed power to challenge the excesses of male sexual and legal privilege, capitalist accumulation, and imperialist domination.

In the most useful recent comparison of these two writers, Mitzi Myers has argued that, despite the partisan political differences between Wollstonecraft's and More's positions, they have much in common.[10] Because, Myers argues, they share a particular historical moment, certain protofeminist interests, and the ideological limits of a certain epistemological ground, Wollstonecraft's and More's positions may not seem to us as radically antithetical as they did to most of their contemporaries. But this argument, grounded in social anthropology rather than social history, depoliticizes the differences between Wollstonecraft and More. Hence Myers insists that "their remedies" merely "differ in many details," and that modern scholarship which stresses distinctions between them "myopically reproduces the anti-Jacobin opposition of More and Wollstonecraft" (Myers, p. 211, p. 201). Defusing what contemporaries read as political conflict allows Myers to offer us a retrospective success story in which protofeminist yet pious – and avowedly class-specific – domestic reform becomes historically validated because it was to win wide support in the nineteenth century while the more radical, egalitarian claims for social revolution fell away. I suggest we focus instead on the shared limits of their ideology, while continuing to recognize the importance of political differences between them. Not a "revolution in female manners" but a testing of the limits of any bourgeois revolutionary program: that is the most important historical lesson we can learn from Wollstonecraft's radicalism, which was to predicate itself exclusively upon the interests of middle-class women because "they appear to be in the most natural state" (*Vindication*, p. 81).

Feminist and democratic ideology at the limit: the case of Ann Yearsley's *To Mira, On The Care Of Her Infant*

The channelling of potentially radical tendencies into bourgeois reformism is illustrated clearly by the texts of Ann Yearsley, who was, as we have seen, briefly patronized by More. Yearsley, who figures herself in her early work as "Lactilla," cannot conceive of an oppositional discourse specific to working-class struggle. "Lactilla," whose name can be traced back at least to the character of the wetnurse for James II and Mary of Modena's "warming-pan" infant in the *Amours of Messalina* of 1689, ends in 1796 by condemning the practice of wet-nursing. Out of the contradictory energies of laboring-class bodies and knowledge, and bourgeois identification that would "do away with" notions of, if not the social convenience and political necessity of, classes altogether, Yearsley writes *To Mira, On The Care Of Her Infant*,[11] a poem that criticizes the whole warlike public sector of political activity and yet founders on the question of class.

If a number of the poems in Yearsley's 1796 volume, *The Rural Lyre*, address the political in a domestic fashion, *To Mira* discloses the theoretical and practical limitations of a politics of domesticity.[12] Written during the war with France, the poem opposes male militancy to a female world of education and nurturance.[13] The women left at home alone to tend infants while the men go off to fight have at their disposal, Yearsley argues, not only the potential for pleasure but for social power in the changes they may bring

about in future generations by taking command of education and transforming its traditionally stultifying programs.

The poem opens with a startling paradox and a very peculiar image of
female nurturing "warmth." The times are hostile ones in which flourish
"war, destruction, crimes that fiends delight" (1). With faint Popean echoes,
Yearsley gives us the globe apocalyptically plunged into *Dunciad*-like darkness: "and millions sink in night" (2); and shattered by opposition and the
will-to-power, as in the first epistle of the *Essay on Man*: "Whilst man to man
oppos'd wou'd shake the world, / And see vast systems into chaos hurl'd"
(5–6). These clashes of will so prodigal of life could be avoided if men turned
the other cheek or spread pacifism by example (7–8), but as it is, women are
left to themselves and the care of the next generation, a more blessed
occupation:

> Let us, whose sweet employ the Gods admire,
> Serenely blest, to softer joys retire!
> Spite of those wars, we will mild pleasure know –
> Pleasure, that, long as woman lives, shall flow!
> We are not made for Mars; we ne'er could bear
> His pond'rous helmet and his burning spear;
>
> 　　　. . .
>
> 　I am no Amazon; nor would I give
> One silver groat by iron laws to live.
> Nay, if, like hers, my heart were iron-bound,
> My warmth would melt the fetters to the ground.　(9–22)

Troping perhaps on reports of Frenchwomen appearing as amazons in the
service of the revolution, Yearsley distances herself from even a specifically
female militancy.[14] So intense is female "warmth," and so inextricable from
desires of unbounded liberty, that the poet claims she would *melt* herself free
from armor and arms – the physical signs of the iron discipline of combat.
Women thus possess a power that undermines mere martial prowess.

Throughout the poem childrearing is represented as a practice demanding
enlightened theorization. The poet addresses Mira in a context of continuing
exchanges about political events, so that the care of infants is presented not as
an isolated, all-absorbing activity, but as integral to a complex scene of social
being informed by public activity and capable of participation in it. The poet's
advice on childrearing will be acted upon "whilst we read, reflect, by turns
converse, / Comment on wars in prose or mimic verse" (27–28), as another
form of affective and intellectual practice. Of what does this advice consist?
Briefly: no swaddling clothes; no wetnurses or fobbing the child off onto
nannies; no harsh discipline or maternal anger or irritation allowed; affection,
stimulation, reading and looking at pictures, the pursuit of knowledge,

indulgence and liberty, rather than restraint, to be encouraged. These are commonly known as "Rousseauian" ideas, but the text represents them as the products of the poet's "long" experience of "A mother's duty" (29–30); if there is intertextuality at work, it has been completely internalized and submerged as the poet's own empirical findings. The purpose of such education is implicitly to counter "Custom" that would "gentle Nature's pow'r destroy" (32) – to produce new experiences of enlightened childhood leading to greater social and affective powers of liberty: to emancipation of the social being, in short. Mothers are to devote themselves to their infants, to breastfeed them, even if that means giving up the social round which seems their only other obligation; the reprehensible Circe, whose infant dies because she will not "renounce" "dress" or "the ball" – "For a child's humour suffer TASTE to fall? / "*Immensely monstrous! singular!*" she cried" (59–61) – is the negative example against which Mira is to measure herself. Such an upbringing will run counter to conservative theory as well as unreflective custom, so that socializing the child in these ways itself marks a break with structure and repression, is itself a movement towards emancipation, and a direct political challenge to the status quo, both represented and upheld here by (oppressed and) repressive "maiden aunts," the Hannah Mores of household politics:

> I grant, when he the distant toy would reach,
> Stern self-denial maiden aunts would preach:
> But, contrary to this cold maxim tried,
> Bestow the gift, Indulgence be thy guide;
> Ay, give unask'd; example has its kind,
> Pouring its image on the ductile mind.
> Hence nobler spirits shall their likeness breed,
> And ONE great virtue take the mental lead.   (171–78)

Thus a distinctly pleasurable pedagogy is being recommended, in which games and not tasks are offered to the child, and the instinctive desire for knowledge is deliberately merged with desire for the mother as both comforting physical presence and chief source of affection and praise:

> Woo to enquiry – strictures long avoid,
> By force the thirst of weakly sense is cloy'd:
> Silent attend the frown, the gaze, the smile,
> To grasp far objects the incessant toil;
> So play life's springs with energy, and try
> The unceasing thirst of knowledge to supply.   (95–100)

We are to repeat the imperative structure of the first line in the last two, so that it is the mother who plays upon "life's springs," and should do so energetically, consciously working to supply, along with mother's milk, the right materials for knowledge – "Indulgence" and an interest in "liberty."

The "mind" or "soul," with its desire "TO KNOW" (which is repeated in the poem four times) and its connection to "instinctive happiness," is personified as feminine, a traditional enough descendant of Psyche, Athena, and Boethius' Dame Philosophy, but with a difference that is interesting in the light of psychoanalytical feminism:

> In infancy, when all her force is young,
> She patient waits behind the useless tongue;
>
> . . .
>
> Till cadence whispers o'er the eager thought,
> And human accents strike, with MEANING fraught;
> Then gentle breathings in the babe inspire
> Joy, pleasure, sympathy, new-born desire.
> He feels instinctive happiness, and tries
> To grasp her fully as she onward flies.
> Hence Mira's soft endearments shall excite
> In her dear Edward exquisite delight.   (141–58)

The mother's seduction of the infant seems enabled by the traditional feminine casting of the "psyche"; the mother becomes the embodiment of all objects that promise the instinctive happiness the psyche is forever seeking. And this crucial complicity between femininity and pleasure significantly occurs before the acquisition of language, before the oedipal crisis and entry into the symbolic order of language, structured by the Father's Law.[15] Through intimate exchanges with the mother, the psychic ground is prepared to receive the structure of meaning before "MEANING" itself becomes linguistically accessible.

Here Yearsley theorizes the relation between mother and child celebrated by Wordsworth in the famous passage of Book II of *The Prelude* in which this "intercourse of touch," this "drinking in" of maternal feeling through nursing and looking into the mother's eyes, is represented as the source of all subsequent social feeling:

> . . . blest the Babe,
> Nursed in his Mother's arms, who sinks to sleep,
> Rocked on his Mother's breast; who with his soul
> Drinks in the feelings of his Mother's eye!
> For him, in one dear Presence, there exists
> A virtue which irradiates and exalts
> Objects through widest intercourse of sense.
> No Outcast he, bewildered and depressed:
> Along his infant veins are interfused
> The gravitation and the filial bond
> Of nature that connect him with the world.
>
> . . .

> . . . From early days,
> Beginning not long after that first time
> In which, a Babe, by intercourse of touch
> I held mute dialogues with my Mother's heart,
> I have endeavoured to display the means
> Whereby this infant sensibility,
> Great birthright of our being, was in me
> Augmented and sustained.[16]   (234–72)

For both Yearsley and Wordsworth, as for Julia Kristeva, the paradigmatic infant is male. Wordsworth's "mute dialogues" sustain the child, apparently independently of the mother's attitude or circumstances; the mystique of her "Presence" is all. Yearsley's text, written from the mother's rather than the infant's point of view, represents the relation more clearly as a narcissistic one, in which the mother and child "mirror" one another's gestures, emotions, desires, and in so doing, affirm and amplify them; hence the mother's silent attendance on the infant's frown, gaze, and smile, the better to mimic them. To succeed as a mother, "Mira" must constitute herself as the perfect "mirror."[17] This amounts to a maternal imperative in Yearsley's program of pleasurable pedagogy: it is up to the mother to instil the experience of pleasure, to "woo," "excite," and "exquisitely delight" the child. Implicitly, the better job she does, the happier, freer, and more affectionate the child will be: a citizen of a new affective and emancipatory polity. And the erotic desire struggled with and rejected elsewhere in Yearsley's verse as a snare that can endanger precious liberty finds some sanctioned compensation here by the cradle, the hearth, and the cottage door.

Mothers are not the only women in this peaceful, progressive paradise, however. Yearsley's production of revolutionary education founders, ironically, on class. Who are the subjects most severely excluded from this already depopulated family circle? – the servants, wetnurses and nannies, who make a living at "mothering." As early as 1622 the Countess of Lincoln had argued against wetnursing not only on the basis of scriptural precedent and the natural evidence of animals, but also on the grounds that it was unfair to play on a nurse's need or desire for wages, and in so doing, to force "a *poorer woman to banish her owne infant*, for the entertaining of a *richer womans child*, as it were, bidding her *unloue her owne to loue yours*."[18] If many early-modern rich women employed wetnurses for reasons cited by the Countess – "it is obiected, that [breastfeeding] is troublesome; that it is noysome to ones clothes; that it makes one looke old, &c." (p. 13) – they also experienced a much higher rate of fertility as a result than did women who breastfed. As Dorothy McLaren has shown, "The choice for wives during their teeming years in pre-industrial England was an infant in the womb or at the breast. Since most wives chose to have an infant at the breast, their fertility lagged

well behind their fecundity."[19] The arguments for maternal lactation associated with a late eighteenth-century discourse of domesticity are clearly not
new, but they are bound up with demographic changes consequent upon the
transition to industrialization. What had been the prerogative of rich women
in previous decades was becoming more common as urbanization disrupted
traditional rural practices. According to McLaren, "Infant mortality had
reached alarming proportions by 1760 and is attributed to incorrect infant
nutrition and the abandonment of breastfeeding" (p. 46). Thus Yearsley's
argument, though not new, may have been produced in response to a
contemporary problem of some urgency. What is perhaps most surprising is
that the Countess of Lincoln's rather modern argument regarding the
enforced deprivation of the nurse's child is conspicuously absent from
Yearsley's account. *To Mira* represents wetnurses and nannies as women
without familial responsibilities of their own for whom childrearing simply
equals wage labor and pleasure servitude. In this respect her argument parallels
certain positions adopted in contemporary French debates. As Marie-France
Morel comments:

In reality, for physicians this contrast between urban culture and peasant beliefs was
reduced to the fundamental dichotomy of good mother/bad wetnurse. The
enlightened mother took physicians' advice; she nursed her own child, refused to put
it to wet-nurse, and closely supervised its upbringing. In contrast, women in the
country took in strangers' infants in order to earn money. Their feelings were, in the
proper sense of the word, *denatured*, since they refused the breast to their own child in
order to sell it to a nursling from the city whom they would never love.[20]

For Yearsley, however, the contrast between mother and wetnurse is specifically a class difference rather than an urban–rural distinction:

> I saw the beauteous Caleb t'other day
> Stretch forth his little hand to touch a spray,
> Whilst on the grass his drowsy nurse inhal'd
> The sweets of Nature as her sweets exhal'd:
> But, ere the infant reach'd the playful leaf,
> She pull'd him back – His eyes o'erflow'd with grief;
> He check'd his tears – Her fiercer passions strove,
> She look'd a vulture cowring o'er a dove!
> "I'll teach you, brat!" The pretty trembler sigh'd –
> When, with a cruel shake, she hoarsely cried –
> "Your Mother spoils you – every thing you see
> "You covet. It shall ne'er be so with me!
> "Here, eat this cake, sit still, and don't you rise –
> "Why don't you pluck the sun down from the skies?

"I'll spoil your sport – Come, laugh me in the face –
"And henceforth learn to keep your proper place.
"You rule me in the house! – to hush your noise
"I, like a spaniel, must run for toys:
"But here, Sir, let the trees alone, nor cry –
"Pluck, if you dare – Who's master? you, or I?

. . .

Hence vice and ignorance (What ills are worse?)
Arise contagious in the artful nurse;
For Virtue's self she ne'er could virtue prize,
O'er THOUGHT deform'd she throws the fair disguise;
Coarse in idea – furious in her ire,
Her passions grow amid their smother'd fire.
O trust not Edward to so warm a breast,
Lest she infuse the evils you detest.   (101–86)

What has become of Yearsley's militantly pacifist female "warmth" in the
person of the nursemaid? The relation between mistress and paid servant only
exacerbates the class-specific effects of inadequate education, thwarted affections, strategic hypocrisy, and hostility towards the privileged. But what is to
be done to emancipate her, or is she merely to be banished from the payroll?
Here the bourgeois family is explicitly consolidated by means of casting out,
scapegoating, or in Kristeva's terms, abjecting, the lower-class nursemaid.[21]

We should recall that, within the *Vindication* at least, Mary Wollstonecraft
was unable to think her way beyond a republican reformist program, in
which domestic happiness depends upon married couples "Raised sufficiently
above abject poverty not to be obliged to weigh the consequence of every
farthing they spend," "with perhaps merely a servant-maid" to take off the
mother's hands "the servile part of the household business" (pp. 254–55). In
the context of writing fiction, Wollstonecraft was able to give the working-
class woman a voice, as we shall see. But in the philosophical mode of the
Vindication she announces herself as addressing precisely the women of the
class to which she herself belongs and which she identifies as the class most
worthy of imitation: "I pay particular attention to those in the middle class,
because they appear to be in the most natural state" (p. 81).

This is precisely the construction Yearsley's text produces and advertises as
a possible solution to the problem of emancipatory and pacifist desires in a
reactionary and militarized historical moment. Lactilla, the savage milkwoman and resentful antagonist of the propertied classes, has been banished
from within "her" own text to the margins of this re-socialization program.
The poet's rebellious "warmth" at the beginning of the poem and the nurse's
"contagious" warmth near the end stand in a contradictory yet mutually
reflective relation. Yearsley would cast off the old mentality of class war

waged on all fronts, including the domestic, the most intimate, for a reliance upon future generations of emancipated youth.

Advocating female militancy in the service of pacifism, not female passivity in the service of militarism, *To Mira* slides without contradiction from the desire for liberty to the hearth where cultural reproduction occurs, safe from material hardship or political strife, both of which have been displaced – from this poem at least – onto a battlefield sufficiently "over there" and occupied solely by men. *To Mira* produces a discourse of domesticity that exalts the will "TO KNOW" as a sovereign subject. That this sovereign subject might also become the subject of empire, and of military repression of popular disturbance at home, need not be recognized textually so long as the fervent warmth of desire for new political arrangements confines itself to the domestic circle, and to women's mutually supporting friendships, in an idealist conception of their function as producers of "the future."

And so we are left with commerce, without the slave trade, and women's confinement to the domestic sphere, without any coercion, a "freely chosen" investment in social change through progressive maternal influence. Lactilla, the figure for the savage laboring–class writer, silently disappears; "coarse" and "furious" nursemaids surface as villains – the return of a repressed, regressive working class. The question of social emancipation becomes confused, is displaced, defused, in the service of vivid representation and the recognition of intractable class differences. Is it merely ironical that one of More's first gestures of material assistance was to provide Yearsley with "a *little* Maid, to help feed her pigs, and nurse the little ones, while she herself sells her Milk"?[22]

The Turkish prejudice

If we examine More's, Wollstonecraft's, and Yearsley's shared ideological ground in search of its limits in other ways, we find a more totalizing exclusion than the suppression of class in the projection of a hostile yet exotic culture of Eastern alterity designated "the Mahometans" or "the Turks." This is a traditional figure for otherness within British culture, perhaps as old as the crusades, but one that recurs with peculiar intensity in the late eighteenth and early nineteenth centuries. Thus Wollstonecraft, when she wishes to villify male tyranny, invokes "the true style of Mahometanism," or "the true Mahometan strain," or "that destructive blast which desolates Turkey, and renders the men, as well as the soil, unfruitful" (*Vindication*, p. 80, p. 100, p. 131). And, for More, it is necessary to remind her audience that they are "neither to train up Amazons nor Circassians, but to form Christians," in direct contrast to "the luxurious dissipation brought in by [the Romans'] Asiatic conquests" (*Strictures*, 1, p. 69, pp. 76–77). However depraved the British may be, it is necessary for More to posit an antipathetic other in order to consolidate her audience's sense of cultural identity. To be British is to be enlightened and free; as for "those fair victims to luxury, caprice, and despotism, whom the laws and the religion of the voluptuous prophet of Arabia exclude from light, and liberty, and knowledge; . . . *they are slaves*" (*Strictures*, 1, p. 3). Recall Jack the Blacksmith's expostulation: "Why I'd sooner go to the Negers to get learning, or to the Turks to get religion, than to the French for freedom and happiness"; More may be playing upon supposed working-class chauvinism and racism here, but her own discourse deploys the same figures.

The language of rights produced by the discourses of revolution at the end of the eighteenth century makes it theoretically possible to imagine general emancipation, the end of privilege and prejudice. British liberty and scientific enlightenment would seem to be antithetical to the perpetuation of both xenophobia and traditional class prejudices. Yet the construction of otherness, of groups beyond the pale of Britishness, or even more narrowly, Englishness, continues in the collective imaginary, generated by imperialism's demands for strategies of subjugation. And within the domestic economy, even radicalism, with its roots in artisanal culture, remains relatively closed to women and the unskilled of both sexes. As Gareth Stedman Jones comments, "If this was the 'republic of artisans', it was a very masculine republic."[23] The constitution of an emancipatory politics sensitive to but not based on class or racial or gender differences and exclusions remains a project for our own moment, one for which an analysis of the limits of available discourses of liberty and emancipation would seem not only advisable but crucial.

A shifting limit: Wollstonecraft's *The Wrongs of Woman: Or, Maria. A Fragment*

Rather than seeking to recuperate a "revolution in female manners" as compensation for the relative political conservatism that followed the upheavals of the 1780s and 1790s, I suggest that we address ourselves to the Derridian notion of "revolutions that as yet have no model." As Gayatri Spivak has suggested, "In order to work with a non-transcendental non-logical (non)-concept (or graphic)," such as Derrida proposes, "one must think a great change of mind-set. Of course a mere change of mind-set, however great, will not bring about revolutions. Yet, without this revolutionary change of mind, revolutionary 'programs' will fall into the same metaphysical bind of idealized and repeatable intention and context that Derrida plots in speech act theory."[24] To effect a deconstructive reversal-displacement of the silent exclusions of class-specific and xenophobic ideology in our readings of the texts of impurely "revolutionary" women might go some way towards a more revolutionary politics than we have yet conceived, within academic disciplines as well as outside them. One of those exclusions is surely the discourse of laboring-class women, marked as it is by "impure" contradictions, incompletely articulated counter-ideologies, and ingrained self-effacement. We might do worse than to begin there to disturb, subvert, and displace (Spivak, p. 38) the limits of the already conventional pieties of much existing feminist research.

Cora Kaplan has argued most persuasively that Wollstonecraft's contradictory positing of feminist emancipation within a class-specific moralization of sexuality prefigures current feminist dilemmas regarding the relations between sexual pleasure, subjectivity, "political correctness," and class, cultural, and racial divisions between women: "Wollstonecraft's project, with its contradictory implications, suggests some of the problems involved in the moralization of sexuality on behalf of any political programme, even a feminist one."[25] Should we not attempt to engage Wollstonecraft's contradictions as boldly as she addressed the ideological predicament of the women of her class in the *Vindication*?

To do Wollstonecraft credit, we should recognize that in her second novel, *The Wrongs Of Woman: or, Maria*, unfinished at her death, she attempted to "write back in" the discourse of sexual pleasure and of working-class women's specific oppressions, two texts of otherness that had been excluded from the *Vindication*. The inset autobiographical narrative by the servant Jemima, who "had felt the crushing hand of power, hardened by the exercise of injustice, and ceased to wonder at the perversions of the understanding, which systematize oppression,"[26] is as scrupulously accurate regarding the wages, hours, and working conditions of laundresses in London as was Mary Collier's *The Woman's Labour* regarding the circumstances of rural washerwomen in the 1730s:

'Not to trouble you,' continued she, 'with a detailed description of all the painful feelings of unavailing exertion, I have only to tell you, that at last I got recommended to wash in a few families, who did me the favour to admit me into their houses, without the most strict enquiry, to wash from one in the morning till eight at night, for eighteen or twenty-pence a day. On the happiness to be enjoyed over a washing-tub I need not comment; yet you will allow me to observe, that this was a wretchedness of situation peculiar to my sex.[27]

Jemima enters the narrative as warder to the eponymous heroine Maria, who has been separated from her child and confined to a private madhouse by her villainous husband Venables. Having married Maria for her dowry of £5,000, the spendthrift Venables has had her locked up to gain control of what little property of hers remains. Jemima, who has been brutalized in a hundred ways, nevertheless responds to Maria's desolation at the loss of her child; once again, maternal affection proves the irresistible sign of a character worthy of sympathy. Jemima's empirical accuracy is complemented by her capacity for strong feeling.

In an exchange with Maria and Darnford, another inmate who will become Maria's lover, Jemima relates her history of exploitation in a manner that Mary Poovey has described as "decidedly *un*sentimental."[28] The product of an unhappy liaison between servants, in which her mother was seduced and abandoned, only to die nine days after giving birth, Jemima has learned to narrate her suffering in a devastatingly understated way. Her tale of female "slavery" chronicles her experiences as domestic drudge, slop-shop apprentice, seduced and cast-off servant, prostitute, mistress of a dissipated man of letters, washerwoman, thief, convict, beggar, workhouse inmate, and madhouse warder. Punctuated with politically astute reflections on the oppression endured by women of her class, Jemima's narrative is an answer to Maria's "often-repeated question," why Jemima's "sentiments and language were superior" to her station (*The Wrongs of Woman*, p. 106, p. 111). Jemima's extreme marginalization and the very intensity of her suffering, mediated by the literacy and exposure to intellectual discussion she had gained from the dissipated man of letters, have forged her complex, politicized subjectivity. As a self-contained narrative of chapter length, Jemima's story is thus inscribed within the middle-class heroine Maria's and serves as a prelude to Maria's inset memoirs and her political and sexual awakening. As symbolically charged as any maid-servant within the bourgeois family romance, Jemima reminds us that the polite world is constructed through the exclusion and the abjection of the "low," and that what is socially peripheral may also be symbolically central, in Stallybrass and White's terms (*The Politics and Poetics of Transgression*, p. 5). The class-specificity of Jemima's struggle to survive as a servant discloses the class-specific construction, or constructedness, of both Maria's and Mary Wollstonecraft's struggles with romance and writing. The placement of Jemima's story thus interrupts what might otherwise have been a narrative too easily assimilable to autobiographical reading, too transparently a rewriting of Wollstonecraft's own life.

Both Poovey and Myers comment on Jemima's text only to dismiss it, to read it as too easily circumscribable within Maria's sentimental plot.[29] By down-playing this intertext's importance, and the radical disruption of the heroine's plot and the autobiographical reading of that plot it represents, they themselves help to dissipate the text's contradictory energies. Wollstonecraft has learned to accommodate the working-class text fictively, if not theoretically: our impure idealization, our incomplete revolution that has and is no model, persists. As an impurely "revolutionary woman," Wollstonecraft the writer remains a contradiction in terms. After Maria follows Jemima's lead in fleeing the asylum to set up house together, Jemima insists on being considered Maria's housekeeper and receiving "the customary stipend." This "freely chosen," contractual servitude represents a certain falling back on the terms of the *Vindication*, the terms of bourgeois compromise, but the urgency of Jemima's presence in the text prevents any easy subsumption of her subjectivity within Maria's. She has been "written back in" with a vengeance.

Analogous to this reinscription of the working-class woman's voice in the debates concerning social justice that mark *The Wrongs of Woman* as an English Jacobin novel is the reinscription of sexuality.[30] The novel's fragmentary conclusion represents the experience of erotic passion as more liberating and much healthier than the "sickly" repressions of romance. What had been excluded from the discourse of the *Vindication* returns, the voice of female labor and the emancipatory possibilities of a less constrained sexuality than British law and social custom of the 1790s would admit. The sexualized Maria who has experienced erotic ecstasy with Darnford is also the politicized Maria born of a close kinship with Jemima. Wollstonecraft goes so far as to connect libidinal repression with social oppression:

The heart is often shut by romance against social pleasure; and, fostering a sickly sensibility, grows callous to the soft touches of humanity.

(*The Wrongs of Woman*, p. 193)

It would seem that Wollstonecraft here is attempting to distinguish between sexuality and domesticity, the eroticism fostered by romance and enshrined in marriage. She would have Maria go beyond a politics of domesticity that elicits female desire only to foreclose it within the domestic circle. This "soft" revolution of consciousness is further dispersed by the text's fragmentary status, its production forever interrupted by Wollstonecraft's death. Wollstonecraft's notes indicate that Darnford was to betray and abandon Maria.[31] And as Michel Foucault has argued, a politics of sexual liberationism, or even of sexual identities, presents no clear way out of the regulation of desire characteristic of bourgeois domesticity, no radical break from a culture organized around a "truth" supposedly "hidden" in sexuality and made to speak itself again and again.[32] And so we are forced to read Maria's exclamation, when she remembers thinking herself in love with Venables – "What a revolution took place, not only in my train of thoughts, but feelings!" (*The Wrongs of Woman*, p. 135) – as both bitterly ironical and historically premature, for the relation with Darnford offers no real alternative to Maria's disastrous marriage. Marriage and motherhood versus sexual pleasure and sensibility: rather than standing in real opposition to each other, Venables and Darnford represent the two sides of a single system into which the sexual/sensible woman is interpellated.[33]

To rewrite Wollstonecraft as offering little in the way of an alternative to More, however, is to forget how far she was able to go in her exploration of new possibilities of feminist consciousness and political articulation, new impure contradictions waiting to be worked through. And to write of either

More or Wollstonecraft without attending to the historical margins, to such coextensive though discontinuous discourses as that represented by laboring-class women's writing is to perpetuate both theoretically and in practice those "perversions of the understanding" that may conspire to systematize oppression. If the history of feminism has been beset by significant forgetting, so that the same arguments have been made repeatedly for several centuries, and always as if for the first time, then a feminist literary history should commit itself both to remembering and to recognizing the difficulty, and the frequent impossibility, of "remembering."

Ironically, this forgetting is already happening within the 1790s. Anna Laetitia Aikin Barbauld (1743–1825), the daughter of a Nonconformist minister, parodies the eighteenth-century Miltonic tradition early in the decade by invoking the "domestic Muse" in order to compose a suitably "female" poem on that major household event, "Washing-Day"[34]:

> The Muses are turned gossips; they have lost
> The buskined step, and clear high-sounding phrase,
> Language of gods. Come then, domestic Muse,
> In slipshod measure loosely prattling on
> Of farm or orchard, pleasant curds and cream,
> Or drowning flies, or shoe lost in the mire
> By little whimpering boy, with rueful face;
> Come, Muse, and sing the dreaded Washing-Day.   (1–8)

Barbauld's perspective is that of the middle-class child whose routines are excitingly disrupted by the monthly wash, when "ere the first gray streak of dawn, / The red-armed washers come and chase repose" (13–14). Who are these Muses who have turned gossips? Not, it would seem, those of the plebeian georgic tradition, for no mention is made of laboring-class women's verse, of Collier's representation of washing-day from the perspective of the "red-armed washers," of Leapor's disclosure of the domestic economy of the country house, of Yearsley's rural prospects seen from the milkwoman's point of view. Barbauld pays no attention to class differences across the scene of women's writing; this self-parodic "women's" poem claims to take its place in a tradition of domestic verse within which the perspective, and the possible articulations, of the "red-armed washers" have become once more invisible, unthinkable. Barbauld writes as if addressing such a domestic topic were newly fashionable, as if the province of such verse belonged to privileged women writers like herself, "loosely prattling on," in ever greater numbers, of domestic events and rural simplicity where Milton once tackled sublimer subjects, but doing so from a leisured perspective, surrounded by and made possible by silent female servants.

Why should we be surprised that Richard Polwhele admitted reading Ann Yearsley, and Anna Laetitia Barbauld, if she read Yearsley, did not? The construction of a female literary tradition, and the convenient examination of women's literary production with respect to gender and without sufficient attention to the operation of class differences, will reproduce this historical problematic again and again. Class-specific forms of forgetting may begin at the very moment of heightened working-class articulacy, of new demands for democratic reforms and increased political participation. When laboring-class resistance is combined with protofeminist protest against gender inequality, a privileged woman writer like Barbauld may back away from seeming to align herself with such volatile opinions.

The effacement of the possibility of those red-armed washerwomen speaking or writing for themselves is coupled in Barbauld's *œuvre* with skepticism about feminist ambitions. In "The Rights Of Woman,"[35] Barbauld concludes her parodic verse redaction of Wollstonecraft's *Vindication* with a command that women abandon their desires for liberty and equality:

> Then, then, abandon each ambitious thought,
> Conquest or rule thy heart shall feebly move,
> In Nature's school, by her soft maxims taught,
> That separate rights are lost in mutual love. (29–32)

Repentance of ambition for political rights, and the substitution of an idealized reconciliation between the sexes – and, by analogy, between the classes – wrought in "mutual love": Polwhele's and More's project would seem to have triumphed over Wollstonecraft's and Yearsley's. But writing in the 1790s, Barbauld at least has to struggle with what is so very desirable within the *Vindication*, its appeal to middle-class women's intellectual aspirations; and she does memorialize the monthly washing-day as a scene of women's power, as Ann Messenger has pointed out. Such male escapades as the Montgolfier brothers' experiments in ballooning are shown to be no greater imaginative achievements than the whimsy represented by women's domestic verse, and achievements of less importance than the material necessity of washing; as Messenger writes, "the assumption that what men do is important and what women do is not, is turned upside down. The women's washing is heroic; the men's exploits are child's play" (Messenger, pp. 188–92). The boldness of such a recognition cannot be sustained. Barbauld's text remains marked by contradictions that she shares with other women writers, including her laboring-class contemporaries.

After 1800: from class combativeness to the dejection of Ann Candler and the conservatism of Elizabeth Bentley

By the end of the century, the discourse of laboring-class women's verse seems to have played itself out, along with much of the radical democratic energy with which it may often have been allied. In 1803, Ann More Candler (1740–1816), a "Suffolk cottager" and then a resident of Tattingstone House of Industry, published a slim volume of verse superficially like those of her predecessors. But this volume is dominated by an autobiographical memoir of twenty pages and entitled, not *Poems on Several Occasions* or *on Various Subjects*, but the less confident, more ingratiating *Poetical Attempts*.[36] We are supposed to be interested in the drama, hardship, and perseverance of Ann Candler, her piety, morality, and industry as such, and not her class-skewed encounter with English verse, her contradictory, sometimes radical appropriation of literary pleasures and prerogatives traditionally above her station. There is a note in the British Library copy of her verses, recording that she was "much respected for her integrity."[37] Similarly, Elizabeth Bentley (1767–1839), whose first volume of *Genuine Poetical Compositions, on Various Subjects* introduced her to the world in 1791 as the daughter of a journeyman cordwainer, a woman who "had no education" and "read only by accident," published in 1821 *Poems; being the Genuine Compositions of Elizabeth Bentley, Of Norwich*, poetical documents that have little to do with the tradition of laboring-class verse.[38] Bentley is now the proprietor of a small school and capable of sentimentalized representations of "peasant life" coupled with blood-drumming militarism in the service of imperial rule. Here we have something like Duck's history: a social rise traceable in the readoption of the conventions of leisured pastoral and georgic poetry that the plebeian poet had begun by questioning and rejecting.

If in "On Health And Liberty. 1787," Bentley could argue that "The want of Liberty each bliss destroys" (23),[39] though she defines liberty rather restrictively as obedience to British law, Bentley in 1821 reiterates Hannah More's message to the poor of the 1790s: frugality and industry signify virtue, and virtue is all that the poor ought to desire:

> How happy in his reed-roof'd cot,
> The rural peasant's humble lot,
>
> . . .
>
> His hut two sister nymphs frequent,
> Ruddy Health and meek Content,
> Led by industry their friend,
> On Temp'rance steps these nymphs attend.[40]   (1–14)

Is this not a reactionary move, especially when combined with the jingoistic rhetoric of poems like her "On the Victory Over The Dutch Fleet, October 11th, 1797":

> HARK! where Joy's triumphant throng
> Ardent pour the grateful song,
>   To Heav'n's Almighty Lord!
> *He* view'd in scorn th' insulting host,
> Who madly threaten'd o'er our coast

> To wave th' ensanguin'd sword:
>
> . . .
>
> Britannia, empress of the main,
> Her pow'r shall undisturb'd maintain,
>   While beams the orb of day;
> Her commerce o'er the globe extend,
> Each distant clime its products send,
>   Each nation bless her sway[41]   (1–30)

and "Song. The Briton's Resolution. August, 1803":

> Fierce foes to every blessing
>   The British peasant shares,
> They'd rob us of each treasure
>   That life to man endears.
>
>   . . .
>
> Is life more dear than freedom?
>   Say, will you bear the yoke,
> Survive your Country's ruin,
>   And crouch beneath the stroke,
>
> The slaves of Gallic tyrants?
>   What heart but answers – No!
> Seize, seize your sword and firelock,
>   And rush to meet the foe.
>
>   . . .
>
> We'll save our Country's freedom,
>   Or in her cause we'll die;
> Brave Britons, when united,
>   The world in arms defy.[42]   (9–40)

Such patriotic rhetoric may seem to speak for itself as a sign of lower-class retrenchment in the wake of a particularly turbulent decade.

If we recontextualize Bentley's jingoism within the discourses of opposition to the latter course of the French revolution and Napoleonic rule, however, her rhetoric can be read as rather more complex, not entirely reactionary. Even artisanal radicalism would refuse to celebrate what had become of France by the end of the 1790s. The Bentley who had praised British liberty in 1787 may still be faintly discerned if we read these poems in the light of such commentary on the revolutionary moment as James Gillray's caricatures. In 1831 John Landseer argued that Gillray was "a reluctant ally of the tory faction . . . his heart was always on the side of whiggism and liberty."[43]

Gillray's pairing of images of *French Liberty* and *British Slavery* (1792) is politically ambivalent; as Ronald Paulson comments, this pair of prints:

pushes Tory England as far to one extreme as it pushes revolutionary France to the other, and England becomes a sleekly-fat, suspiciously Hanoverian-looking lout, complaining about taxes and a government that will make slaves of us all. The starved but lithe Frenchman is talking about liberty as he dines on leeks. The two sides have been polarized until they are equally ridiculous and unacceptable.[44]

Bentley seems to have been a less reluctant ally of the Tories than Gillray, but her texts are not entirely innocent of protest against both British complacency and the authoritarianism of "th' ensanguin'd sword," whoever wields it. To set freedom above life itself may be an ideological move too often employed in the service of British imperialism, but Bentley advocates the defense of British liberties from a French attack, not British determination of French affairs. Paulson argues regarding Gillray, "To ignore the subversive, the radical, the skeptical . . . reading . . . is to miss half the truth" (Paulson, p. 187). In the light of representations like Gillray's of the gap between the revolutionary rhetoric of liberty and actual popular deprivation in France, Bentley's defense of British liberty, however jingoistic, may retain something of a critically populist edge.

So also with Bentley's mixed, potentially contradictory use of various poetic genres. By the time she publishes "The Gleaner's Prayer" in 1821, it may seem that Mary Collier's polemical *The Woman's Labour* has been completely forgotten:

> Fresh as the roseate beams of morn,
>   We children of the cot
> Forsake our home at early dawn,
>   Nor deem severe our lot.[45]   (17–20)

All the furnishings of pastoral otium in georgic guise, including the by now weary "roseate" dawn, which is also vaguely "early," have reappeared as if Duck and Collier had never written. And the voice of protest has been silenced in favor of an insistence on the stoicism of the poor and an appeal to charity. Only in that cursory moment of attributed self-understanding – "Nor deem severe our lot" – do the dignity of rural labor and the refusal of patronizing sympathy, so characteristic of a Collier, a Duck, a Hands, or a Yearsley, surface briefly.

If, however, the newly prized category of working-class writing by 1821 is prose autobiography, in which the cultural difference of the working-class subject is at once sensationally exploited and cancelled, recuperated by the discipline of literary self-representation, might there not be something also productively resistant about the public, explicitly political form of much of

Bentley's verse? She attempts the high style, makes public pronouncements, legislates acceptable behavior for the great as well as the poor. By the middle of the nineteenth century, such a stance by a residually laboring-class woman has become unthinkable, though it was sometimes adopted in the eighteenth century and most fully realized by Ann Yearsley between 1788 and 1796. The constraints imposed on plebeian writing by a neoclassical aesthetic were not necessarily more repressive, more productive of class subjection than the class-specific indoctrination into an autobiographical mode that bespoke resignation to disenfranchisement, the rendering of oneself as an object of sympathy rather than as a participant in the shaping of public discourse and political opinion. But this was a shift that happened gradually and in relation to other shifts in public discourse, in the available political languages.

Indeed a certain tendency towards resignation to the status quo, made possible at least partly by religious belief in a utopian "future state" after death, though, as we have seen, that was not the sole function of religion in this period, had been there from the beginning, in the accommodationism observable in the texts of Collier. But it is important to determine the operations of power within a discourse, and to mark the crucial differences as well as resemblances between the self-presentations of working-class subjects (how the culture speaks through them), where such texts can be recovered, and the ways that they are spoken, and spoken for, by middle- and upper-class subjects in the texts of mainstream culture.

Let us keep in mind the range of discursive possibilities that lie beyond as well as between the figures of Austen's Harriet Smith, naive protégée only capable of being spoken for, and Brontë's Nelly Dean, through whom propertied patriarchal culture speaks. The historical matrices of these figures from fiction are crucial. As a character, Nelly may possess a complex, fully nuanced subjectivity, a class-specific subjectivity of a type apparently of little interest to Austen and her contemporaries. Nelly, the female servant as agent of patriarchy, works in the narrative margins to bring about the repressive closure of property rights and family relations that have formed her subjectivity, taught her to "love" her own subjection, her own exclusion from the novel's class-specific centers of social power, heroic action, and romantic drama reserved for those "born" to them. In her self-exclusion, her perverse laying claim to the power of domestic servitude as surrogate motherhood, we can read the cultural traces of the collapse of a potentially revolutionary democratic movement across class lines, the fragmentation of political opposition, the reinvigoration of gender antagonism within the working class. It is 1847, a moment by which the decline of both Chartism and Owenism is assured, and, according to Stedman Jones, a moment by which the long process of consolidating working-class culture as a defensive culture of consolation, achieved by 1900, has already begun, both within and outside London, through:

the decay of artisan radicalism, the marginal impact of socialism, the largely passive acceptance of imperialism and the throne, and the growing usurpation of political and educational interests by a way of life centred round the pub, the race-course and the music-hall. In sum, its impermeability to the classes above it was no longer threatening or subversive, but conservative and defensive.[46]

In the abjection of Ann Candler's *Poetical Attempts*, and the conflation of British liberties with military rule in Elizabeth Bentley's *Poems*, many of which would protect "freeborn Englishmen" by soliciting the lowliest of rural Britons for Britannia's imperial service, we can trace the waning of class combativeness and the increasing defensiveness of a working class now in considerable fear of threats from within, as the division between those in work and the unemployed or dependent, the "industrious" and the "indigent" poor, sharpened.

Thus Candler at once protests the meanness of the charity she receives and reviles her fellow inmates at Tattingstone House of Industry as "the dregs":

> Within these dreary walls confin'd,
>   A lone recluse, I live,
> And, with the dregs of human kind,
>   A niggard alms receive.
>
> Uncultivated, void of sense,
>   Unsocial, insincere,
> Their rude behaviour gives offence,
>   Their language wounds the ear.[47]   (5–12)

There is evidence here to support Wordsworth's protest against such houses of industry, whose dreary walls imprison the poverty that would be more kindly treated by the open air:

> Reverence the hope whose vital anxiousness
> Gives the last human interest to his heart.
> May never HOUSE, misnamed of INDUSTRY,
> Make him a captive! – for that pent-up din,
> Those life-consuming sounds that clog the air,
> Be his the natural silence of old age!
> Let him be free of mountain solitudes.
>
> (*The Old Cumberland Beggar*, 177–83)

Though not an inhabitant of Cumbrian mountainous splendor, but of East Anglian lowlands, Candler writes as if she would prefer a poverty-stricken independence to the "pent-up din" of uncongenial and "insincere" fellow inmates. Ironically, she is as much a "lone recluse" as any Wordsworthian solitary although she lives confined among many, in enforced sociality. The terseness of her reference to "niggard alms" may well represent a stronger indictment of contemporary charitable practices than Crabbe's indictment of the institution of the poorhouse as itself perpetuating vices in *The Borough*. For Crabbe, it is not upper-class stinginess but the inmates themselves who are responsible for their mutual degradation:

> In this vast Room, each Place by habit fix'd,
> Are Sexes, Families, and Ages mix'd, –
> To Union forc'd by Crime, by Fear, by Need,
> And all in Morals and in Modes agreed; –
>
>   . . .
>
> And Need and Misery, Vice and Danger bind
> In sad alliance each degraded Mind.
>
>   (*Letter XVIII. The Poor and their Dwellings*, 344–53)

Candler boldly criticizes the penny-pinching propertied classes who think their houses of industry constitute suitable solutions to poverty. The struggle to assert her dignity and respectability in such circumstances, however, produces in Candler's text a certain class-conscious snobbery towards the less respectable, the less literate, whose "language wounds the ear."

Against the "rudeness" of her fellow inmates, their vulgarity as well as their lack of sympathy for this lone and poetically-inclined recluse, Candler sets her own cultivation, which has enabled her to focus her misery and work through it by reading and remembering oriental tales, whose fabulous sufferings she identifies with her own experience. In a scene of such isolation and pain, only an appeal to religion seems to offer Candler consolation:

> In youth strange fairytales I've read,
>   Of magic skills and pow'r,
> And mortals, in their sleep, convey'd
>   To some enchanted tow'r.
>
>   . . .
>
> The tales these eastern writers feign
>   Like facts to me appear;
> The fabled suff'rings they contain,
>   I find no fictions here.
>
> And since, in those romantic lays,
>   My miseries combine,
> To bless my lengthen'd wane of days,
>   Their bright reverse be mine.
>
> Look down, O God! in me behold
>   How helpless mortals are,
> Nor leave me friendless, poor, and old,
>   But guide me with thy care. (49–84)

The interweaving of romantic reading with reminders of the writer's empirical hardships gives a highly textualized, "processed" effect to Candler's verse. We are constantly reminded that she has come down in the world, losing her cottage by faithfully following her unreliable husband to London, only to be deserted by him, and to have to make her way back to Suffolk, pregnant again, soon to find herself with seven children to look after. In terms of the fine shades of class feeling in the period, her crossing from respectable cottager to resident of the workhouse has been particularly demoralizing, for the workhouse exists not merely to enforce industry and limit parish relief, but to mark the distinction between the respectable and the dependent poor. At the same time, her history is offered to us as a literary model guaranteed to elicit sympathy: polemical protest has given way to the generation of charitable feeling in projected readers, who will be able to distinguish between Candler as cultivated and "deserving," and her fellow inmates at Tattingstone as the rabble both she and her audience have learned to fear. Appropriately, Candler's autobiography is prefaced by a statement of her piety and authenticity as a humble cottager which turns on a line from Gray's *Elegy*; her *Poetical Attempts* merely supplement her memoir, which is offered to us as an authentic example of "The short and simple annals of the poor."[48]

Yet there had been plebeian alternatives to this discourse of muffled protest, of defeat and cooption, as there would be again. In the political struggles of the 1830s and 1840s, working-class women's activism was crucially important, as Barbara Taylor and Sally Alexander have shown.[49] There would be many radical transformations of sexual relations, capitalism, Chartism, Owenism, socialism, and trade unionism proposed by laboring women, and with mixed success, but no longer proposed between the covers of volumes of verse bearing the class-specific signatures of laboring women poets. "Poetry" itself had also undergone fundamental changes that were relatively autonomous from shifts in class relations.

These poets can in some sense serve us as historians of the construction of the eighteenth-century female subaltern in Britain. Their writing testifies to the contradictions of laboring-class protofeminist and political consciousness, and to the possibilities for writing as a form of critical articulation and resistance to oppression. Within the ideology of natural poetic genius and the complex circuitry of patronage and marketplace, these poets managed some surprising innovations. Unlike Goldsmith's figure of the sad historian, as we have seen, these women were neither abject nor silent.

Notes

Introduction

1 John Gay, "Thursday, Or, The Spell" from *The Shepherd's Week. In Six Pastorals* in *John Gay: Poetry and Prose*, ed. Vinton A. Dearing with the assistance of Charles E. Beckwith, 2 vols. (Oxford: Clarendon, 1974), I, pp. 109–13; lines 1–4, 131–36.

2 Oliver Goldsmith, *The Deserted Village* in *The Poems of Gray, Collins, and Goldsmith*, ed. Roger Lonsdale (London: Longmans, 1969), pp. 669–94; lines 131–36.

3 Gay, "Tuesday, Or, The Ditty," *The Shepherd's Week*, pp. 101–08, lines 11–16.

4 Pat Thane and Anthony Sutcliffe (eds.), "Introduction," *Essays in Social History Volume 2* (Oxford: Clarendon Press, 1986), p. xxviii, p. xxx. See also E. P. Thompson, *The Making of the English Working Class* (London: Gollancz, 1963), pp. 10–11, and for the eighteenth century, "Eighteenth-Century English Society: Class Struggle without Class?" *Journal of Social History* (May 1978), pp. 133–65.

5 Gareth Stedman Jones, *Languages of Class: Studies in English Working Class History 1832–1982* (Cambridge: Cambridge University Press, 1983), p. 2, pp. 21–22.

6 Joan Wallach Scott, "On Language, Gender, and Working-Class History," *Gender and the Politics of History* (New York: Columbia University Press, 1988), pp. 58–60, p. 66.

7 Sally Alexander, "Women, Class and Sexual Differences in the 1830s and 1840s: Some Reflections on the Writing of a Feminist History," *History Workshop Journal* 17 (Spring 1984), p. 128, pp. 133–34.

8 Pierre Macherey, *A Theory of Literary Production*, trans. Geoffrey Wall (London and Boston: Routledge & Kegan Paul, 1978), p. 94.

9 See, for example, Gayatri Chakravorty Spivak, *In Other Worlds: Essays in Cultural Politics* (New York: Methuen, 1987).

10 Louis Althusser, "Ideology and Ideological State Apparatuses (Notes towards an Investigation)" in *Lenin and Philosophy and Other Essays*, trans. Ben Brewster (New York and London: Monthly Review Press, 1971), pp. 162–86.

11 Raymond Williams, *Keywords: A Vocabulary of Culture and Society* (New York: Oxford University Press, 1976), pp. 126–30.

12 Macherey, *A Theory of Literary Production*, esp. pp. 75–101.

13 Mikhail Bakhtin, *The Dialogic Imagination: Four Essays*, trans. Michael Holquist and Caryl Emerson (Austin: University of Texas Press, 1981), pp. 67–68.

14 Leonore Davidoff, "Mastered for Life: Servant and Wife in Victorian and

Edwardian England," *Journal of Social History* 7:4 (1974), pp. 406–28; reprinted in Thane and Sutcliffe, *Essays in Social History Volume 2*, this passage, p. 142.

15 Margaret Anne Doody employs the term "ventriloquism" in the context of English Civil War verse and the Augustan "voice" in *The Daring Muse: Augustan Poetry Reconsidered* (Cambridge: Cambridge University Press, 1985), pp. 44–49. I use it here to emphasize the way in which plebeian women poets could appropriate the language of canonical master texts for their own purposes.

16 *The Death of Amnon. A Poem. With an Appendix: containing Pastorals, and other Poetical Pieces.* By Elizabeth Hands (Coventry: Printed for the author by N. Rollason, 1789), pp. 47–50.

17 Luce Irigaray, *This Sex Which Is Not One*, trans. Catherine Porter with Carolyn Burke (Ithaca: Cornell University Press, 1985), p. 152.

18 Ann Messenger, *His and Hers: Essays in Restoration and Eighteenth-Century Literature* (Lexington, Ky.: The University Press of Kentucky, 1986), p. 5, pp. 9–10.

19 Morag Shiach, *Discourse on Popular Culture: Class, Gender and History in the Analysis of Popular Culture* (Oxford: Polity Press, 1989), pp. 12–13.

20 See Raymond Williams, *Marxism and Literature* (Oxford: Oxford University Press, 1977) on addressing cultural discontinuities through the terms "dominant," "residual," and "emergent," pp. 121–27.

21 *Blackwood's Edinburgh Magazine* 41:257 (March 1837), p. 408. S. Austin Allibone, in *A Critical Dictionary of English Literature and British and American Authors*, 3 vols. (Philadelphia and London: Lippincott and Trübner, 1877), I, p. 1072, silently "corrects" this quotation from *Blackwood's* to read "a shopkeeper in London," no doubt confusing Barber's place of publication and what may read like frequent visits to London with permanent residence there. See Joyce Fullard's entry on Barber in Janet Todd (ed.), *A Dictionary of British and American Women Writers 1660–1800* (London: Methuen, 1984), p. 38.

22 [George Colman and Bonnell Thornton,] *Poems by Eminent Ladies*, 2 vols. (London: R. Baldwin, 1755), I, p. 146. Colman and Thornton take these statements from the preface to Masters's *Poems on Several Occasions* (London: Printed for the Author by T. Browne, 1733). She also published *Familiar Letters and Poems on Several Occasions* (London: Printed for the Author by D. Henry and R. Cave, 1755).

23 Mary Barber, *Poems on Several Occasions* (London: C. Rivington, 1734). The best recent criticism of Barber is to be found in Margaret Doody's essay "Augustan Women? Four Poets of the Eighteenth Century," forthcoming in a collection of Clark Library lectures, edited by Alan Roper. I thank them both for letting me read it in manuscript.

24 *Dictionary of National Biography*, XIII, p. 25 (hereafter *D.N.B.*), and Todd (ed.), *A Dictionary*, pp. 215–16. The entry on Masters suggests that at least her first volume (1733) was revised by the Rev. Thomas Scott, a Dissenting minister.

25 These details come from the prefatory materials to Bentley's two volumes of verse, *Genuine Poetical Compositions, on Various Subjects* (Norwich: Crouse and Stevenson, 1791) and *Poems; being the Genuine Compositions of Elizabeth Bentley, Of Norwich* (Norwich: Sold by the Author and Stevenson, Matchett, and Stevenson; London: Taylor and Hessey; Cambridge: Deightons; "and all other booksellers," 1821). See also Gayle Trusdel Pendleton's entry in Todd (ed.), *A Dictionary*, pp. 46–47.

26 Bentley's conservatism should be considered in the light of frequent identifications of shoemakers with political radicalism; see E. J. Hobsbawm and Joan

Wallach Scott, "Political Shoemakers," *Past and Present* 89 (November 1980), pp. 86–114. Bentley's father must have been severely disabled by his stroke because, as Hobsbawm and Scott comment, "Perhaps the most plausible explanation of the trade's intellectualism derives from the fact that a shoemaker's work was both sedentary and physically undemanding. Probably it was physically the least taxing labour for men in the countryside," p. 96.

27 See Joyce Fullard's entry on Harrison in Todd (ed.), *A Dictionary*, p. 153.

28 In *Emily Brontë* (Oxford: Basil Blackwell, 1985), James H. Kavanagh forcefully characterizes Nelly Dean as a phallic mother in the service of patriarchal law, pp. 31–43.

1 Sensibility and slavery: the discourse of working-women's verse

1 In by far the best single source, *Virtue of Necessity: English Women's Writing 1649–88* (London: Virago, 1988), Elaine Hobby questions the assertions of previous scholarship concerning women sectaries, establishing their central, not auxiliary, status in various sects and the political nature of their demands "for their right to be involved in matters of national government" (p. 27), as well as their activities' specifically feminist implications. She also demonstrates the limitations of the sectarian women's self-authorization, whether they present themselves as instruments of God's will or have their works published, and thus authorized, by men; see the first chapter, pp. 26–53. See also Keith Thomas, "Women and the Civil War Sects," *Past and Present* 13 (1958), pp. 42–62, reprinted in Trevor Ashton (ed.), *Crisis in Europe, 1560–1660* (1965; London: Routledge & Kegan Paul, 1970), pp. 317–40; Christopher Hill, *The World Turned Upside Down: Radical Ideas During the English Revolution* (New York: Viking, 1972), pp. 247–60; Clare Cross, "'He-Goats before the Flocks,' a Note on the Part Played by Women in the Founding of some Civil War Churches," *Studies in Church History* 8 (1972), pp. 195–202; Phyllis Mack, "Women as Prophets During the English Civil War," *Feminist Studies* 8:1 (Spring 1982), pp. 19–45 and "The Prophet and Her Audience: Gender and Knowledge in The World Turned Upside Down," in *Reviving the English Revolution: Reflections and Elaborations on the Work of Christopher Hill*, ed. Geoff Eley and William Hunt (London and New York: Verso, 1988), pp. 139–52. For the nineteenth century, see Barbara Taylor, *Eve and the New Jerusalem: Socialism and Feminism in the Nineteenth Century* (New York: Pantheon, 1983) and Julia Swindells, *Victorian Writing and Working Women: The Other Side of Silence* (Minneapolis: University of Minnesota Press and Oxford: Polity Press, 1986).

2 Shiach briefly discusses the work of Duck, Collier, Tatersal, Leapor, Yearsley, Bryant, Bloomfield, Clare, and William Thom in *Discourse on Popular Culture*, pp. 35–70.

3 Swindells, "Liberating the Subject? Autobiography and 'Women's History': a Reading of *The Diaries of Hannah Cullwick*," a paper presented at a conference on Autobiographies, Biographies, and Life Histories of Women: Interdisciplinary Perspectives, at the University of Minnesota, March, 1986. My thanks to Winnie Woodhull for this reference. See also Swindells, *Victorian Writing and Working Women*, pp. 137–53.

4 When Janet Little publishes a poem "On Reading Lady Mary Wortley Montague And Mrs. Rowe's letters" in 1792, in which Rowe displaces Montagu from her position as a literary star, Little betrays a confused sense of chronology; see *The*

Poetical Works Of Janet Little, The Scotch Milkmaid (Air: John & Peter Wilson, 1792), pp. 157–58, wrongly numbered as pp. [153]–54. The general silence about other women writers within laboring women's poetry of the period would seem to suggest that the seventeenth- and eighteenth-century female literary tradition was still so inaccessible as barely to have established any presence at all beside the male canon of "great English poets" upon whom all the plebeian poets continued to draw.

5 This literary procedure has been theorized by Claudine Herrmann, Hélène Cixous, and other "new French feminists" as a distinguishing feature of *l'écriture féminine*. See Herrmann's *Les Voleuses de langue* (Paris: des Femmes, 1976). Materialist feminism in France, from Simone de Beauvoir and the journal *Questions féministes* to Monique Wittig, Christine Delphy, and Catherine Clément, though not so well known in the United States, is likely to be a more durable project than the psychoanalytical–literary-critical focus of *l'écriture féminine*. I wish to thank Marie-Florine Bruneau for helping me to clarify this point.

6 Spivak, "Subaltern Studies: Deconstructing Historiography," *In Other Worlds*, p. 203.

7 Shiach, *Discourse on Popular Culture*, p. 6.

8 Nigel Cross makes this point in relation to the development of (male) working-class autobiography in the nineteenth century: "If Blackett, Miller, Prince, Ridings, Cooper and Massey are remembered at all it is for their lives rather than their literary works," *The Common Writer: Life in Nineteenth-Century Grub Street* (Cambridge: Cambridge University Press, 1985), p. 126. Unfortunately, he does not treat working-class women writers in his study at all, but discusses middle- and upper-class women writers in a chapter entitled, ironically, "The Female Drudge: Women Novelists and Their Publishers."

9 Dwight L. Durling, *Georgic Tradition in English Poetry* (New York: Columbia University Press, 1935).

10 James Woodhouse, *Spring*, in *Poems On Sundry Occasions. By James Woodhouse, a Journeyman Shoemaker* (London: Printed for the Author by W. Richardson and S. Clark, 1764), pp. [25]–37.

11 See Gerald M. MacLean, *The Woman as Good as the Man*, the 1677 English translation of Poullain de la Barre's *De l'égalité des deux sexes* (1673) (Detroit: Wayne State University Press, 1987) pp. 24–42, and Timothy J. Reiss, "Revolution in Bounds: Wollstonecraft, Women and Reason," in *Gender and Theory: Dialogues on Feminist Criticism*, ed. Linda Kauffman (Oxford: Basil Blackwell, 1989), pp. 11–50.

12 Reasonably persuasive deployments of the concept of patriarchy in materialist feminist analysis include Roisin McDonough and Rachel Harrison, "Patriarchy and Relations of Production," pp. 11–41 and Annette Kuhn, "Structures of Patriarchy and Capital in the Family," pp. 42–67 in *Feminism and Materialism: Women and Modes of Production*, ed. Annette Kuhn and AnnMarie Wolpe (London: Routledge & Kegan Paul, 1978). But see Michèle Barrett, *Women's Oppression Today: Problems in Marxist Feminist Analysis* (London: Verso, 1980), pp. 10–19 for an astute critique of even such sophisticated attempts to apply it without difficulty.

13 Michèle Barrett and Mary McIntosh, "Ethnocentrism and Socialist-Feminist Theory," *Feminist Review* 20 (June 1985), p. 39. Barrett and McIntosh's position is informed by Eugene Genovese's notion of paternalism within the institution of slavery.

14 Ann Cromarty Yearsley, the daughter of Ann and John Cromarty (or

Cromartie), a milkwoman and a laborer, was born on Clifton Hill near Bristol and baptized on July 15, 1753 in Clifton Parish Church, according to the parish register. Yearsley herself, however, appears to have thought or wished others to think that she was born in 1756, the date given in the *D.N.B.*, xxi, pp. 1225–26 and followed by most scholars since. J. M. S. Tompkins in *The Polite Marriage, etc.: Eighteenth-Century Essays* (Cambridge: Cambridge University Press, 1938), p. 60, gives yet another birth date, 1752, but this probably resulted from confusing pagination in the register.

15 Letter from Hannah More to Elizabeth Robinson Montagu, August 27, 1784; Huntington Library manuscript MO 3986, p. 2. Letters from this correspondence in which Yearsley figures, MO 3986–3992, have been published in *The Female Spectator: English Women Writers Before 1800*, ed. Mary R. Mahl and Helene Koon (Bloomington and Old Westbury: Indiana University Press and The Feminist Press, 1977), pp. 277–86.

16 Two good recent studies of Yearsley, which nevertheless argue for two very different versions of her class position and politics, are Moira Ferguson, "Resistance and Power in the Life and Writings of Ann Yearsley," *The Eighteenth Century: Theory and Interpretation* 27:3 (Fall 1986), pp. 247–68 and Mary Waldron, "Ann Yearsley and the Clifton Records," *The Age of Johnson: A Scholarly Annual* 3, ed. Paul J. Korshin (New York: AMS Press, forthcoming, 1990). Waldron argues that Yearsley, who had married a man who was her social superior and the possessor of some unearned income until its mysterious loss, did not "identify herself with the feckless labouring masses, addicted to the instant gratification of unsuitable tastes, which Mrs. Montagu had in mind" (p. 7). Yearsley's grasp of "abstract" financial dealings, her recognition that, unlike the Montagus', "the Mores' prosperity was based entirely on earned income and investment and had so far no comfortable landed background" (p. 10), and her seeing herself as "almost equal in status to Hannah More, in that even as a milkwoman she had been self-employed and that, given the chance, she could again become as independent, if not quite so rich, as the Mores themselves" (p. 10), are cited as evidence that Yearsley should be seen as not "working-class" at all. See chapter 4 below.

17 Yearsley reports that, after her falling out with More, she "became very obnoxious" to her, "on account of a very trifling additional circumstance," the discovery of Yearsley's buying "what is called the hogwash of her kitchen." More apparently "charged" Yearsley with the publicizing of this arrangement, to which charge Yearsley responded: "I told her, when she charged me with it, that I could not see how it could offend her, as it was the perquisite of her Cook, and had been paid for by the person who had it before I had the honour of knowing her." Eventually the cook offered Yearsley back the money she had already paid for the slops, but Yearsley claims that she did not accept it. See Yearsley's "Narrative" addressed "To The Noble and Generous Subscribers, Who so liberally patronized A Book Of Poems, Published under the Auspices of Miss H. More, Of Park-Street, Bristol" in the fourth edition of *Poems, on Several Occasions* (London: Printed for G. G. J. and J. Robinson, 1786), pp. xviii–xxxi. (British Library shelfmark 11644.d.32; spine misleadingly reads: 11644.d.33.). I have quoted from the more common volume in which it appears, *Poems, on Various Subjects. By Ann Yearsley, A Milkwoman Of Clifton, Near Bristol; Being Her Second Work* (London: Printed for the Author, and Sold by G. G. J. and J. Robinson, 1787), pp. xv–xxv; episode above from pp. xvii–xix. Moira Ferguson has published a long excerpt from Yearsley's "Narrative" in *First Feminists: British Women Writers 1578–1799* (Bloomington and Old Westbury: Indiana University Press and The Feminist Press, 1985), pp. 382–86.

18 Dominick LaCapra, *History & Criticism* (Ithaca and London: Cornell University Press, 1985), p. 133.

19 Frank Lentricchia, *Criticism and Social Change* (Chicago and London: University of Chicago Press, 1983), p. 131.

20 In "Liberating the Subject?" Swindells writes, "I presuppose in my paper that we see our study of the life stories of women as part of a project to liberate ourselves as socialist feminist subjects. I show, however, that this cannot be done simply by liberating our sisters from history – either by finding 'authentic' voices where these cannot exist, or by deciding, in our eagerness to liberate their texts from silence, that these sisters led liberated lives." Abstract.

21 See More's "A Prefatory Letter To Mrs. Montagu. By A Friend," in Yearsley's *Poems, on Several Occasions* (London: T. Cadell, 1785), pp. iii–xii.

22 More to Montagu, October 22, 1784; Huntington Library manuscript MO 3988, p. 1, p. 4.

23 More to Montagu, August 27, 1784; Huntington Library manuscript MO 3986, p. 2.

24 Waldron, "Ann Yearsley and the Clifton Records," p. 5 and n. 17.

25 Robert Southey, *Attempts In Verse, By John Jones, An Old Servant: With Some Account Of The Writer, Written By Himself: And An Introductory Essay On The Lives Of Our Uneducated Poets* (London: John Murray, 1831), p. 134, and Tompkins, *The Polite Marriage*, p. 100.

26 Through the eighteenth century, women remained less literate than men. See Margaret Spufford, *Small Books and Pleasant Histories: Popular Fiction and Its Readership In Seventeenth-Century England* (Athens, Ga.: University of Georgia Press, 1981 and Cambridge: Cambridge University Press, 1985), p. 34, and David Cressy, *Literacy and the Social Order: Reading and Writing in Tudor and Stuart England* (Cambridge: Cambridge University Press, 1980), p. 128, pp. 145–56. Since more people could read than could write, women may well have figured significantly in a reading public, "the true size of which we shall never be able to assess," Spufford, *Small Books*, p. 36.

27 More, "Prefatory Letter," p. iv, p. viii.

28 Susan Pedersen, "Hannah More Meets Simple Simon: Tracts, Chapbooks, and Popular Culture in Late Eighteenth-Century England," *Journal of British Studies* 25:1 (January 1986), p. 86, p. 87. In order to strengthen her claims to revisionism, and to make More a culturally if not politically progressive figure, Pedersen artificially reduces "politics" to the debate over English Jacobinism. She would have done better to have distinguished between a narrowly "political" or topical function for the tracts and the inevitably political instrumentality of campaigns for "moral" reform of the poor.

29 Mitzi Myers, "Hannah More's Tracts for the Times: Social Fiction and Female Ideology," in *Fetter'd or Free? British Women Novelists, 1670–1815*, ed. Mary Anne Schofield and Cecelia Macheski (Athens, Ohio and London: Ohio University Press, 1986), p. 269.

30 As E. P. Thompson argues, "The remedies proposed might differ; but the impulse behind Colquhoun, with his advocacy of more effective police, Hannah More, with her halfpenny tracts and Sunday Schools, the Methodists with their renewed emphasis upon order and submissiveness, Bishop Barrington's more humane Society for Bettering the Conditions of the Poor, and William Wilberforce and Dr John Bowdler, with their Society for the Suppression of Vice and Encouragement of Religion, was much the same. The message to be given to the labouring poor was simple, and was summarized by Burke in the famine year of

1795: 'Patience, labour, sobriety, frugality, and religion, should be recommended to them; all the rest is downright fraud'," *The Making of the English Working Class*, pp. 60–61.

31 So Angela Carter describes the "liberal lie in action" in *The Sadeian Woman: An Exercise in Cultural History* (London: Virago, 1979), p. 55.

32 See H. Gustav Klaus, *The Literature of Labour: Two Hundred Years of Working-Class Writing* (New York: St. Martin's Press, 1985), pp. 20–21.

33 More to Montagu, October 22, 1784; Huntington Library manuscript MO 3988, p. 1.

34 More to Montagu, September 27, 1784; Huntington Library manuscript MO 3987, p. 4.

35 More to Montagu, October 22, 1784; Huntington Library manuscript MO 3988, p. 1.

36 I am grateful to Isobel Grundy for the formulation of this point.

37 On high-literary relations between the pastoral and georgic modes, see Annabel Patterson, *Pastoral and Ideology: Virgil to Valéry* (Berkeley and Los Angeles: University of California Press, 1987), Anthony Low, *The Georgic Revolution* (Princeton: Princeton University Press, 1985), and John Barrell, *English Literature in History 1730–80: An Equal, Wide Survey* (London and Melbourne: Hutchinson, 1983), pp. 90–109. None of these studies addresses the tradition of plebeian poetry as such and its different relations to poetic and manual labor. The distinction I make between privileged or leisured, and plebeian, pastoral and georgic modes – though the notion of leisured pastoral may sound redundant, and that of leisured georgic self-contradictory – seems a necessary one.

38 On the triumph of vernacular over strictly neoclassical pastoral and the consequent possibilities for "realistic" representation, see John Barrell, *The Dark Side of the Landscape: The Rural Poor in English Painting 1730–1840* (Cambridge: Cambridge University Press, 1980), pp. 54–58.

39 John Dryden, dedication of the *Georgics* "To The Right Honourable Philip Earl of Chesterfield, &c.," *The Poems of John Dryden*, ed. James Kinsley, 4 vols. (Oxford: Clarendon, 1958), II, p. 913.

40 More to Montagu, August 27, 1784; Huntington Library manuscript MO 3986, p. 3. The only translation of the *Georgics* listed in the catalogue of Yearsley's circulating library is Dryden's; *Catalogue of the Books, Tracts, &c. contained in Ann Yearsley's Public Library, No. 4, Crescent, Hotwells* (Bristol: Printed for the Proprietor, 1793), p. 27; British Library shelfmark s. c. 726 (9.).

41 See, for example, Don E. Wayne, *Penshurst: The Semiotics of Place and the Poetics of History* (Madison: University of Wisconsin Press, 1984), pp. 125–28, James G. Turner, *The Politics of Landscape: Rural Scenery and Society in English Poetry 1630–1660* (Oxford: Basil Blackwell, 1979), pp. 36–48 and pp. 153–85, and Raymond Williams, *The Country and the City* (New York: Oxford University Press, 1973), pp. 13–34.

42 R. S. Neale, *Writing Marxist History: British Society, Economy & Culture since 1700* (Oxford: Basil Blackwell, 1985), p. 76.

43 David Levine, "Proto-Industrialization and Demographic Upheaval," in *Essays on the Family and Historical Change*, ed. Leslie Page Moch (College Station, Tex.: Texas A & M University Press, for the University of Texas at Arlington, 1983), pp. 9–34. See also Levine's extended study, *Family Formation in an Age of Nascent Capitalism* (New York: Academic Press, 1977).

44 Cressy, *Literacy and the Social Order*, pp. 145–49.

45 On the effects of enclosure in relation to working-class subsistence economies and

women's work at the end of the eighteenth century, see Ivy Pinchbeck, *Women Workers and the Industrial Revolution 1750–1850* (1930; London: Virago, 1981), pp. 19–26.

46 K. D. M. Snell, *Annals of the Labouring Poor: Social Change and Agrarian England, 1660–1900* (Cambridge: Cambridge University Press, 1985), p. 22.

47 David Davies, *The Case of Labourers In Husbandry Stated And Considered, In Three Parts* (Bath: R. Cruttwell for G. G. and J. Robinson, London, 1795), p. 122. The Robinsons also published and sold Yearsley's later works.

48 Barrell, *The Dark Side of the Landscape*, p. 51.

49 Pinchbeck, *Women Workers*, p. 12, p. 15.

50 Mary Leapor, *Complaining Daphne. A Pastoral* in *Poems Upon Several Occasions*. By Mrs. Leapor of Brackley in Northamptonshire, 2 vols. (London: J. Roberts, 1748–51), II, pp. 72–79.

51 See, for example, Pinchbeck, *Women Workers*, p. 85: according to a Poor Law Commissioners' report of 1835, "'the custom of the mother of a family carrying her infant with her in its cradle into the field, rather than lose the opportunity of adding her earnings to the general stock, though partially practised before, is becoming very much more general now.'" The exigencies described by these eighteenth-century poets do not seem to have been much mitigated by industrialization.

52 See Ann Kussmaul, *Servants in Husbandry in Early Modern England* (Cambridge: Cambridge University Press, 1981), pp. 3–10 and Snell, *Annals of the Labouring Poor*, pp. 81–84.

53 Dorothy Marshall, *The English Domestic Servant in History* (London: Historical Association, General Series G. 13, George Philip, 1949), pp. 6–7, quoted in John Burnett, *Useful Toil: Autobiographies of Working People from the 1820s to the 1920s* (Harmondsworth: Penguin, 1984), p. 143. See also J. Jean Hecht, *The Domestic Servant Class in Eighteenth-Century England* (London: Routledge & Kegan Paul, 1956).

54 For changes in laboring-class attitudes towards sex and marriage, see Snell, *Annals of the Labouring Poor*, pp. 306–07, pp. 352–57. With the passage of the Marriage Act in 1753, verbal spousals ceased to be binding; only a church wedding which took place in and during the places and times specified by the 1604 canons, had been entered in the parish register, and signed by both parties, counted; parental consent was necessary for couples under twenty-one, and enforcement of the law became the business of the more powerful secular instead of the church courts. As Lawrence Stone comments, "The unknown number of the poor who were unwilling or unable to go through the ceremony in the church were henceforth obliged to live in concubinage, since their private exchanges of verbal promises were no longer legally binding ... After 1754 the law was absolutely clear, although it is by no means certain how many of the poor or the Dissenters were able or willing to comply with it," *The Family, Sex and Marriage In England 1500–1800* (London: Weidenfeld and Nicolson, 1977), p. 35, p. 37. There is some reason to suspect that Hands was a Dissenter: see chapter 5 below.

55 Philo-Philippa, *To the Excellent Orinda*, commendatory poem first included in the second edition of Katherine Philips's poems, *Poems By the most deservedly Admired Mrs. Katherine Philips The matchless Orinda. To which is added Monsieur Corneille's Pompey & Horace, Tragedies. With several other Translations out of French* (London: Printed by J. M. for H. Herringman, 1667), Sig. C2r–D2v (italics reversed), and in subsequent editions (1678, 1710).

56 See, for example, Myra Reynolds, *The Learned Lady in England, 1650–1760*

(Boston: Houghton Mifflin, 1920); Joan Kelly, "Early Feminist Theory and the *Querelle des Femmes, 1400–1789*," *Signs* 8:1 (Autumn 1982), pp. 4–28; Hilda Smith, *Reason's Disciples: Seventeenth-Century English Feminists* (Urbana, Chicago, London: University of Illinois Press, 1982); Katharine M. Rogers, *Feminism in Eighteenth-Century England* (Urbana, Chicago, London: University of Illinois Press, 1982); Patricia Crawford, "Women's Published Writings 1600–1700," in *Women in English Society 1500–1800*, ed. Mary Prior (London and New York: Methuen, 1985), pp. 211–82; Katherine Usher Henderson and Barbara F. McManus, *Half Humankind: Contexts and Texts of the Controversy about Women in England, 1540–1640* (Urbana and Chicago: University of Illinois Press, 1985); Gerald M. MacLean, introduction to *The Woman as Good as the Man* and Hobby, *Virtue of Necessity*.

57 On Cary and other radical sectarian women writers of the 1640s and 1650s, see Hobby, *Virtue of Necessity*, pp. 26–53.

58 [Mary Astell], *A Serious Proposal To the Ladies, For the Advancement of their true and greatest Interest. By a Lover of Her Sex* (London: Printed for K. Wilkin, 1694).

59 Mary Cary (afterward Mary Rande), *A new And More Exact Mappe Or Description Of New Jerusalems Glory* (London: Printed by W. H., 1651), pp. 237–38 (misnumbered as pp. 137–238); also quoted in Doris Mary Stenton, *The English Woman in History* (1957; New York: Schocken, 1977), p. 175, with some modernizations. (Clark Library shelfmark ★BZ C333L 1651.)

60 Astell, *A Serious Proposal To the Ladies*, pp. 64–65.

61 Bridget Hill, "A Refuge from Men: The Idea of a Protestant Nunnery," *Past and Present* 117 (November 1987), pp. 107–30.

62 Mack, "Women as Prophets," p. 38.

63 See, for example, Susan Moller Okin, "Patriarchy and Married Women's Property in England: Questions About Some Current Views," *Eighteenth-Century Studies* 17:2 (Winter 1983/84), pp. 121–38 and Susan Staves, "Pin Money," *Studies in Eighteenth-Century Culture* 14, ed. O. M. Brack, Jr. (Madison: University of Wisconsin Press, 1985), pp. 47–77. Both seek to correct the views of historians like Lawrence Stone and Randolph Trumbach who, in *The Family, Sex and Marriage* and *The Rise of the Egalitarian Family* (New York: Academic Press, 1978), respectively, argue for the rise of affective individualism and the companionate marriage in this period. Okin concludes, "While it is clear that further research needs to be done on this issue, indications are that, until significant changes in marriage and property were effected by the Divorce Act and the Married Women's Property Acts in the latter half of the nineteenth century, both the legal structure of marriage and prevailing attitudes about it were such that only in fantasy can we regard eighteenth-century married life as a situation of companionship between equals," p. 138.

64 [Mary Astell], *Some Reflections Upon Marriage, Occasion'd by the Duke & Dutchess Of Mazarine's Case; which is also consider'd* (London: Printed for John Nutt, 1700), pp. 28–29. Ruth Perry concludes that in terms of conventional politics, Astell was "conservative," and that "The key to Astell's radicalism is radical doubt, not radical politics," *The Celebrated Mary Astell: An Early English Feminist* (Chicago and London: University of Chicago Press, 1986), p. 331, p. 332. See also Bridget Hill, *The First English Feminist: Reflections on Marriage and Other Writings by Mary Astell* (Aldershot: Gower/Maurice Temple Smith, 1986).

65 Jocelyn Harris, *Samuel Richardson* (Cambridge: Cambridge University Press, 1987), p. 18. Harris continues, "'Slavery' is the first word of Locke's first treatise of government, and he defines it as the vile and miserable estate of man under

tyranny, and the exercise of power beyond right when the satisfaction of any irregular passion comes before the preservation of the people (II. 199). The word 'slave' [in Richardson's *Pamela*] refers pointedly to the Turks, whose treatment of women was often in the eighteenth century unfavourably compared to England's," p. 19.

66 Philips, "An Answer to another perswading a Lady to Marriage," *Poems*, p. 155.

67 Philips, "To Mrs. Mary Awbrey," *Poems*, pp. 70–71.

68 Philips, "A Friend," *Poems*, pp. 94–97.

69 Ann Yearsley, note on the sixteenth page of manuscript additions at the end of a copy of her *Poems, on Several Occasions* now in the Central Library in Bristol. Shelfmark B23432.

70 Pope, *Sapho to Phaon*, ed. E. Audra and Aubrey Williams in *The Twickenham Edition of the Poems of Alexander Pope*, gen. ed. John Butt, 11 vols. (London and New Haven: Methuen and Yale University Press, 1939–69), I, pp. 393–404. Hereafter cited as *T.E.*

71 William Blake, "Proverbs of Hell" in *The Marriage of Heaven and Hell, The Poems of William Blake*, ed. W. H. Stevenson and David V. Erdman (London: Longman, 1971), p. 111.

72 On the love that "dare not speak its name" and the historicity of gay and lesbian discourse, see Eve Kosofsky Sedgwick, *Between Men: English Literature and Male Homosocial Desire* (New York: Columbia University Press, 1985), esp. pp. 1–20, pp. 47–48, pp. 94–96, pp. 201–17.

73 Sheila Rowbotham, *Woman's Consciousness, Man's World* (Harmondsworth: Penguin, 1973), p. 124.

74 Montagu to More, 1784, in William Roberts, *Memoirs Of The Life And Correspondence Of Mrs. Hannah More*, 4 vols. (London: R. B. Seeley and W. Burnside, 1834), I, p. 364.

75 Harrison's situation is characterized in the "Preface" to the first edition as follows:

SUFFICE it to say of this Publication, that the Author is a very obscure Young Woman, and quite destitute of the Advantages of Education, as well as under great bodily Affliction. Her Father dying when she was young, and leaving a large Family unprovided for, she went out to Service at sixteen Years of Age; in which Station she continued till *August*, 1772; when Disorders seized her, which ever since have baffled the Power of Medicine and the Skill of Physicians.

See [Susannah Harrison,] "Preface," *Songs In The Night; By a Young Woman under deep Afflictions* (London: Printed by R. Hawes; Sold by T. Vallance and Alexander Hogg, 1780), pp. [iii]–iv.

76 This poem appears in two of the editions I have examined, the fourth British, *Songs In The Night; by a Young Woman under heavy afflictions. The Fourth Edition; with a supplement* (Ipswich: Printed and Sold by Punchard & Jermyn; London: Vallance and Conder, Buckland; Braintree: Smitherman; Bury: Rogers; Woodbridge: Loder, 1788), pp. 186–87 and the fourth American edition, *Songs In The Night: by a young woman under heavy afflictions* (New Brunswick: Lewis Deare, 1813), pp. 201–02.

77 Harrison, "XVIII," *Songs In The Night; By a Young Woman under deep Afflictions* (1780), p. 18. Further quotations are from this edition.

78 One of Gott's works appeared in 1788, the others in the 1790s: *The Midnight Cry, "Behold, the Bridegroom comes!" Or, An Order from God To Get Your Lamps Lighted, Otherwise you must go into Darkness, where there will be weeping, wailing, and gnashing of Teeth. . . . This Is My Experience, Dorothy Gott* (London: Printed for the

Author; Sold at her house, No. 81, Featherstone-street, Bunhill-row; and at J. Watson's, near the Basing-house, Kingland Road, 1788). British Library shelf-mark 4151.f.41.(1.). I owe this reference to Virginia Blain, Patricia Clements, and Isobel Grundy, *The Feminist Companion to Literature in English: Women Writers from the Middle Ages to the Present* (London: Batsford and New Haven: Yale University Press, 1990), who shared some of their findings.

79 The relevant lines are as follows:

> Is there any thing in it worth reading, I pray?
> For your nice attention, there's nothing can 'scape.
> She answer'd, – There's one piece, whose subject's a Rape.
> A Rape! interrupted the Captain Bonair,
> A delicate theme for a female I swear.   (29–33)

80 Lady Mary Wortley Montagu, *Essays and Poems and Simplicity, a Comedy*, ed. Robert Halsband and Isobel Grundy (Oxford: Clarendon, 1977), pp. 273–76, pp. 279–84.

81 Felicity A. Nussbaum's Pope is a milder antifeminist than Ellen Pollak's for Nussbaum's Pope "seems to reveal an unusual awareness of the control that custom and tradition have over women's lives," he represents "his awareness that women's choices were few," and within an asexual (unthreatening) model of ideal femininity, he "keeps [women] forever in unresolved conflict," thus acknowledging the lived force of ideological contradictions; see *The Brink of All We Hate: English Satires on Women 1660–1750* (Lexington, Ky.: The University Press of Kentucky, 1984), p. 137, p. 158. Pollak's critique of Pope's relative compliance with contemporary gender ideology is much more polemical. Unlike Swift, who cannot align himself with philosophical optimism or the ideological assumptions upon which sexual conventions are based, Pope combines philosophical optimism with a seemingly chivalrous misogyny in pleasantly deceptive ways: "Pope's misogyny and philosophic optimism intersect at the point where women, who have fundamentally negative value, are fundamentally impotent," and, "For all her variability, woman in Pope's text[s] invariably functions as at once a sign of her own lack and an alibi for the primacy of a masculine presence," *The Poetics of Sexual Myth: Gender and Ideology in the Verse of Swift and Pope* (Chicago and London: University of Chicago Press, 1985), p. 113, p. 123.

82 Pope, *Epistle to a Lady*, ed. F. W. Bateson in *T.E.* III:ii.

83 As Pollak comments, "Martha is esteemed because, both like and unlike other women, she is not 'other,' because her pleasure has been elided with the imperatives of a masculine pleasure, because essentially her will is not her own . . . For woman, says Pope, whether she remains discreetly hidden inside the law or flamboyantly transgresses its boundaries, inhabits a place of nonmeaning. She has 'No-meaning' in herself (114); she is a lack," *The Poetics of Sexual Myth*, p. 116.

84 [Anne, Viscountess Irwin,] *An Epistle to Mr. Pope, By a Lady. Occasioned by his Characters of Women* in *The Gentleman's Magazine* 6 (December 1736), p. 745. Reprinted as "On Mr. Pope's Characters of Women, by Anne, late Viscountess Irwin, Aunt to the present Earl of Carlisle," in *The New Foundling Hospital for Wit. Being a Collection of Curious Pieces in Verse and Prose, Several of which were never before printed. Part the Sixth* (London: Printed for J. Almon, 1773), pp. 42–46. My thanks to James Turner for this reference.

85 For the best concise discussion of Pope's exclusion from power and privilege on many fronts, see Brean S. Hammond, *Pope* (Brighton: Harvester, 1986), pp. 9–29. For connections between this experience of exclusion and Pope's identification with female powerlessness, see my "The Discourse of Exclusion: Literary and

Social Relations in the Later Career of Alexander Pope" (Ph.D. dissertation, University of Virginia, 1983). Laura Brown powerfully illuminates connections between gender ideology and imperialism in *Alexander Pope* (Oxford: Basil Blackwell, 1985), pp. 8–28.

86 Elizabeth Hands, "On reading Pope's Eloiza to Abelard," *The Death of Amnon*, p. 114.

87 That this gendered ambiguity is not synonymous with an enunciation of protofeminism on Pope's part is made clear by Kristina Straub, in an essay that demonstrates well how the metaphor of rape serves both Pope and Anne Killigrew as a means to literary power, but with crucial political differences: "While in Killigrew's poem the rape metaphor suggests the paradoxical and highly problematic power of the victim's anger, in *Arbuthnot* Pope uneasily attempts to reshape the terms of domination and victimization inherent in the metaphor to express his own ambiguous but finally unresolved role – as both potential victim and rapist – in the paradigm . . . Whereas Killigrew's redistribution of power between the two terms of a binary opposition leads to heightened conflict, an intensified sense of contradiction, Pope's destabilizing of the victim/rapist paradigm seeks resolution, a finally non-revolutionary peace with the social system that defines power as he knows it, as he suffers from it and stands to gain from it." See "Indecent Liberties with a Poet: Audience and the Metaphor of Rape in Killigrew's 'Upon the saying that my Verses' and Pope's *Arbuthnot*," *Tulsa Studies in Women's Literature* 6:1 (Spring 1987), p. 29.

88 Jacques Derrida, ". . . That Dangerous Supplement . . .," in *Of Grammatology*, trans. Gayatri Chakravorty Spivak (Baltimore and London: The Johns Hopkins University Press, 1976), pp. 144–45.

89 See Harold Bloom, *The Anxiety of Influence: A Theory of Poetry* (London, Oxford, and New York: Oxford University Press, 1973) and Sandra M. Gilbert and Susan Gubar, *The Madwoman in the Attic: The Woman Writer and the Nineteenth-Century Literary Imagination* (New Haven: Yale University Press, 1979). Toril Moi gives an astute critique of Gilbert and Gubar in *Sexual/Textual Politics: Feminist Literary Theory* (London and New York: Methuen, 1985), pp. 57–69. Janice Doane and Devon Hodges are right to link the theoretical positions of Bloom and Gilbert and Gubar as follows: "Both accounts, while giving glancing acknowledgment to self-division and repression, insist finally upon psychic integrity and sexual difference"; see *Nostalgia and Sexual Difference: The Resistance to Contemporary Feminism* (New York and London: Methuen, 1987), p. 92.

90 Margaret Anne Doody, "Swift among the Women," *The Yearbook of English Studies* 18 (1988), pp. 68–92.

91 More to Montagu, August 27, 1784; Huntington Library manuscript MO 3986, p. 3.

92 Stephen Duck, *On Richmond Park, and Royal Gardens* in *Poems On Several Occasions* (London: Printed for the Author, 1736), pp. 72–84.

93 Reprinted in Pope, *Miscellany Poems*, 2 vols. (London: Printed for Bernard Lintot and sold by Henry Lintot, 1732), I, pp. 24–29, pp. 2–4.

94 Mary Masters, "To The Right Honourable The Earl of Burlington," *Poems on Several Occasions* (London: Printed by T. Browne for the Author, 1733), pp. 5–7. Pope published his *Epistle to Burlington* in 1731.

95 On Burlington, see Carole Fabricant, *Swift's Landscape* (Baltimore and London: The Johns Hopkins University Press, 1982); she demystifies Burlington's benevolence and claims that Swift saw through him in ways Pope never did. As part of a larger argument about Swift's radical alienation from English aristocratic values,

the contrast with Pope is useful, but it tends to underplay Pope's own criticisms of Burlington and other great landowners; see pp. 1–23, pp. 95–100, p. 116, pp. 196–98. For Burlington's patronage and architectural contributions see James Lees-Milne, *Earls of Creation: Five Great Patrons of Eighteenth-Century Art* (London: Hamish Hamilton, 1962), Fiske Kimball, "Burlington Architectus," *Journal of the Royal Institute of British Architects* October 15, 1927, pp. 675–93, and November 12, 1927, pp. 14–16. For additions to and corrections of Kimball's analysis, see Sir Reginald Blomfield, "Burlington Architectus," *J.R.I.B.A.* November 26, 1927, pp. 45–46.

96 Even that rather unaccomplished poet Mary Caesar, Pope's friend and a Jacobite conspirator, has inadvertently contributed four lines to the Pope canon. See Howard Erskine-Hill, "Under Which Caesar? Pope in the Journal of Mrs. Charles Caesar, 1724–1741," *Review of English Studies* n. s. 33:132 (November 1982), pp. 436–44).

97 But see Doody, "Swift among the Women," pp. 79–82, and *The Connoisseur* 69 (Thursday, May 22, 1755), I, p. 413: "Among the rest I could not but wonder at the astonishing dexterity, with which the admired Mrs. LEAPOR of *Brackley* guided the horse [Pegasus, the poet's steed], though she had not the least direction or assistance from any body."

98 Mary Leapor, "On the Death of a justly admir'd Author," *Poems Upon Several Occasions*. By Mrs. Leapor of Brackley in Northamptonshire, 2 vols. (London: J. Roberts, 1748–51), I, pp. 252–54.

99 E[lizabeth] Bentley, "On Reading Mr. Pope's Poems. 1786," *Genuine Poetical Compositions, on Various Subjects* (Norwich: Crouse and Stevenson, 1791), p. 2.

100 Compare Pope's monosyllabic struggles in the sound and sense manifesto, *An Essay on Criticism*: "And ten low Words oft creep in one dull line" (347) and the *Epistle to Burlington*, which apparently Mary Leapor also liked: "And when up ten steep slopes you've dragg'd your thighs, / Just at his Study-door he'll bless your eyes" (131–32) in *T.E.* I, p. 278, and III:ii, p. 145.

101 Ann Yearsley, "Written On A Visit," *Poems, on Various Subjects*, pp. 139–43.

102 *The Monthly Review; Or, Literary Journal*, 77:ii (July–December 1787), p. 489, pp. 485–86.

2 The resignation of Mary Collier: some problems in feminist literary history

1 Johanna Brenner and Maria Ramas, "Rethinking Women's Oppression," *New Left Review* 144 (March/April 1984), p. 47, n. 37. This distinction holds so far as landed property or capital is concerned. But there remains a sense in which male control of property *in women* links the working class with the feudal and bourgeois social formations from which it can otherwise be distinguished. As Keith Thomas puts it, "Fundamentally, female chastity has been seen as a matter of property; not, however, the property of legitimate heirs, but the property of men in women," "The Double Standard," *Journal of the History of Ideas* 20 (1959), pp. 209–10.

2 See Roger Lonsdale's *The New Oxford Book of Eighteenth Century Verse* (Oxford and New York: Oxford University Press, 1984), pp. 325–26, and his *Eighteenth Century Women Poets: An Oxford Anthology* (Oxford and New York: Oxford University Press, 1989), pp. 171–73; and Moira Ferguson's Augustan Reprint 230, *The Thresher's Labour (Stephen Duck) and The Woman's Labour (Mary Collier)* (Los Angeles: William Andrews Clark Memorial Library, 1985) and her *First Feminists,*

pp. 257–65. Sheila Rowbotham includes short excerpts from *The Woman's Labour* in *Hidden From History: Rediscovering Women In History from the 17th Century to the Present* (New York: Pantheon, 1974), pp. 25–26.

3 A point made by Klaus, *The Literature of Labour*, p. 14. See, for example, Louise A. Tilly and Joan W. Scott, *Women, Work, and Family* (New York: Holt, Rinehart, Winston, 1978).

4 Collier, *The Woman's Labour: An Epistle To Mr. Stephen Duck; In Answer to his late Poem, called The Thresher's Labour. To which are added, The Three Wise Sentences, Taken From The First Book of Esdras, Ch. III. and IV* (London: Printed for the Author; and Sold by J. Roberts, 1739). I have quoted throughout from the British Library copy (shelfmark 1346.f.17).

5 "Piety, Purity, Peace, and an Old Maid" are the concluding words of Collier's brief autobiography; see "Some Remarks of the Author's Life drawn by herself," in *Poems, on Several Occasions* (title-page missing; spine reads: Winchester, 1762), p. v. (British Library shelfmark 11632.f.12.) On the 10 percent of the population who remained single, see Keith Wrightson, *English Society 1580–1680* (London: Hutchinson, 1982), pp. 67–68 and Stone, *The Family, Sex, and Marriage*, p. 652. Single women and widows were the groups most likely to require relief from their parishes. According to Ivy Pinchbeck, "The anxiety shown in some districts [including Sussex, where Collier lived for a number of years] to get single women employed, actually led to the pauperizing of domestic service," *Women Workers*, p. 80. See also Pinchbeck, pp. 79–86 and Bridget Hill, *Eighteenth-Century Women: An Anthology* (London: Allen and Unwin, 1984), pp. 123–34, pp. 156–72.

6 Huntington Library manuscript MO 3986, p. 2, mentions six children, but Mary Waldron in "Ann Yearsley and the Clifton Records" provides evidence for a seventh, Yearsley's first-born son who died in 1779 at the age of four.

7 In "The Sexual Division of Labour in Feudal England," *New Left Review* 113–14 (January/April 1979), pp. 147–68, Christopher Middleton has argued, persuasively, that the subordination of women in social formations like that of feudal England did not depend on their biological capacity to reproduce; it was "rather the direct, personal servicing of men by women that was the fulcrum of domestic labour – both in and out of marriage," p. 164. More recently, he has tried to link these insights with evidence from the early modern period in "Women's Labour and the Transition to Pre-Industrial Capitalism," in *Women and Work in Pre-Industrial England*, ed. Lindsey Charles and Lorna Duffin (London: Croom Helm, 1985), pp. 181–206.

8 Collier, *Poems on Several Occasions*, pp. 30–32.

9 See Martha Vicinus, *The Industrial Muse: A Study of Nineteenth Century British Working-Class Literature* (New York: Barnes and Noble, 1974) for a discussion of how working-class literature is excluded from scholarly "canons of taste," pp. 1–2, pp. 140–84.

10 For these and related debates, see Michèle Barrett, "Feminism and the Definition of Cultural Politics" in *Feminism, Culture and Politics*, ed. Rosalind Brunt and Caroline Rowan (London: Lawrence and Wishart, 1982), pp. 37–58; and Lillian Robinson, "Treason Our Text: Feminist Challenges to the Literary Canon," pp. 105–21, and Rosalind Coward, "Are Women's Novels Feminist Novels?" pp. 225–39, both in *The New Feminist Criticism*, ed. Elaine Showalter (New York: Pantheon, 1985).

11 Relevant texts include: *Common Sense: Or, The Englishman's Journal* 135 (September 1, 1739); "A new Method for making Women as useful and as capable of

maintaining themselves, as the Men are; and consequently preventing their becoming old Maids, or taking ill Courses. By a Lady," in *The Gentleman's Magazine* 9 (October 1739), pp. 525–26; and the "Sophia" pamphlets, of disputed authorship, esp. *Woman Not Inferior to Man: Or, A short and modest Vindication of the natural Right of the Fair-Sex to a perfect Equality of Power, Dignity, and Esteem, with the Men* (1739), collected and republished with two others under the title *Beauty's Triumph: Or, The Superiority of the Fair Sex invincibly proved* in 1751. Ferguson provides excerpts from the first and third pamphlets in *First Feminists*, pp. 266–83. See MacLean's introduction to *The Woman As Good As The Man*, pp. 26–29, for a useful discussion of the "Sophia" controversy. If we go back some months to January 24, 1738, we can include in this debate Lady Mary Wortley Montagu's *The Nonsense of Common Sense* 6, reprinted in *Essays and Poems*, ed. Halsband and Grundy, pp. 130–34.

12 What is most remarkable is how little rural women's wages seem to have changed between 1739 and the nineteenth century, given the rise in prices; see Pinchbeck, *Women Workers*, p. 16, p. 19, p. 24, pp. 53–66, pp. 94–99. As late as 1843, in Wiltshire, Dorset, Devon, and Somerset, the average women's wage remained "six-pence or eight-pence" a day in winter, p. 95.

13 Pinchbeck describes this differential in some detail, especially in relation to amendments in the Poor Laws, without pronouncing on its psychological or political effects in *Women Workers*, pp. 84–102. More recent feminist accounts, making use of twentieth- as well as nineteenth-century data, admit certain social, political, and psycho-sexual effects of this gender-based competition into their analyses, but do not necessarily agree about their specificity. See, for example, Barrett, *Women's Oppression Today*, pp. 152–86; Brenner and Ramas, "Rethinking Women's Oppression," p. 47; Barrett's reply in *New Left Review* 146 (July/August 1984), pp. 123–28; Angela Weir and Elizabeth Wilson, "The British Women's Movement," *New Left Review* 148 (November/December 1984), p. 95.

14 Stephen Duck, *The Thresher's Labour*, in the first authorized edition of *Poems On Several Occasions* (London: Printed for the Author, 1736). On the gendered division of labor in agricultural work (and the symbolically masculine significance of the scythe), see Michael Roberts, "Sickles and Scythes: Women's Work and Men's Work at Harvest Time," *History Workshop Journal* 7 (Spring 1979), pp. 3–28; and his "'Words They Are Women, And Deeds They Are Men': Images of Work and Gender in Early Modern England" in Charles and Duffin (eds.), *Women and Work in Pre-Industrial England*, pp. 122–80.

15 See Williams, *The Country and the City*, pp. 88–89.

16 Not that it had ever really "been" there in the first place, as James Turner has amply demonstrated in *The Politics of Landscape*; see esp. his chapter on "The Vanishing Swain," pp. 173–85.

17 In *The Literature of Labour*, Klaus suggests that in addressing Duck, "who quite obviously did not include the female agricultural workers in his 'we', Collier tentatively approaches another form of solidarity: a sisterhood of the poor, of working women," p. 15. In "Stephen Duck and Mary Collier: Plebejische Kontro-Verse über Frauenarbeit vor 250 Jahren," *Gulliver* 10 (1981), p. 121, Klaus claims that Collier's use of "we" is inconsistent, but it seems to me that in every case she uses it to refer quite precisely to working-class women; I am indebted to Jerold C. Frakes for help with translation here.

18 Similarly, Yearsley closes the "Prologue" to *Earl Goodwin, An Historical Play* (London: G. G. J. and J. Robinson, 1791) with a reminder of her former,

non-literary source of income, to which she can return if the play fails: "That voice, ye patrons of the Muse, is yours / But if e'en there, her airy visions fail, / Her last best refuge is her – milking pail."

19 See Julia Kristeva's *Desire in Language: A Semiotic Approach to Literature and Art*, ed. Leon S. Roudiez, trans. Thomas Gora, Alice Jardine, and Leon S. Roudiez (New York: Columbia University Press, 1980), p. 15 and *passim*. The radical possibilities of the "dialogic" mode have entered critical discourse primarily by way of Bakhtin's *The Dialogic Imagination*.

20 This concept of "defamiliarization" or *ostraneniye* (making strange) is elaborated by the Russian formalist Victor Shklovsky in "Art as Technique" in *Russian Formalist Criticism: Four Essays*, trans. Lee T. Lemon and Marion J. Reis (Lincoln and London: University of Nebraska Press, 1965), pp. 3–24.

21 Collier's reliance here upon the racist trope of the liberty denying "otherness" of the Turks is typical of British assumptions in the period, with the notable exception of Lady Mary Wortley Montagu's *Turkish Embassy Letters*. For more on the "Turkish prejudice," see chapter 7.

22 The feminist critique of the politics of "the authentic voice" is indebted to the work of Foucault. In a culture in which sexuality, far from being silenced, has been enjoined to speak, to speak "as a woman" is to risk playing into the oppressive forces of power one wishes to challenge. See in *Feminism & Foucault: Reflections on Resistance*, ed. Irene Diamond and Lee Quinby (Boston: Northeastern University Press, 1988) the essays by Mary Lydon, "Foucault and Feminism: A Romance of Many Dimensions," pp. 135–47, Winifred Woodhull, "Sexuality, Power, and the Question of Rape," pp. 167–76, and Biddy Martin, "Feminism, Criticism, and Foucault," pp. 3–19.

23 See Pinchbeck, *Women Workers*, pp. 56–57. Interestingly, regarding the "divided care" necessitated by bringing infants to the fields, Pinchbeck cites a Sussex example: according to a Poor Law Commissioners' report of 1835, "'the custom of the mother of a family carrying her infant with her in its cradle into the field, rather than lose the opportunity of adding her earnings to the general stock, though partially practised before, is becoming very much more general now,'" p. 85.

24 See Pinchbeck, *Women Workers*, pp. 19–26.

25 As Barry Reay argues, "Much of women's labour was domestic, and collective, so presumably the entry points for this almost invisible cultural world are the places where, or the times when, women gathered," "Introduction" to *Popular Culture in Seventeenth-Century England* (New York: St. Martin's Press, 1985), p. 12. See also Peter Burke, in *Popular Culture*, p. 50 and Alice Clark, *Working Life of Women in the Seventeenth Century* (1919; London: Routledge & Kegan Paul, 1982), p. xxxiv ("Introduction" by Miranda Chaytor and Jane Lewis), p. 51.

26 See "Some Account Of The Author's Life," in *Poems on Several Subjects: Written by Stephen Duck, Lately a poor Thresher in a Barn in the County of Wilts, at the Wages of Four Shillings and Six Pence per Week* (London: Printed for J. Roberts, 1730), pp. iv–v, in which it is insinuated that male working-class literacy constitutes a kind of sexual impotence: "The courteous Reader must be inform'd, that our Poet is to be unhappily number'd amongst those Men, whose *Learning* and *fine Parts* are not able to give their Yoke-mates that *Satisfaction* and *Content*, which a weak Mind with a vigorous Constitution is generally apt to do. . . . [Duck went on writing and burning his work] and his Wife continually scolding, because he neglected his Labour: And when he was *Scanning* his Lines, she would oftentimes

run out and raise the whole Neighbourhood, telling the People, *That Her Husband dealt with the Devil, and was going mad because he did nothing all day but talk to himself, and tell his Fingers.*" Duck himself refers to this biographical sketch as "a very false Account" in the preface to *Poems on Several Occasions*, p. ix, without specifying any particular inaccuracies.

27 In *The Lives Of Our Uneducated Poets*, Southey comments as follows on Duck's marriage, presumably with reference to the account of Duck in the pirated edition: "It appears that he met with little encouragement for his intellectual ambition from his wife, nor was it likely that he should. . . . It was his lot at this time to be duck-peck'd by his lawful wife, who held herself to be lawful mistress also, and told all the neighbourhood that her husband dealt with the devil, or was going mad, for he did nothing but talk to himself and tell his fingers. Probably she acquitted the devil of any share in her husband's aberrations, and became reconciled to his conduct when she found that he began to be favourably noticed by persons in a higher station," p. 89, p. 93.

28 Shiach, *Discourse on Popular Culture*, p. 50. There is no evidence for these hostile gender stereotypes except for the "Life" which was published in the pirated editions of Duck's poems. Shiach cites Dr. Alured Clarke, one of Duck's patrons, to the contrary: "'He speaks so well of his wife, that I believe it would give him pain to see so indifferent a character of her in writing,'" p. 50.

29 The contrast with Thomson seems almost obligatory; Klaus contrasts Duck and Thomson in *The Literature of Labour*, p. 13. Quotations from Thomson's *The Seasons* are taken from J. Logie Robertson's edition (London: Oxford University Press, 1908).

30 See Roland Barthes, "Operation Margarine," in *Mythologies*, trans. Annette Lavers (New York: Hill and Wang, 1972), pp. 41–42.

31 Collier, *The Poems of Mary Collier, the Washerwoman of Petersfield; To which is prefixed her Life, Drawn By Herself. A New Edition* (Petersfield: W. Minchin, n.d.), "Advertisement," p. iii. (British Library shelfmark 11657.de.53.)

32 As in Collier, *Poems, on Several Occasions, The Happy Husband, And The Old Batchelor. A Dialogue*, pp. 33–40; "A Gentleman's Request to the Author on Reading The Happy Husband and the Old Batchelor," p. 41; and *Spectator Vol. the Fifth. Numb. 375. Versified*, pp. 54–59.

33 As in Collier, *Poems, on Several Occasions*, "On The Marriage of George the Third. Wrote in the Seventy-Second year of her Age," pp. 60–62.

34 As in Collier, *Poems, on Several Occasions, The First and Second Chapters of the First Book of Samuel Versified*, pp. 42–49.

35 Appended to the third edition of Collier, *The Woman's Labour* and *The Three Wise Sentences* (London: Printed for the Author; and Sold by J. Roberts, 1740), as the final page – p. 32. (British Library shelfmark 1509 / 4592.) Also reprinted, as an appendage to the "Advertisement To The First Edition" in *The Poems of Mary Collier . . . A New Edition*, p. vi. (British Library shelfmark 11657.de.53.)

36 Thompson, *The Making of the English Working Class*, pp. 419–27.

37 H. J. Perkin, *The Origins of Modern British Society, 1780–1880* (London and Toronto: Routledge & Kegan Paul and University of Toronto Press, 1969), p. 196, pp. 247–64. For a brief airing of the arguments on both sides, see Edward Royle and James Walvin, *English Radicals and Reformers 1760–1848* (Lexington, Ky.: The University Press of Kentucky, 1982), pp. 183–85.

38 Collier, "An Elegy Upon Stephen Duck," *Poems on Several Occasions*, pp. 50–51.

3   An English Sappho brilliant, young and dead? Mary Leapor laughs at the fathers

1 *Poems, Upon Several Occasions.* By Mrs. Leapor of Brackley in Northamptonshire, 2 vols. (London: J. Roberts, 1748–51). We should note that James Roberts, the publisher and bookseller, had also handled Duck's and Collier's work. The "Rever. Mr. Stephen Duck" is listed as a subscriber to Leapor's first volume. Readers of Leapor are all indebted to the groundbreaking research of Betty Rizzo, particularly her work on the patronage and publication history of Leapor's texts. In "Christopher Smart, the 'C. S.' Poems, and Molly Leapor's Epitaph," *The Library*, sixth series, 5 (March 1983), pp. 22–31 and in her entry on Leapor in Todd (ed.), *A Dictionary*, pp. 192–93, Rizzo establishes that Samuel Richardson printed the second volume, edited by Isaac Hawkins Browne, and that Leapor's chief patron, the writer of the letter of February 21, 1749 to John ★★★★★, Esq. in Leapor's second volume, the document from which most biographical information about Leapor has been derived, is Bridget Freemantle. In "Molly Leapor: An Anxiety for Influence," *The Age of Johnson: A Scholarly Annual* 4, ed. Paul J. Korshin (New York: AMS Press, forthcoming, 1991), Rizzo makes a strong case for John Watts having printed the first volume, pp. 14–15. My thanks to her for having generously shared valuable unpublished research.

2 *Blackwood's Edinburgh Magazine* 41:257 (March 1837), p. 408.

3 I am indebted to Richard Greene for these biographical facts about Leapor; his fund of knowledge and good judgment, and his generous sharing of unpublished work, have saved me from a number of errors. He discovered the existence of the inscribed copy of Leapor's first volume at Weston Hall – the library contains both volumes – and represents her biography most fully in relation to criticism of the poems in his unpublished D.Phil. thesis, "Mary Leapor: A Problem of Literary History," Oxford University, 1989.

4 *The Cruel Parent. A Dream* is a poem in Leapor's first volume; *The Unhappy Father. A Tragedy*, the work of which she was most proud, is a play in her second.

5 For an introduction to some of the theoretical problems posed by such an inquiry, see Monique Wittig, "The Straight Mind," *Feminist Issues* 1:1 (Summer 1980), pp. 103–11; the "Lesbian Issue" of *Signs* 9:4 (Summer 1984); Katie King, "The Situation of Lesbianism as Feminism's Magical Sign: Contests for Meaning and the U.S. Women's Movement, 1968–1972," *Communication* 9 (1986), pp. 65–91; and Biddy Martin, "Lesbian Identity and Autobiographical Difference[s]," in *Life/Lines: Theorizing Women's Autobiography*, ed. Bella Brodzki and Celeste Schenck (Ithaca and London: Cornell University Press, 1989), pp. 77–103. I am especially indebted to Elaine Hobby, whose unpublished paper, "Writing and Deviance in Early-Modern England: Katherine Philips – Was She, Or Wasn't She? And Why Does It Matter?," delivered at the University of Sussex in the spring of 1986, has helped me to place some of these difficulties in a theoretically nuanced historical context.

6 Hobby, with reference to a recent formulation by Jonathan Dollimore, "Writing and Deviance in Early-Modern England," p. 7.

7 See in the second volume of her poems the letter of February 21, 1749 from Leapor's anonymous female patron, Bridget Freemantle, to John ★★★★★, Esq., p. xxxii. At one point in her letter, Freemantle addresses this John ★★★★★, Esq. as if he were instrumental in printing Leapor's verse: ". . . when the Papers were first sent to you, in order to be printed," p. xxv. There are no fewer than fifteen John –––––, Esq.'s among the subscribers to Leapor's first volume, and eight in the list

for volume II, including one John Wowen, Esq. (five asterisks, five letters?) who
subscribed for four copies of the latter, as many as Samuel Richardson, and Isaac
Hawkins Browne and his wife between them, did – and Richardson and Hawkins
Browne were involved in bringing out this second volume. Four copies of the
second volume were as many as were bought by anybody except the Rev. Dr.
Trimnell, Archdeacon of Leicester, who bought six. Betty Rizzo thinks that John
*****, Esq. is John Duncombe: "Molly Leapor: An Anxiety for Influence," p. 16;
Richard Greene thinks he is possibly John Blencowe, of the family for whom
both Leapor and her father had worked.

8 The recovery of Sappho for twentieth-century feminists includes such work as
Joan DeJean's "Fictions of Sappho," *Critical Inquiry* 13 (Summer 1987),
pp. 787–805, Linda S. Kauffman, *Discourses of Desire: Gender, Genre, and Epistolary
Fictions* (Ithaca and London: Cornell University Press, 1986), esp. pp. 50–61, J.
Hallett, "Sappho and Her Social Context: Sense and Sensuality," *Signs* 4 (1979),
pp. 447–64, Eva Stehle Stigers's response, pp. 465–71, and Lawrence Lipking,
Abandoned Women and Poetic Tradition (Chicago and London: University of
Chicago Press, 1988).

9 See, for example, Nicolas Boileau-Despréaux, *Œuvres Diverses Du Sieur
D*** Avec Le Traité Du Sublime . . .* (Paris: Denys Thierry, 1685); *Posthumous
Works Of Monsieur Boileau. Made English by Several Hands* (London: E. Curll,
1713); Ambrose Phillips's translations of Sappho's odes, with a life, in *The
Works Of Anacreon, And Sappho. Done from the Greek, by several Hands* (London:
E. Curll, 1713); and Joseph Addison's *The Works Of Anacreon, Translated Into
English Verse; . . . To which are added the Odes, Fragments, and Epigrams of Sappho*
(London: John Watts, 1735); it is interesting that Watts published Sappho
and printed Leapor's first volume. Longinus quotes an ode of Sappho's in order
to illustrate the potentially sublime representation of eros as engaging not
merely one "passion," but all the passions and all the senses – a description of
erotic feeling endorsed by Longinus as what "any lover undergoes." Some
translators make more of Sappho's addressing this ode to a woman than others;
Ambrose Phillips's "normalizing" headnote reads: "Whatever might have
been the Occasion of this *Ode*, the *English* Reader will enter into the Beauties of
it, if he supposes it to have been written in the Person of a *Lover* sitting by his
Mistress," p. 74.

10 Joseph Addison, *Spectator* no. 223, Thursday, November 15, 1711 in *The Spectator*,
ed. Donald F. Bond, 5 vols. (Oxford: Clarendon, 1965), II, p. 366.

11 See Lipking, *Abandoned Women and Poetic Tradition*, p. 255 for other contenders;
Lipking himself favors Aphra Behn, p. 97.

12 On Leapor's debt to Swift, see Margaret Doody, "Swift among the Women,"
pp. 79–82.

13 "To the Reader," in the first volume of Leapor's poems, Sig. A2v.

14 In the biographical chapter of "Mary Leapor," Richard Greene suggests that such
poems as "The Disappointment," *An Essay on Friendship*, "The Head-Ach. To
Aurelia," and others indicate that Leapor at some point belonged to a circle of
young women, possibly while she was in service at Weston Hall since her father
seems not to have known about them, but Greene also presents a few arguments
against this supposition: "The Sacrifice" and *An Epistle to Artemisia. On Fame*
suggest that she entertained friends at home; Philip Leapor simply may not have
observed his daughter's friendships closely; and Leapor's work in the Jennens's
house would have left little time for socializing, especially if she was using her
leisure to write, pp. 16–17.

15 Greene, "Mary Leapor," p. 19.
16 Bridget Freemantle was the second daughter of Thomas Freemantle, rector of Hinton from 1692 until his death in 1719, and Mary Freemantle, daughter of John Newton, Gent. She and her mother lived together in Hinton, a small village "in a low situation about one mile east from Brackley" until her mother's death some months before Leapor's in 1746. Bridget Freemantle lived on at Hinton until her death in her eighty-first year in 1779. See George Baker, *The History and Antiquities of the County of Northampton*, 2 vols. (London: Nichols, 1822–30), I, pp. 635–38. My thanks to Betty Rizzo for this reference.
17 Greene, "Mary Leapor," p. 17.
18 Letter [from Freemantle] to John *****, Esq., pp. xx–xxii.
19 Hecht, *The Domestic Servant Class in Eighteenth-Century England*, p. 115. My thanks to Richard Greene for this reference.
20 Letter from Leapor [to Freemantle], II, p. 314.
21 *D.N.B.*, XI, p. 766.
22 See Betty Rizzo, "Christopher Smart, the 'C.S.' Poems, and Molly Leapor's Epitaph," pp. 22–31 and "Molly Leapor: An Anxiety for Influence," pp. 13–19; *D.N.B.*, XI, p. 766. The evidence for Samuel Richardson, Isaac Hawkins Browne, and Christopher Smart as involved in the production and promotion of volume II – Smart largely through a projected epitaph – and for the identification of Bridget Freemantle as the author of the letter to John *****, Esq. is in a letter from Richardson to Isaac Hawkins Browne, December 10, 1750, in the Hyde Collection, Four Oaks Farm, Somerville, New Jersey.
23 "Th' autumnal threads that round the branches flew" is a slight alteration of "Colinetta," line 11; *Gentleman's Magazine* 54:ii (September 1784), p. 650. This quotation touches off a discussion in subsequent issues regarding Leapor's identity; we cannot assume that she was widely known, but her reputation lived on.
24 William Cowper, letter of March 19, 1791 in William Hayley, *The Life and Posthumous Writings Of William Cowper, Esqr.*, 4 vols. (Chichester: J. Seagrave for J. Johnson, London, 1806), III, p. 296. This letter favorably compares Elizabeth Bentley's "natural genius" with Leapor's.
25 Letter [from Freemantle] to John *****, Esq., II, pp. xxix–xxx.
26 Pope, *Satire II. i.*, ed. John Butt, *T.E.*, IV: "F. I'd write no more. P. Not write? but then I *think*, / And for my Soul I cannot sleep a wink" (11–12).
27 Letter from Leapor [to Freemantle], II, p. 317.
28 Letter [from Freemantle] to John *****, Esq., II, p. xxviii.
29 Alastair Fowler, "Country House Poems: The Politics of a Genre," *The Seventeenth Century* 1:1 (1986), pp. 1–14.
30 See *The Feminist Companion to Literature in English* and the forthcoming anthology from the Brown University Women Writers Project under the direction of Susanne Woods and Elaine Brennan, *Women Writers in English 1330–1830*. Lanyer does not appear in such otherwise indispensable studies of the genre as George R. Hibbard's "The Country-house Poem of the Seventeenth Century," *Journal of the Warburg and Courtauld Institutes* 19 (1956), pp. 159–74 and Raymond Williams's *The Country and the City*. See, for a critique of Williams and other marxist writers on the genre, Fowler, "Country House Poems." See also Heather Dubrow, "The Country-House Poem: A Study in Generic Development," *Genre* 12 (Summer 1979), pp. 153–79 and, in relation to Pope, Howard Erskine-Hill, *The Social Milieu of Alexander Pope: Lives, Example, and the Poetic Response* (New Haven: Yale University Press, 1975), esp. pp. 279–317.

31 Aemilia Lanyer, *The Description of Cooke-ham* from *Salve Devs Rex Ivdaeorvm* (London: Printed by Valentine Simmes for Richard Bonian, 1611), Sig. H2r–IIr.

32 George Crabbe, *Letter VI. Professions – Law* in *The Borough*, ed. Norma Dalrymple-Champneys and Arthur Pollard, *The Complete Poetical Works*, 3 vols. (Oxford: Clarendon, 1988), I, pp. 419–21 and *Silford Hall; or, The Happy Day* in *Posthumous Tales, The Complete Poetical Works*, III, p. 24.

33 For the historical distortions involved in this view of Burlington, see Carole Fabricant, *Swift's Landscape* (Baltimore and London: The Johns Hopkins University Press, 1982), pp. 109–13.

34 Pope, *The Epistle to Burlington* in *T.E.*, III:ii.

35 The description of the rooms at Weston by Sir George Sitwell in *A Brief History of Weston Hall Northamptonshire and of the Families That Possessed It* (London: privately printed, 1927) suggests that Weston Hall may well have been Leapor's model for the house, but what Leapor satirizes, Sitwell cites as evidence "that some good architect was the designer," p. 13: "At the south-east corner of the house the ground falls away sharply, thus enabling kitchen and offices to be placed in a basement well lighted from the east. From the kitchen wing, a service passage at the same level led under the small paved court in front of the hall, emerging by a stairway through what is now a china cupboard close to the parlour and drawing-room. The windows, half-sunk in the ground, which light the passage, are of the 1680–90 type, and the order in which 'small beer cellar, bottle house, cellar stair door, folding doors by parlour,' follow each other in the list of 1714, indicate that this was the original planning of the house." My thanks to Richard Greene for bringing this book to my attention.

36 Greene, "Mary Leapor," p. 13.

37 Margaret Doody, "Swift among the Women," p. 82.

38 See Michèle Barrett, *Women's Oppression Today*, p. 202, and Mark Poster, *Critical Theory of the Family* (London: Pluto, 1978).

39 Great alterations that sound remarkably reminiscent of Leapor's parlor-building here were made at Weston, though not until 1777, according to Sitwell: "These alterations of 1777 made the house more commodious, but ruined its beauty. A lofty Drawing- or Dining room was gained, with three airy bedchambers of the new fashion. On the other hand, the Great Parlour disappeared, the ceiling in this part being lowered to gain height for the storey above, while the hall was deprived of afternoon sun and of its view over the flower-garden," *A Brief History*, p. 72.

4   The complex contradictions of Ann Yearsley: working-class writer, bourgeois subject?

1 *The Amours Of The French King With The Late Queen of Albion. Being The Fourth and Last Part of the History of Messalina.* By a Woman of Quality (London: John Lyford, 1689), p. 34. My thanks to Rachel Weil for this reference.

2 *Earl Goodwin, An Historical Play.* By Ann Yearsley, Milk-Woman, Of Clifton, Near Bristol. Performed With General Applause At The Theatre-Royal, Bristol (London: G. G. J. and J. Robinson, 1791) and *The Royal Captives: A Fragment of Secret History. Copied From An Old Manuscript.* By Ann Yearsley (London: G. G. and J. Robinson, 1795).

3 See Rubenstein's entry on Yearsley in Todd (ed.), *A Dictionary*, pp. 336–37.

4 *Stanzas of Woe, addressed from the Heart On A Bed Of Illness, to Levi Eames, Esq. Late Mayor Of The City Of Bristol.* By Ann Yearsley, A Milk-Woman Of Clifton, Near Bristol (London: G. G. J. and J. Robinson, 1790).

5 Yearsley, *The Rural Lyre; A Volume Of Poems: Dedicated To The Right Honourable The Earl Of Bristol, Lord Bishop Of Derry* (London: G. G. and J. Robinson, 1796).

6 On the abandonment of eighteenth-century laboring poets by their patrons, see Vicinus, *The Industrial Muse*, p. 168 and Klaus, *The Literature of Labour*, pp. 20–21.

7 Cathy N. Davidson, *Revolution and the Word: The Rise of the Novel in America* (New York and Oxford: Oxford University Press, 1986), p. 41.

8 William Roberts, *Memoirs Of The Life And Correspondence Of Mrs. Hannah More*, 4 vols. (London: R. B. Seeley and W. Burnside, 1834), II, p. 366. Roberts dates this letter from July or August, 1793, but G. H. Spinney in "Cheap Repository Tracts: Hazard and Marshall Edition," *Transactions of the Bibliographical Society, London*, n.s., 20:3 (December 1939), p. 297, thinks it was written in August or September, 1794.

9 Roberts, *Memoirs of Hannah More*, II, p. 294. In fact the Birmingham riot of 1791 displayed an excess of loyalist fervor against the republicanism of the "Constitutional Society" and the Dissenter Joseph Priestley. Southey, in *Letters From England: By Don Manuel Alvarez Espriella*, 3 vols. (London: Longman, Hurst, Rees and Orme, 1807), II, pp. 122–23, comments on the volatility of the Birmingham mob as follows, "In no other place are there so many ingenious mechanics, in no other place is trade so precarious. War ruins half the manufacturers of Birmingham by shutting their markets." E. P. Thompson discusses the Birmingham riots as "transitional" between eighteenth-century mob violence, and the politicized protests of Jacobin working people in the 1790s, in *The Making of the English Working Class*, pp. 79–80, pp. 114–15.

10 Roberts, *Memoirs of Hannah More*, II, pp. 188–89.

11 More's ballad *The Riot; Or, Half a Loaf is better than no Bread* (London: J. Marshall and R. White, etc., n.d.) was said to have stopped a riot among colliers near Bath: "The plan was thoroughly settled; they were resolved to work no more, but to attack first the mills, and then the gentry. A gentleman of large fortune got into their confidence, and a few hundreds were distributed and sung with the effect, as they say, mentioned above," Roberts, *Memoirs of Hannah More*, II, p. 386.

12 More, *Cheap Repository. The Sunday School* (London: J. Marshall and R. White, etc., n.d.), p. 10.

13 Roberts, letter from More to Dr. Beadon, Bishop of Bath and Wells, 1801, in *Memoirs of Hannah More*, III, p. 133.

14 Roberts, *Memoirs of Hannah More*, III, p. 133.

15 Roberts, letter from More to William Wilberforce, 1823, in *Memoirs of Hannah More*, IV, p. 211.

16 Ferguson, "Resistance and Power," p. 226.

17 Rubenstein, astonishingly, dismisses Yearsley's poetry as "remarkable primarily for its sustained note of self-pity" in Todd (ed.), *A Dictionary*, p. 336. But see Ferguson, "Resistance and Power," for a vindication of Yearsley's "confrontational politics," p. 252, pp. 256–66.

18 For these concepts of ideology and sovereign subjectivity see Louis Althusser, "Ideology and Ideological State Apparatuses (Notes towards an Investigation)," *Lenin and Philosophy and Other Essays*, trans. Ben Brewster (New York and London: Monthly Review Press, 1971), pp. 127–86 and Gayatri Chakravorty Spivak, "The Politics of Interpretations," *In Other Worlds*, pp. 118–33.

19 In "Ann Yearsley and the Clifton Records," Waldron suggests that Yearsley failed to behave towards More with the "commendable submissiveness" (p. 7) with which other female laboring poets like Mary Collier and Phillis Wheatley had behaved towards their patrons because she belonged to the class immediately below More's own: "It looks likely that Yearsley reacted differently from other 'uneducated' writers because she felt less removed socially from her patron and more in command of the realities of the situation" (p. 10). Wheatley's status as not a freeborn white English servant but a black slave is not taken into account here; her "submissiveness," or lack of it, is located in a different field of power from Collier's or Yearsley's. And Waldron does not consider the possibility that social antagonism and class resistance may take different forms in different historical situations, that Yearsley might feel entitled to a more democratic social exchange with her patron than Collier had done because of historical shifts in the discourses of class privilege generally.

20 Royle and Walvin, *English Radicals and Reformers*, p. 189.

21 In *Poems, on Several Occasions* (1785), hereafter *P.O.S.O.*

22 "To the Same [i.e., To Stella]; on her Accusing The Author Of Flattery, and of Ascribing to the Creature that Praise which is due only to the Creator," in *P.O.S.O.*

23 In *Poems, on Various Subjects* (1787), hereafter *P.O.V.S.* Young, without having low-born poets in mind, and while taking only ancient and modern "greats" as his examples, goes so far as to write, "As it is said in *Terence, Pecuniam negligere interdum maximum est lucrum*; so to neglect of learning, genius sometimes owes its greater glory," in *Conjectures On Original Composition. In A Letter To The Author Of Sir Charles Grandison* (London: A. Millar and R. and J. Dodsley, 1759), p. 29.

24 Rubenstein, seeming both needlessly unsympathetic towards Yearsley's achievements and unreflectively bound to a post-Romantic veneration of "originality," fails to acknowledge the relatively "highly derivative" qualities of eighteenth-century verse in Todd (ed.), *A Dictionary*, p. 336.

25 James Beattie, "Advertisement" to *The Minstrel: Or, The Progress Of Genius. A Poem. Book The First* (London: E. & C. Dilly, etc., 1771), p. [v].

26 Beattie, *The Minstrel: Book II* in *The Minstrel; Or, The Progress Of Genius: And Other Poems* (London: John Sharpe, 1816), stanza XLVI, lines 7–8; LVI, 1–5.

27 Beattie, *The Minstrel . . . Book The First* (1771), stanza VI, lines 3, 5–6.

28 More to Montagu, August, 27, 1784; Huntington Library manuscript MO 3986, p. 3.

29 More, "Prefatory Letter," *P.O.S.O.*, p. ix.

30 More, "Prefatory Letter," *P.O.S.O.*, pp. vi–vii.

31 More to Montagu, September 27, 1784; Huntington Library manuscript MO 3987, p. 4.

32 More to Montagu, October 22, 1784; Huntington Library manuscript MO 3988, p. 2.

33 More to Montagu, December 7, 1784; Huntington Library manuscript MO 3989, pp. 1–2.

34 John Dyer, *Grongar Hill* (first octosyllabic text), ed. Richard C. Boys (Baltimore: The Johns Hopkins Press, 1941).

35 More to Montagu, August 7, 1784; Huntington Library manuscript MO 3986, p. 2. See Waldron, "Ann Yearsley and the Clifton Records," pp. 4–6, for details about John Yearsley's family and income.

36 *The Gentleman's Magazine* 54:ii (December 1784), p. 897.

37 John Clare, *The Autobiography 1793–1824* in *The Prose of John Clare*, ed. J. W. and Anne Tibble (New York: Barnes & Noble, 1970), pp. 23–24.

38 Clare, *Autobiography*, p. 24.

39 As reported to Joseph Cottle, the Bristol bookseller, in *Early Recollections; Chiefly Relating to the late Samuel Taylor Coleridge, during his long residence in Bristol*, 2 vols. (London: Longman, Rees and Co. and Hamilton, Adams and Co., 1837), I, pp. 76–77.

40 Tompkins, *The Polite Marriage*, p. 101.

41 Gray's *Elegy* commemorates the "frail memorials" of the poor, "With uncouth rhymes and shapeless sculpture decked." These headstones also carry "holy texts" "That teach the rustic moralist to die"; see *The Poems of Thomas Gray, William Collins, and Oliver Goldsmith*, ed. Roger Lonsdale (London: Longmans, 1969), lines 78–84. Clare, *Autobiography*, p. 29. Tompkins surmises that this early experience of reading graveyard verse in her mother's company was clearly what first kindled Yearsley's "genius," *The Polite Marriage*, p. 60.

42 *The Gentleman's Magazine* 54:ii, p. 897.

43 More to Montagu, August 27, 1784; Huntington Library manuscript MO 3986, p. 3.

44 Henry Thompson, *The Life of Hannah More: with Notices Of Her Sisters* (London: T. Cadell and Edinburgh: W. Blackwood and Sons, 1838), p. 49.

45 Brean Hammond has demonstrated well Pope's departures from the historical specificity of Heloise and Abelard in the interests of erotic psychodrama in the fifth chapter of *Pope* (Brighton: Harvester, 1986), pp. 174–84. Crucially, Pope removes Heloise's intellectual status and her capacity for "principled conceptualism" from Eloisa, leaving her a slave to passion, p. 178. And, we might add, leaving women's experience marginalized as definitively and reductively erotic. See also Gillian Beer's fine article "'Our unnatural No-voice': The Heroic Epistle, Pope, and Women's Gothic," *The Yearbook of English Studies* 12 (1982), pp. 125–51, to which Hammond is indebted.

46 The manuscript of "Clifton Hill" in More's hand here reads: "the sparkling flame of love." This is the only substantive variant, suggesting that More may have made few, if any, substantive changes to Yearsley's verse in her capacity as editor. Huntington Library manuscript MO 6085, p. 16.

47 See Foucault, *Madness and Civilization: A History of Insanity in the Age of Reason*, trans. Richard Howard (New York: Vintage, 1973) and Deleuze and Guattari, *Anti-Oedipus: Capitalism and Schizophrenia*, trans. Robert Hurley, Mark Seem, Helen R. Lane (Minneapolis: University of Minnesota Press, 1983).

48 John Wesley in the *Journal*, September 25, 1789, according to the *D.N.B.*, ix, p. 401.

49 Thompson, *Life of Hannah More*, pp. 48–55.

50 [Horace Walpole], "The Translator's Preface," *The Castle of Otranto, A Story. Translated by William Marshall, Gent. From the Original Italian of Onuphrio Muralto, Canon of the Church of St. Nicholas at Otranto* (London: Tho. Lownds, 1765), p. vi.

51 Samuel Johnson, *Life of Savage*, ed. Clarence Tracy (Oxford: Clarendon, 1971), p. 140.

52 Roberts, *Memoirs of Hannah More*, I, p. 360.

53 More to Montagu, July 7, 1789; Huntington Library manuscript MO 3997, p. 2.

54 *The Monthly Review; Or, Literary Journal* 73:ii (July–December 1785), p. 219, p. 221.

55 See *The Monthly Review* 77:ii (July–December 1787), pp. 485–89; *The Monthly Review* (enlarged series) 16:i (January–April 1795), pp. 112–14; *The Monthly*

Review 19:i (January–April 1796), pp. 452–53. According to Tompkins in *The Polite Marriage*, p. 89, in reviewing Yearsley's novel *The Royal Captives*, both the *Monthly* and the *Critical Review* were generous and enthusiastic: "The *Critical* spoke of genius, which was a word of wider application in the eighteenth century than it is now, and both reviews were certainly inclined to graciousness by the liberal sentiments, the just abhorrence of tyranny which the book reveals."

56 See Yearsley, "Narrative" addressed "To The Noble and Generous Subscribers . . ." first published in the fourth edition of *P.O.S.O.*, pp. xviii–xxxi, and more accessible in *P.O.V.S.*, pp. xv–xxv; this episode on p. xx of the latter.

57 Cottle, *Early Recollections*, I, p. 75.

58 Some of these details appear in Yearsley's "Narrative" and the rest in Huntington Library manuscripts HM 1837, MO 3990, and MO 3994.

59 More to Montagu, July 21, 1785; Huntington Library manuscript MO 3991, pp. 3–4.

60 More to Montagu, October 20, 1785; Huntington Library manuscript MO 3993, p. 3.

61 Yearsley's "Narrative" in *P.O.V.S.*, p. xx.

62 Yearsley's "Narrative," *P.O.V.S.*, p. xviii.

63 In More to Montagu, September 16, 1785; Huntington Library manuscript MO 3992, pp. 1–2.

64 Cottle, *Early Recollections*, I, pp. 74–75.

65 More to Montagu, October 20, 1785; Huntington Library manuscript MO 3993, p. 2.

66 For conservative vituperation against Hervey on these grounds, see *Memoirs Of Lady Hamilton; With Illustrative Anecdotes Of Many Of Her Most Particular Friends And Distinguished Contemporaries* (London: Henry Colburn, 1815), pp. 122–25. The anonymous memoirist implies that Hervey had a particular fondness for such women of "menial" or lower-class origins as Emma Hamilton and the Countess of Lichtenau, p. 118.

67 Robert Dunlop writes: "At a time when sectarian jealousies ran high, Hervey did much by his example to soften their asperities and to cultivate a spirit of toleration . . . His popularity with every class of the community . . . his enormous wealth and undoubted ability soon raised him to a prominent position among the volunteers of the north. Like most of the intelligent politicians of the time, he was strongly convinced of the necessity of supplementing the legislative enactments of 1782 by a radical reform of the representation of the Irish House of Commons; but, unlike the majority of them, he would gladly have seen the elective franchise extended to the Roman catholics . . . His views, although extreme, showed a keener preception of the critical nature of the situation than those of Grattan and Charlemont," *D.N.B.*, IX, pp. 731–32.

68 Yearsley, "Dedication," *P.O.V.S.*, p. v; "Dedication," *Earl Goodwin, An Historical Play*, Sig. A2r; "Dedication," *The Rural Lyre*, p. viii.

69 See "To Frederick Yearsley, On his return from the Sacred Font, where the Right Honourable the Earl of Bristol stood Sponsor, the Child being distinguished by taking his Lordship's Name" and "On The Death Of Frederick Yearsley," *P.O.V.S.*, pp. 61–64, pp. 65–66. Hervey was not Yearsley's only patron at this time. Ferguson has identified the support given Yearsley by Eliza (Dawson) Fletcher in "Resistance and Power," p. 225.

70 Roberts, *Memoirs of Hannah More*, II, p. 81.

71 Pope, *An Essay on Man*, ed. Maynard Mack, *T.E.*, III:i.

72 Raymond Dexter Havens, in *The Influence of Milton on English Poetry* (New York:

Russell & Russell, 1961), p. 655, lists several of Yearsley's poems in his "Appendix" of poems influenced by *Paradise Lost*, not including this one.

73 The quotation marks placed at the end of this line appear to be a compositor's mistake, so I have omitted them from the text for the sake of clarity.

74 Doody, *The Daring Muse*, p. 123, p. 130.

75 See, for example, Neil McKendrick, John Brewer, and J. H. Plumb, *The Birth of a Consumer Society: The Commercialization of Eighteenth-Century England* (Bloomington: Indiana University Press, 1982).

76 *D.N.B.*, XIV, pp. 467–68.

77 Tompkins, *The Polite Marriage*, p. 99.

78 Yearsley, *A Poem On The Inhumanity Of The Slave-Trade* (London: G. G. J and J. Robinson, 1788).

79 Yearsley, "Advertisement," *Stanzas of Woe*, Sig. A3r–Sig. A3v.

80 William Godwin, *Caleb Williams*, ed. David McCracken (London: Oxford University Press, 1970), p. 73. My thanks to Peter Manning for suggesting this connection between Yearsley's situation and the events Godwin represents.

81 Yearsley, *The Dispute. Letter to the Public From The Milkwoman* [1791]; British Library shelfmark 1501/67.

82 Ferguson, "Resistance and Power," pp. 259–62.

83 Thompson, *Whigs and Hunters: The Origin of the Black Act* (New York: Pantheon, 1975), pp. 260–69.

84 Yearsley, "Advertisement," *Stanzas of Woe*, Sig. A3v.

85 Thompson, *Whigs and Hunters*, pp. 265–66.

86 Tompkins, *The Polite Marriage*, p. 98. On the organized repression of radical movements and the circulation of radical ideas in this period, see J. R. Western, "The Volunteer Movement as an Anti-Revolutionary Force, 1793–1801," *The English Historical Review* 71:281 (October 1956), pp. 603–14.

87 According to a manuscript in Yearsley's hand at the Huntington, "Goodwin a Tragedy. By Mrs. Yearsley the Bristol Milkwoman," the play was written in October, 1789; Huntington Library manuscript LA 846.

88 See "Reflections on the Death of Louis XVI." By Ann Yearsley (Bristol: Printed for, and Sold by the Author, at her Public-Library, Crescent, Hotwells, 1793) and "Sequel to Reflections on the Death of Louis XVI." By Ann Yearsley (Bristol: Printed for the Author [etc.], 1793). The latter poem is dated February 12, 1793; Louis XVI was executed on 21 January.

89 Yearsley, "An Elegy on Marie Antoinette, of Austria, Ci-Devant Queen of France: with a Poem on the Last Interview Between The King of Poland and Loraski" (n.p.: Printed (by J. Rudhall) for the Author, [1793]), lines 39–40.

90 Gayatri Spivak, "Explanation and Culture: Marginalia," *In Other Worlds*, p. 103.

91 See Nancy Armstrong, *Desire and Domestic Fiction: A Political History of the Novel* (New York and Oxford: Oxford University Press, 1987), esp. pp. 3–27.

92 Royle and Walvin, *English Radicals and Reformers*, p. 187.

93 Stedman Jones, *Languages of Class*, pp. 126–27.

94 Taylor, *Eve and the New Jerusalem*, p. 18.

95 Stedman Jones, *Languages of Class*, pp. 124–25.

96 Tompkins, *The Polite Marriage*, p. 94.

97 Yearsley, "Argument" to *The Consul C. Fannius To Fannius Didius*, *Rural Lyre*, p. 47.

98 Yearsley, *Lucy, A Tale For The Ladies*, *P.O.V.S.*

99 Here I disagree with Waldron, who finds *Poems, on Various Subjects* "perhaps the

high point of Yearsley's achievement," in "Ann Yearsley and the Clifton Records," p. 14.

100 Tompkins, *The Polite Marriage*, p. 96.

101 Rubenstein, in Todd (ed.), *A Dictionary*, p. 337.

102 Yearsley, *The Genius Of England, On the Rock of Ages, Recommending Order, Commerce And Union To The Britons*, line 107, *Rural Lyre*.

103 *D.N.B.*, XVII, pp. 480–85.

104 More's *The Riot*, we are told, was "Written in 1795, a Year of Scarcity and Alarm"; *Poems of Hannah More* (London: T. Cadell & W. Davies, 1816), p. 334.

105 William Blake, "London," *The Poems of William Blake*, ed. W. H. Stevenson and David V. Erdman (London: Longman, 1971), pp. 213–14.

106 *Catalogue Of The Books, Tracts, &c. Contained In Ann Yearsley's Public Library, No. 4, Crescent, Hotwells* (Bristol: Printed for the Proprietor, 1793), p. 17, p. 22, p. 23. The last items in the catalogue, numbers 664–66, are listed simply as volumes of Yearsley's own verse, without titles; what might it signify that she assigned herself the "number of the beast?" British Library shelfmark s.c. 726 (9.).

107 This is Williams's term for a whole historical process traceable globally but also within the history of Britain – "the struggle for democracy, the development of industry, the extension of communications, and the deep social and personal changes" that accompany and help bring about these politico-material shifts – as analyzed in *The Long Revolution* (Harmondsworth: Penguin, 1971), p. 12. See Juliet Mitchell's *Women: The Longest Revolution: Essays in Feminism, Literature and Psychoanalysis* (London: Virago, 1984) for a feminist reformulation.

5   Laboring in pastures new: the two Elizabeths

1 In a letter to John Johnson of March 19, 1791, William Cowper writes: "You ask, if it may not be improper to solicit Lady Hesketh's subscription to the poems of the Norwich maiden? To which I reply, it will be by no means improper . . . [F]or she is much an admirer of poesy, that is worthy to be admired, and such I think, judging by the specimen, the poesy of this maiden, Elizabeth Bentley of Norwich, is likely to prove . . . The fact is, that though strong natural genius is always accompanied with strong natural tendency to its object, yet it often happens that the tendency is found where the genius is wanting. In the present instance however (the poems of a certain Mrs. Leapor excepted, who published some forty years ago) I discern, I think, more marks of true poetical talent than I remember to have observed in the verses of any other male or female, so disadvantageously circumstanced. I wish her therefore good speed, and subscribe to her with all my heart"; in William Hayley, *The Life And Posthumous Writings, Of William Cowper, Esqr. With An Introductory Letter To The Right Honourable Earl Cowper. A New And Enlarged Edition*, 4 vols. (Chichester: J. Seagrave for J. Johnson, London, 1806), III, pp. 295–96.

2 *The Death of Amnon. A Poem, with an Appendix: containing Pastorals, and other Poetical Pieces*. By Elizabeth Hands (Coventry: Printed for the Author by N. Rollason, 1789). Lonsdale includes five poems by Hands in *Eighteenth Century Women Poets*, pp. 422–29.

3 See, for example, *Proletarianization and Family History*, ed. David Levine (London and Orlando: Academic Press, 1984) and, for some useful criticism of the concept, Rab Houston and K. D. M. Snell, "Proto-Industrialization? Cottage Industry, Social Change, and Industrial Revolution," *The Historical Journal* 27:2 (1984), pp. 473–92.

4 Letter from Henry Homer to Richard Bisse Riland (November 4, 1788) in W. K. Riland Bedford, *Three Hundred Years of a Family Living, Being A History of the Rilands of Sutton Coldfield* (Birmingham: Cornish Brothers, 1889), pp. 112–14; cited by Hecht, *The Domestic Servant Class*, p. 191. I owe this reference to Richard Greene.

5 *D.N.B.*, VIII, p. 475. Bertie Greatheed was the son of Samuel Greatheed of Guy's Cliffe, near Warwick, and his wife Lady Mary Bertie, daughter of Peregrine, second duke of Ancaster. His career as a dramatist seems to have been rather undistinguished; his blank-verse tragedy *The Regent* was performed at Drury Lane in 1788, supported by John Kemble and Mrs. Siddons, and withdrawn after nine nights.

6 Hands, dedication, *The Death of Amnon*, Sig. A1r.

7 Letter from Homer to Riland; Homer attributes Hands's discovery largely to his son, Philip Bracebridge Homer (1765–1838), who had shown James *The Death of Amnon*.

8 Grace Isobel Clark in her entry on Hands in Todd (ed.), *A Dictionary*, pp. 149–50, claims that she was "possibly a Dissenter." Riland Bedford, in *Three Hundred Years of a Family Living*, describes an Edward Hands, cordwainer, who, as a "Protestant Dissenter," in 1785 had his house licensed as a place of worship, p. 69. Given their shared locale, Edward and Elizabeth Hands may well have been related.

9 Barrell, *The Dark Side of the Landscape*, p. 21, p. 64. Note the slide from "the poor" to the activities of poor men, as if poor women ("wenches") were not really part of the laboring classes at all, and certainly not as conscious subjects or historical agents.

10 On the Marriage Act of 1753 and its probable relation to the poor, see Erica Harth, "The Virtue of Love: Lord Hardwicke's Marriage Act," *Cultural Critique* (Spring 1988), pp. 123–54, John R. Gillis, *For Better, For Worse: British Marriages, 1600 to the Present* (New York and Oxford: Oxford University Press, 1985), esp. pp. 140–42, and Stone, *The Family, Sex and Marriage*, pp. 35–37. Hands's texts would seem to offer evidence that runs counter to Stone's sweeping assumptions about a lack of affective as opposed to economic ties among the lower classes, e.g. p. 393. Snell discusses changes in working-class attitudes towards sex and marriage in *Annals of the Labouring Poor*, pp. 306–07, pp. 352–57. Perhaps we can find in Hands evidence to support Michel Foucault's thesis regarding working-class resistance to bourgeois interference in working-class sexual behavior, resistance to "a whole technology of control which made it possible to keep that body and sexuality, finally conceded to them, under surveillance (schooling, the politics of housing, public hygiene, institutions of relief and insurance, the general medicalization of the population, in short, an entire administrative and technical machinery made it possible to safely import the deployment of sexuality into the exploited class . . .) Whence no doubt the proletariat's hesitancy to accept this deployment and its tendency to say that this sexuality was the business of the bourgeoisie and did not concern it," *The History of Sexuality, Vol. I: An Introduction*, trans. Robert Hurley (New York: Pantheon, 1978), pp. 126–27.

11 Bakhtin, *The Dialogic Imagination*, p. 293.

12 Lady Mary Wortley Montagu, "The Lover; a Ballad," in *Essays and Poems*, ed. Halsband and Grundy, pp. 234–36. Of this fourth stanza, Byron wrote, "Is not her '*Champaigne and Chicken*' worth a forest or two? Is it not poetry?" See the *Letters and Journals*, ed. R. E. Prothero, 1898–1901, 5. 566; cited in Halsband and Grundy, p. 171.

13 E[lizabeth] Bentley, *Genuine Poetical Compositions, on Various Subjects*, Dedicated, by permission, to Wm. Drake, Jun. Esq. M.P. (Norwich: Crouse and Stevenson, 1791).

14 As Gayle Trusdel Pendleton points out in her entry on Bentley in Todd (ed.), *A Dictionary*, p. 46.

6   Other others: the marginality of cultural difference

1 Letter from Robert Burns to George Thomson, October, 1794, in *The Letters of Robert Burns*, ed. G. Ross Roy, 2 vols. (Oxford: Clarendon, 1985), II, p. 318.

2 [Margaretta Matilda Oddell,] "Memoir" of Phillis Wheatley (Boston, 1834) reprinted as Appendix D in William H. Robinson, *Phillis Wheatley and Her Writings* (New York and London: Garland, 1984), p. 431.

3 See Gayatri Chakravorty Spivak, "The Rani of Sirmur," in *Europe and Its Others: Proceedings of the Essex Conference on the Sociology of Literature, 1984*, ed. Francis Barker, Peter Hulme, Margaret Iversen, and Diana Loxley, 2 vols. (Colchester: University of Essex, 1985), I, pp. 128–51, and "Subaltern Studies: Deconstructing Historiography," *In Other Worlds*, pp. 197–221. See also *"Race," Writing, and Difference*, ed. Henry Louis Gates, Jr. (Chicago and London: University of Chicago Press, 1986) which includes Spivak's essay "Three Women's Texts and a Critique of Imperialism," pp. 262–80, and a fine essay by Mary Louise Pratt, "Scratches on the Face of the Country; or, What Mr. Barrow Saw in the Land of the Bushmen," pp. 138–62; *Black Literature and Literary Theory*, ed. Henry Louis Gates, Jr. (London and New York: Methuen, 1984); and Edward Said, *Orientalism* (New York: Pantheon, 1978).

4 Spivak, "The Rani of Sirmur," p. 130.

5 Homi K. Bhabha, "Signs Taken for Wonders: Questions of Ambivalence and Authority under a Tree outside Delhi, May 1817," *Europe and Its Others*, p. 97, p. 104; an earlier version is included in *"Race," Writing, and Difference*, ed. Gates, pp. 163–84. See also Bhabha, "The other question: difference, discrimination and the discourse of colonialism" in *Literature, Politics and Theory: Papers from the Essex Conference 1976–84*, ed. Francis Barker, Peter Hulme, Margaret Iversen, and Diana Loxley (London and New York: Methuen, 1986), pp. 148–72.

6 Thompson, *The Making of the English Working Class*, p. 14.

7 For English reports of Scottish slovenliness, see Caroline Davidson, *A Woman's Work Is Never Done: A History of Housework in the British Isles 1650–1950* (London: Chatto & Windus, 1982), pp. 115–17.

8 James Currie, "Prefatory Remarks on the Character and Condition of the Scottish Peasantry" in *The Works of Robert Burns*, 4 vols. (Liverpool: J. M'Creery for T. Cadell, Jun. and W. Davies, London and W. Creech, Edinburgh, 1800), I, pp. 3–4.

9 [James Paterson,] *The Contemporaries Of Burns, And The More Recent Poets Of Ayrshire, With Selections From Their Writings* (Edinburgh: Hugh Paton, 1840), p. 79. This is the best account of Little, but there are also useful entries on her by Maurice Lindsey in *The Burns Encyclopedia* (New York and London: St. Martin's Press and Robert Hale, 1980), pp. 218–19, and by Jocelyn Harris in Todd (ed.), *A Dictionary*, p. 199.

10 "Besides being the most skilful, the work of the dairywoman was without question the most arduous of all women's labours in the agricultural sphere," and "The financial value of women's work was far greater on a dairy farm than in any other branch of agriculture, since the prosperity of such a farm depended almost entirely on their results," Pinchbeck, *Women Workers*, p. 12, p. 15.

11 *The Poetical Works Of Janet Little, The Scotch Milkmaid* (Air: John & Peter Wilson, 1792). Copies cited include those in the Glasgow University Library (shelfmark Sp. Coll. 95), the British Library (shelfmark 11646.h.10), and the Huntington Library (shelfmark 441921). Lonsdale includes one poem by Little in *Eighteenth Century Women Poets*, pp. 453–55.

12 Paterson, *Contemporaries of Burns*, p. 83. Flora, "the little Countess," was the only daughter of James Muir Campbell, fifth Earl of Loudoun, who "shot himself on account of financial troubles in 1786," *Robert Burns and Mrs. Dunlop: Correspondence Now Published In Full For The First Time*, ed. William Wallace, 2 vols. (New York: Dodd, Mead and Company, 1898), I, p. 301.

13 Paterson, *Contemporaries of Burns*, p. 87.

14 See, for example, Wallace, *Robert Burns and Mrs. Dunlop*, I, p. 275; II, p. 169, p. 170. When Mrs. Henri leaves Loudoun Castle for France in 1792, Little marries John Richmond, an elderly laborer at the castle who survives her by six years; Paterson, *Contemporaries of Burns*, p. 87, p. 98, and Wallace, I, p. 191, n. 2; p. 276, n. 4. Little's life and circumstances are completely circumscribed by the family and feudal household relations.

15 Wilson is Alexander Wilson, "born at Paisley in 1766; published a volume of poems in 1790; emigrated to America in 1793, wrote the *American Ornithology* and died at Philadelphia in 1813," Wallace, *Robert Burns and Mrs. Dunlop*, II, pp. 188–89. The poems went through two editions in 1790 and a reappearance in 1791 as *Poems, Humorous, Satirical, and Serious*, D.N.B., XXI, p. 546.

16 To Burns, Dunlop writes, regarding Little's "merit" and becoming sense of place: "I thought to tell you of a humble poetess who came from Ecclesfechan to be my chamber-maid on the merit of her attempting what seemed beyond her line in the way of writing or thinking. I parted with her to my daughter, thinking a child's maid, if she was fit for it, a better place than I had to offer . . . She is industrious, and seems good-temper'd and discreet . . .," Wallace, *Robert Burns and Mrs. Dunlop*, I, p. 274. Little's promotion to running the dairy at Loudoun represents a further betterment of her position within this extended family.

17 In "Burns and Heteroglossia," *The Eighteenth Century: Theory and Interpretation* 28:1 (Winter 1987), pp. 3–27, David B. Morris provides a fine demonstration of the usefulness of Bakhtin for reading texts like Burns's. Morris argues that Burns's poetry exemplifies the dialogic mode, and the socio-cultural polyphony to be found within literary discourses and even within individual words, that Bakhtin identifies as heteroglossia. Morris both draws attention to the linguistic conflicts and uncertainties to which Burns was heir as an eighteenth-century Scottish poet and seeks to recuperate his "freedom of speech" (p. 23) both via and contra Bakhtin (who privileges the novel as the locus of heteroglossia to the near exclusion of poetry). I am puzzled as to why Morris adopts only the term heteroglossia, and not also Bakhtin's term polyglossia, which describes a cultural situation in which more than one language is operative, as with Latin and the various European vernaculars in the Middle Ages, and Scottish, Gaelic and English poetry in this period. See Bakhtin, *The Dialogic Imagination*, pp. 61–68.

18 While Morris puts paid to such critical assumptions as Burns's lack of "originality" (p. 21), he discloses another common literary-historical prejudice when he claims, without quoting any particular texts as evidence, and without mentioning any women poets of the period, that Burns's "songs offer what seems a more authentic rendering of women's voices than the work of any other eighteenth-century poet" (p. 22). However inadvertently, Morris would seem to be assuming here that all eighteenth-century poets (of importance? of interest?) were men.

19 Linda Kauffman, *Discourses of Desire*, pp. 20–22, p. 318. See also Janet Gurkin

Altman, *Epistolarity: Approaches to a Form* (Columbus: Ohio State University Press, 1982).

20 I owe these references to the authors of *The Feminist Companion to Literature in English.*

21 Wallace, *Robert Burns and Mrs. Dunlop,* II, p. 140.

22 Hannah More, *Slavery, A Poem* (London: T. Cadell, 1788) and Ann Yearsley, *A Poem On The Inhumanity Of The Slave-Trade* (London: G. G. J. and J. Robinson, 1788). Moira Ferguson reprints Yearsley's poem in *First Feminists,* pp. 386–96. In her forthcoming study, *Subject to Others: British Women Writers and Colonial Slavery 1760–1834,* Ferguson analyzes crucial connections between the emergence of feminism and abolitionist politics.

23 Tompkins, *The Polite Marriage,* p. 77.

24 *Poems On Various Subjects, Religious And Moral.* By Phillis Wheatley, Negro Servant to Mr. John Wheatley, of Boston, in New England (London: Printed for A. Bell, Aldgate; sold by Cox and Berry, Boston, 1773). The Clark Library copy (shelfmark *PS 866 W5P7) is inscribed "one of the earliest books by a negro." Wheatley was the first African to publish a book of poetry in English. Juan Latino, a black slave of Granada, published three volumes of verse in Latin between 1573 and 1576; see Charles T. Davis and Henry Louis Gates, Jr. (eds.), *The Slave's Narrative* (Oxford and New York: Oxford University Press, 1985), pp. xxvii–xxviii.

25 Thomas Jefferson, "Query XIV" in *Notes on Virginia* (1784), quoted in Julian D. Mason, Jr., *The Poems of Phillis Wheatley* (Chapel Hill: University of North Carolina Press, 1966), p. xliii.

26 Ironically, Gilbert Imlay, who enters feminist literary history primarily through his less than enlightened behavior towards Mary Wollstonecraft, defended Wheatley against Jefferson's charges. Citing her poem "On Imagination," Imlay writes: "Indeed, I should be glad to be informed what white upon this continent has written more beautiful lines," in *A Topographical Description of The Western Territory of North America* (New York, 1793), I, pp. 185–86, reprinted in Mason, *The Poems of Phillis Wheatley,* p. xliv. Mason, p. xliv, also reports Henri Grégoire and Samuel Stanhope Smith as challenging Jefferson's racist remarks on Wheatley's behalf in *An Enquiry Concerning The Intellectual and Moral Faculties, And Literature of Negroes & Mulattoes, Distinguished in Science, Literature And The Arts,* trans. D. B. Warden (Brooklyn, 1810), pp. 44–45, and *An Essay on the Causes of the Variety of Complexion and Figure in the Human Species* (New Brunswick and New York, 1810), p. 269, n., respectively.

27 James Parton, "Antipathy to the Negro," *The North American Review* 127 (November–December 1878), pp. 487–88, quoted in Mason, *The Poems of Phillis Wheatley,* p. xlv.

28 Mason, *The Poems of Phillis Wheatley,* p. xxxii.

29 Charles W. Akers, 'Our Modern Egyptians': Phillis Wheatley and the Whig Campaign Against Slavery in Revolutionary Boston," *The Journal of Negro History* (July 1975), p. 399.

30 William H. Robinson, *Phillis Wheatley and Her Writings,* p. 97, p. 108.

31 A recent collection of critical essays not only handily documents this general history of Wheatley criticism, but helps break new ground in the legitimation of Wheatley's *œuvre* as an object of serious study, attending to such questions as Popean influence, the elegiac mode, the sublime, and contemporary definitions of "the Negro." See especially the essays by Albertha Sistrunk, Mukhtar Ali Isani, John C. Shields, and Henry Louis Gates, Jr. in *Critical Essays on Phillis Wheatley,* ed. William H. Robinson (Boston: G. K. Hall and Company, 1982). The

collection is usefully reviewed by Valerie Smith in *Early American Literature* 18:1 (Spring 1983), pp. 110–11.

32 Phillis Wheatley, letter to the Rev. Samson Occom, February 11, 1774, reprinted in Robinson, *Phillis Wheatley and Her Writings*, p. 332, as it appeared in *The Massachusetts Spy* for March 24, 1774. Robinson reminds us that Wheatley had been a freed woman for several months by the time she composed this letter, and notes its "politely sarcastic scoring of the patently absurd Christian racists," pp. 120–21. Akers, in "'Our Modern Egyptians,'" pp. 406–07, reprints the letter as it appeared in the *Boston Post-Boy (Massachusetts Gazette)*, March 21, 1774, p. 3/2 and the *Boston News-Letter (Massachusetts Gazette)*, March 24, 1774, p. 1/3. Akers comments, "Thus, in Boston as in Virginia, elitist patriots cried for the rights of man while they continued to enjoy the labor of their African slaves," p. 402.

33 See, for example, Anne Lane (ed.), *The Debate Over Slavery: Stanley Elkins and His Critics* (Urbana: University of Illinois Press, 1971), esp. pp. 5–7, pp. 348–61. Erlene Stetson provides a black feminist perspective on the whole question of slavery in "Studying Slavery: Some Literary and Pedagogical Considerations on the Black Female Slave," in *All the Women Are White, All the Blacks Are Men, But Some of Us Are Brave: Black Women's Studies*, ed. Gloria T. Hull, Patricia Bell Scott, Barbara Smith (Old Westbury, N.Y.: The Feminist Press, 1982), pp. 61–84. See also Angela Davis, *Women, Race & Class* (New York: Vintage, 1981).

34 Oddell, "Memoir," in Robinson, *Phillis Wheatley and Her Writings*, pp. 431–32.

35 Letter from "L" to the editor, *The London Magazine* (March 1772), quoted in Robinson, *Phillis Wheatley and Her Writings*, p. 25.

36 June Jordan, "The Difficult Miracle of Black Poetry in America, or Something Like a Sonnet for Phillis Wheatley," *On Call: Political Essays* (Boston, Mass.: South End Press, 1985), p. 90.

37 Wheatley, "An address to the Deist 1767," manuscript in the Massachusetts Historical Society, reprinted in Robinson, *Phillis Wheatley and Her Writings*, pp. 133–34.

38 Citing this poem as an example, Margaret Doody has suggested in "Augustan *Women*? Four Poets of the Eighteenth Century" that there may be more than mere commonplace wisdom in the idea that classical narratives have an apparently "universal appeal" when we come to such unlikely appropriators of classical sources as Wheatley. I would add that there seems to be a convergence between classical subjects and intellectual ambition in eighteenth-century women's verse, especially for the more "unlikely" imitators.

39 Henry Louis Gates, Jr., "Editor's Introduction: Writing 'Race' and the Difference It Makes," *"Race," Writing, and Difference*, pp. 8–9. See also his *Figures in Black: Words, Signs, and the "Racial" Self* (New York and Oxford: Oxford University Press, 1987), pp. 61–79, and *The Signifying Monkey: A Theory of Afro-American Literary Criticism* (New York and Oxford: Oxford University Press, 1988), pp. 89–92.

40 See Robinson, *Phillis Wheatley and her Writings*, p. 271, n. 1.

41 Robert Hayden, "A Letter from Phillis Wheatley, *London*, 1773" in *American Journal: Poems* (New York and London: Liveright, 1982), pp. 3–4. My thanks to Anca Vlasopolos for this reference.

42 Jordan, "The Difficult Miracle," pp. 96–97.

43 Houston A. Baker, Jr., "Caliban's Triple Play," in Gates (ed.), *"Race," Writing, and Difference*, p. 383.

44 I owe this formulation of such an argument to Howard Erskine-Hill.

45 See Jerome J. McGann, *A Critique of Modern Textual Criticism* (Chicago and London: University of Chicago Press, 1983), p. 81, p. 93.

7   The 1790s and after: revolutions that as yet have no model

1 Mary Wollstonecraft, *The Wrongs of Woman: or, Maria. A Fragment* (1798) in *Mary and The Wrongs of Woman*, ed. Gary Kelly (Oxford and New York: Oxford University Press, 1976), p. 135.

2 Roberts, *Memoirs of Hannah More*, II, p. 189.

3 [Richard Polwhele], *The Unsex'd Females: A Poem, Addressed To The Author Of The Pursuits Of Literature* (London: Cadell and Davies, 1798), p. [3], n.

4 [Polwhele], *The Unsex'd Females*, p. 28, n.: "I know nothing of Miss Wollstone-craft's character or conduct, but from the Memoirs of Godwin, with whom this lady was afterwards connected."

5 This notion of comparability is not unlike the "logic of equivalence" proposed by Ernesto Laclau and Chantal Mouffe in *Hegemony and Socialist Strategy: Towards a Radical Democratic Politics*, trans. Winston Moore and Paul Cammack (London and New York: Verso, 1985): "In the case of women we may cite as an example the role played in England by Mary Wollstonecraft, whose book *Vindication of the Rights of Women* [*sic*], published in 1792, determined the birth of feminism through the use made in it of the democratic discourse, which was thus displaced from the field of political equality between citizens to the field of equality between the sexes," p. 154. See also Reiss, "Revolution in Bounds: Wollstonecraft, Women, and Reason," in *Gender and Theory*, pp. 11–50 for a discussion of contradictions in Wollstonecraft's position.

6 Wollstonecraft, Dedication "To M. Talleyrand-Périgord, Late Bishop of Autun," *Vindication of the Rights Of Woman: With Strictures on Political And Moral Subjects*, ed. Miriam Brody Kramnick (London: J. Johnson, 1792; Harmonds-worth: Penguin, 1982), pp. 88–89.

7 *D.N.B.*, XIII, p. 866.

8 More, *Strictures On The Modern System Of Female Education. With A View Of The Principles And Conduct Prevalent Among Women Of Rank And Fortune*, 2 vols. (London: Cadell and Davies, 1799), I, pp. 165–66.

9 [Hannah More], *Village Politics. Addressed To All The Mechanics, Journeymen, And Day Labourers, In Great Britain. By Will Chip, A Country Carpenter* (London: F. and C. Rivington, 1793), p. 5.

10 Mitzi Myers, "Reform or Ruin: 'A Revolution in Female Manners,'" *Studies in Eighteenth-Century Culture* 11, ed. Harry C. Payne (Madison: University of Wisconsin Press, 1982), p. 203, p. 211: "'It is amazing,' observed their contempo-rary Mary Berry, studying More and Wollstonecraft in tandem, how much the two 'agree on all the great points of female education. H. More will, I dare say, be very angry when she hears this.' . . . Though their remedies differ in many details, Wollstonecraft and More each diagnose England's moral – and almost mortal – illness in analogous terms. Perceiving a society infected with fashionable corrup-tion, both preach a militantly moral middle-class reform grounded in women's potentiality . . . It is certainly true that conservatives identified feminist and male radicals who dared to reassess family structure and the relationship between the sexes as a threat . . . But radicals like Wollstonecraft . . . were equally anxious for a renovated domestic ideal."

11 Yearsley, *To Mira, On The Care Of Her Infant*, in *The Rural Lyre*, pp. 113–24.

12 What I am posing here as a limit of theoretical and political conceptualization in

the discourse of 1790s feminism and radicalism, Nancy Armstrong traces as crucial to the development of the English domestic novel as instrumental in the establishment of bourgeois cultural hegemony; see *Desire and Domestic Fiction*, esp. pp. 3–95.

13 The poem is signed "Bristol Wells, September 16, 1795"; *The Rural Lyre*, p. 124.

14 But see John Robison's *Proofs of a Conspiracy against all the Religions and Governments of Europe, carried on in the secret meetings of Free Masons, Illuminati, and Reading Societies* (Edinburgh: William Creech and London: Cadell and Davies, 1797), in which he rails against French "amazonian" fashion as a product of revolutionary licentiousness rather than revolutionary militancy; Yearsley would wish to be associated with neither of these: "Are not the accursed fruits of Illumination to be seen in the present humiliating condition of woman in France? pampered in every thing that can reduce them to the mere instrument of animal pleasure ... It was no doubt with the same adherence to *serious principle*, that Mademoiselle Therouanne was most beautifully dressed *à l'Amazonne* on the 5th of October 1789, when she turned the heads of so many young officers of the regiments at Versailles," pp. 251–53.

15 Yearsley comes close here to giving us a version of Julia Kristeva's notion of an infantile semiotic *chora*, which, though repressed by language acquisition and the Law, remains a potential source of resistance to and subversion of the symbolic order. See the excerpt from *Revolution in Poetic Language* in *The Kristeva Reader*, ed. Toril Moi (Oxford: Basil Blackwell, 1986), pp. 93–98.

16 Wordsworth, *Book Second: School-Time (continued), The Prelude* in *Poetical Works*, ed. Thomas Hutchinson and Ernest de Selincourt (London: Oxford University Press, 1936).

17 In Lacanian terms, however, this stage of mirroring should not be confused with "the mirror stage" that formalizes our split subjectivity. For the mother's body as affirming and amplifying "mirror" is not perceived by the infant at this stage as "other" from itself; it takes the spectral image in the mirror proper to force this re-cognition; see Jacques Lacan, "The Mirror Stage as Formative of the Function of the I as Revealed in Psychoanalytic Experience," *Ecrits: a Selection*, trans. Alan Sheridan (New York: Norton, 1977), pp. 1–7.

18 Elizabeth Clinton, Countess of Lincoln, *The Covntess Of Lincolnes Nvrserie* (Oxford: John Lichfield and James Short, 1622), p. 19.

19 Dorothy McLaren, "Marital Fertility and Lactation 1570–1720," *Women in English Society 1500–1800*, ed. Mary Prior (London and New York: Methuen, 1985), p. 46. See also Barbara B. Harrell, "Lactation and Menstruation in Cultural Perspective," *American Anthropologist* 83:4 (1981), pp. 796–823.

20 Marie-France Morel, "City and Country in Eighteenth-Century Medical Discussions about Early Childhood," in *Medicine and Society in France: Selections from the Annales: Economies, Sociétés, Civilisations, Vol. 6*, ed. Robert Forster and Orest Ranum, trans. Elborg Forster and Patricia M. Ranum (Baltimore and London: The Johns Hopkins University Press, 1980), pp. 51–52. I owe this reference to Mary Jacobus.

21 See Peter Stallybrass and Allon White, "Below Stairs: the Maid and the Family Romance," in *The Politics and Poetics of Transgression* (Ithaca: Cornell University Press, 1986), pp. 149–70, and Julia Kristeva, *Powers of Horror: An Essay on Abjection*, trans. Leon S. Roudiez (New York: Columbia University Press, 1982).

22 Letter from Hannah More to Elizabeth Montagu, October 22, 1784; Huntington Library manuscript MO 3988, p. 1.

23 Stedman Jones, *Languages of Class*, p. 217. Stedman Jones continues, "Even if

some artisans discussed politics with their wives, women were excluded *de facto* from the focal institutions of this culture."

24 Spivak, "Revolutions That As Yet Have No Model: Derrida's *Limited Inc*," *Diacritics* 10 (December 1980), p. 38.
25 Cora Kaplan, "Wild Nights: Pleasure/Sexuality/Feminism," in *Sea Changes: Essays on Culture and Feminism* (London: Verso, 1986), p. 50.
26 Wollstonecraft, *The Wrongs of Woman*, p. 80.
27 Wollstonecraft, *The Wrongs of Woman*, p. 115. Gary Kelly (ed.), suggests that we compare this passage with M. Dorothy George, *London Life in the Eighteenth Century* (1966), p. 207.
28 Mary Poovey, *The Proper Lady and the Woman Writer: Ideology as Style in the Works of Mary Wollstonecraft, Mary Shelley, and Jane Austen* (Chicago and London: University of Chicago Press, 1984), p. 103.
29 Poovey, in *The Proper Lady*, no sooner labels Jemima's story "a radical, indeed feminist, story" than she describes it as thoroughly "reabsorbed into Maria's sentimentalism" (p. 104). In "Unfinished Business: Wollstonecraft's *Maria*," *Wordsworth Circle* 11:2 (Spring 1980), pp. 107–14, Myers eloquently describes the novel as both "unfinished business" and "the culmination" of Wollstonecraft's career "in more than one sense" (p. 107). But she claims that "Everyone ... compliments the stark record of the proletarian woman's trials in Jemima, Maria's warder in the asylum" (p. 110) as if such an oft-repeated assessment rendered Jemima's story a negligible part of Wollstonecraft's achievement.
30 Poovey argues that Jemima's time as a prostitute represents an interlude of "anarchy" and a "brief assertion of female sexuality," but I think she overeroticizes Jemima's relative economic "independence" in this episode, *The Proper Lady*, p. 104.
31 As Tania Modleski has observed in *Loving with a Vengeance: Mass-Produced Fantasies for Women* (London: Methuen, 1984), p. 84.
32 Foucault, *The History of Sexuality, Vol. I*, p. 127: "We must return, therefore, to formulations that have long been disparaged; we must say that there is a bourgeois sexuality, and that there are class sexualities. Or rather, that sexuality is originally, historically bourgeois, and that, in its successive shifts and transpositions, it induces specific class effects"; and p. 157: "We must not think that by saying yes to sex, one says no to power; on the contrary, one tracks along the course laid out by the general deployment of sexuality. It is the agency of sex that we must break away from, if we aim – through a tactical reversal of the various mechanisms of sexuality – to counter the grips of power with the claims of bodies, pleasures, and knowledges, in their multiplicity and their possibility of resistance. The rallying point for the counterattack against the deployment of sexuality ought not to be sex-desire, but bodies and pleasures."
33 My thanks to Mary Jacobus for offering this formulation.
34 Anna Laetitia Barbauld, "Washing-Day" in *The Works of Anna Laetitia Barbauld. With A Memoir By Lucy Aikin*, 2 vols. (London: Printed for Longman, Hurst, Rees, Orme, Brown, and Green, 1825), I, pp. 202–06. For an interesting discussion of Barbauld and access to the complete text of this poem, see Ann Messenger, *His and Hers*, pp. 172–96, pp. 244–46.
35 Barbauld, "The Rights Of Woman," *Works*, I, pp. 185–87.
36 *Poetical Attempts, By Ann Candler, A Suffolk Cottager; with a short Narrative Of Her Life* (Ipswich: John Raw; also sold in London by T. Hurst, 1803). (British Library shelfmark 11632.aa.11.)
37 The note reads: "Thursday last died at Holton, aged 74 years, Ann Candler, (a

Suffolk Cottager) much respected for her integrity. Ipsw. Journ. Sept: 17. 1816."

38 Prefatory letter from Elizabeth Bentley to the Rev. Mr. Walker in Norwich and "Preface" to E. Bentley, *Genuine Poetical Compositions, on Various Subjects*, Sig. A3v and Sig. A1v; and *Poems; being the Genuine Compositions of Elizabeth Bentley, Of Norwich* (Norwich: Sold by the Author and Stevenson, Matchett, and Stevenson; London: Taylor and Hessey; Cambridge: Deightons; "and all other booksellers," 1821).

39 Bentley, "On Health And Liberty. 1787," in *Genuine Poetical Compositions*, pp. 6–7.

40 Bentley, "The Rural Life" in *Poems*, p. 30.

41 Bentley, "On the Victory Over The Dutch Fleet, October 11th, 1797" in *Poems*, pp. 56–57.

42 Bentley, "Song. The Briton's Resolution. August, 1803" in *Poems*, pp. 96–97.

43 John Landseer, *Athenaeum* 207 (15 October 1831), p. 667; cited in Ronald Paulson, *Representations of Revolution (1789–1820)* (New Haven and London: Yale University Press, 1983), p. 184.

44 Paulson, *Representations of Revolution*, p. 185.

45 Bentley, "The Gleaner's Prayer" in *Poems*, pp. 104–05.

46 Stedman Jones, *Languages of Class*, p. 215, and p. 237.

47 Candler, "Reflections On My Own Situation, Written in T–tt–ngst–ne House of Industry, February 1802," in *Poetical Attempts*, p. 53.

48 "Memoirs of the life of Ann Candler," *Poetical Attempts*, Sig. B1r.

49 Taylor, *Eve and the New Jerusalem* and Alexander, "Women, Class and Sexual Differences in the 1830s and 1840s: Some Reflections on the Writing of a Feminist History," *History Workshop Journal* 17 (Spring 1984), pp. 135–46.

Index